Lecture Notes in Computer Science   **9686**

Commenced Publication in 1973
Founding and Former Series Editors:
Gerhard Goos, Juris Hartmanis, and Jan van Leeuwen

More information about this series at http://www.springer.com/series/7408

Alberto Lluch Lafuente · José Proença (Eds.)

Coordination Models and Languages

18th IFIP WG 6.1 International Conference, COORDINATION 2016
Held as Part of the 11th International Federated Conference
on Distributed Computing Techniques, DisCoTec 2016
Heraklion, Crete, Greece, June 6–9, 2016
Proceedings

 Springer

Editors
Alberto Lluch Lafuente
Technical University of Denmark
Lyngby
Denmark

José Proença
University of Minho
Braga
Portugal

ISSN 0302-9743   ISSN 1611-3349   (electronic)
Lecture Notes in Computer Science
ISBN 978-3-319-39518-0   ISBN 978-3-319-39519-7   (eBook)
DOI 10.1007/978-3-319-39519-7

Library of Congress Control Number: 2016939929

LNCS Sublibrary: SL2 – Programming and Software Engineering

Printed on acid-free paper

This Springer imprint is published by Springer Nature
The registered company is Springer International Publishing AG Switzerland

Foreword

The 11th International Federated Conference on Distributed Computing Techniques (DisCoTec) took place at the Aquila Atlantis Hotel in Heraklion, Greece, during June 6–9, 2016. It was organized by the Institute of Computer Science of the Foundation for Research and Technology – Hellas and the University of Ioannina, Greece. The DisCoTec series is one of the major events sponsored by the International Federation for Information Processing (IFIP). It comprises three conferences:

COORDINATION, the IFIP WG 6.1 International Conference on Coordination Models and Languages
- DAIS, the IFIP WG 6.1 International Conference on Distributed Applications and Interoperable Systems
- FORTE, the IFIP WG 6.1 International Conference on Formal Techniques for Distributed Objects, Components and Systems

Together, these conferences cover a broad spectrum of distributed computing subjects, ranging from theoretical foundations and formal description techniques to systems research issues.

Each day of the federated event began with a plenary speaker nominated by one of the conferences. The three invited speakers were Tim Harris (Oracle Labs, UK), Catuscia Palamidessi (Inria, France), and Vijay Saraswat (IBM T.J. Watson Research Center, USA).

Associated with the federated event were also two satellite workshops, that took place during June 8–9, 2016:

- The 9th Workshop on Interaction and Concurrency Experience (ICE) with keynote lectures by Uwe Nestmann (Technische Universität Berlin, Germany) and Alexandra Silva (University College London, UK)
- The Final Public Workshop from the LeanBigData and CoherentPaaS projects

Sincere thanks go to the chairs and members of the Program and Steering Committees of the involved conferences and workshops for their highly appreciated efforts. Organizing DisCoTec 2016 was only possible thanks to the dedicated work of the Organizing Committee, including George Baryannis (Publicity Chair) and Vincenzo Gulisano (Workshops Chair), with excellent support from Nikos Antonopoulos and Alkis Polyrakis of PCO-Convin. Finally, many thanks go to IFIP WG 6.1 for sponsoring this event, Springer *Lecture Notes in Computer Science* for their support and sponsorship, and to EasyChair for providing the refereeing infrastructure.

Kostas Magoutis

Preface

This volume contains the proceedings of COORDINATION 2016: the 18th IFIP WG 6.1 International Conference on Coordination Models and Languages held during June 6–9, 2015, in Heraklion, Crete. The conference was co-located with FORTE and DAIS, as part of the DisCoTec federated conferences on distributed computing techniques.

COORDINATION is the premier forum for publishing research results and experience reports on software technologies for collaboration and coordination in concurrent, distributed, and complex systems. The key focus of the conference is the quest for high-level abstractions that can capture interaction patterns and mechanisms occurring at all levels of the software architecture, up to the end-user domain. COORDINATION 2016 solicited high-quality contributions on the usage, study, formal analysis, design, and implementation of languages, models, and techniques for coordination in distributed, concurrent, pervasive, and parallel software-intensive computing systems. COORDINATION 2016 also solicited contributions aimed at adapting and integrating traditional COORDINATION techniques in the realm of multi-agent systems (MAS), which typically involve more coarse-grained (cognitive, intelligent, goal-oriented) components.

The Program Committee (PC) of COORDINATION 2016 consisted of 32 prominent researchers from 19 different countries. We received 44 submissions out of which the PC selected 16 full papers for inclusion in the program. All submissions were reviewed by at least three independent referees; papers were selected based on their quality, originality, contribution, clarity of presentation, and relevance to the conference topics. The review process included an in-depth discussion phase, during which the merits of all papers were discussed by the PC. The selected papers constituted a program covering a varied range of topics and techniques related to system coordination, including: programming and communication abstractions; communication protocols and behavioral types; actors and concurrent objects; tuple spaces; games, interfaces, and contracts; information flow policies and dissemination techniques; and probabilistic models and formal verification. The program was further enhanced by an invited talk by Vijay Saraswat from IBM T.J. Watson Research Lab (USA).

The success of COORDINATION 2016 was due to the dedication of many people. We would like to thank the Steering Committee for inviting us to chair the conference, the authors for submitting high-quality papers, the PC and their subreviewers for their careful reviews and lively discussions during the final selection process, and the invited speaker for his keynote. We also thank the providers of the EasyChair conference management system, which was used to run the review process and to generate the proceedings. Finally, we thank the Organizing Committee from Heraklion, led by Kostas Magoutis, for its contribution in making the logistic aspects of COORDINATION 2016 a success.

June 2016

Alberto Lluch Lafuente
José Proença

Organization

Program Committee Chairs

Alberto Lluch Lafuente   Technical University of Denmark, Denmark
José Proença   KU Leuven/University of Minho, Belgium/Portugal

Program Committee

Gul Agha   University of Illinois at Urbana-Champaign, USA
Luís Barbosa   University of Minho, Portugal
Jacob Beal   BBN Technologies, USA
Simon Bliudze   EPFL, Switzerland
Olivier Boissier   ENS Mines Saint-Etienne, France
Roberto Bruni   Università di Pisa, Italy
Tevfik Bultan   University of California at Santa Barbara, USA
Carlos Canal   University of Málaga, Spain
Dave Clarke   Uppsala University, Sweden
Stephen Crancfield   University of Otago, New Zealand
Ferruccio Damiani   Università di Torino, Italy
Frank De Boer   CWI, The Netherlands
Rocco De Nicola   IMT - Institute for Advanced Studies Lucca, Italy
José Luiz Fiadeiro   Royal Holloway, University of London, UK
Tom Holvoet   KU Leuven, Belgium
Valerie Issarny   Inria, France
Einar Broch Johnsen   University of Oslo, Norway
Rania Khalaf   IBM T.J. Watson Research Center, USA
Ramtin Khosravi   University of Tehran, Iran
Natallia Kokash   Leiden University, The Netherlands
Mieke Massink   CNR-ISTI, Italy
Hernán Melgratti   Universidad de Buenos Aires, Argentina
Flemming Nielson   Technical University of Denmark, Denmark
Munindar P. Singh   NCSU, USA
Marjan Sirjani   Reykjavik University, Iceland
Meng Sun   Peking University, China
Vasco T. Vasconcelos   University of Lisbon, Portugal
Carolyn Talcott   SRI International, USA
Emilio Tuosto   University of Leicester, UK
Mirko Viroli   Università di Bologna, Italy
Takuo Watanabe   Tokyo Institute of Technology, Japan
Martin Wirsing   Ludwig-Maximilians-Universität München, Germany

Steering Committee

Gul Agha	University of Illinois at Urbana Champaign, USA
Farhad Arbab	CWI and Leiden University, The Netherlands
Dave Clarke	Uppsala University, Sweden
Tom Holvoet	KU Leuven, Belgium
Jean-Marie Jacquet	University of Namur, Belgium
Christine Julien	The University of Texas at Austin, USA
Eva Kühn	Vienna University of Technology, Austria
Wolfgang De Meuter	Vrije Universiteit Brussels, Belgium
Rocco De Nicola	IMT - Institute for Advanced Studies Lucca, Italy
Rosario Pugliese	Università di Firenze, Italy
Marjan Sirjani	Reykjavik University, Iceland
Carolyn Talcott	SRI International, California, USA
Vasco T. Vasconcelos	University of Lisbon, Portugal
Gianluigi Zavattaro	University of Bologna, Italy
Mirko Viroli	University of Bologna, Italy

Additional Reviewers

Abd Alrahman, Yehia
Akkaya, Ilge
Aldini, Alessandro
Azadbakht, Keyvan
Bagheri, Maryam
Basile, Davide
Belzner, Lenz
Bernardo, Marco
Bezirgiannis, Nikolaos
Charalambides, Minas
Chen, Xiaohong
Ciancia, Vincenzo
Cimoli, Tiziana
Coppo, Mario
Desai, Nirmit
Dezani-Ciancaglini, Mariangiola
Dokter, Kasper
Gkolfi, Anastasia
Ishakian, Vatche

Jaghoori, Mohammad Mahdi
Khamespanah, Ehsan
Li, Yi
Lienhardt, Michael
Mariani, Stefano
Martins, Francisco
Mechitov, Kirill
Mostrous, Dimitris
Murphy, Amy
Palmskog, Karl
Pianini, Danilo
Ricci, Alessandro
Sabouri, Hamideh
Schlatte, Rudolf
Serbanescu, Vlad Nicolae
Shaver, Chris
Spaccasassi, Carlo
Tesei, Luca

(Logical and Imperative)
Calculi for Distributed Coordination
(Abstract)

Vijay Saraswat

IBM T.J. Watson, USA

Abstract. We review work over the last thirty years on simple, formal models capturing the essence of (realistic) views of distributed coordination. We trace a path through work on concurrent constraint programming, its linear version, connections with the asynchronous pi-calculus, and, more recently, through the imperative resilient X10. As always, the virtue of clean and powerful abstractions is that they can ease design of real systems that address tricky technical concerns. We illustrate with the calculus for resilient X10, designing which forced us to a semantic principle, Happens Before Invariance, which is useful in practice.

Contents

Multilevel Transitive and Intransitive Non-interference, Causally

Paolo Baldan[1]([⊠]) and Alessandro Beggiato[2]

[1] Dipartimento di Matematica, Università di Padova, Padova, Italy
baldan@math.unipd.it
[2] IMT School for Advanced Studies Lucca, Lucca, Italy
alessandro.beggiato@imtlucca.it

Abstract. We develop a theory of non interference for multilevel security domains based on causality, with Petri nets as a reference model. We
first focus on transitive non-interference, where the relation representing
the admitted flow is transitive. Then we extend the approach to intransitive non-interference, where the transitivity assumption is dismissed,
leading to a framework which is suited to model a controlled disclosure
of information. Efficient verification algorithms based on the unfolding
semantics of Petri nets stem out of the theory.

1 Introduction

Starting with [1], the notion of non-interference has been widely used in the
study of information flow security. In the simplest scenario, entities are classified
according to two levels, a confidential level *High* and a public level *Low*. Information is allowed to flow from *Low* to *High*, but not vice-versa. When dealing with
formalisms describing concurrent components that can interact and synchronize,
like process calculi and Petri nets, a popular formulation of non-interference is
Non-Deducibility on Composition (NDC). It states that a component S is free of
interference whenever S running in isolation, seen from the low level, is behav-
iorally equivalent to S interacting with any parallel high level component [2–9].
Intuitively, the behavior of the *High* part of the system is required not to cause
any modification in the behavior of the *Low* part.

This informal reference to causality is made formal in [7] that, relying on some
previous work [5], provides a causal characterization of BNDC (Bisimulation-
based NDC) on Petri nets, in terms of the unfolding semantics [10]. The interest
for a causal characterization is not only of theoretical nature. On the pragmatic
side the use of a true concurrent semantics, like the unfolding, which represents
interleaving only implicitly, is helpful to face the state explosion problem which
affects the verification of concurrent systems.

The approach in [7] works in a two-level setting, possibly with downgrading [11], while since its infancy (see, e.g., [12]) information flow security has

Supported by MIUR project CINA and the Padua University project ANCORE.

A. Lluch Lafuente and J. Proença (Eds.): COORDINATION 2016, LNCS 9686, pp. 1–17, 2016.
DOI: 10.1007/978-3-319-39519-7_1

recognized the usefulness of dealing with multilevel security domains where a relation between levels, referred as a security policy, specifies the admitted flows. The transitive nature of information flow – if information flows from level A to level B and from B to C then it necessarily flows from A to C – naturally leads to work in domains where the security policy is a partial order, only allowing a flow of information from lower to higher levels (no read-up, no write-down). The order can be total, expressing a hierarchy of confidentiality degrees (e.g., top secret, secret, confidential and unclassified in a military setting). It can also be partial, typically when various confidentiality criteria are combined into a single domain. E.g., an administration could keep public and sensitive citizen data concerning taxes and civil status. Independent access rights to sensitive tax and civil status data naturally leads to a lattice of security levels.

As argued, e.g., in [13] it can also be natural to consider *intransitive* policies, in a way that a direct flow between two levels, say from A to B, can be forbidden, while a flow mediated through a third level, say D, is admitted. Intransitive policies are suited, for instance, for representing downgrading of confidential information. This allows for a controlled form of leakage, making such policies more realistic than pure non-interference policies that require the complete isolation of confidential levels. More generally, intransitive policies allow one to describe the (possibly cyclic) paths on which information is allowed to flow in a system.

In this paper the approach of [7], providing a causal characterization of the BNDC (Bisimulation-based NDC) property for (safe) Petri nets based on the unfolding semantics, is extended to deal with multilevel transitive policies. Generalizing [11] we also treat the intransitive case, namely we develop a multilevel theory for BINI [6], an adaptation of BNDC to intransitive domains. The non-interference properties of interest are characterized in terms of the absence of suitable causal dependencies in the unfolding, witnessed by places where illegal interactions occur. This enables the definition of algorithms that checks the non-interference properties on a suitably defined complete prefix of the unfolding.

The unfolding-based algorithms are implemented in a tool MultiUBIC [14]. Compared to tools that exploit the reachability graph of the net, like ANICA (Automated Non-Interference Check Assistant) [15] and PNSC (Petri Net Security Checker) [16], thanks to the partial order representation of concurrency, MultiUBIC - as its predecessor UBIC – leads to a gain of efficiency for highly concurrent systems where the unfolding prefix can be exponentially smaller than the complete state space (see e.g. [17]). The verification of multilevel policies can be also reduced to a number of problems on two-level security domains (enriched with a downgrading level in the intransitive case). MultiUBIC comes equipped with facilities for performing the reduction. The experiments suggest that, in general, a direct multilevel verification is more efficient when the number of levels increases, but situations are singled out where the reduction is convenient.

Synopsis. In Sect. 2 we define multilevel security domains and we review some Petri net notions. In Sect. 3 we focus on transitive policies, providing a causal characterization of the BNDC property and a verification algorithm. In Sect. 4

we extend the results to intransitive policies. In Sect. 5 we describe the tool MultiUBIC. In Sect. 6 we draw some conclusions.

2 Multilevel Security Domains and Petri Nets

In this section, after introducing multilevel security domains, we review some basic notions about Petri nets, with special attention to their unfolding semantics, later used to provide a causal characterization of the non-interference properties.

2.1 Multilevel Security Domains

Definition 1 (multilevel security domain). *A multilevel security domain (MSD) $(\mathscr{L}, \rightsquigarrow)$ is a finite set of security levels $\mathscr{L}$, endowed with a reflexive relation $\rightsquigarrow \subseteq \mathscr{L} \times \mathscr{L}$ called a security policy. When $\rightsquigarrow$ is transitive we call $(\mathscr{L}, \rightsquigarrow)$ a transitive multilevel security domain.*

The security policy specifies the legal information flows. It is reflexive because entities at the same level should be able to freely exchange information. Without loss of generality, a transitive MSD will be assumed to be a partial order. In fact, if $\rightsquigarrow$ is a proper preorder (i.e., not antisymmetric), we can equivalently consider the partial order obtained as its quotient under the equivalence $\rightsquigarrow \cap \rightsquigarrow^{-1}$. Since equivalent levels can communicate in either direction, they can be safely collapsed. Examples of MSD will be discussed later, after introducing also net systems. Given $S \subseteq \mathscr{L}$ we write $\overline{S}$ for its complement $\mathscr{L} \setminus S$.

Definition 2 (upper sets and targets). *Let $(\mathscr{L}, \rightsquigarrow)$ be a MSD. An upper set is a subset $U \subseteq \mathscr{L}$ such that if $L \in U$ and $L \rightsquigarrow L'$ then $L' \in U$. Given a security level $L \in \mathscr{L}$ its set of targets is $\uparrow L = \{L' \in \mathscr{L} \mid L \rightsquigarrow L'\}$, while the strict targets are $\mathord{\uparrow} L = \uparrow L \setminus \{L\}$.*

An entity (user, program, variable, instruction) with associated security level L has permission to influence, or to write, or to pass information only to entities with security level in $\uparrow L$. Any other information flow is a violation of the policy. Targets are defined on sets $U \subseteq \mathscr{L}$ by letting $\uparrow U = \bigcup_{L \in U} \uparrow L$ and $\mathord{\uparrow} U = \uparrow U \setminus U$.

2.2 Petri Nets and Net Systems

A *(Petri) net* is a tuple $N = (P, T, F)$ where P, T are disjoint sets of *places* and *transitions*, respectively, and $F : (P \times T) \cup (T \times P) \rightarrow \{0, 1\}$ is the *flow function*. Graphically places and transitions are drawn as circles and rectangles, respectively, while the flow function is rendered by means of directed arcs connecting places and transitions. For $x \in P \cup T$ we define its *pre-set* ${}^{\bullet}x = \{y \in P \cup T : F(y, x) = 1\}$ and its *post-set* $x^{\bullet} = \{y \in P \cup T : F(x, y) = 1\}$. A *marking* of N is a function $m : P \rightarrow \mathbb{N}$. A transition $t \in T$ is *enabled* at a marking m, denoted $m[t\rangle$, if $m(p) \geq F(p, t)$ for all $p \in P$. If $m[t\rangle$ then t can be *fired* leading to a new marking m', written $m[t\rangle m'$, defined by $m'(p) = m(p) + F(t, p) - F(p, t)$

for all places $p \in P$. The enabling and firing relations are extended to $\sigma \in T^*$ (finite sequences of elements of T) by defining $m[\varepsilon\rangle m$ (where ε is the empty sequence) and $m[\sigma\rangle m'[t\rangle m''$ imply $m[\sigma t\rangle m''$. Markings are represented as black dots, called *tokens*, inside places. A *marked net* is a pair $\mathbf{N} = (N, m_0)$ where N is a net and m_0 is a marking of N. A marking m' is *reachable* if there exists $\sigma \in T^*$ such that $m_0[\sigma\rangle m'$. The set of reachable markings of $\mathbf{N}$ is denoted by $[m_0\rangle$. When $m[t\rangle m'$, the marking m', uniquely determined by m and t, is denoted by $\langle m[t\rangle$. Analogously, for $\sigma \in T^*$, if $m[\sigma\rangle$ we can define the marking $\langle m[\sigma\rangle$. A net $\mathbf{N}$ is *safe* if for every $p \in P$ and every $m \in [m_0\rangle$ we have $m(p) \leq 1$.

In order to formalize information flow properties in the setting of Petri nets, an MSD $\mathscr{L}$ is fixed and, as in [5,6], transitions are associated with security levels.

Definition 3 (net system). *A net system is a tuple $N = (P, T, F, \lambda)$ where (P, T, F) is a Petri net and $\lambda : T \to \mathscr{L}$ is a function that assigns a security level to each transition. For $S \subseteq \mathscr{L}$ we define $T_S = \{t \in T \mid \lambda(t) \in S\}$, the set of transitions whose security level is in S. An S-system is a net system such that $T = T_S$, i.e. a system only capable of performing actions whose security level belongs to S.*

Consider the net system and security domain in Fig. 1. It represents a device consisting of two independent sensors getting new measures for a processor, that, in turn, can poll them to acquire more recent data. Each sensor has a cyclic behavior. For instance, the left sensor is capable to get a measure (get_A). Such measure can be exposed at its interface ($show_A$) and then removed after a while (rem_A), restarting the cycle. Alternatively, the measure can be sent to a shared cache ($send_A$) which is thus updated ($upd\,i_C$). Note that when a place is both in the pre- and post-set of a transition (like *cache* for $upd\,i_C$) instead of an ingoing and an outgoing arrow, we draw a single double arrow. The presence or

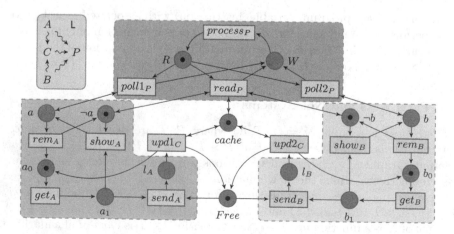

Fig. 1. A non-BNDC net system under the security domain $\mathscr{L}$ (top left).

absence of a datum at the interface is represented by a token in place a or $\neg a$, respectively. The access to the cache by the two sensors via transitions $upd\, i_C$ is mutually exclusive (the cache stores a single measure), as guaranteed by the use of place *Free*, consumed by transitions $send_X$ and produced by $upd\, i_C$. The processor cyclically gets some value for the measure. If a value is exposed at the interfaces of the sensors (places a or b marked) then one of such values is taken ($poll\, i_P$), otherwise (places $\neg a$ and $\neg b$ marked) the cached value is read ($read_P$).

The security level of transitions is given by their subscript (namely, $\lambda(t_L) \mapsto L$). Transitions modeling the left and right sensors have security level A and B. The processor and the cache have security levels P and C, respectively. The intuition is that the two sensors should not interfere with each other, and they can send information to the processor directly or through the cache. The processor and the cache should not affect the behavior of the sensors.

In order to formalize the non-interference notions we will need some operations on net systems, specifically (parallel) composition and restriction [6].

Definition 4 (composition). *Let N and N' be two net systems such that $P \cap P' = \emptyset$ and for all $t \in T \cap T'$ it holds $\lambda t = \lambda' t$. The composition of N and N' is the net system $N|N' = (P \cup P', T \cup T', \lambda \cup \lambda', F \cup F')$. The composition of $\mathbf{N} = (N, m_0)$ and $\mathbf{N}' = (N', m_0')$ is the marked net system $\mathbf{N}|\mathbf{N}' = (N|N', m_0 \cup m_0')$.*

Definition 5 (restriction). *Given a net system N and a subset $T_1 \subseteq T$, the restriction of N by T_1 is the net system $N \setminus T_1 = (P, T - T_1, \lambda', F')$ where λ' and F' are the obvious restrictions of λ and F. For a marked net system $\mathbf{N}$, the restriction $\mathbf{N} \setminus T_1$ is $(N \setminus T_1, m_0)$.*

Intuitively $N|N'$ is the parallel composition of N and N', synchronized on the common transitions. Restriction simply removes the restricted transitions.

2.3   Unfolding Semantics and Related Notions

The behavior of a Petri net can be represented by its unfolding $\mathcal{U}(\mathbf{N})$ [10], an acyclic net constructed inductively starting from the initial marking of $\mathbf{N}$ and then adding, at each step, an occurrence of each enabled transition of $\mathbf{N}$. In what follows we indicate by π_1 the projection over the first component of pairs.

Definition 6 (unfolding). *Let $\mathbf{N} = ((P, T, F), m_0)$ be a marked net. Define the net $U^{(0)} = (P^{(0)}, T^{(0)}, F^{(0)})$ as $T^{(0)} = \emptyset$, $P^{(0)} = \{(p, \bot) : p \in m_0\}$ and $F^{(0)} = \emptyset$, where $\bot$ is an element not belonging to P, T or F. The unfolding is the least net $\mathcal{U}(\mathbf{N}) = (P^{(\omega)}, T^{(\omega)}, F^{(\omega)})$ containing $U^{(0)}$ and such that*

- *if $t \in T$ and $X \subseteq P^{(\omega)}$ with X reachable, and $\pi_1(X) = {}^\bullet t$, then $(t, X) \in T^{(\omega)}$;*
- *for any $e = (t, X) \in T^{(\omega)}$, the set $Z = \{(p, e) : p \in \pi_1(e)^\bullet\} \subseteq P^{(\omega)}$; moreover ${}^\bullet e = X$ and $e^\bullet = Z$.*

Places and transitions in the unfolding represent tokens and firing of transitions, respectively, of the original net. Each place in the unfolding is a tuple

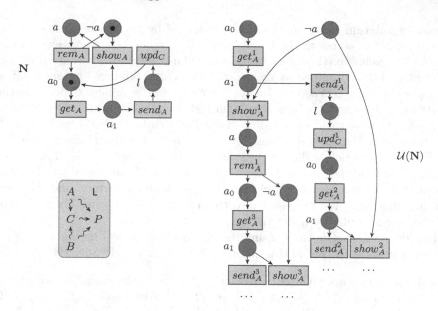

Fig. 2. A net system and the initial part of its unfolding.

recording the place in the original net and the "history" of the token. For historical reasons transitions and places in the unfolding are also called *events* and *conditions*, respectively. The projection π_1 over the first component maps places and transitions of the unfolding to the corresponding items of the original net **N**. The initial marking is implicitly identified as the set of minimal places.

As an example, consider the net system in Fig. 2 (top left), a slightly simplified version of the subnet of Fig. 1 modeling one of the sensors. A fragment of its unfolding is provided in Fig. 2(right). Conditions and events are labeled with the name of the corresponding place and transition in the original net. Different occurrences of a transition are distinguished using a numeric superscript. The conditions labeled by a_0 and $\neg a$ on the top, according to Definition 6, are $(a_0, \bot)$ and $(\neg a, \bot)$, respectively. Event get_A^1 is $(get_A, \{(a_0, \bot)\})$ and the condition a_1 in its post-set is (a_1, get_A^1). Similarly, event $show_A^1$ is $(show_A, \{(a_1, get_A^1), (\neg a, \bot)\})$.

Definition 7 (causality, conflict). *Causality $<$ is the least transitive binary relation on $P^{(\omega)} \cup T^{(\omega)}$ such that $x < y$ if $x \in {}^{\bullet}y$. By $\leq$ we denote the reflexive closure of $<$. Conflict is the least symmetric binary relation $\sharp$ on $P \cup T$ such that if $t, t' \in T$, $t \neq t'$ and ${}^{\bullet}t \cap {}^{\bullet}t' \neq \emptyset$ then $t \sharp t'$ and if $x < x'$ and $x \sharp y$ then $x' \sharp y$.*

In the running example, $get_A^1 \leq show_A^1$ and $get_A^1 \leq send_A^1$, while $send_A^1 \sharp show_A^1$ and $show_A^1 \sharp rem_A^1$.

The runs of **N** are represented by the configurations of $\mathcal{U}(\mathbf{N})$, i.e., subsets of $T^{(\omega)}$ that are causally closed and conflict-free. For a transition $t \in T^{(\omega)}$ we define its *causes* $[t] = \{t' \in T^{(\omega)} : t' \leq t\}$ and its *strict causes* $[t) = [t] - \{t\}$.

Definition 8 (configuration). *A configuration of* $\mathcal{U}(\mathbf{N})$ *is a finite subset* $C \subseteq$ $T^{(\omega)}$ *such that* $(C \times C) \cap \sharp = \emptyset$ *and* $[e] \subseteq C$ *for all* $e \in C$. *The set of all configurations of* $\mathcal{U}(\mathbf{N})$ *is denoted by* $\mathcal{C}(\mathcal{U}(\mathbf{N}))$.

The transitions of a configuration C can be fired in any order compatible with causality, producing a marking called the frontier $C^\circ = (P^{(0)} \cup \bigcup_{t \in C} t^\bullet) -$ $(\bigcup_{t \in C} {}^\bullet t)$; in turn, this corresponds to a marking of $\mathbf{N}$ given by $\mathsf{M}(C) = \pi_1(C^\circ)$. For instance, in Fig. 2, the set $\{get_A^1, show_A^1, rem_A^1\}$ is a configuration, while $\{show_A^1, rem_A^1\}$ and $\{get_A^1, show_A^1, rem_A^1, show_A^2\}$ are not since the first is not causally closed $(get_A^1 < show_A^1)$ and the second has a conflict $(show_A^1 \# show_A^2)$.

The unfolding has been shown to be marking complete in the sense that $m \in [m_0\rangle$ iff there exists $C \in \mathcal{C}(\mathcal{U}(\mathbf{N}))$ such that $\mathsf{M}(C) = m$ (see [10,18]).

3 Transitive Multilevel Non-interference

In this section we focus on transitive multilevel security domains and we define the reference security property in the paper as an instance of (Bisimulation-based) Non-Deducibility on Composition (BNDC) [5].

3.1 Bisimilarity-Based Non-deducibility on Composition

Let $(\mathcal{L}, \leadsto)$ be a transitive MSD, fixed throughout the section. The definition of BNDC can be obtained by adapting that in [5,7] to the multilevel setting. First, in order to formalize the idea of variations of the behavior which are visible at a given security level we introduce a *view function* (or purge function [19]).

Definition 9 (view function). *Given a subset of the domain* $S \subseteq \mathcal{L}$ *and a net system* N, *the* view function $S(\cdot) : T^* \to T_S^*$, *is defined inductively by* $S(\epsilon) = \epsilon$, $S(t\sigma') = tS(\sigma')$ *if* $\lambda(t) \in S$ *and* $S(t\sigma') = S(\sigma')$ *otherwise.*

The view function filters out transitions whose level is not in S. It is used to define a bisimulation capturing the observation power of a user able to observe only events with security level in a given set.

Definition 10 (S-view bisimulation). *Let* $\mathbf{N}$, $\mathbf{N}'$ *be marked systems and* $S \subseteq$ $\mathcal{L}$. *An* S-*view simulation of* $\mathbf{N}$ *by* $\mathbf{N}'$ *is a relation* $R \subseteq [m_0\rangle \times [m_0'\rangle$ *such that:*

- $(m_0, m_0') \in R$;
- *if* $(m, m') \in R$ *and* $m[\sigma\rangle$ *then there exists* σ' *such that* $S(\sigma) = S(\sigma')$, $m'[\sigma'\rangle$ *and* $(\langle m[\sigma\rangle, \langle m'[\sigma'\rangle) \in R$.

An S-*view bisimulation between* $\mathbf{N}$ *and* $\mathbf{N}'$ *is a relation* $R \subseteq [m_0\rangle \times [m_0'\rangle$ *such that* R *and* R^{-1} *are* S-*view simulations. If there exists an* S-*view bisimulation between* $\mathbf{N}$ *and* $\mathbf{N}'$, *we say that they are* S-*view bisimilar and write* $\mathbf{N} \approx_S \mathbf{N}'$.

In a two-level setting, i.e., in the domain $\{Low \rightsquigarrow High\}$, a system is non-interferent when the low level behavior is not influenced by high level interactions. Formally, a net system $\mathbf{N}$ is BNDC when $\mathbf{N} \approx_{Low} (\mathbf{N}|\mathbf{N}') \setminus (T_{High} - T')$ for any $\{High\}$-net $\mathbf{N}'$, i.e., the "low level" view of the behavior of $\mathbf{N}$ remains unchanged when the net interacts with any high level net system [6].

The generalization to the multilevel setting considers any partition of the security domain in an upper set $U \subseteq \mathscr{L}$ and its complement $\overline{U}$, and requires that U does not influence the view of $\overline{U}$.

Definition 11 (BNDC). *Let $\mathbf{N}$ be a marked net system. For an upper set $U \subseteq \mathscr{L}$, we say that $\mathbf{N}$ is U-BNDC if $\mathbf{N} \approx_{\overline{U}} (\mathbf{N}|\mathbf{N}') \setminus (T_U - T')$ for all marked U-systems $\mathbf{N}'$. The system is BNDC if it is U-BNDC for any upper set $U \subseteq \mathscr{L}$.*

The definition can be understood as follows. Given an upper set U, if the system is not U-BNDC then there is a flow from some level $L \in U$ to $L' \in \overline{U}$. This is a security violation since $L \not\rightsquigarrow L'$ otherwise L' would be in U. Vice versa, if there is a security violation, it will consist of a flow from some security level L to a level L' which cannot be influenced by L, namely $L \not\rightsquigarrow L'$. This is captured by the definition above when considering the upper set $U = \uparrow L$, since $L' \in \overline{U}$.

Note that the BNDC property for a multilevel domain reduces to the validity of BNDC in a number of two-level domains, one for each upper set, with U and its complement $\overline{U}$ playing the role of the high and low part of the system, respectively. Actually, as suggested by the considerations above, any security violation can be detected by analyzing upper sets of the kind $U = \uparrow L$ for $L \in \mathscr{L}$.

Proposition 1. *A net system $\mathbf{N}$ is BNDC iff $\mathbf{N}$ is $\uparrow L$-BNDC for every $L \in \mathscr{L}$.*

3.2 BNDC Through Causal and Conflict Places

The characterization of BNDC based on causal and conflict places for the two-level case in [5,7], can be generalized to multilevel security domains. Roughly, a net system is BNDC when transitions with different security levels are never in conflict and there is no causal flow which is not allowed by the security policy.

Hereafter we focus on safe nets, which admit simpler and more effective notions of causal and conflict place (a weakening of those for general nets, whence the qualification "weak").

Notation. Given a net system $\mathbf{N}$ and a transition $t \in T$, we denote by $t^- = {}^\bullet t \setminus t^\bullet$ and, dually, $t^+ = t^\bullet \setminus {}^\bullet t$ the sets of places where the firing of t decrease and increase, respectively, the number of tokens.

Definition 12 (weak causal place). *A weak causal place in a net system $\mathbf{N}$ is any place $p \in {}^\bullet l \cap h^+$, for some $l, h \in T$ such that $\lambda h \not\rightsquigarrow \lambda l$, and some marking $m \in [m_0\rangle$ such that $m[h\tau l\rangle$, with $\tau \in T^*$.*

Intuitively, the firing sequence $h\tau l$ and the place $p \in {}^\bullet l \cap h^+$ witness a firing of l that depends on a token produced by the firing of h, representing an illegal flow from level λh to level λl. Conflict places are defined along the same lines.

Definition 13 (weak conflict place). *A weak conflict place in a net system* **N** *is any place* $p \in {}^\bullet l \cap h^-$, *for some* $l, h \in T$ *such that* $\lambda h \not\leadsto \lambda l$, *and some reachable marking* $m \in [m_0\rangle$ *such that* $m[h\rangle$ *and* $m[\tau l\rangle$, *with* $\tau \in T^*$.

The presence of weak causal or conflict places witnesses the failure of BNDC.

Theorem 1 (BNDC through weak causal/conflict places). *A safe net system* **N** *is BNDC iff* **N** *contains no weak causal nor weak conflict place.*

Consider the running example in Fig. 1. The system is not BNDC. In fact place a_0 is causal, as witnessed by the firing sequence $get_A\, send_A\, upd1_C\, get_A$, with $a_0 \in upd1_C{}^+ \cap {}^\bullet get_A$ and $\lambda(upd1_C) = C \not\leadsto A = \lambda(get_A)$. Analogously, place b_0 is causal and place *Free*, is both causal and conflict. The interference seems unavoidable given that the cache is accessed in mutual exclusion and a value sent to the cache must determine an update. In Sect. 4 we will show how these occurrences of interference can be amended with the use of intransitive policies.

3.3   Non-interference in the Unfolding

Occurrences of causal and conflict places in the unfolding of safe net systems can be given a structural characterization, which, thanks to Theorem 1, leads to a unfolding-based characterization of the BNDC property.

Notation. For a condition b and an event t in the unfolding $\mathcal{U}(\mathbf{N})$ we set $t^+ = \{b \in P^{(\omega)} : \pi_1(b) \in \pi_1(t)^+\}$ and $t^- = \{b \in P^{(\omega)} : \pi_1(b) \in \pi_1(t)^-\}$.

Proposition 2 (BNDC in the unfolding). *A safe net system* **N** *is not BNDC iff there are events* h', l' *such that* $\lambda h' \not\leadsto \lambda l'$ *and a condition* b *in* $\mathcal{U}(\mathbf{N})$ *such that either*

(i) $b \in {}^\bullet l' \cap h'^+$ *or*
(ii) $b \in {}^\bullet l' \cap h'^-$ *and* $[h'] \cup [l'] \in \mathcal{C}(\mathcal{U}(\mathbf{N}))$.

Note that condition (ii) is harder to check than (i), as it involves an exploration of the history of the interacting transitions. In the verification procedure it is convenient to look only for causal interference. This can be done, thanks to the fact that for safe nets all occurrences of interference can be reduced to causal ones. We omit the details which largely overlap with those for the two-level case [7]. We only remark that the causal reduction causes an expansion of the size of the net that is at most quadratic in the number of transitions.

Proposition 3 (BNDC in the causal reduct). *Let* **N** *be a safe net system. It is possible to build a safe net* $\gamma(\mathbf{N})$, *called* causal reduct *of* **N**, *such that* **N** *is BNDC iff* $\gamma(\mathbf{N})$ *has no weak causal places.*

3.4   Unfolding-Based Algorithm for BNDC

The unfolding of a net can be infinite (when it includes a cycle). Starting with [18] techniques have been developed for efficiently constructing finite prefixes of the unfolding which are complete with respect to properties of interest [20].

Here, as a first step, we identify a completeness criterion ensuring that an unfolding prefix includes at least a representative for a causal interference, when a net system is not BNDC. This is used for developing an algorithm for checking BNDC for a safe net. Interestingly, while Definition 11 reduces multilevel non-interference to a number of checks in a two-level setting, here the verification is performed by constructing a single unfolding prefix.

As discussed in the two-level case [7], a prefix complete for reachability could omit information relevant for interference. In order to capture all occurrences of interference, in the two-level case, markings were enriched by recording which tokens were generated by high transitions. Here we record the level of transitions generating the tokens, adapting the notion of completeness accordingly.

Definition 14 (c-marking, c-complete prefix). *Let* N *be a safe net system and let* $C \in \mathcal{C}(\mathcal{U}(N))$. *The* confidentiality marking (c-marking) *of* C *is* $M^*(C) = \langle M(C), \Lambda_C \rangle$, *where* $\Lambda_C : M(C) \to \mathscr{L}$ *is a partial function defined as follows. For any* $b \in C^\circ$, *if* $^\bullet b = \{t'\}$ *then* $\Lambda_C(\pi_1(b)) = \lambda t'$, *otherwise, if* $^\bullet b = \emptyset$ *then* $\Lambda_C(\pi_1(b))$ *is undefined. A prefix* U *of* $\mathcal{U}(N)$ *is* complete for c-marking reachability, *or simply* c-complete, *when for any configuration* $C \in \mathcal{C}(\mathcal{U}(N))$ *there exists* $C' \in \mathcal{C}(U)$ *such that* $M^*(C) = M^*(C')$.

In words, Λ_C maps each marked place to the level of the transition that generated the corresponding token. It is undefined on tokens of the initial marking.

When checking BNDC on a complete prefix U, we need to consider also events at the "border" of U, i.e., events that are enabled by configurations of U and which could be could be added by a further unfolding step. In the procedure for generating the prefix these transitions will be added and marked as cut-offs. The prefix obtained from U by adding such transitions is denoted $U^\triangleright$.

We can now show that a c-complete prefix U of $\mathcal{U}(N)$, includes sufficient information for deciding whether or not N contains a weak causal place.

Theorem 2 (weak causal places in c-complete prefixes). *Let* N *be a safe net system and let* U *be a c-complete prefix of* $\mathcal{U}(N)$. *Then* p *is a weak causal place in* N *iff there exists in* $U^\triangleright$ *a condition* b *and events* h', l' *such that* $\pi_1(b) = p$, $b \in {}^\bullet l' \cap h'^+$ *and* $\lambda h' \not\rightsquigarrow \lambda l'$.

The above result and Proposition 3 implies that, given a safe net system, one can check for BNDC on a c-complete prefix of the unfolding of its causal reduct.

Corollary 1 (BNDC on c-complete prefixes). *Let* N *be a safe net system and let* U *be a c-complete prefix of* $\mathcal{U}(\gamma(N))$. *Then* N *is not BNDC iff there exist events* $h', l' \in U^\triangleright$ *such that* $\lambda h' \not\rightsquigarrow \lambda l'$ *and* ${}^\bullet l' \cap h'^+ \neq \emptyset$.

Corollary 1 leads to an algorithm for checking BNDC on safe net systems. Given $\mathbf{N}$ first it computes its causal reduct $\gamma(\mathbf{N})$. Then it builds a c-complete prefix of the unfolding $\mathcal{U}(\gamma(\mathbf{N}))$ by adding, at each step, a transition occurrence and checking if its direct causalities satisfy the conditions in Corollary 1.

Corollary 2 (correctness of the algorithm for BNDC). *Let* $\mathbf{N}$ *be a safe net system. The algorithm outlined above always terminates and answers 'yes' iff* $\mathbf{N}$ *is BNDC.*

4 Intransitive Multilevel Non-interference

In this section we focus on intransitive policies. The idea is that some information flows between levels that cannot communicate directly become allowed if they are mediated by a chain of trusted intermediaries.

4.1 Bisimilarity-Based Intransitive Non-interference

Inspired by the idea of separability in [19], in order to check whether there are illegal flows from a set of levels U, we artificially isolate that set by removing from the system all of its legal targets in $\uparrow U$. If, afterwards, the levels in U can still influence other levels in the rest of the system, the influence is certainly illegal. In fact, it cannot be mediated by a chain of legal intermediaries since any such chain has been certainly broken by the construction. This leads to a multilevel generalization of BINI (Bisimulation-based Intransitive Non-Interference) [6].

Definition 15 (BINI). *Given* $U \subseteq \mathcal{L}$, *a net system* $\mathbf{N}$ *is U-BINI if for all reachable markings* $m \in [m_0\rangle$ *the system* $(N \setminus T_{\uparrow U}, m)$ *is U-BNDC in the domain* $\mathcal{L}' = (\mathcal{L} \setminus \uparrow U, \rightsquigarrow^*)$. *The system* $\mathbf{N}$ *is BINI if it is U-BINI for all* $U \subseteq \mathcal{L}$.

As explained above, for each set of levels U we consider the net $N \setminus T_{\uparrow U}$, obtained by pruning the transitions with level in $\uparrow U$, to which a flow from U is admitted. The presence of an illegal flow from U is thus reduced to the presence of any flow from U in the pruned subsystem. In turn, the presence of a flow from U is formalized by resorting to the notion of BNDC previously introduced (Definition 11). It is easy to see that the definition is well-given, i.e., U is an upper set in $\mathcal{L}' = (\mathcal{L} \setminus \uparrow U, \rightsquigarrow^*)$. Note that an illegal flow from U could occur at any reachable marking m of the original system, but clearly the pruning operation can make m unreachable. This is the reason why the pruned net $N \setminus T_{\uparrow U}$ is checked with any marking reachable in the original net system $\mathbf{N}$.

Consider the running example in Fig. 1, which is not BNDC due to an interference between the cache and the sensors, and between the sensors themselves. In both cases the interference stem out from the mutually exclusive access to the cache. If this mode of access is an hardware constraint, it might be the case that the designer intends to ignore such occurrences of interference, deeming them inevitable and not problematic. This can be modeled by adding a number of

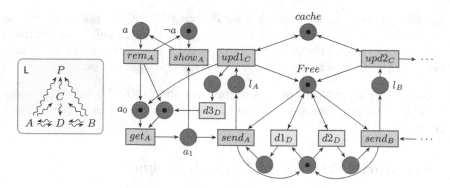

Fig. 3. A fix for the sensor net that makes it BINI. Only part of the system is shown, and as usual $\lambda(x_L) = L$. The downgrading transitions are highlighted in green. (Color figure online)

"downgrading" levels to the domain, and modifying the net adding downgrading transitions. In Fig. 3 we show how this can be done in order to make the old net BINI (we only show a part of the system: the processor is unchanged and the second sensor is symmetric to the first one). Note, e.g., that $C \not\rightsquigarrow A$ but transition $upd1_C$ can obviously influence get_A, since we can have a causal chain $upd1_C \, d3_D \, get_A$. However, this is not a violation of BINI because the interference occurs through $d3_D$, which is a legitimate intermediary ($C \rightsquigarrow D \rightsquigarrow A$). More formally, if we take $U = \{C\}$, according to Definition 15, we have to consider the net $N \setminus T_{\uparrow U}$, where legal intermediaries for C, namely transitions with level in $\uparrow\{C\} = \{D, P\}$ are pruned. In particular, the pruned net does not include transition $d3_D$ and thus the interference of $upd1_C$ on get_A is correctly hidden. Similarly, transitions $d1_D$ and $d2_D$ mediate the conflict between $send_A$ and $send_B$.

Although not immediate, as a sanity check, it can be proved that BINI and BNDC coincide on transitive domains.

Proposition 4 (BINI is BNDC on transitive domains). *In a transitive MSD $\mathscr{L}$, a net system $\mathbf{N}$ is BINI if and only if $\mathbf{N}$ is BNDC.*

Additionally, BINI can be characterized by replacing the quantification over all subsets $U \subseteq \mathscr{L}$ of Definition 15 with a quantification over single levels.

Proposition 5 (multilevel BINI on single levels). *A net system $\mathbf{N}$ is BINI iff $\mathbf{N}$ is $\{L\}$-BINI for each $L \in \mathscr{L}$.*

4.2 BINI Through Causal and Conflict Places

A characterization of BINI amenable of effective verification in the unfolding of safe nets, relies on intransitive variants of weak causal and conflict places.

Definition 16 (intransitive weak causal/conflict place). *Let* $\mathbf{N}$ *be a safe net system. An* intransitive weak causal place *is* $p \in {}^{\bullet}l \cap h^{+}$, *for* $l, h \in T$ *such that* $\lambda h \nrightarrow \lambda l$, *and there is a reachable* $m \in [m_0\rangle$ *such that* $m[h\tau l\rangle$, *with* $\tau \in T^{*}_{\overline{\uparrow \lambda h}}$. *An* intransitive weak conflict place *is* $p \in {}^{\bullet}l \cap h^{-}$, *for* $l, h \in t$ *such that* $\lambda h \nrightarrow \lambda l$, *and there is a reachable* $m \in [m_0\rangle$ *such that* $m[h\rangle$ *and* $m[\tau l\rangle$, *with* $\tau \in t^{*}_{\overline{\uparrow \lambda h}}$.

The difference with respect to the notions of weak causal and conflict place in Sect. 3.2 for transitive policies is that here τ is required not to contain any transition to which information can could legally flow from h. Intuitively, the reason is that, otherwise, the flow from h to l would be mediated by such transition, possibly amending the violation represented by p. As an example, in Fig. 3 place *Free* is not an intransitive conflict place, despite the fact that *Free* $\in {}^{\bullet}send_A \cap send_B^{-}$ and $B \nrightarrow A$. The reason is that, in any firing sequence starting from place *Free* marked, an occurrence of $send_A$ is necessarily preceded by $d1_D$.

Theorem 3 (BINI through intransitive weak places). *A safe net system* $\mathbf{N}$ *is BINI iff it contains no intransitive weak causal or conflict place.*

4.3   BINI in the Unfolding

Occurrences of intransitive weak causal places can be characterized in the unfolding of safe nets.

Theorem 4 (intransitive weak causal places in the unfolding). *Let* $\mathbf{N}$ *be a safe net system. A place* p *in* $\mathbf{N}$ *is an intransitive weak causal place iff there exists a condition* b *in* $\mathcal{U}(\mathbf{N})$ *such that* $\pi_1(b) = p$ *and there are events* h', l' *such that (i)* $b \in {}^{\bullet}l' \cap h'^{+}$ *and (ii)* $\forall t' : h' < t' \leq l'. \lambda h' \nrightarrow \lambda t'$.

The above, together with the possibility of resorting, as in the intransitive case, to the causal reduct, leads to the following characterization of BINI.

Proposition 6 (BINI in the causal reduct). *Let* $\mathbf{N}$ *be a net system. Then* $\mathbf{N}$ *is BINI iff the causal reduct* $\gamma(\mathbf{N})$ *contains no intransitive causal places.*

For building a complete prefix, we still need to enrich the marking associated with a configuration C with a function Λ_C, mapping each token to the security level of the generating transition. However, due to the intransitivity of the policy, this is no longer sufficient to detect a violation. In fact, assume that an event l of level L consumes a token of level H such that $H \nrightarrow L$. Apparently this is a violation of the policy since the presence of a token of level H reveals that an event, say h, of the same level has been executed before, and this fact is visible at level L. However, this might not be a problem, since it could be that a token of a level D such that $H \rightsquigarrow D \rightsquigarrow L$, is also in the pre-set of l, produced by an event d such that $h < d < l$. In this case, the flow of information from L to H is legitimately mediated by D. Roughly, we can think that the token of level D absorbs the token of level H to its level. We then enrich the markings with an *absorbing relation* δ over the conditions in the frontier of a configuration.

Definition 17 (i-marking, i-complete prefix). *Let* $\mathbf{N}$ *be a safe net system and let* $C \in \mathcal{C}(\mathcal{U}(\mathbf{N}))$. *The* intransitive confidentiality marking (i-marking) *of* C *is* $\mathsf{M}_i^*(C) = \langle \mathsf{M}(C), \Lambda_C, \delta_C \rangle$, *where* $\Lambda_C : P \to \mathscr{L}$ *is as in Definition 14 and* $\delta_C : \pi_1(C^\circ) \times \pi_1(C^\circ)$ *is the relation:*

$$\{(\pi_1(p), \pi_1(q)) \mid \exists t, t' \in C . q \in t'^\bullet \wedge \lambda(t') \rightsquigarrow \lambda t \wedge t' < t \leq p\}$$

A prefix U *of* $\mathcal{U}(\mathbf{N})$ *is* complete for i-marking reachability *(*i-complete*), when for any configuration* $C \in \mathcal{C}(\mathcal{U}(\mathbf{N}))$ *there is* $C' \in \mathcal{C}(U)$ *such that* $\mathsf{M}_i^*(C) = \mathsf{M}_i^*(C')$.

Intuitively, whenever $\delta(p, q)$ the token in p absorbs the token in q to its level, if they are used in the same pre-set.

It can be proved that an i-complete prefix U of $\mathcal{U}(\mathbf{N})$ includes sufficient information for deciding whether $\mathbf{N}$ contains a weak intransitive causal place. This fact, with Theorem 4 and Proposition 6, implies that one can check BINI for a net system on an i-complete prefix of the unfolding of its causal reduct.

Corollary 3 (BINI on i-complete prefixes). *Let* $\mathbf{N}$ *be a safe net system and let* U *be a i-complete prefix of* $\mathcal{U}(\gamma(\mathbf{N}))$. *Then* $\mathbf{N}$ *is not BINI iff there exists in* $U^\triangleright$ *a condition* b *and events* h', l' *such that* $b \in {}^\bullet l' \cap h'^+$, $\lambda h' \not\rightsquigarrow \lambda l'$, *and furthermore* $\forall b' \in {}^\bullet l' . \neg(b' \delta_{[l']} b)$.

In words, an interference is witnessed by an event l' that uses a token b of a non accessible level such that b is not absorbed. As in the transitive case, this result is used for designing an algorithm that checks BINI on safe net systems.

5   The Tool MultiUBIC

The unfolding-based algorithms outlined in the previous sections are implemented in MultiUBIC [14]. It extends a previous tool UBIC, which was limited to two level security domains (possibly with downgrading). MultiUBIC inputs a security policy (transitive or intransitive) and a safe net system, and it checks whether BNDC (transitive policies) or BINI (intransitive policies) is satisfied.

Compared to PNSC [21] and ANICA [22], "interleaving competitors" based on the work [5], MultiUBIC inherits the good performance of its ancestor UBIC: the use of a partial order semantics leads to a gain of efficiency especially for highly concurrent systems, where the state explosion problem is more serious.

The verification of multi-level security policies can be reduced to a number of checks in a two-level setting (possibly with downgrading, in the intransitive case). MultiUBIC comes equipped with facilities for performing such reduction. The definition of BNDC suggests that such reduction can be expensive, since the two-levels problems arise from partitions of the security domain whose number can be exponential in the number of levels. For net systems it can be actually shown that we can limit to a linear number of two-level checks, one for each level (see Proposition 1 for the transitive case and Proposition 5 for the intransitive case). Still, some preliminary experiments reveal that solving directly the original multi-level problem, typically provides a linear gain of efficiency at the price of an increase of memory usage. The performances of MultiUBIC can degrade for net systems where a relevant number of places have input transitions of different levels, a fact that potentially causes an exponential blow of the number of enriched markings. A precise characterization of this pathological situations is under investigation. Due to space limitations, a presentation of the experimental results and a more extensive discussion are deferred to the full version.

6 Conclusions

We studied non-interference in a multilevel setting, for transitive and intransitive security domains, focusing on Petri nets. Generalizing [7,11], we showed that Bisimilarity-based Non-Deducibility on Composition (BNDC) and its intransitive extension BINI [6], admit a causal characterizations in the unfolding of safe net systems. This led to verification algorithms for BNDC and BINI on safe net systems with multilevel policies, implemented in the tool MultiUBIC.

Causal semantics have been used in [23] for deducing the occurrence of non-observable transitions in the diagnosis of discrete event systems. There is a clear conceptual relation relation between diagnosability properties and non-interference, despite the fact that the former are trace-based while our non-interference is bisimulation-based. The work on intransitive non-interference in [24], that relies on automata models and language theory could be helpful for establishing a formal relation.

In the setting of Petri nets other classes of information flow properties have been studied, like opacity properties [25] (which include non-interference) and selective non-interference [26]. Exploring the use of causal semantics in this general setting appears as an interesting and challenging venue of future research.

A huge literature exists on non-interference for various formalisms, including process calculi and imperative languages (see, e.g., [2,27] for surveys). Fruitful connections could emerge investigating a causal characterizations of non-interference in these settings, possibly through encodings into Petri nets.

We also plan to consider formalizations of non-interference obtained from the classical ones, by replacing interleaving observational semantics with true-concurrent ones [28]. The higher distinguishing power of such semantics could allow to identify new forms of interference which cannot be captured in an interleaving setting. Interesting reflections in this directions are reported in [29].

References

1. Goguen, J.A., Meseguer, J.: Security policies and security models. In: Proceedings of the Symposium on Security and Privacy, pp. 11–20. IEEE Computer Society (1982)
2. Focardi, R., Gorrieri, R.: Classification of security properties (Part I: information flow). In: Focardi, R., Gorrieri, R. (eds.) FOSAD 2000. LNCS, vol. 2171, pp. 331–396. Springer, Heidelberg (2001)

3. Ryan, P., Schneider, Y.: Process algebra and non-interference. J. Comput. Secur. **9**(1/2), 75–103 (2001)
4. Mantel, H.: Possibilistic definitions of security - an assembly kit. In: Proceedings of CSFW 2000, pp. 185–199. IEEE Computer Society (2000)
5. Busi, N., Gorrieri, R.: Structural non-interference in elementary and trace nets. Math. Struct. Comput. Sci. **19**(6), 1065–1090 (2009)
6. Best, E., Darondeau, P., Gorrieri, R.: On the decidability of non interference over unbounded Petri nets. In Chatzikokolakis, K., Cortier, V. (eds.) Proceedings of SecCo 2010. EPTCS, vol. 51, pp. 16–33. Open Publishing Association (2010)
7. Baldan, P., Carraro, A.: A causal view on non-intereference. Fundamenta Informaticae **140**(1), 1–38 (2015)
8. McCullough, D.: Noninterference and the composability of security properties. In: Symposium on Security and Privacy, pp. 178–186. IEEE Computer Society (1988)
9. Wittbold, J., Johnson, D.: Information flow in nondeterministic systems. In: Symposium on Security and Privacy, pp. 148–161. IEEE Computer Society (1990)
10. Nielsen, M., Plotkin, G., Winskel, G.: Petri nets, event structures and domains, part 1. Theoret. Comput. Sci. **13**, 85–108 (1981)
11. Baldan, P., Burato, F., Carraro, A.: Intransitive non-interference by unfolding. In: Lanese, I., Madelaine, E. (eds.) FACS 2014. LNCS, vol. 8997, pp. 269–287. Springer, Heidelberg (2015)
12. Denning, D.E.: A lattice model of secure information flow. Commun. ACM **19**(5), 236–243 (1976)
13. Rushby, J.M.: Design and verification of secure systems. In: Proceedings of SOSP 1981, pp. 12–21. ACM (1981)
14. Beggiato, A.: MultiUBIC. https://github.com/AlessandroBeggiato/MultiUbic/releases
15. Service Technology: ANICA: Automated Non-Interference Check Assistant. http://service-technology.org/anica
16. Gorrieri, R., Vernali, M.: On intransitive non-interference in some models of concurrency. In: Aldini, A., Gorrieri, R. (eds.) FOSAD 2011. LNCS, vol. 6858, pp. 125–151. Springer, Heidelberg (2011)
17. Esparza, J., Heljanko, K.: Unfoldings - A Partial order Approach to Model Checking. EACTS Monographs in Theoretical Computer Science. Springer, New York (2008)
18. McMillan, K.L.: A technique of state space search based on unfolding. Form. Methods Syst. Des. **6**(1), 45–65 (1995)
19. Rushby, J.: Noninterference, transitivity, and channel-control security policies. Technical report, December 1992
20. Khomenko, V., Koutny, M., Vogler, W.: Canonical prefixes of Petri net unfoldings. Acta Informatica **40**, 95–118 (2003)
21. Frau, S., Gorrieri, R., Ferigato, C.: Petri net security checker: structural non-interference at work. In: Degano, P., Guttman, J., Martinelli, F. (eds.) FAST 2008. LNCS, vol. 5491, pp. 210–225. Springer, Heidelberg (2009)
22. Accorsi, R., Lehmann, A.: Automatic information flow analysis of business process models. In: Barros, A., Gal, A., Kindler, E. (eds.) BPM 2012. LNCS, vol. 7481, pp. 172–187. Springer, Heidelberg (2012)
23. Haar, S.: Types of asynchronous diagnosability and the reveals-relation in occurrence nets. IEEE Trans. Autom. Control **55**(10), 2310–2320 (2010)
24. Hadj-Alouane, B.N., Lafrance, S., Lin, F., Mullins, J., Yeddes, M.M.: On the verification of intransitive noninterference in multilevel security. IEEE Trans. Syst. Man Cybernetics Part B **35**(5), 948–958 (2005)

25. Bryans, J., Koutny, M., Ryan, P.: Modelling dynamic opacity using Petri nets with silent actions. In: Dimitrakos, T., Martinelli, F. (eds.) FAST 2005. IFIP, vol. 173, pp. 159–172. Springer, Boston (2005)
26. Best, E., Darondeau, P.: Deciding selective declassification of Petri nets. In: Degano, P., Guttman, J.D. (eds.) POST 2012. LNCS, vol. 7215, pp. 290–308. Springer, Heidelberg (2012)
27. Mantel, H., Sands, D.: Controlled declassification based on intransitive noninterference. In: Chin, W.-N. (ed.) APLAS 2004. LNCS, vol. 3302, pp. 129–145. Springer, Heidelberg (2004)
28. van Glabbeek, R., Goltz, U.: Refinement of actions and equivalence notions for concurrent systems. Acta Informatica **37**(4/5), 229–327 (2001)
29. Fröschle, S.: Causality, behavioural equivalences, and the security of cyberphysical systems. In: Meyer, R., Platzer, A., Wehrheim, H. (eds.) Olderog-Festschrift. LNCS, vol. 9360, pp. 83–98. Springer, Heidelberg (2015)

A Game Interpretation of Retractable Contracts

Franco Barbanera[1]([✉]) and Ugo de' Liguoro[2]

[1] Dipartimento di Matematica e Informatica, University of Catania, Catania, Italy
barba@dmi.unict.it
[2] Dipartimento di Informatica, University of Torino, Torino, Italy
ugo.deliguoro@unito.it

Abstract. In the setting of contract theory, retractable contracts have been defined to formalize binary session protocols where the partners can go back to certain particular synchronization points when the session gets stuck, looking for a successful state, if any.

In the present paper we propose a three-party game-theoretic interpretation of client/server systems of retractable contracts. In particular, we show that a client is retractable-compliant with a server if and only if there exists a winning strategy for a particular player in a game-theoretic model of contracts. Such a player can be looked at as a *mediator*, driving the choices in the retractable points. We show that winning strategies for the mediator player correspond to orchestrators in a system of orchestrated client/server sessions, and vice versa.

The notion of *contract* has been proposed as an abstraction to formally specify and check the behaviour of software systems, and especially of web services. In particular, in the setting of service-oriented architectures the concept of agreement, often called *compliance*, is of paramount importance while searching components and ensuring that they will properly collaborate with each other. The main challenge is that compliance has to meet the contrasting requirements of guaranteeing correctness of interactions w.r.t. certain safety and liveness conditions, while remaining coarse enough to maximize the possibilities of finding compliant components in a library or services through the web.

The main conceptual tool to face the issue is that of relaxing the constraint of a perfect correspondence among contracts through *contract refinement*, also called sub-contract [8,9] and sub-behaviour [3] relations, that is pre-order relations such that processes conforming to more demanding contracts (which are lower in the pre-order) can be safely substituted in contexts allowing more permissive ones. Indeed contract refinement closely resembles subtyping, as it is apparent in the case of session types [3,10], and it is related to (but doesn't coincide with) observational pre-orders and *must-testing* in process algebra [6,11].

However, since the first contributions to the theory of contracts [9], a rather different approach has been followed, based on the idea of filtering out certain actions that, although unmatched on both sides of a binary interaction, can be

This work was partially supported by the COST Action IC1405 of the European Union and by the Project FIR 1B8C1 of the University of Catania.

A. Lluch Lafuente and J. Proença (Eds.): COORDINATION 2016, LNCS 9686, pp. 18–34, 2016.
DOI: 10.1007/978-3-319-39519-7_2

neglected or prevented by the action of a mediating process called the *orchestrator* [13,14], without compromising the reaching of the goals of the participants, like the satisfaction of all client requests in a client-server architecture.

An alternative route for the same purpose is to change the semantics of contracts so that interacting processes can adapt each other by means of a rollback mechanism: these are the *retractable contracts* proposed in [4]. Although compliance can be decided in advance, interaction among processes exposing retractable contracts undergoes a sequence of failures and backtracks that might be avoided by extracting information from the compliance check.

The contribution of the present paper is to show that the two approaches of orchestrated and retractable compliance are indeed equivalent, at least in the case of *session contracts* (see [2,3], where they are dubbed "session behaviours"), which are contracts that limit the non-determinism by constraining both external and internal choices to a more regular form. More precisely, we consider contracts that are syntactically the same as retractable ones, but instead of adding rollback to the usual contract semantics, we abstractly define outputs in an external choice as *affectible* actions: their actual sent can be influenced by the partner in a binary session or by some entity external to the system. Affectible actions correspond to retractable actions in [4].

The essence of the construction is that (an appropriate restriction of) orchestrators correspond to winning strategies in certain concurrent games that naturally model retractable contracts. In [5] the theory of contracts has been grounded on games over event structures among multiple players; applying this framework to retractable contracts, the interaction among a client and a server can be seen as a play in a three-party game. Player A moves according to the unaffectible actions of the client; player B moves according to the unaffectible actions of the server, whereas moves by player C correspond to affectible actions on both sides, namely the retractable agreement points of the system. The client ρ is hence affectible-compliant with the server σ whenever C has a winning strategy in the game with players A and B, where player C wins when she succeeds to lead the system $\rho\|\sigma$ to a successful state (the client terminates) or the interaction proceeds indefinitely without deadlocking.

The payoff of the game theoretic interpretation is that there is a precise correspondence between winning strategies for player C and elements of a class of orchestrators in the sense of [14]. Such a correspondence is of interest on its own, since strategies are abstract entities while orchestrators are terms of a process algebra and concrete witnesses of the agreement among participants of a session. Moreover, we can decide whether a client-server pair is reversible-compliant by means of an algorithm that synthesizes an orchestrator if any, or reports failure.

1   Affectible Contracts and Retractable Compliance

Affectible session contracts (affectible contracts for short) are a variant of *retractable contracts* in [4]; they are syntactically the same, but affectible session contracts have a different, and more abstract semantics. Nonetheless compliance coincides in both settings as we show in this section.

Definition 1 (Affectible session contracts). *Let $\mathcal{N}$ (set of names) be some countable set of symbols and let $\overline{\mathcal{N}} = \{\,\overline{a} \mid a \in \mathcal{N}\,\}$ (set of conames), with $\mathcal{N} \cap \overline{\mathcal{N}} = \emptyset$. The set* ASC *of* **affectible session contracts** *is defined as the set of the* **closed** *(with respect to the binder* rec *) expressions generated by the following grammar,*

$$\sigma, \rho := \mid \mathbf{1} \qquad\qquad\quad success$$
$$\mid \textstyle\sum_{i \in I} a_i.\sigma_i \quad input$$
$$\mid \textstyle\sum_{i \in I} \overline{a}_i.\sigma_i \quad affectible\ output$$
$$\mid \textstyle\bigoplus_{i \in I} \overline{a}_i.\sigma_i \quad unaffectible\ output$$
$$\mid x \qquad\qquad\quad variable$$
$$\mid \mathsf{rec}\, x.\sigma \qquad\quad recursion$$

where I is non-empty and finite, the names and the conames in choices are pairwise distinct and σ is not a variable in rec $x.\sigma$.

Affectible as well as retractable contracts stem from *session behaviours* of [3] also called *session contracts* in [6]. With respect to session behaviors, affectible contracts add the affectible output construct, which is called retractable output in [4]. The affectible output represents points where the client-server interaction can be influenced by the partner process, or can be guided by a third party; consequently they are represented by the CCS external choice operator as it is the case of the input branching (which is always affectible). Outputs in an internal choice are regarded as unaffectible actions and treated as unretractable in the setting of retractable contracts. The transitions representing an internal choice have no label; note that any $\bigoplus_{i \in I} \overline{a}_i.\sigma_i$ just reduces to one of its summands.

In the following we consider recursion up-to unfolding, that is we equate rec $x.\sigma$ with $\sigma\{x/\mathsf{rec}\,x.\sigma\}$. The symbol α will be used as a variable ranging over $\mathcal{N} \cup \overline{\mathcal{N}}$.

Definition 2 (LTS for ASC**).** *Let* $\mathbf{Act} = \mathcal{N} \cup \overline{\mathcal{N}} \cup \{\,\overline{a}^+ \mid \overline{a} \in \overline{\mathcal{N}}\,\}$.

$$(+)\ a.\sigma + \sigma' \xrightarrow{a} \sigma \qquad\qquad (\overline{+})\ \overline{a}.\sigma + \sigma' \xrightarrow{\overline{a}^+} \sigma$$
$$(\oplus)\ \overline{a}.\sigma \oplus \sigma' \longrightarrow \overline{a}.\sigma \qquad\qquad (\alpha)\quad \alpha.\sigma \xrightarrow{\alpha} \sigma$$

A client/server system (system for short) is a pair of contracts in ASC that we denote by $\rho \parallel \sigma$.

Definition 3 (LTS for systems). *Let* $\mathbf{csAct} = \{\,+, \tau\,\}$.

$$\frac{\rho \to \rho'}{\rho \parallel \sigma \to \rho' \parallel \sigma} \qquad\qquad \frac{\sigma \to \sigma'}{\rho \parallel \sigma \to \rho \parallel \sigma'}$$

$$\frac{\rho \xrightarrow{a} \rho' \quad \sigma \xrightarrow{\overline{a}^+} \sigma'}{\rho \parallel \sigma \xrightarrow{+} \rho' \parallel \sigma'} \qquad\qquad \frac{\rho \xrightarrow{\overline{a}^+} \rho' \quad \sigma \xrightarrow{a} \sigma'}{\rho \parallel \sigma \xrightarrow{+} \rho' \parallel \sigma'}$$

$$\frac{\rho \xrightarrow{\alpha} \rho' \quad \sigma \xrightarrow{\overline{\alpha}} \sigma'}{\rho \parallel \sigma \xrightarrow{\tau} \rho' \parallel \sigma'}$$

We define $\Longrightarrow\ =\ \rightarrow^* \circ \xrightarrow{\tau}$ and $\overset{+}{\Longrightarrow}\ =\ \rightarrow^* \circ \xrightarrow{+}$. In the last rule, $\overline{\alpha}$ is the CCS involution of names and co-names.

The semantics of $\rho \parallel \sigma$ is reminiscent of CCS parallel composition as used to define testing preorders in [12], but for the usage of the labels $+$ and τ and for the absence of a success marker (there is a set of success states instead: see below). We use labels $+$ and τ to distinguish among affectible and unaffectible communications respectively, although they are both unobservable as the only observable facts are termination and the resulting state.

Lemma 1. *Let* $\rho, \sigma \in \mathsf{ASC}$. $\rho \parallel \sigma \Longrightarrow$ *and* $\rho \parallel \sigma \overset{+}{\Longrightarrow}$ *can never both occur.*

The affectible compliance relation can be now coinductively defined as follows.

Definition 4 (Affectible Compliance Relation $\dashv^A$).

(i) Let $\mathcal{H} : \mathcal{P}(\mathsf{ASC} \times \mathsf{ASC}) \to \mathcal{P}(\mathsf{ASC} \times \mathsf{ASC})$ *be such that, for any* $\mathcal{R} \subseteq \mathsf{ASC} \times \mathsf{ASC}$, *we get* $(\rho, \sigma) \in \mathcal{H}(\mathcal{R})$ *if the following conditions hold:*

(1) $[\ \rho \parallel \sigma \not\Longrightarrow$ *and* $\rho \parallel \sigma \overset{+}{\not\Longrightarrow}\ ]$ *implies* $\rho = \mathbf{1}$;
(2) $\forall \rho', \sigma'.\ [\ \rho \parallel \sigma \Longrightarrow \rho' \parallel \sigma'$ *implies* $\rho'\ \mathcal{R}\ \sigma'\ ]$;
(3) $\rho \parallel \sigma \overset{+}{\Longrightarrow}$ *implies* $\exists \rho', \sigma'.\ [\ \rho \parallel \sigma \overset{+}{\Longrightarrow} \rho' \parallel \sigma'$ *and* $\rho'\ \mathcal{R}\ \sigma'\ ]$.

(ii) A relation $\mathcal{R} \subseteq \mathsf{ASC} \times \mathsf{ASC}$ *is an* affectible compliance relation *if* $\mathcal{R} \subseteq \mathcal{H}(\mathcal{R})$. $\dashv^A$ *is the greatest solution of the equation* $X = \mathcal{H}(X)$, *that is* $\dashv^A\ =\ \nu\mathcal{H}$.

In words the client ρ is affectible-compliant with the server σ if either ρ and σ cannot communicate because $\rho = \mathbf{1}$, namely all client requirements have been satisfied; or all unaffectible communications of the system $\rho \parallel \sigma$ lead to compliant systems; or there exists an affectible communication leading to a compliant system. By Lemma 1 the last two conditions cannot be simultaneously satisfied.

Because of conditions *(i2)* and *(i3)*, the affectible compliance relation is an abstract concept; but it can be made concrete via the characterization in terms of retractable computations, provided in Sect. 1.

Let us consider the following example from [4]. A Buyer is looking for a bag ($\overline{\mathsf{bag}}$) or a belt ($\overline{\mathsf{belt}}$); she will decide how to pay, either by credit card ($\overline{\mathsf{card}}$) or by cash ($\overline{\mathsf{cash}}$), after knowing the price from the Seller.

$$\mathsf{Buyer} = \overline{\mathsf{bag}}.\mathsf{price}.(\overline{\mathsf{card}} \oplus \overline{\mathsf{cash}}) + \overline{\mathsf{belt}}.\mathsf{price}.(\overline{\mathsf{card}} \oplus \overline{\mathsf{cash}})$$

The Seller does not accept credit card payments for items of low price, like belts, but only for more expensive ones, like bags:

$$\mathsf{Seller} = \mathsf{belt}.\overline{\mathsf{price}}.\mathsf{cash} + \mathsf{bag}.\overline{\mathsf{price}}.(\mathsf{card} + \mathsf{cash})$$

From the previous definition it is not difficult to check that $\mathsf{Buyer} \dashv^A \mathsf{Seller}$.

Retractable Contracts. Let us recall the formalism of retractable contracts; the following definitions and Theorem 1 below are from [4]. As said before, retractable and affectible contracts are syntactically the same, but the operational semantics of the formers is based on a rollback operation, acting on the recording of certain discarded branches of an interaction. The notion of *contracts with histories* is defined as follows:

Definition 5 (Contracts with histories). *Let* Histories *be the set of expressions (referred to also as* stacks*) generated by the grammar:*

$$\gamma ::= [\,] \mid \gamma : \sigma \quad where \, \sigma \in \mathsf{ASC} \cup \{\circ\}.$$

Then the set of contracts with histories *is defined by:*

$$\mathsf{RCH} = \{\gamma \prec \sigma \mid \gamma \in \mathsf{Histories}, \sigma \in \mathsf{ASC} \cup \{\circ\}\,\}.$$

Histories are finite lists of contracts representing the branches which have been discarded because of a retractable synchronization action. The effect of retracting such an action is modeled by restoring the last contract on the history as the actual contract and by trying a different branch, if any. This is formalised by the operational semantics of contracts with histories that is defined as follows.

Definition 6 (LTS of Contracts with Histories).

$(+)\ \gamma \prec \alpha.\sigma + \sigma' \xrightarrow{\alpha} \gamma{:}\sigma' \prec \sigma$ $(\oplus)\ \gamma \prec \bar{a}.\sigma \oplus \sigma' \xrightarrow{\tau} \gamma \prec \bar{a}.\sigma$

$(\alpha)\ \gamma \prec \alpha.\sigma \xrightarrow{\alpha} \gamma{:}\circ \prec \sigma$ $(\mathsf{rb})\ \gamma{:}\sigma' \prec \sigma \xrightarrow{\mathsf{rb}} \gamma \prec \sigma'$

When selecting a branch of an external choice, the discarded branches are memorised on top of the new stack (the last contract of the history) in the right-hand side of rule $(+)$; on the contrary, when an internal choice occurs, the stack remains unchanged in rule $(\oplus)$. When a single action is executed, the history is modified by adding a '$\circ$', meaning that the only available branch has been tried and no alternative is left. Rule (rb) recovers the contract on the top of the stack (if the stack is different than $[\,]$) by replacing the current one with it. Note that the combined effect of rules $(\oplus)$ and (α) is that the alternative branches of an internal choice are unrecoverable.

The interaction of a client with a server is modeled by the reduction of their parallel composition, that can be either forward, consisting of CCS style synchronisations and single internal choices, or backward if there is no possible forward reduction, the client is different than **1** (the fulfilled contract) and rule (rb) is applicable on both sides.

Definition 7 (TS of Client/Server Pairs). *We define the relation* $\longrightarrow$ *over pairs of retractable contracts with histories by the following rules:*

$$\frac{\delta \prec \rho \xrightarrow{\alpha} \delta' \prec \rho' \quad \gamma \prec \sigma \xrightarrow{\overline{\alpha}} \gamma' \prec \sigma'}{\delta \prec \rho \,\|\, \gamma \prec \sigma \longrightarrow \delta' \prec \rho' \,\|\, \gamma' \prec \sigma'} \ (comm)$$

$$\frac{\delta \prec \rho \xrightarrow{\tau} \delta \prec \rho'}{\delta \prec \rho \,\|\, \gamma \prec \sigma \longrightarrow \delta \prec \rho' \,\|\, \gamma \prec \sigma} \ (\tau)$$

$$\frac{\gamma \prec \rho \xrightarrow{rb} \gamma' \prec \rho' \quad \delta \prec \sigma \xrightarrow{rb} \delta' \prec \sigma' \quad \rho \neq 1}{\gamma \prec \rho \,\|\, \delta \prec \sigma \longrightarrow \gamma' \prec \rho' \,\|\, \delta' \prec \sigma'} \ (rbk)$$

plus the rule symmetric to (τ) w.r.t. $\|$. Moreover, rule (rbk) applies only if neither $(comm)$ nor (τ) do.

Up to the rollback mechanism, compliance in the retractable setting is defined as usually done with client/server contracts.

Definition 8 (Retractable Compliance, $\dashv^{\mathsf{ttk}}$).

(i) The relation $\dashv^{\mathsf{ttk}}$ on contracts with histories is defined as follows: for any $\delta', \rho', \gamma', \sigma'$, $\delta \prec \rho \dashv^{\mathsf{ttk}} \gamma \prec \sigma$ holds whenever

$$\delta \prec \rho \,\|\, \gamma \prec \sigma \xrightarrow{\;*\;} \delta' \prec \rho' \,\|\, \gamma' \prec \sigma' \nrightarrow \ implies \ \rho' = 1$$

(ii) The relation $\dashv^{\mathsf{ttk}}$ on contracts is defined by: $\rho \dashv^{\mathsf{ttk}} \sigma$ if $[\,] \prec \rho \dashv^{\mathsf{ttk}} [\,] \prec \sigma$.

In Buyer/Seller example we have that, in case a belt is agreed upon and the buyer decides to pay using her credit card, the system gets stuck in an unsuccessful state. This causes a rollback enabling a successful state to be reached. So Buyer $\dashv^{\mathsf{ttk}}$ Seller.

Retractable compliance can be axiomatised in terms of derivability in a formal system whose statements do not mention histories.

Definition 9 (Formal System $\triangleright$ for Retractable Compliance).

$$(\textsc{Ax}) : \overline{\Gamma \triangleright 1 \dashv^{\prec} \sigma} \qquad (\textsc{Hyp}) : \overline{\Gamma, \rho \dashv^{\prec} \sigma \triangleright \rho \dashv^{\prec} \sigma}$$

$$(+\cdot+) : \frac{\Gamma, \alpha.\rho + \rho' \dashv^{\prec} \overline{\alpha}.\sigma + \sigma' \triangleright \rho \dashv^{\prec} \sigma}{\Gamma \triangleright \alpha.\rho + \rho' \dashv^{\prec} \overline{\alpha}.\sigma + \sigma'}$$

$$(\oplus \cdot +) : \frac{\forall i \in I. \ \Gamma, \bigoplus_{i \in I} \overline{a}_i.\rho_i \dashv^{\prec} \sum_{j \in I \cup J} a_j.\sigma_j \triangleright \rho_i \dashv^{\prec} \sigma_i}{\Gamma \triangleright \bigoplus_{i \in I} \overline{a}_i.\rho_i \dashv^{\prec} \sum_{j \in I \cup J} a_j.\sigma_j}$$

$$(+ \cdot \oplus) : \frac{\forall i \in I. \ \Gamma, \sum_{j \in I \cup J} a_j.\sigma_j \dashv^{\prec} \bigoplus_{i \in I} \overline{a}_i.\rho_i \triangleright \rho_i \dashv^{\prec} \sigma_i}{\Gamma \triangleright \sum_{j \in I \cup J} a_j.\sigma_j \dashv^{\prec} \bigoplus_{i \in I} \overline{a}_i.\rho_i}$$

Let us formally show that $\emptyset \triangleright$ Buyer $\dashv^\times$ Seller

$$
\cfrac{
\cfrac{
\cfrac{}{\Gamma'' \triangleright 1 \dashv^\times 1}\text{(Ax)} \qquad
\cfrac{}{\Gamma'' \triangleright 1 \dashv^\times 1}\text{(Ax)}
}{\Gamma' \triangleright \overline{\text{card}} \oplus \overline{\text{cash}} \dashv^\times \text{card} + \text{cash}}(\oplus,+)
}{
\cfrac{
\text{Buyer}' \dashv^\times \text{Seller} \triangleright \text{price}.(\overline{\text{card}} \oplus \overline{\text{cash}}) \dashv^\times \overline{\text{price}}.(\text{card} + \text{cash})
}{\triangleright \text{Buyer} \dashv^\times \text{Seller}}(+,+)
}(+,+)
$$

where $\Gamma' = $ Buyer $\dashv^\times$ Seller, $\text{price}.(\overline{\text{card}} \oplus \overline{\text{cash}}) \dashv^\times \overline{\text{price}}.(\text{card} + \text{cash})$
and $\Gamma'' = \Gamma', \overline{\text{card}} \oplus \overline{\text{cash}} \dashv^\times \text{card} + \text{cash}$

The formal system $\triangleright$ completely axiomatises retractable compliance:

Theorem 1 (Soundness and Completeness of system $\triangleright$ w.r.t $\dashv^{tbk}$).

$$\rho \dashv^{tbk} \sigma \quad \text{if and only if} \quad \triangleright \rho \dashv^\times \sigma.$$

Equivalence of $\dashv^A$ and $\dashv^{tbk}$. As previously observed, the judgements of system $\triangleright$ abstract away from histories, which are essential in the definition of rollback. This is possible because rollback is just a backtracking mechanism, which is however limited to the exploration of alternative branches of the reduction tree of a system rooted at retractable communications. Since affectible and retractable communications are the same, it is natural to look at system $\triangleright$ to establish the equivalence among $\dashv^A$ and $\dashv^{tbk}$.

Lemma 2. *If $\rho \dashv^A \sigma$, then one of the following conditions holds:*

1. $\rho = 1$;
2. $\rho = \sum_{i \in I} \alpha_i.\rho_i$, $\sigma = \sum_{j \in J} \overline{\alpha}_j.\sigma_j$ *and* $\exists h \in I \cap J. \rho_h \dashv^A \sigma_h$;
3. $\rho = \bigoplus_{i \in I} \overline{a}_i.\rho_i$, $\sigma = \sum_{j \in J} a_j.\sigma_j$, $I \subseteq J$ *and* $\forall h \in I. \rho_h \dashv^A \sigma_h$;
4. $\rho = \sum_{i \in I} a_i.\rho_i$, $\sigma = \bigoplus_{j \in J} \overline{a}_j.\sigma_j$, $I \supseteq J$ *and* $\forall h \in J. \rho_h \dashv^A \sigma_h$.

In Theorem 1, soundness and completeness of system $\triangleright$ has been proved when the symbol $\dashv^\times$ is interpreted as the retractable compliance relation $\dashv^{tbk}$. We now show that system $\triangleright$ is sound and complete also when the symbol $\dashv^\times$ is interpreted as the affectible compliance relation $\dashv^A$. The equivalence of the relations $\dashv^{tbk}$ and $\dashv^A$ follows then as an immediate corollary.

Definition 10. (A $\dashv^A$-semantics for system $\triangleright$). *Let Γ be a set of statements of the form $\rho \dashv^\times \sigma$. We define*

(i) $\models^A \Gamma$ *if* $\forall(\rho' \dashv^\times \sigma') \in \Gamma. [\rho' \dashv^A \sigma']$;
(ii) $\Gamma \models^A \rho \dashv^\times \sigma$ *if* $\models^A \Gamma \Rightarrow \rho \dashv^A \sigma$.

The proof of the following Lemma is inspired to [7].

Lemma 3. (Soundness of $\triangleright$ w.r.t $\dashv^A$). *If $\Gamma \triangleright \rho \dashv^\times \sigma$, then $\Gamma \models^A \rho \dashv^\times \sigma$.*

We write $\mathcal{D} :: \Gamma \rhd \rho \dashv^\times \sigma$ when $\mathcal{D}$ is a derivation in the system $\rhd$ with conclusion $\Gamma \rhd \rho \dashv^\times \sigma$. We can easily implement a backward proof search (from conclusion to premises) in the formal system $\rhd$ by means of a procedure **Prove**.

Lemma 4. (i) **Prove**$(\Gamma \rhd \rho \dashv^\times \sigma) = \mathcal{D} \neq \textbf{\textit{fail}}$ implies $\mathcal{D} :: \Gamma \rhd \rho \dashv^\times \sigma$; (ii) **Prove**$(\Gamma \rhd \rho \dashv^\times \sigma)$ terminates for all judgments $\Gamma \rhd \rho \dashv^\times \sigma$.

Lemma 5 (Completeness of $\rhd$ w.r.t $\dashv^A$). If $\rho \dashv^A \sigma$, then $\rhd \rho \dashv^\times \sigma$.

Proof (Sketch). If $\rho \dashv^A \sigma$ then by Lemma 2 there are four possibilities; disregarding the contexts Γ's, we see that each of these cases corresponds exactly to one rule in system $\rhd$, where **Prove** is recursively applied to the respective premises, but for rule (HYP), that corresponds to an exit clause in **Prove**. It follows that **Prove**$(\rhd \rho \dashv^\times \sigma) \neq \textbf{fail}$, so that the thesis follows by Lemma 4, since **Prove** always terminates either returning a correct derivation or **fail**.

Corollary 1. $\dashv^{tbk} = \dashv^A$

Proof. By Lemmas 3 and 5 and Theorem 1

2 Game-Theoretic Interpretation of Retractable Contracts

Following [5] we interpret affectible contracts as certain games over event structures. This yields a game-theoretic interpretation of affectible contracts, and hence of retractable contracts by Corollary 1. For the reader's convenience we briefly recall the basic notions of event structure and game associated to an LTS.

Definition 11 (Event structure [15]). *Let* $\mathbf{E}$ *be a denumerable universe of events and let* $\mathbf{A}$ *be a universe of* action labels. *Besides, let* $\# \subseteq E \times E$ *be an irreflexive and symmetric relation (called* conflict relation).

(i) *The predicate CF on sets* $X \subseteq E$ *and the set Con of finite* conflict-free *sets are defined by* $CF(X) = \forall e, e' \in X. \neg(e \# e')$ $Con = \{ X \subseteq_{fin} E \mid CF(X) \}$
(ii) *An* event structure *is a quadruple* $\mathcal{E} = (E, \#, \vdash, l)$ *where*
  $-\ \vdash\ \subseteq Con \times E$ *is a relation such that* $sat(\vdash) = \vdash$ (*i.e.* $\vdash$ *is saturated),*
    where $sat(\vdash) = \{ (Y, e) \mid X \vdash e \& X \subseteq Y \in Con \}$;
  $- \ l : E \to \mathbf{A}$ *is a labelling function.*

Given a set E of events, E^∞ denotes the set of sequences (both finite and infinite) of its elements. We denote by $e = \langle e_0 e_1 \cdots \rangle$ a sequence of events[1]. Given e, we denote by $\widehat{e}$ the set of its elements, by $|e|$ its length (either a natural number or ∞) and by $e_{/i}$ for $i < |e|$ the subsequence $\langle e_0 e_1 \cdots e_{i-1} \rangle$ of its first i elements. Given a set X we denote by $|X|$ its cardinality. $\mathbb{N}$ is the set of natural numbers.

---

[1] Differently than in [5], we use the notation e for sequences instead of σ, which refers to a contract here.

Definition 12 (LTS over configurations [5]). *Given an event structure*
$\mathcal{E} = (E, \#, \vdash, l)$, *we define the LTS* $(\mathcal{P}_{fin}(E), E, \rightarrow_{\mathcal{E}})$ *as follows:*

$$C \xrightarrow{e} C \cup \{e\} \qquad if \quad C \vdash e, e \notin C \ and \ CF(C \cup \{e\})$$

Given an LTS $(S, \rightarrow)$ and a state $s \in S$, we denote by $(s, \rightarrow)$ the restriction of
$\rightarrow$ to the transitions starting with the state s, and by $\mathsf{Tr}(s, \rightarrow)$ the set of the
(finite or infinite) traces in $(s, \rightarrow)$ out of s.

Multi-player Games. All the subsequent definitions and terminology are from
[5], except in the case of games that we call multi-player instead of "contracts",
which would be confusing in the present setting.

A set of participants (players) to a game will be denoted by $\mathfrak{P}$, whereas
the universe of partecipants is denoted by $\mathfrak{P}_{\mathfrak{U}}$. We shall use A, B,... as variables
ranging over $\mathfrak{P}$ or $\mathfrak{P}_{\mathfrak{U}}$. The symbols A, B, ... will denote particular elements of $\mathfrak{P}$
or $\mathfrak{P}_{\mathfrak{U}}$. We assume that each event is associated to a player by means of a function
$\pi : \mathbf{E} \rightarrow \mathfrak{P}_{\mathfrak{U}}$. Moreover, given $A \in \mathfrak{P}_{\mathfrak{U}}$ we define $\mathbf{E}_A = \{e \in \mathbf{E} \mid \pi(e) = A\}$.

Definition 13 (Multi-player game).

*(i) A game $\mathcal{G}$ is a pair $(\mathcal{E}, \Phi)$ where $\mathcal{E} = (E, \#, \vdash, l)$ is an event structure and
$\Phi : \mathfrak{P}_{\mathfrak{U}} \rightharpoonup E^{\infty} \rightarrow \{-1, 0, 1\}$ associates each participant and trace with a
payoff. Moreover, for all $X \vdash e$ in $\mathcal{E}$, $\Phi(\pi(e))$ is defined. We say that $\mathcal{G}$ is a
game with partecipants $\mathfrak{P}$ whenever ΦA is defined for any player A in $\mathfrak{P}$.*
*(ii) A play of a game $\mathcal{G} = (\mathcal{E}, \Phi)$ is a (finite or infinite) trace of $(\emptyset, \rightarrow_{\mathcal{E}})$ i.e. an
element of $\mathsf{Tr}(\emptyset, \rightarrow_{\mathcal{E}})$.*

Definition 14 (Strategy and conformance). *A strategy Σ for a participant
A in a game $\mathcal{G}$ is a function which maps each finite play $e = \langle e_0 \cdots e_n \rangle$ to a
(possibly empty) subset of $\mathbf{E}_A$ such that: $e \in \Sigma(e) \Rightarrow ee$ is a play of $\mathcal{G}$.
A play $e = \langle e_0 e_1 \cdots \rangle$ conforms to a strategy Σ for a partecipant A in $\mathcal{G}$ if, for
all $i \geq 0$, $e_i \in \mathbf{E}_A \Rightarrow e_i \in \Sigma(e_{/i})$.*

Although events, namely moves, are associated to players via the map π, this
is not injective in general, so that players can share moves. In general there are
neither a turn rule nor alternation of players, similarly to concurrent games in
[1]. A strategy Σ provides "suggestions" to some player on how to legally move
continuing finite plays (also called "positions" in game-theoretic literature). But
Σ may be ambiguous at some places, since $\Sigma(e)$ may contain more than an
event; in fact it can be viewed as a partial mapping which is undefined when
$\Sigma(e) = \emptyset$.

We refer to [5] for the general definition of winning strategy for multi-player
games (briefly recalled also in Remark 1 below), since it involves the conditions
of fairness and innocence, which will be trivially satisfied in our interpretation of
affectible client/server systems, where the notion of winning strategy corresponds
to the one given in Definition 19.

Turn-Based Operational Semantics and Compliance. Toward the game theoretic interpretation of a client/server system $\rho \parallel \sigma$, we introduce a slightly different description of the semantics of affectible contracts, making explicit the idea of a three-player game. We interpret the internal choices and the input actions of the client as moves of a player A and the internal choices and the input actions of the server as moves of a player B. The synchronisations due to affectible choices are instead interpreted as moves of the third player C.

From a technical point of view this is a slight generalization and adaptation to our scenario of the turn-based semantics of "session types" in [5], Sect. 5.2. The changes are needed both because we have three players instead of two, and because session types are just session contracts, that is affectible contracts without affectible outputs.

Definition 15 (Single-buffered ASC). *The set* $\mathsf{ASC}^{[]}$ *of* single-buffered *affectible contracts is defined by* $\mathsf{ASC}^{[]} = \mathsf{ASC} \cup \{\mathbf{0}\} \cup \{[\bar{a}_k]\sigma_k \mid \oplus_{i \in I}\bar{a}_i.\sigma_i \in \mathsf{ASC}, k \in I\}$

We use the symbols $\tilde{\rho}, \tilde{\sigma}, \tilde{\rho}', \tilde{\sigma}' \ldots$ to denote elements of $\mathsf{ASC}^{[]}$. A *turn-based configuration* (configuration for short) is a pair $\tilde{\rho} \parallel\!\parallel \tilde{\sigma}$, where $\tilde{\rho}, \tilde{\sigma} \in \mathsf{ASC}^{[]}$.

As in [5], we have added the "single buffered" contracts $[\bar{a}]\sigma$ to represent the situation in which $\bar{a}$ is the only output offered after an internal choice. Since the actual synchronization takes place in a subsequent step, $\bar{a}$ is "buffered" in front of the continuation σ.

Definition 16 (Turn-based operational semantics of configurations). Let $\mathbf{tbAct} = \{A, B, C\} \times (\mathbf{Act} \cup \{\checkmark\})$. *In Fig. 1 we define the LTS* $\longrightarrow$ *over turn-based configurations, with labels in* $\mathbf{tbAct}$.

Comparing $\longrightarrow$ with the LTS for affectible contracts, we observe that $[\bar{a}]\sigma$ is a duplicate of $\bar{a}.\sigma$, with the only difference that now there is a redundant step in $\oplus_{i \in I}\bar{a}_i.\rho_i \parallel\!\parallel \tilde{\sigma} \xrightarrow{A:\bar{a}_k} [\bar{a}_k]\rho_k \parallel\!\parallel \tilde{\sigma}$ when I is the singleton $\{k\}$. Also we have the new reduction $\mathbf{1} \parallel\!\parallel \tilde{\rho} \xrightarrow{C:\checkmark} \mathbf{0} \parallel\!\parallel \tilde{\rho}$ to signal when player C wins.

Let $\beta = \langle \beta_1 \cdots \beta_n \rangle \in \mathbf{tbAct}^*$. We shall use the notation $\xrightarrow{\beta} = \xrightarrow{\beta_1}$ $\circ \cdots \circ \xrightarrow{\beta_n}$

Definition 17 (Turn-Based Compliance Relation $\dashv^{\mathbf{tb}}$).

(i) Let $\mathcal{H} : \mathcal{P}(\mathsf{ASC}^{[]} \times \mathsf{ASC}^{[]}) \rightarrow \mathcal{P}(\mathsf{ASC}^{[]} \times \mathsf{ASC}^{[]})$ be such that, for any $\mathcal{R} \subseteq \mathsf{ASC}^{[]} \times \mathsf{ASC}^{[]}$, we get $(\tilde{\rho}, \tilde{\sigma}) \in \mathcal{H}(\mathcal{R})$ if:

(1) $\tilde{\rho} \parallel\!\parallel \tilde{\sigma} \nrightarrow$ implies $\rho = \mathbf{0}$;

(2) $\forall \tilde{\rho}', \tilde{\sigma}'.$ $[\ \tilde{\rho} \parallel\!\parallel \tilde{\sigma} \xrightarrow{\beta} \tilde{\rho}' \parallel\!\parallel \tilde{\sigma}'$ implies $\tilde{\rho}'\,\mathcal{R}\,\tilde{\sigma}'\ ]$,
    where $\beta \in \{A{:}a, A{:}\bar{a}, B{:}a, B{:}\bar{a} \mid a \in \mathcal{N}\}$;

(3) $\exists a \in \mathcal{N}.\tilde{\rho} \parallel\!\parallel \tilde{\sigma} \xrightarrow{C:a}$ implies $\exists \tilde{\rho}', \tilde{\sigma}', a.\ [\tilde{\rho} \parallel\!\parallel \tilde{\sigma} \xrightarrow{C:a} \tilde{\rho}' \parallel\!\parallel \tilde{\sigma}'$ and $\tilde{\rho}'\,\mathcal{R}\,\tilde{\sigma}']$;

$$\oplus_{i \in I} \bar{a}_i.\rho_i \,\|\!|\!|\, \tilde{\sigma} \xrightarrow{\text{A}:\bar{a}_k} [\bar{a}_k]\rho_k \,\|\!|\!|\, \tilde{\sigma} \qquad \Sigma_{i \in I} a_i.\rho_i \,\|\!|\!|\, [\bar{a}_k]\sigma \xrightarrow{\text{A}:a_k} \rho_k \,\|\!|\!|\, \sigma$$

$$\tilde{\rho} \,\|\!|\!|\, \oplus_{i \in I} \bar{a}_i.\sigma_i \xrightarrow{\text{B}:\bar{a}_k} \tilde{\rho} \,\|\!|\!|\, [\bar{a}_k]\sigma_k \qquad [\bar{a}_k]\rho \,\|\!|\!|\, \Sigma_{i \in I} a_i.\sigma_i \xrightarrow{\text{B}:a_k} \rho \,\|\!|\!|\, \sigma_k$$

$$\bar{a}.\rho + \rho' \,\|\!|\!|\, a.\sigma + \sigma' \xrightarrow{\text{C}:a} \rho \,\|\!|\!|\, \sigma \qquad a.\rho + \rho' \,\|\!|\!|\, \bar{a}.\sigma + \sigma' \xrightarrow{\text{C}:a} \rho \,\|\!|\!|\, \sigma$$

$$1 \,\|\!|\!|\, \tilde{\rho} \xrightarrow{\text{C}:\checkmark} 0 \,\|\!|\!|\, \tilde{\rho}$$

where $(k \in I)$

Fig. 1. Turn-based operational semantics of turn-based configurations

(ii) A relation $\mathcal{R} \subseteq \mathsf{ASC}^{[]} \times \mathsf{ASC}^{[]}$ *is a* turn-based compliance relation *if* $\mathcal{R} \subseteq \mathcal{H}(\mathcal{R})$. $\dashv^{\text{tb}}$ *is the greatest solution of the equation* $X = \mathcal{H}(X)$, *that is* $\dashv^{\text{tb}} = \nu\mathcal{H}$.
(iii) For $\rho, \sigma \in \mathsf{ASC}$, *we say that* ρ *is* turn-based compliant *with* σ *if* $\rho \dashv^{\text{tb}} \sigma$.

Turn-based compliance is equivalent to affectible compliance

Theorem 2. *Let* $\rho, \sigma \in \mathsf{ASC}$. $\qquad \rho \dashv^{\text{tb}} \sigma \quad \Leftrightarrow \quad \rho \dashv^{\text{A}} \sigma$.

Three-Player Game Interpretation for ASC Client/Server Systems.
Using the turn-based semantics, we associate to any client/server system an event structure, and then a three-player game[2], extending the treatment of session types with two-player games in [5]. For our purposes we just consider the LTS of a given client/server system instead of an arbitrary one.

Definition 18. (ES of affectible-contracts systems). *Let* $\rho \,\|\, \sigma$ *be a client/server system of affectible contracts. We define the event structure* $[\![\rho \,\|\, \sigma]\!] = (E, \#, \vdash, l)$, *where*

- $E = \{\, (n, \beta) \mid n \in \mathbb{N}, \beta \in \mathbf{tbAct} \,\}$
- $\# = \{\, ((n, \beta_1), (n, \beta_2)) \mid n \in \mathbb{N}, \beta_1, \beta_2 \in \mathbf{tbAct}, \beta_1 \neq \beta_2 \,\}$
- $\vdash = sat\vdash_{\rho \| \sigma}$

  where $\vdash_{\rho \| \sigma} = \{\, (X, (n, \beta)) \mid \rho \,\|\, \sigma \xrightarrow{snd(X)} \tilde{\rho}' \,\|\!|\!|\, \tilde{\sigma}' \xrightarrow{\beta} \text{ and } n = |X| + 1 \,\}$
- $l(n, \beta) = \beta$.

where the partial function $snd(\text{-})$ *maps any* $X = \{\, (i, \beta_i) \,\}_{i=1..n}$ *to* $\langle \beta_1 \cdots \beta_n \rangle$, *and it is undefined over sets not of the shape of* X.

Events in $[\![\rho \,\|\, \sigma]\!]$ are actions in **tbAct** paired with time stamps. Two events are in conflict if different actions should be performed at the same time, so that configurations must be linearly ordered w.r.t. time. The relation $X \vdash_{\rho \| \sigma} (n, \beta)$ holds if X is a trace in the LTS of $\rho \,\|\, \sigma$ of length $n - 1$; therefore the enabling

---

[2] Such interpretation is called *semantic-based* in [5] and it applies quite naturally to our context. Instead the *syntax-based* approach (which is equivalent to the semantic-based one in a two-players setting; see [5] Sect. 5.3.2) cannot be straightforwardly extended to a three-player game.

$Y \vdash (n, \beta)$ holds if and only if Y includes a trace of length $n - 1$ that can be prolonged by β, possibly including (n, β) itself and any other action that might occur after β in the LTS.

So, by the above, $\vdash_{\mathsf{Buyer}\|\mathsf{Seller}}$ in $[\![\mathsf{Buyer} \| \mathsf{Seller}]\!]$ corresponds to

$\{ \ \emptyset \vdash_{\mathsf{Buyer}\|\mathsf{Seller}} (1, (\mathsf{C} : \mathtt{belt})), \ \emptyset \vdash_{\mathsf{Buyer}\|\mathsf{Seller}} (1, (\mathsf{C} : \mathtt{bag})),$

$\quad \{(1, (\mathsf{C:belt}))\} \vdash_{\mathsf{Buyer}\|\mathsf{Seller}} (2, (\mathsf{B:\overline{price}})), \{(1, (\mathsf{C:bag}))\} \vdash_{\mathsf{Buyer}\|\mathsf{Seller}} (2, (\mathsf{B:\overline{price}})),$

$\quad \{(1, (\mathsf{C:belt})), (2, (\mathsf{Seller:\overline{price}}))\} \vdash_{\mathsf{Buyer}\|\mathsf{Seller}} (3, (\mathsf{A:price})), \dots$

$\quad \dots X_1 \vdash_{\mathsf{Buyer}\|\mathsf{Seller}} (6, (\mathsf{C}, \checkmark)) \qquad\qquad\qquad\qquad\qquad\qquad\qquad \}$

where $X_1 = \{(1, (\mathsf{C:bag})), (2, (\mathsf{B:\overline{price}})), (3, (\mathsf{A:price})), (4, (\mathsf{A:\overline{cash}})), (5, (\mathsf{B:cash})) \}$ The $\vdash_{\rho\|\sigma}$ of this simple example is finite. It is not so in general for systems with recursive contracts.

The following definition is a specialisation of Definitions 4.6 and 4.7 in [5]. We use $\mathsf{MaxTr}(s, \rightarrow)$ and $\mathsf{FinMaxTr}(s, \rightarrow)$ to denote the set of maximal traces and finite maximal traces, respectively, of $\mathsf{Tr}(s, \rightarrow)$.

Definition 19. *Given $\rho, \sigma \in \mathsf{ASC}$, we define the game $\mathcal{G}_{\rho\|\sigma}$ as $([\![\rho \| \sigma]\!], \Phi)$, where $\pi(n, \beta) = A$ if $\beta = A{:}\alpha$, ΦA is defined only if $A \in \{\mathsf{A}, \mathsf{B}, \mathsf{C}\}$ and*

$$\Phi A e = \begin{cases} 1 & \text{if } \ \mathbf{P}(A, e) \\ -1 & \text{otherwise} \end{cases}$$

where $\mathbf{P}(A, e)$ holds whenever

$$e \in \mathsf{Tr}(\emptyset, \rightarrow_{[\![\rho\|\sigma]\!]}) \ \& \ [e \in \mathsf{FinMaxTr}(\emptyset, \rightarrow_{[\![\rho\|\sigma]\!]}) \ \Rightarrow \ \exists e', n. \ e = e'(n, (A{:}\checkmark))]$$

A player A wins in the sequence of events e if $\Phi A e > 0$. A strategy Σ for player A is winning if A wins in all plays conforming to Σ.

Note that, $\mathbf{P}(A, e)$ holds for any A and infinite element e of $\mathsf{Tr}(\emptyset, \rightarrow_{[\![\rho\|\sigma]\!]})$.

For the game $\mathcal{G}_{\mathsf{Buyer} \| \mathsf{Seller}}$, it is possible to check that, for instance,

$$\Phi \mathsf{C} s_1 = 1, \quad \Phi \mathsf{A} s_1 = -1, \quad \Phi \mathsf{B} s_2 = -1, \quad \Phi \mathsf{C} s_3 = -1$$

where
$s_1 = (1, (\mathsf{C:bag}))(2, (\mathsf{B:\overline{price}}))(3, (\mathsf{A:price}))(4, (\mathsf{A:\overline{cash}}))(5, (\mathsf{B:cash}))(6, (\mathsf{C}, \checkmark))$,
$s_2 = (4, (\mathsf{A:bag}))(1, (\mathsf{C:\overline{price}}))$
$s_3 = (1, (\mathsf{C:bag}))(2, (\mathsf{B:\overline{price}}))(3, (\mathsf{A:price}))(4, (\mathsf{A:\overline{cash}}))(5, (\mathsf{B:cash}))$
Let us define a particular strategy $\widetilde{\Sigma}$ for C in $\mathcal{G}_{\mathsf{Buyer} \| \mathsf{Seller}}$ as follows:

$$\widetilde{\Sigma}(s) = \begin{cases} \{\, (1, (\mathsf{C:bag})) \,\} & \text{if } s = \langle\rangle \\ \{\, (6, (\mathsf{C}, \checkmark)) \,\} & \text{if } s = s_3 \\ \emptyset & \text{for any other play} \end{cases}$$

The strategy $\widetilde{\Sigma}$ for C in $\mathcal{G}_{\mathsf{Buyer} \| \mathsf{Seller}}$ is winning.

Remark 1. According to [5], A wins in a play if $\mathcal{W}\!Ae > 0$, where $\mathcal{W}\!Ae = \Phi\!Ae$ if all players are "innocent" in e, while if A is "culpable", $\mathcal{W}\!Ae = -1$, and if A is innocent and someone else culpable, $\mathcal{W}\!Ae = +1$. A strategy Σ of A is winning if A wins in all *fair* plays conforming to Σ. A play e is "fair" for a strategy Σ of a player A if any event in E_A which is infinitely often enabled is eventually performed. Symmetrically A is "innocent" in e if she eventually plays all persistently enabled moves of her in e, namely if she is fair to the other players, since the lack of a move by A might obstacle the moves by others; she is "culpable" otherwise. As said above, Definition 19 is a particularisation of the general definitions in [5]. In fact in a game $\mathcal{G}_{\rho\|\sigma}$ no move of any player can occur more than once in a play e because of time stamps. Therefore no move can be "persistently enabled", nor it can be prevented since it can be enabled with a given time stamp only if there exists a legal transition in the LTS with the same label. Hence any player is innocent in a play e of $\mathcal{G}_{\rho\|\sigma}$ and all plays are fair. Therefore $\mathcal{W}$ coincides with Φ.

It is possible to characterize affectible and retractable compliance in terms of the existence of a winning strategy for C in $\mathcal{G}_{\rho\|\sigma}$.

Theorem 3. $\rho \dashv^{\mathsf{A}} \sigma$ *(or, equivalently, $\rho \dashv^{\text{rtk}} \sigma$) if and only if player C has a winning strategy in the three-player game $\mathcal{G}_{\rho\|\sigma}$.*

3 Strategies as Orchestrators

In the present section we show that a client ρ is retractable-compliant with a server σ if and only if their interactions can be led to a successful state by means of the mediation of an orchestrator. To do that we show how an orchestrator can be obtained out of a "univocal" winning strategy (see Definition 24 below) for player C in the game $\mathcal{G}_{\rho\|\sigma}$, and vice versa. For a detailed discussion on orchestrators for contracts and orchestrators for session-contracts, we refer to [13,14] and [2] respectively. In the present setting, our orchestrators, that we dub *strategy-orchestrators*, are defined as a variant of the session-orchestrators of [2], which in turn are a restriction of orchestrators in [14]. The task of a strategy orchestrator is to mediate the interactions between two affectible session contracts by selecting one of the possible affectible choices and constraining non-affectible ones.

We consider two sorts of orchestration actions, having the following shapes: $\langle \alpha, \overline{\alpha} \rangle$, enabling the unaffectible synchronization $\rho \| \sigma \overset{\tau}{\longrightarrow} \rho' \| \sigma'$; $\langle \alpha, \overline{\alpha} \rangle^{+}$, enabling the affectible synchronization $\rho \| \sigma \overset{+}{\longrightarrow} \rho' \| \sigma'$.

Definition 20 (Strategy Orchestrators).

*(i) The set **OrchAct** of strategy-orchestration actions is defined by*

$$\mathbf{OrchAct} = \{\, \langle \alpha, \overline{\alpha} \rangle \mid \alpha \in \mathcal{N} \cup \overline{\mathcal{N}} \,\} \cup \{\, \langle \alpha, \overline{\alpha} \rangle^{+} \mid \alpha \in \mathcal{N} \cup \overline{\mathcal{N}} \,\}$$

*We let $\mu, \mu', \ldots$ range over elements of **OrchAct** with the shape $\langle \alpha, \overline{\alpha} \rangle$, and $\mu^{+}, \mu'^{+}, \ldots$ range over elements of **OrchAct** with the shape $\langle \alpha, \overline{\alpha} \rangle^{+}$.*

(ii) *We define the set* Orch *of strategy orchestrators, ranged over by* $f, g, \ldots$, *as the* closed *(with respect to the binder* rec *) terms generated by the following grammar:*

$$f, g \ ::= 1 \qquad\qquad\qquad idle$$
$$| \ \mu^+.f \qquad\qquad\qquad prefix$$
$$| \ \mu_1.f_1 \vee \ldots \vee \mu_n.f_n \quad disjunction$$
$$| \ x \qquad\qquad\qquad\qquad variable$$
$$| \ \mathsf{rec}\, x.f \qquad\qquad\qquad recursion$$

where the μ_i *in a disjunction are pairwise distinct. Moreover, we impose strategy orchestrators to be* contractive, *i.e. the* f *in* $\mathsf{rec}\, x.f$ *is assumed not to be a variable.*

We write $\bigvee_{i \in I} \mu_i.f_i$ as short for $\mu_1.f_1 \vee \ldots \vee \mu_n.f_n$, where $I = \{1, \ldots, n\}$. If not stated otherwise, we consider recursive orchestrators up-to unfolding, that is we equate $\mathsf{rec}\, x.f$ with $f\{x/\mathsf{rec}\, x.f\}$. We omit trailing 1's.

Strategy orchestrators are "simple orchestrators" in [14] and "synchronous orchestrators" in [13], but for the kind of prefixes which are allowed in a single prefix or in a disjunction. In fact a prefix $\langle \alpha, \overline{\alpha} \rangle^+$ cannot occur in disjunctions, where all the orchestrators must be prefixed by $\langle \alpha, \overline{\alpha} \rangle$ actions.

Definition 21 (Strategy orchestrators LTS). *We define the labelled transition system* (Orch, **OrchAct**, $\mapsto$) *by*

$$\mu^+.f \overset{\mu^+}{\mapsto} f \qquad\qquad\qquad (\bigvee_{i \in I} \mu_i.f_i) \overset{\mu_k}{\mapsto} f_k \quad (k \in I)$$

An orchestrated system, represented by $\rho \, \|_f \, \sigma$, is client/server system whose interaction is mediated by an orchestrator.

Definition 22 (LTS for orchestrated-systems). *Let* $\rho, \sigma \in$ ASC *and* $f \in$ Orch.

$$\frac{\rho \to \rho'}{\rho \, \|_f \, \sigma \to \rho' \, \|_f \, \sigma} \qquad\qquad\qquad \frac{\sigma \to \sigma'}{\rho \, \|_f \, \sigma \to \rho \, \|_f \, \sigma'}$$

$$\frac{\rho \overset{a}{\longrightarrow} \rho' \quad f \overset{\langle \overline{a}, a \rangle^+}{\mapsto} f' \quad \sigma \overset{\overline{a}^+}{\longrightarrow} \sigma'}{\rho \, \|_f \, \sigma \overset{+}{\longrightarrow} \rho' \, \|_{f'} \, \sigma'} \qquad \frac{\rho \overset{\overline{a}^+}{\longrightarrow} \rho' \quad f \overset{\langle a, \overline{a} \rangle^+}{\mapsto} f' \quad \sigma \overset{a}{\longrightarrow} \sigma'}{\rho \, \|_f \, \sigma \overset{+}{\longrightarrow} \rho' \, \|_{f'} \, \sigma'}$$

$$\frac{\rho \overset{\alpha}{\longrightarrow} \rho' \quad f \overset{\langle \overline{\alpha}, \alpha \rangle}{\mapsto} f' \quad \sigma \overset{\overline{\alpha}}{\longrightarrow} \sigma'}{\rho \, \|_f \, \sigma \overset{\tau}{\longrightarrow} \rho' \, \|_f \, \sigma'} \ (\alpha \in \mathcal{N} \cup \overline{\mathcal{N}})$$

Moreover, we define $\Longrightarrow \ = \ \to^* \circ (\overset{\tau}{\longrightarrow} \ \cup \ \overset{+}{\longrightarrow}).$

In both transitions $\overset{+}{\longrightarrow}$ and $\overset{\tau}{\longrightarrow}$ synchronization may happen only if the orchestrator has a transition with the appropriate pair of actions. This is because in an orchestrated interaction both client and server are committed to the synchronizations allowed by the orchestrator only. It is then clear that an orchestrator always selects one synchronisation of affectible actions on client and server side, while the disjunction of orchestrators represents the constraint that only certain synchronisations of unaffectible actions are permitted.

Definition 23 (Strategy-orchestrated Compliance).

(i) $f : \rho \dashv^{\text{Orch}} \sigma$ if   for any ρ' and σ', the following holds:

$$\rho \parallel_f \sigma \Longrightarrow^* \rho' \parallel_{f'} \sigma' \not\Longrightarrow \quad implies \quad \rho' = \mathbf{1}.$$

(ii) $\rho \dashv^{\text{Orch}} \sigma$ if $\exists f. \, [f : \rho \dashv^{\text{Orch}} \sigma]$.

Definition 24 (Univocal strategies). Σ is univocal if $\forall e. \, |\Sigma(e)| \le 1$.

The strategy $\widetilde{\Sigma}$ for C in $\mathcal{G}_{\text{Buyer} \parallel \text{Seller}}$, defined in the previous section, is univocal.

The proof of the following theorem relies on the fact that any orchestrator f such that $f : \rho \dashv^{\text{Orch}} \sigma$ corresponds to a univocal winning strategies for player C in $\mathcal{G}_{\rho \parallel \sigma}$. Vice versa a univocal winning strategy Σ for C always induces an orchestrator f_Σ. It is not restrictive to look at univocal strategies only, as established in the next lemma.

We say that Σ *refines* Σ', written $\Sigma \le \Sigma'$, if and only if $\Sigma(e) \subseteq \Sigma'(e)$ for all e.

Lemma 6. *If C has a winning strategy Σ, then C has a univocal winning strategy Σ' such that $\Sigma' \le \Sigma$.*

Theorem 4.
$\exists f. \, [f : \rho \dashv^{\text{Orch}} \sigma]$ $\Leftrightarrow$ *there exists a winning strategy for player C in $\mathcal{G}_{\rho \parallel \sigma}$. In particular, a winning strategy for player C in $\mathcal{G}_{\rho \parallel \sigma}$ can be obtained out of an orchestrator f such that $f : \rho \dashv^{\text{Orch}} \sigma$, and vice versa.*

The orchestrator that can be obtained out of the strategy $\widetilde{\Sigma}$ is

$$\langle \mathsf{bag}, \overline{\mathsf{bag}} \rangle^+ . \langle \overline{\mathsf{price}}, \mathsf{price} \rangle (\langle \mathsf{cash}, \overline{\mathsf{cash}} \rangle \vee \langle \mathsf{card}, \overline{\mathsf{card}} \rangle).$$

Remark 2. Univocal strategies correspond to strategy-orchestrators and are technically easier to work with. On the other hand, we can recover a full correspondence among C strategies and orchestrators by allowing disjunctions of affectible synchronization actions $\langle \alpha, \overline{\alpha} \rangle^+$. In a session-based scenario, however, we expect any nondeterminism to depend solely on either the client or the server. By allowing $f = \langle \overline{a}, a \rangle^+ . f_1 \vee \langle \overline{b}, b \rangle^+ . f_2$ in the system $a.\rho_1 + b.\rho_2 \parallel_f \overline{a}.\sigma_1 + \overline{b}.\sigma_2$, the nondeterminism would depend on the orchestrator too.

Based on the formal system of Definition 9, the algorithm **Synth** in Fig. 2 takes a (initially empty) set of assumptions Γ, and the affectible contracts ρ and σ, and it returns a set O of orchestrators (and hence a set of strategies by the above) if any, such that for any $f \in O$ we have $f : \rho \dashv^{\text{Orch}} \sigma$; the algorithm returns the empty set otherwise. In the algorithm **Synth** we consider orchestrators as explicit terms, that is we do not consider recursion up-to unfolding.

$\textbf{Synth}(\Gamma, \rho, \sigma) =$

    if $x : \rho \dashv^{\text{Orch}} \sigma \in \Gamma$ **then** $\{x\}$

    else if $\rho = 1$ **then** $\{1\}$

    else if $\rho = \sum_{i \in I} \overline{\alpha}_i.\rho_i$ **and** $\sigma = \sum_{j \in J} \alpha_j.\sigma_j$ (where $\alpha \in \mathcal{N} \cup \overline{\mathcal{N}}$) **then**
        let $\Gamma' = \Gamma, x{:}\rho \dashv^{\text{Orch}} \sigma$ **in**
            $\bigcup_{i \in I} \{\, \text{rec } x.\langle \alpha_i, \overline{\alpha}_i \rangle^+.f \mid f \in \textbf{Synth}\,(\Gamma', \rho_i, \sigma_i) \,\}$

    else if $\rho = \bigoplus_{i \in I} \overline{a}_i.\rho_i$ **and** $\sigma = \sum_{j \in I \cup J} a_j.\sigma_j$ **then**
        let $\Gamma' = \Gamma, x{:}\rho \dashv^{\text{Orch}} \sigma$ **in**
        $\{\, \text{rec } x. \bigvee_{i \in I} \langle a_i, \overline{a}_i \rangle.f_i \mid \forall i \in I.f_i \in \textbf{Synth}(\Gamma', \rho_i, \sigma_i) \,\}$

    else if $\rho = \sum_{j \in I \cup J} \overline{a}_j.\rho_i$ **and** $\sigma = \bigoplus_{i \in I} a_i.\sigma_i$ **then**
        let $\Gamma' = \Gamma, x{:}\rho \dashv^{\text{Orch}} \sigma_i$ **in**
        $\{\, \text{rec } x. \bigvee_{i \in I} \langle a_i, \overline{a}_i \rangle.f_i \mid \forall i \in I.f_i \in \textbf{Synth}(\Gamma', \rho_i, \sigma_i) \,\}$

    else $\emptyset$

Fig. 2. The algorithm **Synth**.

Theorem 5 (Soundness and Completeness of *Synth*). *The algorithm* **Synth** *is correct and complete in the following sense:*

(i) **Synth**(Γ, ρ, σ) *terminates for any* Γ, ρ *and* σ.
(ii) *If* $f \in$ **Synth**$(\emptyset, \rho, \sigma) \neq \emptyset$ *then* $f : \rho \dashv^{\text{Orch}} \sigma$.
(iii) *If* $f : \rho \dashv^{\text{Orch}} \sigma$ *then there exists* $g \in$ **Synth**$(\emptyset, \rho, \sigma) \neq \emptyset$ *such that the (possibly infinite) unfolding of* f *and* g *yields the same regular tree.*

It is not difficult to check that by computing **Synth**$(\emptyset, \textsf{Buyer}, \textsf{Seller})$ we get a set just consisting of the orchestrator corresponding to the strategy $\widetilde{\Sigma}$, namely

$$\textbf{Synth}(\emptyset, \textsf{Buyer}, \textsf{Seller}) = \{\, \langle \textsf{bag}, \overline{\textsf{bag}} \rangle^+.\langle \overline{\textsf{price}}, \textsf{price} \rangle(\langle \textsf{cash}, \overline{\textsf{cash}} \rangle \vee \langle \textsf{card}, \overline{\textsf{card}} \rangle) \,\}$$

Using the previous results and Lemma 6 we get the following:

Corollary 2. (i) *The relation* $\dashv^{\text{Orch}}$ *is decidable.*
(ii) *For any* $\rho, \sigma \in$ ASC, *it is decidable whether there exists a winning strategy for player* C *in* $\mathcal{G}_{\rho \parallel \sigma}$.
    Moreover, in case a winning strategy exists, it is possible to effectively compute a univocal winning strategy.

4   Conclusion and Future Work

We have studied two approaches to loosening compliance among a client and a server in contract theory, based on the concepts of dynamic adaptation and of mediated interaction respectively. We have seen that these induce equivalent notions of compliance, which can be shown via the abstract concept of winning strategy in a suitable class of games.

The byproduct is that the existence of the agreement among two contracts specifying adaptive behaviours is established by statically synthesizing the proper orchestrator, hence avoiding any trial and error mechanism at run time. The study in this paper has been limited to the case of binary sessions since this is the setting in which both orchestrators and retractable contracts have been introduced. However strategy based concepts of agreement have been developed in the more general scenario of multiparty interaction, which seems a natural direction for future work.

Acknowledgments. The authors wish to thank Massimo Bartoletti for an insightful discussion, Mariangiola Dezani for her everlasting support and the three anonymous referees for their help in improving the final version of the paper.

References

1. Abramsky, S., Mellies, P.A.: Concurrent games and full completeness. In: Proceedings of the 14th Symposium on Logic in Computer Science, pp. 431–442 (1999)
2. Barbanera, F., van Bakel, S., de' Liguoro, U.: Orchestrated session compliance. In: Proceedings ICE 2015. EPTCS, vol. 189, pp. 21–36 (2015)
3. Barbanera, F., de' Liguoro, U.: Sub-behaviour relations for session-based client/server systems. MSCS **25**(6), 1339–1381 (2015)
4. Barbanera, F., Dezani-Ciancaglini, M., Lanese, I., de' Liguoro, U.: Retractable contracts. In: PLACES. EPTCS, vol. 203, pp. 61–72. Open Publishing Ass. (2015)
5. Bartoletti, M., Cimoli, T., Pinna, G.M., Zunino, R.: Contracts as games on event structures. J. Logical Algebraic Methods Progr. **85**(3), 399–424 (2016)
6. Bernardi, G., Hennessy, M.: Compliance and testing preorders differ. In: Counsell, S., Núñez, M. (eds.) SEFM 2013. LNCS, vol. 8368, pp. 69–81. Springer, Heidelberg (2014)
7. Brandt, M., Henglein, F.: Coinductive axiomatization of recursive type equality and subtyping. Fundam. Inform. **33**(4), 309–338 (1998)
8. Bravetti, M., Zavattaro, G.: A theory of contracts for strong service compliance. Math. Struct. Comput. Sci. **19**(3), 601–638 (2009)
9. Castagna, G., Gesbert, N., Padovani, L.: A theory of contracts for web services. ACM Trans. Prog. Lang. Sys. **31**(5), 19:1–19:61 (2009)
10. Gay, S., Hole, M.: Subtyping for session types in the Pi-Calculus. Acta Informatica **42**(2/3), 191–225 (2005)
11. Laneve, C., Padovani, L.: The *Must* preorder revisited. In: Caires, L., Vasconcelos, V.T. (eds.) CONCUR 2007. LNCS, vol. 4703, pp. 212–225. Springer, Heidelberg (2007)
12. Nicola, R.D., Hennessy, M.: Testing equivalence for processes. In: Díaz, J. (ed.) ICALP 1983. LNCS, vol. 154, pp. 548–560. Springer, Heidelberg (1983)
13. Padovani, L.: Contract-based discovery and adaptation of web services. In: Bernardo, M., Padovani, L., Zavattaro, G. (eds.) SFM 2009. LNCS, vol. 5569, pp. 213–260. Springer, Heidelberg (2009)
14. Padovani, L.: Contract-based discovery of web services modulo simple orchestrators. Theoret. Comput. Sci. **411**, 3328–3347 (2010)
15. Winskel, G.: Event structures. In: Brauer, W., Reisig, W., Rozenberg, G. (eds.) Advances in Petri Nets 1986, Part II. LNCS, vol. 255, pp. 325–392. Springer, Heidelberg (1987)

Where Do Your IoT Ingredients Come From?

Chiara Bodei, Pierpaolo Degano, Gian-Luigi Ferrari, and Letterio Galletta[✉]

Dipartimento di Informatica, Università di Pisa, Pisa, Italy
{chiara,degano,giangi,galletta}@di.unipi.it

Abstract. The Internet of Things (IoT) is here: smart objects are pervading our everyday life. Smart devices automatically collect and exchange data of various kinds, directly gathered from sensors or generated by aggregations. Suitable coordination primitives and analysis mechanisms are in order to design and reason about IoT systems, and to intercept the implied technology shifts. We address these issues by defining IoT-LySA, a process calculus endowed with a static analysis that tracks the provenance and the route of IoT data, and detects how they affect the behaviour of smart objects.

1   Introduction

This is the era of the Internet of Things (IoT), where digitally connected devices are intruding into our everyday life. "Software is eating the world" is the vivid slogan referring to the *smartification* of the objects and devices around us. As buzzword, the IoT is indeed simple and accurate: a global network of things ranging from light bulbs to cars, equipped with suitable software allowing things to interact each other and coordinate their behaviour. For instance, our smart alarm clock can drive our coffeemaker to prepare us a cup of coffee in the morning, while our smart TV can suggest us some movies for the evening. Furthermore, smart devices can automatically exchange information of various kinds gathered from different sources (e.g. sensors) or generated by aggregating several data sets.

More connected smart devices and more applications available on the IoT mean more software bugs and vulnerabilities to identify and fix. For instance, a bug can cause you to wake up into a cold house in winter or an attacker can enter into your smart TV and break your bank account. This is not a big surprise: every advance in information technology has exposed software to new challenges.

Smart devices exhibit and require *open-endedness* to achieve full interactive and cooperative behaviour, and thus they generalise the so-called "embedded systems." These are essentially controllers of machines and are *closed* systems. Therefore, we cannot simply rely on standard techniques for supporting the design and development of IoT, and new software solutions have emerged, e.g. Amazon AWS for IoT and Google Brillo. We argue that the formal techniques and tools need to be adapted in order to support open-endedness of IoT applications and the new complex phenomena that arise in this hybrid scenario.

Partially supported by Università di Pisa PRA_2016_64 Project *Through the fog*.

A. Lluch Lafuente and J. Proença (Eds.): COORDINATION 2016, LNCS 9686, pp. 35–50, 2016.
DOI: 10.1007/978-3-319-39519-7_3

Here, we contribute to this new line of research by introducing the kernel of a formal design framework for IoT, which will provide us with the foundations to develop verification techniques and tools for certifying properties of IoT applications.

Our starting point is the process calculus IoT-LySa, a dialect of LySa [4, 6], within the process calculi approach to IoT [8, 15]. It has primitive constructs to describe the activity of sensors and of actuators, and suitable primitives for managing the coordination and communication capabilities of smart objects. More precisely, our calculus is made up from:

1. Systems of nodes, consisting of (a representation of) the physical components, i.e. sensors and actuators, and of software control processes for specifying the *logic* of the node, including the manipulation of data gathered from sensors and from other nodes. Intra-node generative communications are implemented through a shared store à la Linda [7, 12]. The adoption of this coordination model supports a smooth implementation of the *cyber-physical control architecture*: physical data are made available to software entities that analyse them and trigger the relevant actuators to perform the desired behaviour.
2. An asynchronous multi-party communication among nodes, which can be easily tuned to take care of various constraints, mainly those concerning proximity;
3. Functions to process and aggregate data.

A further contribution of this paper is the definition of an analysis for IoT-LySa to statically predict the run time behaviour of smart systems. We introduce a Control Flow Analysis (CFA) that safely approximates the abstract behaviour of a system of nodes. Essentially, it describes the interactions among nodes, tracks how data spread from sensors to the network, and how data are manipulated.

Technically, our CFA abstracts from the concrete values and only considers their provenance and how they are put together. In more detail, it returns for each node ℓ in the network:

- An abstract store $\hat{\Sigma}_\ell$ that records for sensors and variables a super-set of the abstract values that they may denote at run time;
- A set $\kappa(\ell)$ that over-approximates the set of the messages received by the node ℓ, and for each of them its sender;
- A set $\Theta(\ell)$ of possible abstract values computed and used by the node ℓ.

The result of the analysis can be exploited as the basis for checking and certifying various properties of IoT systems. As it is, the components κ and Θ track how data may flow in the network and how they influence the outcome of functions. An example of property that can be statically checked using the component κ is the detection of redundant communications, thus providing the means for refactoring the system to avoid message storms. Further, the analysis can be used to check whether the values produced by a certain classified sensor reaches an untrusted node. This helps evaluating the security level of the system and detecting potential vulnerabilities.

The paper is organised as follows. The next section introduces our approach with the help of an illustrative example. In Sect. 3 we briefly introduce the process calculus IoT-LySa, while we present our CFA in Sect. 4. Concluding remarks and related work are in Sect. 5.

2 A Smart Street Light Control System

The IoT European Research Cluster (IERC) has recently identified *smart lighting* in *smart cities* [14] as one of most relevant applications for the Internet of Things. Recent studies, e.g. [10,11], show that smart street light control systems represent effective solutions to improve energy efficiency. Many proposed solutions are based on sensors that acquire data about the physical environment and regulate the level of illumination according to the detected events. In this section we show how this kind of scenario can be easily modelled in IoT-LySa and what kind of information our CFA provides to designers.

We consider a simplified system made of two integrated parts, working on a one-way street. The first consists of smart lamp posts that are battery powered and can sense their surrounding environment and can communicate with their neighbours to share their views. If (a sensor of) the lamp post perceives a pedestrian and there is not enough light in the street it switches on the light and communicates the presence of the pedestrian to the lamp posts nearby. When a lamp post detects that the level of battery is low, it informs the supervisor of the street lights, N_s, that will activate other lamp posts nearby. The second component of the street light controller uses the electronic access point to the street. When a car crosses the checkpoint, besides detecting if it is enabled to, a message is sent to the supervisor of the street accesses, N_a, that in turn notifies the presence of the car to N_s. This supervisor sends a message to the lamp post closest to the checkpoint that starts a forward chain till the end of the street. The structure of our control light system is in Fig. 1.

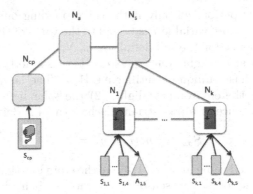

Fig. 1. The organisation of nodes in our street light control system.

We first define the checkpoint N_{cp} as an IoT-LySa node that only contains a visual sensor S_{cp} to take a picture of the car detected in the street, defined as

$$S_{cp} = \mu h.(\tau.1 := v_p).\tau.\ h$$

where v_p is the picture of the car. The sensor communicates the picture to the node by storing it in the location 1 of the shared store. In our model we assume that each sensor has a reserved store location in which records its readings. The action τ denotes internal actions of the sensor, which we are not interested to model, e.g. reading from the environment; the construct $\mu h.$ implements the iterative behaviour of the sensor. Then, the taken picture is enhanced by the process P_{cp} and sent to the supervisor N_a

$$P_{cp} = \mu h.(z := 1).(z' := noiseRed(z)).\langle\langle z'\rangle\rangle \rhd \{\ell_a\}.\ h$$

where ℓ_a is the label of the node N_a (note that 1 is the identifier of the sensor S_{cp} in the assignment $z := 1$). Hence, the checkpoint N_{cp} is defined as

$$N_{cp} = \ell_{cp} : [P_{cp} \parallel S_{cp} \parallel B_{cp}]$$

where ℓ_{cp} is the identifier of N_{cp} and B_{cp} abstracts other components we are not interested in. The node N_a (checks if the car is allowed to enter the street and) communicates its presence to the lamp posts supervisor N_s:

$$N_a = \ell_a : [\mu h.(;\ x). \langle\langle car, x\rangle\rangle \rhd \{\ell_s\}.\ h \parallel B_a]$$

where ℓ_s is the identifier of N_s (see below for the intuition of the general format of the input $(;x)$). The supervisor N_s contains the process $P_{s,1}$ that receives the picture from N_a and sends a message to the node closest to the checkpoint, call it N_1, labelled with ℓ_1:

$$P_{s,1} = \mu h.(car;\ x). \langle\langle x\rangle\rangle \rhd \{\ell_1\}.\ h$$

The input $(car;x)$ is performed only if the corresponding output matches the constant car, and the store variable x is bound to the value of the second element of the output (see below for the full definition of N_s).

In our intelligent street light control system there is a node N_p for each lamp post, each of which has a unique identifier $p \in [1, k]$. The lamp posts have four sensors to sense (1) the environment light, (2) the solar light, (3) the battery level and (4) the presence of a pedestrian. Each of them is defined as follows

$$S_{p,i} = \mu h.(i := v).\ \tau.\ h$$

where v is the perceived value and $i \in [1, 4]$ are the store locations for the sensors. After some internal actions τ, the sensor $S_{p,i}$ iterates its behaviour. The actuator for the lamp post p is defined as

$$A_5 = \mu h.(\!| 5, \{\text{turnon}, \text{turnoff}\}|\!).\ h$$

It only accepts a message from N_c whose first element is its identifier (here 5) and whose second element is either command turnon or turnoff and executes it.

The control process of a lamp post node is composed by two parallel processes. The first process $P_{p,1}$ is defined as follow

$$P_{p,1} = \mu h.(x_1 := 1. x_2 := 2. x_3 := 3. x_4 := 4).$$
$$(x_4 = true) \ ?$$
$$(x_1 \leq th_1 \wedge x_2 \leq th_2) \ ?$$
$$(x_3 \geq th_3) \ ? \ \langle 5, \mathsf{turnon} \rangle. \langle\langle x_4 \rangle\rangle \triangleright L_p. \ h$$
$$: \ \langle\langle \mathsf{err}, \ell_p \rangle\rangle \triangleright \{\ell_s\}. \ h$$
$$: h$$
$$: \ \langle 5, \mathsf{turnoff} \rangle. h$$

The process reads the current values from the sensors and stores them into the local variables x_i. The actuator is turned on if (i) a pedestrian is detected in the street (x_4 holds), (ii) the intensity of environment and solar lights are greater than the given thresholds th_1 and th_2, and (iii) there is enough battery (at least th_3). In addition, the presence of the pedestrian is communicated to the lamp posts nearby, whose labels, typically ℓ_{p-1} and ℓ_{p+1}, are in L_p. Instead, if the level battery is insufficient, an error message, including its identifier ℓ_p, is sent to the supervisor node, labelled ℓ_s. The second process $P_{p,2}$ is defined as follows:

$$P_{p,2} = \mu h.(; \ x).(x = true \vee is\_a\_car(x)) \ ? \ (\langle 5, \mathsf{turnon} \rangle. \langle\langle x \rangle\rangle \triangleright L_p).h : \langle 5, \mathsf{turnoff} \rangle. h$$

It waits for messages from its neighbours or from the supervisor node N_s. When one of them is notified the presence of a pedestrian ($x = true$) or of a car ($is\_a\_car(x)$ holds), the current lamp post orders the actuator to switch the light on. Each lamp post p is described as the IoT-LySA node below:

$$N_p = \ell_p : [\Sigma_p \ \| \ P_{p,1} \ \| \ P_{p,2} \ \| \ S_{p,1} \ \| \ S_{p,2} \ \| \ S_{p,3} \ \| \ S_{p,4} \ \| \ A_{p,5}]$$

where Σ_p is the store of the node ℓ_p, shared with its components. The supervisor node N_s of lamp posts is defined as

$$N_s = \ell_s : [\mu h. \ (err; \ x). \langle\langle true \rangle\rangle \triangleright L_x. \ h \ \| \ P_{s,1} \ \| \ B_s]$$

where $P_{s,1}$ is the process previously defined. As above the input $(err; x)$ is performed only if the corresponding output matches the constant err, and the store variable x is bound to the value of the second element of the output i.e. the label of the relevant lamp post. If this is the case, after some internal elaborations N_s warns the lamp posts nearby x (included in L_x) of the presence of a pedestrian.

Therefore, the whole intelligent controller N of the street lights is described as the parallel composition of the checkpoint node N_{cp}, the supervisors nodes N_a and N_s, and the nodes of lamp posts N_p, with $p \in [1, k]$:

$$N = N_{cp} \ | \ N_a \ | \ N_s \ | \ N_1 \ | \cdots | \ N_k$$

We would like to statically predict how the system behaves at run time. In particular, we want to compute: (i) how nodes interact each other; (ii) how data spread from sensors to the network (tracking); and (iii) which computations each node performs on the received data. To do that, we define a Control Flow Analysis (CFA), which abstracts from the concrete values by only considering their provenance and how they are manipulated. Consider e.g. the picture sent by the camera of S_{cp} to its control process P_{pc}. In the analysis we are only interested in tracking where the picture comes from, and not in its actual value; so we use the abstract value $1^{\ell_{cp}}$ to record the camera that took it. The process P_{pc} reduces the noise in the pictures and sends the result to N_a. Our analysis keeps track of this manipulation through the abstract value $noiseRed^{\ell_{cp}}(1^{\ell_{cp}})$, meaning that the function $noiseRed$, computed by the node ℓ_{cp}, is applied to data coming from the sensor with identifier 1 of ℓ_{cp}.

In more detail, our CFA returns for each node ℓ in the network: an abstract store $\hat{\Sigma}_\ell$ that records for each variable a super-set of the abstract values that it may denote at run time; a set $\kappa(\ell)$ that approximates the set of the messages received by the node ℓ; and the set $\Theta(\ell)$ of possible abstract values computed and used by the node ℓ.

In our example, for each lamp post labelled ℓ_p, the analysis returns in $\kappa(\ell_p)$ both the abstract value $noiseRed^{\ell_{cp}}(1^{\ell_{cp}})$ and the sender of that message, i.e. ℓ_{p+1}. The result of our analysis can be exploited to perform several verifications. For instance, since the pictures of cars are sensitive data, one would like to check whether they are kept secret. By inspecting κ and Θ we discover that the sensitive data of cars is sent to all lamp posts, so possibly violating privacy. Another example is detecting whether there are redundant communications, e.g. since the street is one-way, when a car is present the lamp post at position p needs not to alert the one at $p - 1$. From κ it is easy to detect a redundant communication from the next lamp post.

3   The Calculus IoT-LySa

We adapt the LySa calculus [3,4,6], based on the π- [17] and Spi-calculus [1], to model IoT applications. For that we introduce: (i) systems of nodes, in turn consisting of sensors, actuators and control processes, plus a shared store Σ within each node for internal communications; (ii) primitives for reading from sensors, and for triggering actuator actions; (iii) an asynchronous multi-party communication modality among nodes, subject to constraints, mainly concerning proximity; (iv) functions to process data; (v) explicit conditional statements. For brevity, we do not include here encryption and decryption primitives as in LySa.

Syntax. Systems have a two-level structure and consist of a fixed number of labelled nodes, hosting a store, control processes, sensors and actuators. The label ℓ uniquely identifies the node $\ell : [B]$ and may represent further character-ising information (e.g. its location or other contextual information). Finally, the operator | describes a node system of nodes obtained by parallel composition. The syntax of nodes is as follows.

$\mathcal{N} \ni N ::=$ *systems of nodes*

0	inactive node
$\ell : [B]$	single node ($\ell \in \mathcal{L}$, the set of labels)
$N_1 \mid N_2$	parallel composition of nodes

$\mathcal{B} \ni B ::=$ *node components*

Σ_ℓ	node store
P	process
S	sensor, with a unique identifier $i \in \mathcal{I}_\ell$
A	actuator, with a unique identifier $i \in \mathcal{J}_\ell$
$B \parallel B$	parallel composition of node components

We impose that in $\ell : [B]$ there is a *single* store $\Sigma_\ell : \mathcal{X} \cup \mathcal{I}_\ell \rightarrow \mathcal{V}$, where $\mathcal{X}, \mathcal{V}$ are the sets of variables and of values, respectively. Our store is essentially an array of fixed dimension, so intuitively a variable is the index in the array and an index $i \in \mathcal{I}_\ell$ corresponds to a single sensor (no need of α-conversions). We assume that store accesses are atomic, e.g. through CAS instructions [13]. The other node components are obtained by the parallel composition of control processes P, and of a fixed number of (less than $\#(\mathcal{I}_\ell)$) sensors S, and actuators A (less than $\#(\mathcal{J}_\ell)$). The syntax of processes is as follows

$\mathcal{P} \ni P ::=$ *control processes*

0	inactive process
$\langle\!\langle E_1, \cdots, E_k \rangle\!\rangle \triangleright L.\, P$	asynchronous multi-output $L \subseteq \mathcal{L}$
$(E_1, \cdots, E_j; x_{j+1}, \cdots, x_k).\, P$	input (with matching)
$E?P : Q$	conditional statement
h	iteration variable
$\mu h.\, P$	tail iteration
$x := E.\, P$	assignment to $x \in \mathcal{X}$
$\langle j, \gamma \rangle.\, P$	output of action γ to actuator j

The prefix $\langle\!\langle E_1, \cdots, E_k \rangle\!\rangle \triangleright L$ implements a simple form of multi-party communication among nodes: the tuple $E_1, \ldots, E_k$ is asynchronously sent to the nodes with labels in L and that are "compatible" (according, among other attributes, to a proximity-based notion). The input prefix $(E_1, \cdots, E_j; x_{j+1}, \cdots, x_k)$ is willing to receive a k-tuple, provided that its first j elements match the input ones, and then binds the remaining store variables (separated by a ";") to the corresponding values (see [2,6] for a more flexible choice). Otherwise, the k-tuple is not accepted. A process repeats its behaviour, when defined through the tail iteration construct $\mu h.\, P$, where h is the iteration variable.

A sensor can perform an internal action τ or store the value v, gathered from the environment, into its store location i. An actuator can perform an internal action τ or execute one of its action γ, possibly received from its controlling process. Both sensors and actuators can iterate. For simplicity, here we neither provide an explicit operation to read data from the environment, nor to describe the impact of actuator actions on the environment. Sensors and actuators (uniquely labelled) have the form:

$$\mathcal{S} \ni S ::= sensors \qquad\qquad \mathcal{A} \ni A ::= actuators$$

0	inactive sensor		0	inactive actuator
$\tau.S$	internal action		$\tau.A$	internal action
$i := v.\,S$	store of $v \in \mathcal{V}$		$(\!| j, \Gamma |\!).\,A$	command for actuator j
	by the ith sensor		$\gamma.A$	triggered action $(\gamma \in \Gamma)$
h	iteration var.		h	iteration var.
$\mu\,h\,.\,S$	tail iteration		$\mu\,h\,.\,S$	tail iteration

The syntax of terms follows.

$$\mathcal{E} \ni E ::= terms$$

v	value $(v \in \mathcal{V})$
i	sensor location $(i \in \mathcal{I}_\ell)$
x	variable $(x \in \mathcal{X})$
$f(E_1, \cdots, E_n)$	function on data

The term $f(E_1, \cdots, E_n)$ is the application of function f to n arguments; we assume given a set of primitive functions, typically for aggregating or comparing values, be them computed or representing data in the environment.

Operational Semantics. Our reduction semantics assumes the following *structural congruence* $\equiv$ on nodes, processes and sensors. It is standard except for the last rule that equates a multi-output with no receivers to the inactive process.

- $(\mathcal{N}/_\equiv, |, 0)$ and $(\mathcal{B}/_\equiv, \|, 0)$ are commutative monoids
- $\mu h\,.\,X \equiv X\{\mu h\,.\,X/h\}$ for $X \in \{P, A, S\}$
- $\langle\!\langle E_1, \cdots, E_k \rangle\!\rangle : \emptyset.\,0 \equiv 0$.

We have a two-level *reduction relation* defined as the least relation on nodes and its components, denoted by $\rightarrow$, satisfying the set of inference rules in Table 1. We assume the standard denotational interpretation $[\![E]\!]_\Sigma$ for evaluating terms.

The first two rules implement the (atomic) asynchronous update of shared variables inside nodes, by using the standard notation $\Sigma\{-/-\}$. According to (S-store), the ith sensor uploads the value v, gathered from the environment, into the store location i. According to (Asgm), a control process updates the variable x with the value of E. The rules (Ev-out) and (Multi-com) drive asynchronous multi-communications among nodes. In the first a node labelled ℓ willing to send a tuple of values $\langle\!\langle v_1, ..., v_k \rangle\!\rangle$, obtained by the evaluation of $\langle\!\langle E_1, ..., E_k \rangle\!\rangle$, spawns a new process, running in parallel with the continuation P; its task is to offer the evaluated tuple to all its receivers L. In the rule (Multi-com), the message coming from ℓ_1 is received by a node labelled ℓ_2. The communication succeeds, provided that (i) ℓ_2 belongs to the set L of possible receivers, (ii) the two nodes are compatible according to the compatibility function *Comp*, and (iii) that the first j values match with the evaluations of the first j terms in the input.

Table 1. Reduction semantics, where $X \in \{S, A\}$ and $Y \in \{N, B\}$.

(S-store)

$$\Sigma \parallel i := v.\, S_i \parallel B \rightarrow \Sigma\{v/i\} \parallel S_i \parallel B$$

(Asgm)

$$\frac{\llbracket E \rrbracket_\Sigma = v}{\Sigma \parallel x := E.\, P \parallel B \rightarrow \Sigma\{v/x\} \parallel P \parallel B}$$

(Ev-out)

$$\frac{\bigwedge_{i=1}^{k} v_i = \llbracket E_i \rrbracket_\Sigma}{\Sigma \parallel \langle\!\langle E_1, \cdots, E_k \rangle\!\rangle \triangleright L.\, P \parallel B \;\rightarrow\; \Sigma \parallel \langle\!\langle v_1, \cdots, v_k \rangle\!\rangle \triangleright L.\, 0 \parallel P \parallel B}$$

(Multi-com)

$$\frac{\ell_2 \in L \wedge \; Comp(\ell_1, \ell_2) \wedge \bigwedge_{i=1}^{j} v_i = \llbracket E_i \rrbracket_{\Sigma_2}}{\begin{array}{c} \ell_1 : [\langle\!\langle v_1, \cdots, v_k \rangle\!\rangle \triangleright L.\, 0 \parallel B_1] \mid \ell_2 : [\Sigma_2 \parallel (E_1, \cdots, E_j; x_{j+1}, \cdots, x_k).Q \parallel B_2] \\ \rightarrow \\ \ell_1 : [\langle\!\langle v_1, \cdots, v_k \rangle\!\rangle \triangleright L \setminus \{\ell_2\}.\, 0 \parallel B_1] \mid \ell_2 : [\Sigma_2\{v_{j+1}/x_{j+1}, \cdots, v_k/x_k\} \parallel Q \parallel B_2] \end{array}}$$

(Cond)

$$\frac{\llbracket E \rrbracket_\Sigma = b_1}{\Sigma \parallel E?\, P_1 : P_2 \parallel B \;\rightarrow\; \Sigma \parallel P_i \parallel B} \quad \text{where } b_1 = \mathtt{true}, b_2 = \mathtt{false}$$

(A-com)

$$\frac{\gamma \in \Gamma}{\langle j, \gamma \rangle.\, P \parallel (\!(j, \Gamma)\!).\, A \parallel B \;\rightarrow\; P \parallel \gamma.\, A \parallel B}$$

(Act)

$$\gamma.\, A \;\rightarrow\; A$$

(Int)

$$\tau.\, X \;\rightarrow\; X$$

(Node)

$$\frac{B \rightarrow B'}{\ell : [B] \;\rightarrow\; \ell : [B']}$$

(ParN)

$$\frac{N_1 \rightarrow N_1'}{N_1 \mid N_2 \rightarrow N_1' \mid N_2}$$

(ParB)

$$\frac{B_1 \rightarrow B_1'}{B_1 \parallel B_2 \rightarrow B_1' \parallel B_2}$$

(CongrY)

$$\frac{Y_1' \equiv Y_1 \rightarrow Y_2 \equiv Y_2'}{Y_1' \rightarrow Y_2'}$$

Moreover, the label ℓ_2 is removed by the set of receivers L of the tuple. The spawned process terminates when all its receivers have received the message (see the last congruence rule). The role of the compatibility function $Comp$ is crucial in modelling real world constraints on communication. A basic requirement is that inter-node communications are proximity-based, i.e. that only nodes that are in the same transmission range can directly exchange messages. This is easily encoded here by defining a predicate (over node labels) yielding true only when two nodes are in the same transmission range. Of course, this function could be enriched in order to consider finer notions of compatibility expressing various policies, e.g. topics for event notification. Note that if $Comp$ varies along time, we recover a simple way of expressing dynamic network topologies. According to the evaluation of the expression E, the rule (Cond) says that the process continues as P_1 (if $\llbracket E \rrbracket_\Sigma$ is true) or as P_2 (otherwise). A process commands the jth actuator through the rule (A-com), by sending it the pair $\langle j, \gamma \rangle$; γ prefixes the actuator, if it is one of its actions. The rule (Act) says that the actuator performs the action γ. Similarly, for the rules (Int) for internal actions. The last rules propagate reductions across parallel composition ((ParN) and (ParB)) and nodes (Node), while the (CongrY) are the standard reduction rules for congruence.

4   Control Flow Analysis

Our CFA aims at safely approximating the abstract behaviour of a system of nodes N. The analysis follows the same schema of that for LySA [4], and for the time being we only conjecture that computing its results requires the same low polynomial time complexity. Here, we track the usage of sensor values inside the local node where they are gathered and their propagation in the network of nodes both as raw data or processed via suitable functions. We resort to abstract values for sensor and functions on abstract values, as follows, where $\ell \in \mathcal{L}$:

$$\hat{\mathcal{V}} \ni \hat{v} ::= \textit{abstract terms}$$

$\top^\ell$	special abstract value denoting cut
i^ℓ	sensor abstract value ($i \in \mathcal{I}_\ell$)
v^ℓ	node abstract value
$f^\ell(\hat{v}_1, \cdots, \hat{v}_n)$	function on abstract data

Since the dynamic semantics may introduce function terms with an arbitrarily nesting level, we have new special abstract values $\top^\ell$ that denote all those function terms with a depth greater that a given d. In the clauses defining our analysis, we will use $\lfloor - \rfloor_d$ to keep the maximal depth of abstract terms less or equal to d, defined as expected. Note that, once given the set of functions f occurring in a node N, the abstract values are finitely many.

The result of our CFA is a triple $(\hat{\Sigma}, \kappa, \Theta)$ (a pair $(\hat{\Sigma}, \Theta)$ for terms E, resp.), called *estimate* for N (for E, resp.), that satisfies the judgements defined by the rules of Tables 3 and 2. For this we introduce the following *abstract domains*:

- *abstract store* $\hat{\Sigma} = \bigcup_{\ell \in \mathcal{L}} \hat{\Sigma}_\ell : \mathcal{X} \cup \mathcal{I}_\ell \rightarrow 2^{\hat{\mathcal{V}}}$ where each *abstract local store* $\hat{\Sigma}_\ell$ approximates the concrete local store Σ_ℓ, by associating with each location a set of abstract values that represent the possible concrete values that the location may store at run time.
- *abstract network environment* $\kappa : \mathcal{L} \rightarrow \mathcal{L} \times \bigcup_{i=1}^{k} \hat{\mathcal{V}}^i$ (with $\hat{\mathcal{V}}^{i+1} = \hat{\mathcal{V}} \times \hat{\mathcal{V}}^i$ and k maximum arity of messages), that includes all the messages that may be received by the node labelled ℓ.
- *abstract data collection* $\Theta : \mathcal{L} \rightarrow 2^{\hat{\mathcal{V}}}$ that, for each node labelled ℓ, approximates the set of values that the node computes.

For each term E, the judgement $(\hat{\Sigma}, \Theta) \models_\ell E : \vartheta$, defined by the rules in Table 2, expresses that $\vartheta \in \hat{\mathcal{V}}$ is an acceptable estimate of the set of values that E may evaluate to in $\hat{\Sigma}_\ell$. A sensor identifier and a value evaluate to the set ϑ, provided that their abstract representations belong to ϑ. Similarly a variable x evaluates to ϑ, if this includes the set of values bound to x in $\hat{\Sigma}_\ell$. The last rule analyses

Table 2. Analysis of terms $(\hat{\Sigma}, \Theta) \models_\ell E : \vartheta$.

$$\frac{i^\ell \in \vartheta \subseteq \Theta(\ell)}{(\hat{\Sigma}, \Theta) \models_\ell i : \vartheta} \qquad \frac{v^\ell \in \vartheta \subseteq \Theta(\ell)}{(\hat{\Sigma}, \Theta) \models_\ell v : \vartheta} \qquad \frac{\hat{\Sigma}_\ell(x) \subseteq \vartheta \subseteq \Theta(\ell)}{(\hat{\Sigma}, \Theta) \models_\ell x : \vartheta}$$

$$\frac{\bigwedge_{i=1}^k (\hat{\Sigma}, \Theta) \models_\ell E_i : \vartheta_i \ \wedge}{\forall \hat{v}_1, \cdots, \hat{v}_k : \bigwedge_{i=1}^k \hat{v}_i \in \vartheta_i \ \Rightarrow \ \lfloor f^\ell(\hat{v}_1, \cdots, \hat{v}_k)\rfloor_d \in \vartheta \subseteq \Theta(\ell)}{(\hat{\Sigma}, \Theta) \models_\ell f(E_1, \cdots, E_k) : \vartheta}$$

the application of a k-ary function f to produce the set ϑ. Recall that the special abstract value $\top^\ell$ will end up in ϑ if the depth of the abstract functional term exceeds d, and it represents all the functional terms with nesting greater than d. To do that (i) for each term E_i, it finds the sets ϑ_i, and (ii) for all k-tuples of values $(\hat{v}_1, \cdots, \hat{v}_k)$ in $\vartheta_1 \times \cdots \times \vartheta_k$, it checks if the abstract values $f^\ell(\hat{v}_1, \cdots, \hat{v}_k)$ belong to ϑ. Moreover, in all the rules for terms, we require that $\Theta(\ell)$ includes all the abstract values included in ϑ. This guarantees that only those values actually used are tracked by Θ, in particular those of sensors.

In the analysis of nodes we focus on which values can flow on the network and which can be assigned to variables. The judgements have the form $(\hat{\Sigma}, \kappa, \Theta) \models N$ and are defined by the rules in Table 2. The rules for the *inactive node* and for *parallel composition* are standard. Moreover, the rule for a single node $\ell : [B]$ requires that its component B is analysed, with the further judgment $(\hat{\Sigma}, \kappa, \Theta) \models_\ell B$, where ℓ is the label of the enclosing node. The rule connecting actual stores Σ with abstract ones $\hat{\Sigma}$ requires the locations of sensors to contain the corresponding abstract values. The rule for sensors is trivial, because we are only interested in who will use their values, and so is that for actuators. The rules for processes are in Table 3, and all require that an estimate is also valid for the immediate sub-processes. The rule for k-ary *multi-output* (i) finds the sets ϑ_i, for each term E_i; and (ii) for all k-tuples of values $(\hat{v}_1, \cdots, \hat{v}_k)$ in $\vartheta_1 \times \cdots \times \vartheta_k$, it checks if they belong to $\kappa(\ell' \in L)$, i.e. they can be received by the nodes with labels in L. In the rule for *input* the terms $E_1, \cdots, E_j$ are used for matching values sent on the network. Thus, this rule checks whether (i) these first j terms have acceptable estimates ϑ_i; (ii) the two nodes can communicate $(Comp(\ell', \ell))$; and whether (iii) for each message $(\ell', \langle\!\langle \hat{v}_1, \cdots, \hat{v}_j, \hat{v}_{j+1}, \ldots, \hat{v}_k \rangle\!\rangle)$ in $\kappa(\ell)$ (i.e. in any message predicted to be receivable by the node with label ℓ) the values $\hat{v}_{j+1}, \ldots, \hat{v}_k$ are included in the estimates for the variables $x_{j+1}, \cdots, x_k$. The rule for *assignment* requires that all the values $\hat{v}$ in ϑ, the estimate for E, belong to $\hat{\Sigma}_\ell(x)$. The rule for $\mu h. P$ reflects our choice of limiting the depth of function applications: the iterative process is unfolded d times. The remaining rules are as expected.

To show our analysis at work, consider again the example in Sect. 2 and the process $P_{cp} = \mu h.(z := 1).(z' := noiseRed(z)).\langle\!\langle z' \rangle\!\rangle \triangleright \{\ell_a\}. h$. Every valid CFA

Table 3. Analysis of nodes $(\hat{\Sigma}, \kappa, \Theta) \models N$, and of node components $(\hat{\Sigma}, \kappa, \Theta) \models_\ell B$.

$$\frac{}{(\hat{\Sigma}, \kappa, \Theta) \models 0} \qquad \frac{(\hat{\Sigma}, \kappa, \Theta) \models_\ell B}{(\hat{\Sigma}, \kappa, \Theta) \models \ell : [B]} \qquad \frac{(\hat{\Sigma}, \kappa, \Theta) \models N_1 \wedge (\hat{\Sigma}, \kappa, \Theta) \models N_2}{(\hat{\Sigma}, \kappa, \Theta) \models N_1 \mid N_2}$$

$$\frac{\forall i \in \mathcal{I}_\ell.\ i^\ell \in \hat{\Sigma}_\ell(i)}{(\hat{\Sigma}, \kappa, \Theta) \models_\ell \Sigma} \qquad \frac{}{(\hat{\Sigma}, \kappa, \Theta) \models_\ell S} \qquad \frac{}{(\hat{\Sigma}, \kappa, \Theta) \models_\ell A}$$

$$\frac{\bigwedge_{i=1}^{k} (\hat{\Sigma}, \Theta) \models_\ell E_i : \vartheta_i \wedge (\hat{\Sigma}, \kappa, \Theta) \models_\ell P \wedge}{\forall \hat{v}_1, \cdots, \hat{v}_k : \bigwedge_{i=1}^{k} \hat{v}_i \in \vartheta_i \Rightarrow \forall \ell' \in L : (\ell, \langle\!\langle \hat{v}_1, \cdots, \hat{v}_k \rangle\!\rangle) \in \kappa(\ell')}{(\hat{\Sigma}, \kappa, \Theta) \models_\ell \langle\!\langle E_1, \cdots, E_k \rangle\!\rangle \triangleright L.\, P}$$

$$\frac{\bigwedge_{i=1}^{j} (\hat{\Sigma}, \Theta) \models_\ell E_i : \vartheta_i \wedge Comp(\ell', \ell) \wedge}{\forall (\ell', \langle\!\langle \hat{v}_1, \cdots, \hat{v}_k \rangle\!\rangle) \in \kappa(\ell) : \bigwedge_{i=j+1}^{k} \hat{v}_i \in \hat{\Sigma}_\ell(x_i) \wedge}{(\hat{\Sigma}, \kappa, \Theta) \models_\ell P}{(\hat{\Sigma}, \kappa, \Theta) \models_\ell (E_1, \cdots, E_j;\ x_{j+1}, \cdots, x_k).\, P}$$

$$\frac{(\hat{\Sigma}, \Theta) \models_\ell E : \vartheta \wedge}{\forall \hat{v} \in \vartheta \Rightarrow \hat{v} \in \hat{\Sigma}_\ell(x) \wedge (\hat{\Sigma}, \kappa, \Theta) \models_\ell P}{(\hat{\Sigma}, \kappa, \Theta) \models_\ell x := E.\, P} \qquad \frac{(\hat{\Sigma}, \kappa, \Theta) \models_\ell P}{(\hat{\Sigma}, \kappa, \Theta) \models_\ell \langle j, \gamma \rangle.\, P}$$

$$\frac{(\hat{\Sigma}, \Theta) \models_\ell E : \vartheta \wedge (\hat{\Sigma}, \kappa, \Theta) \models_\ell P_1 \wedge (\hat{\Sigma}, \kappa, \Theta) \models_\ell P_2}{(\hat{\Sigma}, \kappa, \Theta) \models_\ell E?P_1 : P_2}$$

$$\frac{}{(\hat{\Sigma}, \kappa, \Theta) \models_\ell 0} \qquad \frac{(\hat{\Sigma}, \kappa, \Theta) \models_\ell \lfloor \mu h.\, P \rfloor_d}{(\hat{\Sigma}, \kappa, \Theta) \models_\ell \mu h.\, P} \qquad \frac{}{(\hat{\Sigma}, \kappa, \Theta) \models_\ell h}$$

estimate must include at least the following entries (assuming $d = 4$):

(a) $\hat{\Sigma}_{\ell_{cp}}(z) \supseteq \{1^{\ell_{cp}}\}$ (b) $\hat{\Sigma}_{\ell_{cp}}(z') \supseteq \{noiseRed^{\ell_{cp}}(1^{\ell_{cp}}), 1^{\ell_{cp}}\}$

(c) $\Theta(\ell_{cp}) \supseteq \{1^{\ell_{cp}}, noiseRed^{\ell_{cp}}(1^{\ell_{cp}})\}$ (d) $\kappa(\ell_a) \supseteq \{(\ell_{cp}, \langle\!\langle noiseRed^{\ell_{cp}}(1^{\ell_{cp}}) \rangle\!\rangle)\}$

Indeed, all the following checks must succeed:

- $(\hat{\Sigma}, \kappa, \Theta) \models_{\ell_{cp}} \mu h.(z := 1).(z' := noiseRed(z)).\langle\!\langle z' \rangle\!\rangle \triangleright \{\ell_a\}.h$ because
- $(\hat{\Sigma}, \kappa, \Theta) \models_{\ell_{cp}} (z := 1).(z' := noiseRed(z)).\langle\!\langle z' \rangle\!\rangle \triangleright \{\ell_a\}$, that in turn holds
- because (i) $1^{\ell_{cp}}$ is in $\hat{\Sigma}_{\ell_{cp}}(z)$ by (a) $((\hat{\Sigma}, \Theta) \models_\ell 1 : \vartheta \ni 1^{\ell_{cp}})$; and because (ii) $(\hat{\Sigma}, \kappa, \Theta) \models_{\ell_{cp}} (z' := noiseRed(z)).\langle\!\langle z' \rangle\!\rangle \triangleright \{\ell_a\}$, that in turn holds
- because (i) $noiseRed^{\ell_{cp}}(1^{\ell_{cp}})$ is in $\hat{\Sigma}_{\ell_{cp}}(z')$ by (b) since $(\hat{\Sigma}, \Theta) \models_{\ell_{cp}} noiseRed(z) : \vartheta \ni noiseRed^{\ell_{cp}}(1^{\ell_{cp}})$; and because (ii) $(\hat{\Sigma}, \kappa, \Theta) \models_{\ell_{cp}} \langle\!\langle z' \rangle\!\rangle \triangleright \{\ell_a\}$ that holds because $(\ell_{cp}, \langle\!\langle noiseRed^{\ell_{cp}}(1^{\ell_{cp}}) \rangle\!\rangle)$ is in $\kappa(\ell_a)$ by (d).

Correctness of the Analysis. Our CFA respects the operational semantics. The proof of this fact benefits from an instrumented denotational semantics for expressions, the values of which are pairs $\langle v, \hat{v} \rangle$. Consequently, the store (Σ^i_ℓ with a $\perp$ value) and its updates are accordingly extended (the semantics used in Table 1 is $[\![v]\!]^i_{\downarrow_1}$, the projection on the first component of the instrumented one).

Just to give an intuition, we will have $[\![v]\!]^i_{\Sigma^i_\ell} = (v, v^\ell)$, and the assignment $x :=$ E will result in the updated store $\Sigma^i_\ell\{(v, v^\ell)/x\}$, where E evaluates to (v, v^ℓ). Clearly, the semantics of Table 1 is $[\![v]\!]^i_{\downarrow_1}$, the projection on the first component of the instrumented one. In our example, the assignment $z' := noiseRed(z)$ of the process P_{cp} stores the pair $(v, noiseRed^{\ell_{cp}}(1^{\ell_{cp}}))$ made of the actual value v and of its abstract counterpart.

Since the analysis only considers the second component of the extended store, it is immediate defining when the concrete and the abstract stores agree: $\Sigma^i_\ell \bowtie \hat{\Sigma}_\ell$ iff $w \in \mathcal{X} \cup \mathcal{I}_\ell$ such that $\Sigma^i_\ell(w) \neq \perp$ implies $(\Sigma^i_\ell(w))_{\downarrow_2} \in \hat{\Sigma}_\ell(w)$.

The following theorems establish the correctness of our CFA and the existence of a minimal estimate. Their proofs have the usual schema.

Theorem 1 (Subject reduction). *If $(\hat{\Sigma}, \kappa, \Theta) \models N$ and $N \to N'$ and $\forall \Sigma^i_\ell$ in N it is $\Sigma^i_\ell \bowtie \hat{\Sigma}_\ell$, then $(\hat{\Sigma}, \kappa, \Theta) \models N'$ and $\forall \Sigma^{i'}_\ell$ in N' it is $\Sigma^{i'}_\ell \bowtie \hat{\Sigma}_\ell$.*

Theorem 2 (Existence of estimates). *Given N, its estimates form a Moore family that has a minimal element.*

The following corollary of subject reduction justifies the title of this paper: we do track the ingredients of IoT data. The first item makes it evident that our analysis determines whether the value of a term may indeed be used along the computations of a system, and clarifies the role of the component Θ; the second item guarantees that κ predicts all the possible inter-node communications.

Corollary 1.

- *Let $N \xrightarrow{E_1,...,E_n}_\ell N'$ denote a reduction in which all E_i are evaluated at node ℓ. If $(\hat{\Sigma}, \kappa, \Theta) \models N$ and $N \xrightarrow{E_1,...,E_n}_\ell N'$ then $\forall k \in [0, n]$ it is $([\![E_k]\!]^i_{\Sigma^i_\ell})_{\downarrow_2} \in \Theta(\ell)$.*

- *Let $N \xrightarrow{\langle\langle v_1,...,v_n \rangle\rangle}_{\ell_1, \ell_2} N'$ denote a reduction in which the message sent by node ℓ_1 is received by node ℓ_2. If $(\hat{\Sigma}, \kappa, \Theta) \models N$ and $N \xrightarrow{\langle\langle v_1,...,v_n \rangle\rangle}_{\ell_1, \ell_2} N'$ then it holds $(\ell_1, \langle\langle \hat{v}_1, ..., \hat{v}_n \rangle\rangle) \in \kappa(\ell_2)$, where $\hat{v}_i = v_{i \downarrow_2}$.*

Back again to our example, we have that $1^{\ell_{cp}} \in \Theta(\ell_{cp})$, where $([\![1]\!]^1_{\Sigma^1_{\ell_{cp}}})_{\downarrow_2} = 1^{\ell_{cp}}$, and where v is the actual value received by the first sensor. Similarly, we have that $(\ell_{cp}, \langle\langle \hat{v} \rangle\rangle) \in \kappa(\ell_a)$, where $\hat{v} = v_{\downarrow_2}$.

Extending the Analysis. For simplicity, above we have presented a CFA that only tracks the ingredients of the data handled by IoT nodes. Now, we sketch a few possible extensions.

As it is, our analysis tracks the actual usage of sensor data through the component Θ. It is straightforward to also detect which actions of actuators are actually triggered. The result might suggest to use a simpler actuator if some of its actions are never exercised, or even to remove it if it is never used. Technically, a new analysis component α suffices, that for every actuator j collects the actions γ triggered by the control process in the node ℓ. Then, one has only to change the rule for the command to the actuator, as follows:

$$\frac{\gamma \in \alpha_\ell(j) \wedge (\hat{\Sigma}, \kappa, \alpha, \Theta) \models_\ell P}{(\hat{\Sigma}, \kappa, \alpha, \Theta) \models_\ell \langle j, \gamma \rangle . P}$$

To improve the precision of our CFA, we can refine the abstract store by replacing it with the pair $\hat{\Sigma}_{in}, \hat{\Sigma}_{out}$, similarly to the treatment of side effects in [19]. This extension is more invasive, because it requires modifying the rules for accurately handling the store updates. We can obtain a further improvement of the precision by making the analysis more context-sensitive. In particular, an additional component can record the sequence of choices made in conditionals while traversing the node under analysis. One can thus obtain better approximations of the store or detect causal dependencies among the data sent by sensors and the actions carried out by actuators, as well as casuality among nodes.

5   Conclusions

This paper is a first step towards a formal design framework for IoT, which will support the definition of techniques and tools for certifying properties of IoT applications. We proposed the process calculus IoT-LySa, with primitive constructs to describe the activity of sensors and of actuators, and suitable primitives for managing the coordination and communication capabilities of smart objects. We equipped our calculus with a CFA that statically predicts the interactions among nodes, how data spread from sensors to the network, and how data are put together. We sketched how the result of the analysis can be exploited as the basis for checking and certifying various properties of IoT systems.

Besides the extensions mentioned at the end of Sect. 4, we plan to accurately investigate the exact complexity of the analysis and to implement it. We intend to address with our analysis security and privacy "since IoT deals not only with huge amount of sensitive data (personal data, business data, etc.) but also has the power of influencing the physical environment with its control abilities" [14]. In particular, we can assign specific confidentiality levels to sensors and nodes and by inspecting the result of the analysis, we can detect if nodes with a lower level can access data of entities with a higher level. Also, we will enrich our design framework with security policies, e.g. for access control. By tracking the actions of actuators as suggested in Sect. 4, one can predict if an actuator is maliciously triggered by an attacker, as happened in the recent attack performed through a vehicular infotainment network (http://www.wired.com/2015/07/hackers-remotely-kill-jeep-highway/). For brevity, we neglected here the cryptographic primitives LySa offers natively, although both the current operational semantics and the static analysis can easily be extended to cover them. An analysis that identifies where encryption and decryption are really needed would be very useful for designers of IoT systems, because cryptography is expensive since many smart devices have limited battery power. Beneficial to such an analysis may be the preliminary work on an enhanced version of IoT-LySa [5] that estimates costs of cryptographic primitives. Finally, in the IERC words: "there is still a lack of research on how to adapt and tailor existing research on autonomic computing to the specific characteristics of IoT" [14]. To contribute to these issues, we plan to extend our calculus with linguistic mechanisms and a verification machinery to deal with adaptivity in the style of [9].

To the best of our knowledge, only a limited number of papers addressed the specification and verification of IoT systems from a process calculi perspective, within the formal methods approach. The IoT-calculus [15] is one of the first proposals in this setting. It explicitly includes sensors and actuators, and smart objects are represented as point-to-point communicating nodes of heterogeneous networks. Differently from ours, their interconnection topology can vary at run time. The authors propose two notions of bisimilarity that capture system behaviour from the point of view of end-users and of the other devices. The timed process calculus CIoT [8] specifies physical and logical components, addresses both timing and topology constraints, and allows for node mobility. Furthermore, communications are either short-range or internet-based. The focus of this paper is mainly on an extensional semantics that provides a *fully abstract* characterisation of the proposed contextual equivalence.

Many design choices of the above-discussed proposals are similar to ours. The main difference is that our coordination model is based on a shared store à la Linda instead of a message-based communication à la π-calculus. Furthermore, differently from [8,15], we are here mainly interested in developing a design framework that includes a static semantics to support verification techniques and tools for certifying properties of IoT applications.

The calculi above and ours are built upon those previously introduced for wireless, sensor and ad hoc networks ([16,18,20] to cite only a few). In particular, the calculus in [18] is designed to model so-called broadcast networks, with a dynamically changing topology. It presents some features very similar to ours: an asynchronous local broadcast modality, while intra-node communication relies on a local tuple space. Also, the analysis of the behaviour of broadcast networks is done by resorting to a multi-step static machinery.

References

1. Abadi, M., Gordon, A.: A calculus for cryptographic protocols: the spi calculus. In: Proceedings of the 4th ACM Conference on Computer and Communications Security, CCS 1997, pp. 36–47. ACM (1997)
2. Bodei, C., Brodo, C., Focardi, R.: Static evidences for attack reconstruction. In: Bodei, C., Ferrari, G.-L., Priami, C. (eds.) Programming Languages with Applications to Biology and Security. LNCS, vol. 9465, pp. 162–182. Springer, Heidelberg (2015). doi:10.1007/978-3-319-25527-9_12

3. Bodei, C., Buchholtz, M., Degano, P., Nielson, F., Nielson, H.R.: Automatic valida-tion of protocol narration. In: Computer Security Foundations Workshop (CSFW-16 2003), pp. 126–140. IEEE Computer Society (2003)
4. Bodei, C., Buchholtz, M., Degano, P., Nielson, F., Nielson, H.R.: Static validation of security protocols. J. Comput. Secur. **13**(3), 347–390 (2005)
5. Bodei, C., Galletta, L.: Securing IoT communications: at what cost?. In: Cortier, V. (ed.) Proceeding HotSpot 2016 (2016). http://www.loria.fr/cortier/HotSpot2016/ HotSpot2016-proceedings.pdf
6. Buchholtz, M., Nielson, H.R., Nielson, F.: A calculus for control flow analysis of security protocols. Int. J. Inf. Secur. **2**(3), 145–167 (2004)
7. Carriero, N., Gelernter, D.: A computational model of everything. Commun. ACM **44**(11), 77–81 (2001)
8. Castiglioni, V., Lanotte, R., Merro, M.: A semantic theory for the internet of things, CoRR abs/1510.04854 (2015)
9. Degano, P., Ferrari, G.L., Galletta, L.: A two-component language for adapta-tion: design, semantics, and program analysis. IEEE Trans. Softw. Eng. **42** (2016). doi:10.1109/TSE.2015.2496941
10. Elejoste, P., Perallos, A., Chertudi, A., Angulo, I., Moreno, A., Azpilicueta, L., Astrain, J., Falcone, F., Villadangos, J.E.: An easy to deploy street light control system based on wireless communication and led technology. Sensors **13**(5), 6492–6523 (2013)
11. Escolar, S., Carretero, J., Marinescu, M., Chessa, S.: Estimating energy savings in smart street lighting by using an adaptive control system. In: IJDSN 2014 (2014)
12. Gelernter, D.: Generative communication in linda. ACM Trans. Program. Lang. Syst. **7**(1), 80–112 (1985)
13. Herlihy, M.: Wait-free synchronization. ACM Trans. Program. Lang. Syst. **13**(1), 124–149 (1991)
14. IERC: The Internet of Things 2012 - New Horizons (2012). http://www. internet-of-things-research.eu/pdf/IERC_Cluster_Book_2012_WEB.pdf
15. Lanese, I., Bedogni, L., Felice, M.D.: Internet of things: a process calculus approach. In: Proceeding of the 28th Annual ACM Symposium on Applied Computing, SAC 2013, pp. 1339–1346. ACM (2013)
16. Lanese, I., Sangiorgi, D.: An operational semantics for a calculus for wireless sys-tems. Theor. Comput. Sci. **411**(19), 1928–1948 (2010)
17. Milner, R., Parrow, J., Walker, D.: A calculus of mobile processes. I. Inf. Comput. **100**(1), 1–40 (1992)
18. Nanz, S., Nielson, F., Nielson, H.R.: Static analysis of topology-dependent broad-cast networks. Inf. Comput. **208**(2), 117–139 (2010)
19. Riis Nielson, H., Nielson, F.: Flow Logic: a multi-paradigmatic approach to static analysis. In: Mogensen, T.Æ., Schmidt, D.A., Sudborough, I.H. (eds.) The Essence of Computation. LNCS, vol. 2566, pp. 223–244. Springer, Heidelberg (2002)
20. Singh, A., Ramakrishnan, C.R., Smolka, S.: A process calculus for mobile ad hoc networks. Sci. Comput. Program. **75**(6), 440–469 (2010)

Tuple Spaces Implementations and Their Efficiency

Vitaly Buravlev$^{(\boxtimes)}$, Rocco De Nicola, and Claudio Antares Mezzina

IMT School for Advanced Studies Lucca, Piazza S. Francesco, 19, 55100 Lucca, Italy
{vitaly.buravlev,rocco.denicola,claudio.mezzina}@imtlucca.it

Abstract. Among the paradigms for parallel and distributed computing, the one popularized with Linda and based on tuple spaces is the least used one, despite the fact of being intuitive, easy to understand and to use. A tuple space is a repository of tuples, where process can add, withdraw or read tuples by means of atomic operations. Tuples may contain different values, and processes can inspect the content of a tuple via pattern matching. The lack of a reference implementations for this paradigm has prevented its widespread. In this paper, first we do an extensive analysis on what are the state of the art implementations and summarise their characteristics. Then we select three implementations of the tuple space paradigm and compare their performances on three different case studies that aim at stressing different aspects of computing such as communication, data manipulation, and cpu usage. After reasoning on strengths and weaknesses of the three implementations, we conclude with some recommendations for future work towards building an effective implementation of the tuple space paradigm.

1 Introduction

Distributed computing is getting increasingly pervasive, with demands from various applications domains and highly diverse underlying architectures from the multitude of tiny things to the very large cloud-based systems. Several paradigms for programming parallel and distributed computing have been proposed so far. Among them we can list: distributed shared memory, message passing, actors, distributed objects and tuple spaces. Nowadays, the most used paradigm seems to be message passing, with MPI [2] being its latest incarnation, while the least popular one seems to be the one based on tuple space that was proposed by David Gelernter for the Linda coordination model [8].

As the name suggests, message passing provides coordination abstractions based on the exchange of messages between distributed processes, where message delivery is often mediated via brokers and messages consist of a header and a body. In its simplest incarnation, message-passing provides a rather low-level programming abstraction for building distributed systems. Linda, instead provides a higher level of abstraction by defining operations for synchronization and exchange of values between different programs that can share information by accessing common repositories named *tuple spaces*.

Published by Springer International Publishing Switzerland 2016. All Rights Reserved
A. Lluch Lafuente and J. Proença (Eds.): COORDINATION 2016, LNCS 9686, pp. 51–66, 2016.
DOI: 10.1007/978-3-319-39519-7_4

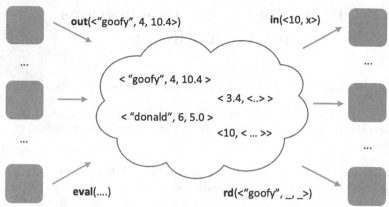

The key ingredients of Linda are few basic operations which can be embedded into different programming languages. These are atomic operations used for writing (out), withdrawing (in), reading (rd) tuples into/from a tuple space. The operations for reading and withdrawing select tuples via *pattern-matching*. Another operation eval is used to spawn new processes. The figure above illustrates an example of tuples space with different, structured, values. For example tuple $\langle$"goofy",4,10.4$\rangle$ is produced by a process via the out($\langle$"goofy",4,10.4$\rangle$) operation, and it is read by the operation rd("goofy", _,_) after pattern-matching: that is the process reads any tuple of three elements whose first one is exactly the string "goofy". Moreover, tuple $\langle 10, \langle \ldots \rangle \rangle$ is consumed (atomically retracted) by operation in($10, x$) which consumes a tuple whose first element is 10 and binds its second element (whatever it is) to the variable x. Patterns are sometimes referred as *templates*.

The simplicity of this coordination model makes it very intuitive and easy to use. Some synchronization primitives, e.g. semaphores, barrier synchronization, can be implemented easily in Linda (cf. [6], Chapter 3). Unfortunately Linda's implementations of tuple space have turned out to be quite inefficient, and this has led researchers to opt for different approaches such Open MP or MPI, which are nowadays offered, as libraries, for many programming languages. When considering distributed applications, the limited use of Linda coordination model is also due to the need of keeping tuple spaces consistent. In fact, in this case, control mechanisms that can affect scalability are needed [7].

In our view, tuple spaces can be effectively exploited as a basis for the broad range of the distributed applications with different domains (from lightweight applications to large cloud based systems). However, in order to be effective, we need to take into account that performances of a tuple space system may vary depending on the system architecture and the type of interaction between its components. The aim of this paper is to examine the state of the art implementations of tuple spaces, and to find out strengths and weaknesses.

We start by cataloguing the existing implementations according to their features, and then we focus on the most recent Linda based systems that are still maintained, while paying specific attention to those featuring decentralized tuples space. For the selected systems, we compare their performances on three different case studies that aim at stressing different aspects of computing such as communication, data manipulation, and cpu usage. After reasoning on strength and weakness of the three implementations, we conclude with some recommendation for future work towards building effective implementation of the tuple space paradigm.

2 Tuple Space Systems

In this Section, first we review several existing tuple space systems by briefly describing each of them, and single out the main features of their implementations, then we summarise these features in Table 1. Later, we focus on the implementations that enjoy the characteristics we consider important for a tuple space implementation: code mobility, distribution of tuples and flexible tuples manipulation.

JAVASPACES. JAVASPACES [13] is one of the first implementations of the tuple space developed by Sun Microsystems. It is based on a number of Java technologies (Jini, RMI). As a commercial system, JAVASPACES supports transactions and mechanism of tuple leases. A tuple, called entry in JAVASPACES, is an instance of a Java class and its fields are the public fields of the class. This means that tuples are restricted to contain only objects but not primitive values. The tuple space is implemented by using a simple Java collection. Pattern matching is performed on the byte level, and the byte level comparison of data supports object-oriented polymorphism.

TSPACES. TSPACES [12] is an implementation of the Linda model at the IBM Almaden Research Center. It combines asynchronous messaging with database features. Like JAVASPACES, TSPACES provides transactional support and mechanism of tuple leases. Moreover, the embedded mechanism for access control to tuple spaces is based on access permission. It checks whether a client is able to perform specific operations in the specific tuples space. Pattern matching is performed using either standard `equals` method or `compareTo` method. Pattern matching uses SQL-like queries, allowing to match tuples regardless of their structure (e.g. the order in which fields are stored).

GIGASPACES. GIGASPACES [9] is a contemporary commercial implementation of tuple space. Nowadays, the core of that system is GIGASPACES XAP, a scale-out application server and any user application should interact with it for creating and manipulating its own tuple space. The main areas where GIGASPACES can be applied are concerned with big data analythics. GIGASPACES main features are: linear scalability, optimization of RAM usage, synchronization with databases and several database-like operations such as complex queries, transactions and replication.

TUPLEWARE. TUPLEWARE [1] is specially designed for array-based applications in which an array is decomposed into several parts each of which can be processed in parallel. It aims at developing a scalable distributed tuple space with good performance on a computing cluster and provides clear and simple programming facilities for dealing with distributed tuple space as well as with centralized one. The tuple space is implemented as a hashtable, containing pairs consisting of a key and a vector of tuples. Due to the nature of Jave hashtable, it is possible to access concurrently several elements of the hashtable, since synchonisation is at the level of hashtable element. To speed up the search in the distributed tuple space, an algorithm based on the history of communication is used. Its main aim is to minimize the number of communications between nodes for tuples retrieval. The algorithm uses *success factor*, a real number between 0 and 1, expressing the likelihood of the fact that a node can find a tuple in the tuple space of other nodes. Each instance of TUPLEWARE calculates success factor on the basis of past attempts to get information from other nodes and tuples are first searched in nodes with greater success factor.

GRINDA. GRINDA [5] is a distributed tuple space which was designed for large scale infrastructures. It combines Linda coordination model with grid architecture aiming at improving performance of distributed tuple space, especially with a large amount of tuples. To boost the search of tuples, GRINDA utilizes spatial indexing schemes (X-Tree, Pyramid) which are usually used in spatial databases and Geographical Information Systems. Distribution of tuple spaces is based on the grid architecture and implemented using structured P2P network (based on Content Addressable Network and tree based).

BLOSSOM. BLOSSOM [15] is a C++ implementation of Linda which was developed to achieve high performance and correctness of the programs using Linda model. In BLOSSOM all tuple spaces are homogeneous with predefined structure, and this allows spending less time for type comparison during the search. To improve scalability, BLOSSOM uses distributed tuple spaces and each processor is assigned a particular tuple space by considering tuple values. The technique of prefetching allows a process to send a request for some tuples to the tuple space and to continue its work while the search continues. When the process needs the requested tuples, it receives them without waiting and spending time for their search which have been already done.

DTUPLES. DTUPLES [10] is designed for peer-to-peer networks and based on distributed hash table (DHT), a scalable and efficient approach. Key points of DHT are autonomy and decentralization. There is no central server and each node of DHT is in charge of storing a part of hash table and of keeping routing information about other nodes. As the basis of the DTH's implementation DTUPLES uses FreePastry[1]. DTUPLES also supports transactions and guarantees fault-tolerance via replication mechanisms. DTUPLES supports multi tuple spaces and distinguishes *public* and *subject* tuple spaces. Public tuple space is a space shared among all the processes and all of them can perform any operation on it. Subject tuple space is a private space accessible only by the processes that are bound to it. Any subject space can be bound to several processes and can

---

[1] FreePastry is an open-source implementation of Pastry, a substrate for peer-to-peer applications (http://www.freepastry.org/FreePastry/).

be removed if no process is bound to it. Due to the two types of tuple spaces, pattern matching is specific for each of them. Templates in the subject tuple space can match tuples in the same subject tuple space and in the common tuple space. However, the templates in the common tuple space cannot match the tuple in the subject tuple spaces.

LUATS. LUATS [11] is a reactive event-driven tuple space system written in Lua. Its main features are associative mechanism of tuple retrieving, fully asynchronous operations and support of code mobility. LUATS provides centralized management of the tuple space which can be logically partitioned into several parts using indexing. LUATS combines Linda model with event-driven programming paradigm. This paradigm was chosen to simplify program development which allows avoiding the use of synchronization mechanisms for tuple retrieval and makes more transparent programming and debugging of multi-thread program. Tuples can contain any data which can be serialized in Lua, including strings with function code. In order to obtain a more flexible and intelligent search, function code can be sent to the server and once executed it can returns the matched tuples. Reactive tuple space is implemented as a hashtable, in which along with data also information supporting the reactive nature of that tuple space (templates, client addresses, ids of callback and so on) is stored.

KLAIM. KLAIM [3] (the Kernel Language for Agents Interaction and Mobility) is an extension of Linda supporting processes migration. The emphasis of KLAIM is on process mobility, which means that processes as any data can be moved from one locality to another and they can be executed in any localities. Klava is a Java implementation of KLAIM [4]. KLAIM supports multiple tuple spaces and operates with explicit localities where processes and tuples are allocated. In this way, several tuples can be grouped and stored in one locality. Moreover, all the operations on tuple spaces are parametric to localities. Emphasis is put also on access control which is important for mobile applications. For this reason KLAIM introduces type system which allows checking whether a process can perform an operation at specific localities.

In order to compare the implementations we have discussed so far, we have singled out the following criteria:

Distributed Tuple Space. This criterion denotes whether tuple spaces are stored in one single node of the distributed network or they are spread across the network.

Decentralized Management. Distributed systems rely on a node that controls the others or the control is shared among several nodes. Usually, systems with the centralized control have bottlenecks which limit their performance.

Tuples Clustering. This criterion determines whether some tuples are grouped by particular parameters that can be used to determine where to store them in the network.

Domain Specificity. Many of implementations have specific area in which they can be used. If the implementation is domain specific it can be good because it is more suitable for it and has an advantage over other ones. On another side, this feature could be considered a limitation if one aims at generality.

Table 1. Results of the comparison

	JSP	TSP	GSP	TW	GR	BL	DTP	LTS	KL
Distributed tuple space			?	✓	✓	✓	✓		✓
Decentralized management			?	✓	✓		✓		
Tuple clustering			?	✓				✓	✓
Domain specificity				✓				✓	
Scalability		✓		✓	✓		✓		
Security	✓	✓							✓
eval operation								✓	✓

JAVASPACES (**JSP**), TSPACES (**TSP**), GIGASPACES (**GSP**), TUPLEWARE
(**TW**), GRINDA (**GR**), BLOSSOM (**BL**), DTUPLES (**DTP**), LUATS (**LTS**),
KLAIM (**KL**)

Scalability. This criterion implies that system based on particular Linda implementation can cope with the increasing amount of data and nodes while
maintaining acceptable performance.

Security. This criterion specifies whether an implementation has security features or not.

eval Operation. This criterion denotes whether the tuple space system has
implemented the eval operation.

Table 1 summarises the result of our comparison: ✓ means that the implementation enjoys the property and ? means that we were not able to provide an
answer, since the source code was not available.

An extra requirement to be able to compare implementations (especially in
terms of time) is that they have to be written in the same language. We have
chosen Java, since nowadays it is the most used language. Moreover, using a
single programming language allows us to develop case studies as *skeletons*:
the code remains the same for all the implementations, only the invocations of
different library methods do change. This choice, guarantees also the possibility
of performing better comparisons of the time performances exhibited by the
different tuple systems which could be significantly depend the chosen language.

After considering the results in Table 1, to perform our detailed experiments
we have chosen: TUPLEWARE which enjoys most of the selected features; KLAIM
since it offers distribution, clustering of tuple spaces and code mobility. Finally,
we have chosen GIGASPACES because it is the most modern among the commercial systems; it will be used as a yardstick to compare the performance of
TUPLEWARE and KLAIM. We would like to add that DTUPLES has not been
considered for the more detailed comparison because we have not been able to
obtain its libraries or source code, and that GRINDA has been dropped because
it seems to be the less maintained one.

In all our implementations of the case studies, we have structured the systems by assigning each process a local tuple space. Because GIGASPACES is a

centralized tuple space, in order to satisfy this rule we do not use it as centralized one, but as distributed: each process is assigned its own tuple space in the GIGASPACES server.

3   Experiments

3.1   Case Studies

In order to compare different tuple space systems we have chosen 3 case studies: *Password search, Sorting* and *Ocean model.* The first case study is a communication intensive task where the number of tuples is large and it requires doing many reading and writing operations. The second case study is computation intensive, since each node spends more time for sorting elements than for communicating with the other nodes. This case study has been considered because it needs structured tuples that contain both basic values (with primitive type) and complex data structures that impact on the speed of the inter-process communication. The third case has been taken into account since it introduces particular dependencies among nodes, which if exploited can improve the application performances. This was considered to check whether adapting a tuple space system to the specific inter-process interaction pattern of a specific class of the applications could lead to significative performance improvements. All the case studies are implemented using master-worker paradigm [6]. Now we briefly describe them.

Password Search. The main aim of the distributed application for password search is to find a password using its hashed value in the predefined distributed database. We have generated that database in the form of the files containing pairs of password and hashed value, for each password. The application creates a master process and several worker processes: the master keeps asking to the workers passwords corresponding to a specific hashed values, by issuing tuples of the form:

$$\langle \text{``search\_task''}, dd157c03313e452ae4a7a5b72407b3a9 \rangle$$

Each worker first loads its part of the distributed database, and after, it obtains from the master a task to look for the password corresponding to a hash value. Once it has found the password, it sends the result back to the master process, with a tuple of the form:

$$\langle \text{``found\_password''}, dd157c03313e452ae4a7a5b72407b3a9, 7723567 \rangle$$

For multi tuple spaces implementations it is necessary to start searching in one local tuple space and then to check the tuple spaces of other workers. The application terminates its execution when all the tasks have been processed and the master has received all results.

Sorting. This distributed application consists of sorting arrays of integers. The master is responsible for loading initial data and for collecting the final sorted data, while workers are directly responsible for the sorting. At the beginning, the master loads predefined initial data to be sorted and sends them to one worker to start the sorting process. Afterwards, the master waits for the sorted arrays from the workers: when any sub-array is sorted the master receives it and builds the whole sorted sequence when all sub-arrays are collected. The behavior of workers is different; when they are instantiated, each of them starts searching for the unsorted data in local and remote tuple spaces. When a worker finds a tuple with data, it checks whether it is possible to sort these data (the size of the data is less than particular threshold). If it is possible to sort them, the worker does the computation, sends the result to the master and starts searching for other unsorted data. Otherwise, the worker splits the array into two parts: one part is stored into its local tuple space while the other is processed.

Ocean Model. The ocean model is a simulation of the enclosed body of water. The core of that case study was given in [1]. The two-dimensional surface of water in the model is represented as a 2-D grid and each cell of the grid represents one point. The parameters of the model are current velocity and surface elevation which are based on a given wind velocity and bathymetry. In order to parallelize the computation, the whole grid is divided into vertical panels, and each worker owns one panel in order to compute its parameters. The aim of the case study is to simulate the body of water during several time-steps. At each time-step, in order to compute the new panel parameters, each worker has to take into account its neighbouring panels.

The mission of the master and workers are similar to the previous case studies. In the application the master instantiates the whole grids, divides it into parts and sends them to the workers. After all iterations, it receives all parts of the grid. Each worker receives its share of the grid and at each iteration it communicates with workers which have adjacent grid parts in order to update and recompute the parameters of its model; in the end it sends its data to the master.

Implementing Case Studies. Since we have chosen Java-based tuple space systems, all case studies are implemented in Java. Implementations of the three case studies require the use of synchronization to avoid conflicts while accessing to the same tuple space. GIGASPACES and TUPLEWARE have built in synchronization mechanisms, while KLAIM does not. To cope with it, for KLAIM we implemented synchronizations, using standard Java synchronized blocks [14], at the node/process level instead of modifying the source code of the core operation and applied it to local tuple space.

There is a difference in the implementation of the search among distributed tuple spaces. TUPLEWARE has a built in operation with notification mechanism: it searches in local and remote tuple spaces once and then waits for the notification that the wanted tuple appears in one of the tuple spaces. The implementation of this operation for KLAIM and GIGASPACES requires to continuously check each tuple space until the wanted tuple is found.

3.2   Methodology

All the conducted experiments are parametric with respect to two parameters. The first one is the number of workers taken into account with values $1, 5, 10, 15$ and it tests how the different implementations scale up with concurrency. The second parameter is application specific, but its meaning is the same: testing the implementation when the workload increases. For the case study *Password search* we vary the number of the entries in the database (10000, 1000000 and 1 million passwords) where it is necessary to search the password. This parameter directly affects the number of local entries each worker has. Moreover, for this case study the number of password to find was fixed to 100. For the *Sorting* case, the second parameter is the number of elements in an array to be sorted (100000, 1 million, 10 million elements). In this case the number of elements does not correspond to the number of tuples because parts of array are transferred also as arrays of smaller size. For the case study *Ocean model* the second parameter is the grid size (300, 600 and 1200) which is related with computational size of the initial task.

Remark 1 (Execution Environment). Our test were conducted on a server with 4 processors Intel Xeon E5620 (4 cores, 12 M Cache, 2.40 GHz, Hyper-Threading Technology) with 32 threads in total, 40 GB RAM and installed Ubuntu 14.04.3. All applications are programmed in Java 8 (1.8.0).

Measured Metrics. For measurement of metrics Clarkware Profiler[2] is used. We use manual method of profiling and insert methods `Profiler.begin(label)` and `Profiler.end(label)` surrounding parts of the code we are interested into program code in order to begin and stop counting time respectively. This sequence of the actions can be repeated many times and in the end we receive report which includes the number of calls, overall and average time. For each metrics the label is different and it is possible to use several of them simultaneously. Each set of experiments was conducted 10 times with randomly generated input and average values of each metrics were computed. To extensively compare the different implementations, we have chosen the following measures:

Local writing time: required time to write one tuple into local tuple space.
Local reading time: required time to read or take one tuple from local tuple space using template. The parameter checks how fast pattern matching works.
Remote writing time: time of the writing to the tuple space plus the time of communication with process associated with tuple space.
Remote reading time: similarly to the previous one, this time is a sum of the time of the search in tuple space and the time of the communication with it.
Search time: when the application has several workers we introduce the time which is required to find a tuple in a several separated tuple spaces.

---

[2] The profiler was written by Mike Clark; source code is available in GitHub.com: https://github.com/akatkinson/Tupleware/tree/master/src/com/clarkware/ profiler.

Total time: total execution time. This time does not include initial creation of tuple spaces or starting tuple space server as in the case of GIGASPACES.

Number of visited nodes: number of visited before a necessary tuple was found.

Please notice that, all plots used in the paper report results of our experiments in a logarithmic scale. When describing the outcome, we have only used those plots which are more relevant to evidence the difference between the three tuple space systems[3].

3.3   Results

Password Search. As shown in Fig. 1 GIGASPACES exhibits better performances than the other two tuple space systems.

Figure 2 depicts the local writing time for each implementation, with different numbers of workers. As we can see, by increasing the number of workers (which implies reducing the amount of local data to consider), the local writing time decreases. This is more evident in TUPLEWARE, which really suffers when a big number of tuples (e.g. 1 million) is stored in a single local tuple space. The writing time of KLAIM is the lowest among other systems and does not change significantly during any variation in the experiments.

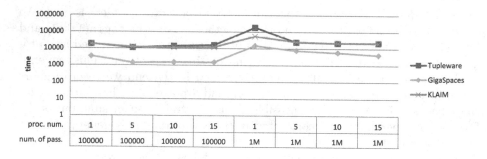

Fig. 1. Password search. Local total time

Local reading time is shown in Fig. 3 and KLAIM is the one that exhibits the worst performance for searching in local space. Indeed, if there is just one worker, the local reading time is 10 times greater than TUPLEWARE. We conjecture that the pattern matching mechanism of KLAIM is less effective than others. By increasing the number of workers the difference becomes less evident, even if it remains four times bigger than TUPLEWARE. Since this case study requires little synchronization among workers, performance improves when the level of parallelism (the number of workers) increases.

---

[3] Plots with more detailed (numeric) information are reported as bar charts at http://sysma.imtlucca.it/coord16_appendix/.

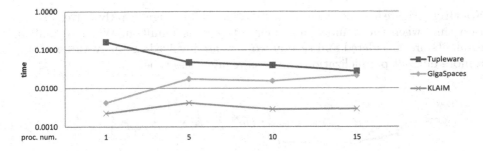

Fig. 2. Password search. Local writing time (1 million passwords)

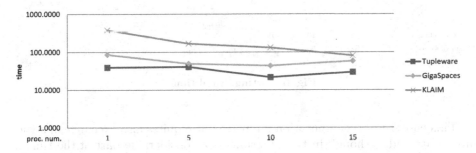

Fig. 3. Password search. Local reading time (1 million passwords)

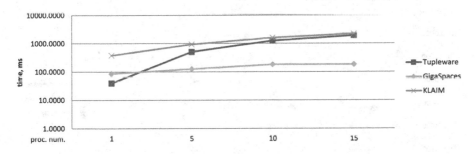

Fig. 4. Password search. Search time (1 million passwords)

Search time is similar to local reading time, but takes into account searching in remote tuple spaces. When considering just one worker, the search time is the same as the reading time in local tuple space, however, when the number of workers increases the search time of TUPLEWARE and KLAIM grows faster than the time of GIGASPACES. Figure 4 shows that GIGASPACES is more sensitive to the number of tuples than to the number of accesses to the tuple space.

It is worth to remark that the local tuple spaces of the three systems exhibit different performances depending on the operation on them: the writing time of KLAIM is always significantly smaller than the others, while the pattern matching mechanism of TUPLEWARE allows faster local searching.

Sorting. Figure 5 shows that GIGASPACES exhibits significantly better execution time when the number of elements to sort is 1 million. When 10 million elements are considered and several workers are involved, TUPLEWARE exhibits a more efficient parallelization and thus requires less time.

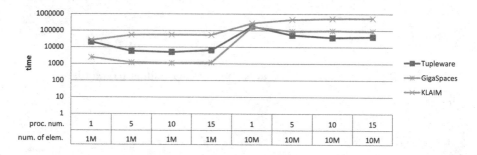

Fig. 5. Sorting. Total time

This case study is computation intensive but requires also exchange of structured data and, although in the experiments a considerable part of the time is spent for sorting, we have that performances do not significantly improve when the number of workers increases.

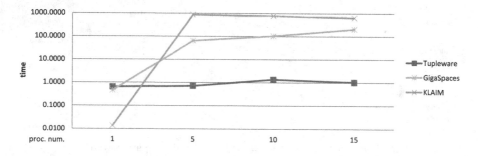

Fig. 6. Sorting. Local writing time (10 million elements)

The performance of KLAIM is visibly worse than others even for one worker. In this case, the profiling of the KLAIM application showed that a considerable amount of time was spent to transmit initial data from the master to the worker. Inefficient implementation of data transmission seems to be the reason the total time of KLAIM differs from the total time of TUPLEWARE.

By comparing Figs. 2 and 6, we see that, when the number of workers increases, GIGASPACES and KLAIM suffer more from synchronization in the current case study than in the previous one; there no other operation was performed in parallel to writing and thus no conflict handling was required.

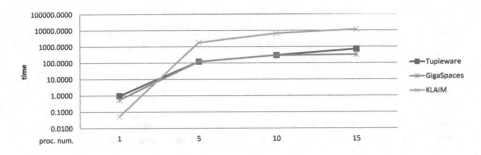

Fig. 7. Sorting. Search time (10 million elements)

In addition to experimenting with case studies, we measured the time required by reading and writing operations on remote tuple space for all three systems. For KLAIM and TUPLEWARE these times were similar and significantly greater than those of GIGASPACES. KLAIM and TUPLEWARE communications rely on TCP and to handle any remote tuple space one needs to use exact addresses and ports. GIGASPACES, that has a centralized implementation, most likely does not use TCP for data exchange but relies on a more efficient memory-based approach.

As shown in Fig. 7, search time directly depends on the number of the workers and grows with it. Taking into account that KLAIM and TUPLEWARE spend more time accessing remote tuple space, GIGASPACES suffers more because of synchronization. KLAIM has the same problem, but its inefficiency is hampered by data transmission cost.

Ocean Model. This case study was chosen to examine behavior of tuple systems when specific patterns of interactions are used. Out of the three considered systems, only TUPLEWARE has a method for reducing the number of visited nodes during search operation which helps in lowering search time. Figure 8 depicts the number of visited nodes for different grid size and different number of workers. The curve depends only weakly on the size of the grid for all systems, and much more on the number of workers. Indeed, from Fig. 8 we can appreciate that TUPLEWARE performs a smaller number of nodes visits, and that when the number of workers increases the difference is even more evident[4].

The difference in the number of visited nodes does not affect significantly the total time of execution (Fig. 9) mostly because the case study requires many read operations from remote tuple spaces (Fig. 10). But, as it was mentioned before, GIGASPACES implements read operation differently from TUPLEWARE and KLAIM and it is more effective when working on a single computer.

Figure 9 provides evidence of the effectiveness of TUPLEWARE when its total execution time is compared with the KLAIM one. Indeed, KLAIM visits more

---

[4] Figure 8, the curves for KLAIM and GIGASPACES are overlapping and purple wins over blue.

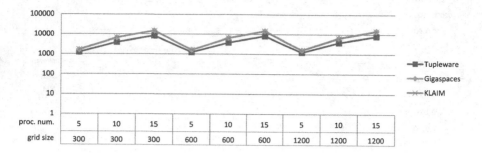

Fig. 8. Ocean model. Number of visited nodes (Color figure online)

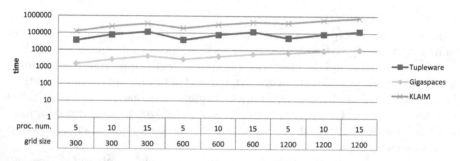

Fig. 9. Ocean model. Total time

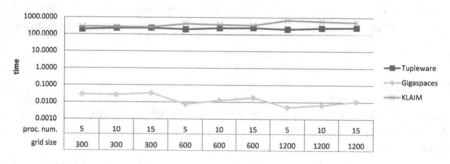

Fig. 10. Ocean model. Remote reading time

nodes and spends more time for each read operation, and the difference increases when the grid size grows and more data have to be transmitted.

This case study suggests that devising an appropriate mechanism for taking advantage of the underlying communication pattern can make cooperative work of distributed tuple spaces more effective.

4   Conclusions

Distributed computing is getting increasingly pervasive, with demands from various applications domains and highly diverse underlying architectures from the multitude of tiny things to the very large cloud-based systems. Tuple spaces certainly feature valuable characteristics to help develop scalable distributed applications/systems. This paper has first surveyed and evaluated a number of tuple space systems, then it has analyzed more closely three different systems. We considered GIGASPACES, because it is one of the few currently used commercial products, KLAIM, because it guarantees code mobility and flexible manipulation of tuple spaces, and TUPLEWARE, because it is the one that turned out to be the best in our initial evaluation. We have then compared the three system by evaluating their performances over three case studies: a communication-intensive one, a computational-intensive one, and one with a specific communication pattern.

Our work follows the lines of [16] but we have chosen more recent implementations and conducted more extensive experiments.

The commercial system GIGASPACES differs from the other two systems for the use of a memory based interprocess communication for data exchange, that guarantees considerably smaller access time to data. Therefore, using this mechanism in the scope of one machine can increase effectiveness of work when different tuple spaces are needed. When working with networked machines, it is not possible to use that mechanism and we need to use approaches to reduce the number of inter-machine communication (e.g. TUPLEWARE approach) and to make that communication effective. Another issue to which we need to pay to attention is related to the implementation of local tuple spaces including pattern matching algorithms and mechanisms to prevent conflicts when accessing the spaces.

Performances of a tuple space system vary depending on the chosen system architectures and on the type of interaction between their components. We did not consider different architectures but we noted problems (data transmission, synchronization, etc.) which may occur in different systems for different types of interaction. We plan to use the results of this work as the basis to design an efficient tuple space system which offers programmer the possibility of selecting (e.g. via a dashboard) the desired features of the tuple space according to the specific application. In this way, one could envisage a distributed middleware with different tuple spaces implementations each of them devised with the best characteristic, in terms of efficiency, to perform the required tasks.

References

1. Atkinson, A.: Tupleware: A Distributed Tuple Space for the Development and Execution of Array-based Applications in a Cluster Computing Environment. University of Tasmania School of Computing and Information Systems thesis, University of Tasmania (2010)
2. Barker, B.: Message Passing Interface (MPI). In: Workshop: High Performance Computing on Stampede (2015)
3. Bettini, L., Kannan, R., De Nicola, R., Ferrari, G.-L., Gorla, D., Loreti, M., Moggi, E., Pugliese, R., Tuosto, E., Venneri, B.: The Klaim project: theory and practice. In: Priami, C. (ed.) GC 2003. LNCS, vol. 2874, pp. 88–150. Springer, Heidelberg (2003)
4. Bettini, L., De Nicola, R., Loreti, M.: Implementing mobile and distributed applications in X-Klaim. Scalable Comput. Pract. Experience 7(4), 13–35 (2006)

5. Capizzi, S.: A Tuple Space Implementation for Large-Scale Infrastructures. Department of Computer Science Univ. Bologna thesis, University of Bologna (2008)
6. Carriero, N., Gelernter, D.: How to Write Parallel Programs - A First Course. MIT Press, Cambridge (1990)
7. Ceriotti, M., Murphy, A.L., Picco, G.P.: Data sharing vs. message passing: Synergy or incompatibility? an implementation-driven case study. In: Proceedings of the 2008 ACM Symposium on Applied Computing, pp. 100–107 (2008)
8. Gelernter, D.: Generative communication in Linda. ACM Trans. Program. Lang. Syst. **7**(1), 80–112 (1985)
9. GigaSpaces. Concepts - XAP 9.0 Documentation - GigaSpaces Documentation-Wiki. http://wiki.gigaspaces.com/wiki/display/XAP9/Concepts (2016). Accessed 25 Jan 2016
10. Jiang, Y., Jia, Z., Xue, G., Dtuples, J.Y.: A distributed hash table based tuple space service for distributed coordination. Fifth International Conference on Grid and Cooperative Computing 2006, GCC 2006, pp. 101–106 (2006)
11. Leal, M.A., Rodriguez, N., Ierusalimschy, R.: Luats a reactive event-driven tuple space. J. Univ. Comput. Sci. **9**(8), 730–744 (2003)
12. Lehman, T., McLaughry, S., Wyckoff, P.: Tspaces: The next wave, vol. 8 (1999)
13. S. Microsystems. JS - JavaSpaces Service Specification. https://river.apache.org/doc/specs/html/js-spec.html (2016). Accessed 25 Jan 2016
14. Oracle. The Java Tutorials. https://docs.oracle.com/javase/tutorial/essential/concurrency/sync.html (2015). Accessed 25 Jan 2016
15. Van Der Goot, R.: High Performance Linda Using a Class Library. Ph.D thesis. Erasmus Universiteit Rotterdam (2001)
16. Wells, G., Chalmers, A., Clayton, P.G.: Linda implementations in java for concurrent systems. Concurrency Pract. Experience **16**(10), 1005–1022 (2004)

On-the-Fly Mean-Field Model-Checking
for Attribute-Based Coordination

Vincenzo Ciancia, Diego Latella$^{(\boxtimes)}$, and Mieke Massink

CNR-ISTI, Pisa, Italy
{V.Ciancia,D.Latella,M.Massink}@cnr.it

Abstract. Typical Collective Adaptive Systems (CAS) consist of a large
number of interacting objects that coordinate their activities in a decentralised and often implicit way. The design of such systems is challenging,
as it requires scalable analysis tools and methods to check properties of
proposed system designs before they are put into operation. A promising technique is Fast Mean-Field Approximated Model-checking. The
FlyFast model-checker uses an on-the-fly algorithm for bounded PCTL
model-checking of selected individuals in the context of very large popu-
lations whose global behaviour is approximated using deterministic limit
techniques. Recently, specific modelling languages have been proposed
for CAS. A key feature of such languages is the *attribute-based* interaction paradigm. In this paper we present an attribute-based coordination
language as a front-end for FlyFast. Its formal probabilistic semantics is
provided and a translation to the original FlyFast language is given and
proved correct. Application examples are also provided.

Keywords: Collective Adaptive Systems · Probabilistic on-the-fly
model-checking · Mean-Field Approximation · Discrete time Markov
chains

1 Introduction and Related Work

Collective Adaptive Systems (CAS) consist of a large number of entities with
decentralised control and varying degrees of complex autonomous behaviour.
CAS are at the core of the envisioned smart cities of the future and encompass
systems like smart urban transport and smart grids. The pervasive nature of CAS
and thus their impact on society requires the development of reliable rigorous
design models as well as *a priori* analysis techniques of such models—covering all
relevant aspects of their behaviour, including quantitative and emergent ones—
before they are put into operation[1].

Model-checking has been widely recognised as a powerful approach to the
automatic verification of concurrent and distributed systems. It consists of an

---

Research partially funded by the EU project QUANTICOL (nr. 600708).

[1] See, e.g. www.focas.eu/adaptive-collective-systems and www.quanticol.eu.

A. Lluch Lafuente and J. Proença (Eds.): COORDINATION 2016, LNCS 9686, pp. 67–83, 2016.
DOI: 10.1007/978-3-319-39519-7_5

efficient procedure that, given an abstract model of the system, decides whether the model satisfies a logical formula, typically drawn from a temporal logic. Unfortunately, traditional model-checking suffers from the so called *state-space explosion* problem which hampers scalability of the approach. In particular, its application to *very large* models, like those typical of CAS, is infeasible. In [15,17] Latella et al. presented a scalable mean-field model-checking procedure for verifying bounded PCTL (Probabilistic Computation Tree Logic) [11] properties of selected individuals in the context of systems consisting of a large number of similar, but independent, interacting objects; a limited form of global system properties can be treated as well. The procedure can be used with huge population sizes, as typical of analysis techniques based on mean-field approximation; the average behaviour of the population is approximated using a population Discrete Time Markov Chain (DTMC) convergence result [21] and is used for representing the context in which the selected individuals operate (see [15,17,21] for details). The model-checking procedure is implemented in the tool FlyFast as an instantiation of a probabilistic on-the-fly model-checker; the latter is parametric on (the semantic model of) the modelling language [15,16].

FlyFast comes with simple modelling language. An agent[2] is a finite state process, a generic state C of which is specified by a *state defining equation* like $C := a_1.C_1 + \ldots + a_r.C_r$. Intuitively, the above notation defines state C of the agent and postulates that there are r outgoing transitions from C, with action a_j labelling a transition going from C to C_j. A probability value is assigned to each action a by means of a *probability function definition $a :: E$*, where the actual probability is given by the value of expression E in the current *occupancy measure vector* **m**. Assume a system is composed of N instances of the agent and that the states of the agent are $C_1, \ldots C_S$. The occupancy measure vector at the current time is the vector $(m_1, \ldots, m_S)$ s.t. m_j yields the *fraction* of agents currently in state C_j over the total number N of agents. A *system specification* is a triple composed by an *agent specification*—given as a set of state defining equations—a set of probability function definitions, and an initial global state. Finally, FlyFast provides the user with *formula declarations* which allow for the interpretation of bounded PCTL atomic propositions in the model at hand. The computational model is *clock-synchronous*; at each step each agent must perform an independent step (which may be an idle self-loop) so that the global state probabilities are given as the product of agent step probabilities, and a new occupancy measure vector can be computed. The global system behaviour is thus a DTMC as well as the stochastic process given by the occupancy measure vector. Notably, for N sufficiently large, the latter can be approximated deterministically, i.e. by a *function* of time. This brings to a dramatic decrease in size of the global state space: at each step, the total number of potential next states drops from S^N to S, which makes bounded PCTL model-checking of very large population systems possible (the interested reader is referred to [15,17,21] for details).

Recently, modelling and programming languages have been proposed specifically for autonomic computing systems and CAS [3,9,12]. Typically, in such

---

[2] In the context of FlyFast we use the words *agent, process* and *object* as synonyms.

frameworks, a system is composed of a set of independent *components* where a component is a process equipped with a set of *attributes* describing features of the component. A classical example of attribute is the component *location*. An additional *environment* is often used for the specification of common or global features. The attributes of a component can be *updated* during its execution so that the association between attribute *names* and attribute *values* is mantained in the dynamic *store* of the component. Attributes can be used in *predicates* appearing in language constructs for component interaction. For instance a component may *broadcast* a message to *all those components satisfying* a given predicate; similarly a component may wait for a message from *any of those components satisfying* a given predicate.

In the present paper, we propose an extension of the FlyFast front-end modelling language for dealing with *components* and *predicate-based interaction*. The extension has been inspired by CARMA [3]. Components are expressed as pairs *process-store*; actions are *predicate based multi-cast* output and input primitives[3]. Associated to each action there is also an (atomic) probabilistic store-update. For instance, assume components have an attribute named loc which takes values in the set of points of a space type. The following action models a multi-cast via channel α to all components in the same location as the sender, making it change location randomly: $\alpha^*[\text{loc} = \mathbf{my}.\text{loc}]\langle\rangle\{\text{loc} \leftarrow \text{randomLoc}(\text{loc})\}$. Here randomLoc is assumed to be a random generator of points in the space[4]. The computational model is *clock-synchronous* as well, but at the component level. In addition, each component is equipped with a local *outbox*. The effect of an output action $\alpha^*[\pi_r]\langle\rangle\sigma$ is to deliver output label $\alpha\langle\rangle$ to the local outbox, together with the predicate π_r, which receiver components will be required to satisfy, as well as the current store γ of the component executing the action; the current store is updated according to update σ. Note that output actions are *non-blocking* and that successive output actions of the same component rewrite its outbox. An input action $\alpha^*[\pi_s]\langle\rangle\sigma$ by a component will be executed with a probability which is proportional to the *fraction* of all those components whose outboxes currently contain the label $\alpha\langle\rangle$, a predicate π_r which is satisfied by the component, and a store γ which satisfies in turn predicate π_s. If such a fraction is zero, then the input action will not take place (input is blocking), otherwise the action takes place, the store of the component is updated via σ, and its outbox cleared. Thus, as in the original FlyFast language, component interaction is probabilistic, but now the *fraction* of the components satisfying the relevant predicates plays a role in the computation of transition probabilities. We provide the formal probabilistic semantics of the extended language and a translation to the original FlyFast language which makes the model-checker support the extended language. The translation is proved correct.

---

[3] For the sake of notational simplicity, in this paper we present a non value-passing version of the FlyFast front-end; the complete, value-passing, approach is described in [8].

[4] *Multi-cast* interaction is denoted using the _* notation, as in CARMA.

Related Work. As we mentioned before, this work has been inspired by CARMA [3], which in turn shares features with SCEL [9]. There are several aspects of either languages that are not present in our proposal. The main reason for the absence of most of them is the fact that this work is intended as a proof of concept rather than the realisation of a ready-to-use tool for reasoning about CAS. So we aim at keeping the language minimal and focussing only on attribute-based interaction in the context of stochastic and mean-field semantics and model-checking. A feature of CARMA not considered here is the notion of *global* environment, since it represents a singularity point that does not fit well with limit approximation techniques. Finally, we point out that the stochastic semantics of CARMA are based on *time inhomogeneous* CTMCs, due to the fact that action parameters may be time dependent, while we use DTMCs as semantic basis. The notion of the outbox is reminiscent of the notion of the ether in PALOMA [10] in the sense that the collection of all outboxes together can be though of as a kind of ether; but such a collection is intrinsically distributed among the components so that it cannot represent a bottleneck in the execution of the system neither a singularity point in the deterministic approximation. Fluid model-checking for *continuous time* systems is addressed in [4] where a global model-checking procedure for the Continuous Stochastic Logic (CSL, [2]) is given, which is based on continuous limit approximated semantics. Fluid semantics have proved very useful for reasoning about large coordination systems (see e.g. [6,18,23]). Predicate-/attribute-based inter-process communication has been originally proposed in [19] where several variants of predicate-/attribute-based communication primitives—including blocking / non-blocking, bounded / unbounded—are discussed in the context of a study on high-level language constructs for distributed systems with decentralised control (see for instance [22]). The notion of predicate-/attribute-based interaction is central in the definition of SCEL [9] where its synchronous-communication variant has been given formal semantics. Asynchronous-communication variants have been defined for stochastic versions of SCEL [20]. An attribute-interaction based calculus is proposed in [1] where broadcast communication links among components are dynamically established on the basis of the interdependences determined by predicates over attributes. A reduction semantics approach is adopted where each transition involves the group composed of both sender and receivers. Attribute π-Calculus has been proposed in [14] and extended to Imperative π-Calculus in [13]; in both calculi, which inherit the classical point-to-point communication paradigm of the π-Calculus, as opposed to multi-cast, attributes are related to messages rather than to processes. None of the above mentioned works on predicate-/attribute-based languages addresses mean-field approximated model-checking so, to the best of our knowledge, the present paper is the first proposal on the subject.

2   Attribute-Based Coordination Language and Logic

In this section we define an attribute-based population description language and related logic. A *system* is defined as a population of N identical interacting components[5] in a *clock-synchronous* fashion. Each component is equipped with a finite set of *attributes*; the current *store* $\gamma \in \Gamma$ of the component maps each attribute *name* to an attribute *value*.

2.1 Syntax

A *component specification* is a pair (Δ, F) where Δ is a finite set of *state-defining* equations, one for each *state* of the component and F is a set of auxiliary function definitions[6]. We let $\mathcal{S}$, ranged over by $C, C', C_1, \ldots$ denote the (denumerable, non-empty) set of all states which can be used in equations. Each equation defines the transitions from the state to other states of the component; each transition is labelled by the *action* the component performs when the transition takes place. The general format of a state defining equation is: $C := [g_1]P_1 \mid \ldots \mid [g_r]P_r$ where each *guard* $[g]$ is a *predicate* π defined according to the following grammar: $\pi ::= \top \mid \bot \mid e_1 \bowtie e_2 \mid \neg\pi \mid \pi_1 \wedge \pi_2$.
$\top$ ($\bot$, resp.) stands for the truth value *true* (*false* resp.), while $\bowtie \in \{\geq, >, \leq, <\}$; we let $\bowtie \in \{>, <\}$. An *expression* e can be an attribute name a, or **my**.a referring to the value of a in the component where it occurs, or a value v in given set $\mathcal{V}$. In defining equations as above, we abbreviate $[\top]P_j$ with P_j and we omit summands of the form $[\bot]P_j$. Each P_j in a state defining equation as above is of the form $p_j :: act_j.C_j$, where p_j is a probability expression, i.e. an expression with value in $[0, 1]$, built from constants $v \in [0, 1]$ and the special operator $\mathsf{frc}\,C$, combined using standard arithmetic operators; for state C, $\mathsf{frc}\,C$ returns the *fraction* of the components that are currently in state C, over the total of N components. Clearly, the use of the frc operator allows action (and, ultimately, transition) probability to depend on the global state of the system. Actions act_j can be *output* actions $\alpha^*[\pi]\langle\rangle\sigma$ or *input* actions $\alpha^*[\pi]()\sigma$. We assume a countable set of *action types* $\mathcal{A}$, with $\alpha \in \mathcal{A}$. The effect of an *output* action $\alpha^*[\pi]\langle\rangle\sigma$ is a broadcast to all those components satisfying predicate π and which are willing to accept the interaction. This is achieved by means of delivering $\alpha\langle\rangle$, together with some additional information, to the outbox of the component executing the action, as we will discuss in detail in Sect. 2.2. In addition, the store of the component executing the action is updated according to the *update* σ, which is a function from Γ to the class of probability distributions over Γ—i.e., in the general case, the update may be probabilistic. Similarly, an *input* action $\alpha^*[\pi]()\sigma$ is used to receive an α-message sent by a component satisfying predicate π. More specifically, the probability of executing the input action will be proportional to the fraction of components which have sent the α-message while satisfying predicate π and requiring a predicate which is satisfied by the component executing the input action. Also input actions are provided with a store

---

[5] In practice, the fact that the components are identical is not a strong limitation since each component may consist of several different sets of states, with each state in a given set being unreachable from states of other sets. Each such a set of states can be seen as a component with a different behaviour.

[6] The specific syntax of auxiliary function definitions is irrelevant and left out here.

update σ whereas the component outbox is cleared as (a side) effect of their execution. In the sequel, we shall call *address predicates* the predicates $[\pi]$ used for identifying the partners in input/output actions. For updates, we use the following notation: $\{a_1 \leftarrow e_1^\gamma, \ldots, a_t \leftarrow e_t^\gamma\}$ where e_j^γ is an expression which may also include functions—the definition of which are to be provided in F—which may depend on the component store γ and produce random results, as we shall see below. Attributes different from $a_1, \ldots, a_t$ are left unchanged by the update. We require that any attribute name a occurring in a guard $[g]$, or in the expressions $e_1^\gamma, \ldots, e_t^\gamma$, must appear in the form **my**.a (thus referring to the value of the attribute in the local store of the component). An attribute name a may appear both with and without the **my**. prefix in the address predicate π. Intuitively, equation $C := [g_1]P_1 + \ldots + [g_r]P_r$ defines state C of the component at hand and postulates that there are r potential outgoing transitions from C, with action act_j labelling a transition going from C to C_j. The actual transitions will be determined by the value of the guards and the action probabilities. Note that it may happen that the current cumulative probability value of the enabled transitions is less than 1; for this reason, the language provides the construct **rest** :: $\alpha[\pi]\langle\rangle\sigma.C$, where **rest** is defined as the residual probability; it is required that there is at most one **rest**-branch (typically the last one) in every state defining equation. Only output actions are allowed in **rest**-branches; this ensures that the residual probability is not affected by the fraction of those components in the system satisfying the address predicate. Obviously, in a given component specification there is exactly one defining equation for each state of the component. We let $\mathcal{S}_\Delta$ denote the finite set of states defined by Δ. Similarly, Γ_Δ, $\mathcal{A}_\Delta$ and Π_Δ denote the set of all stores associated to Δ, the action types and the predicates occurring in (the equations of) Δ. Finally, we let $\mathcal{V}_\Delta$ denote the set of values which can be taken by the attributes of a component specified by Δ. Note that we assume $\mathcal{V}_\Delta$ is a finite set—thus also Γ_Δ is finite; model finiteness is a common assumption for modelling languages supported by automatic analysis and verification tools.

Example 1 (A spatially distributed Computer Epidemic Model). We enrich the Computer Epidemic Model of [5], SEIR, with infection communication and a *bi-dimen-sional Regular GRID* [7] model for space, where for each point ℓ the following specific operators are defined, with the usual North, South, East, West meaning: $N(\ell), S(\ell), E(\ell), W(\ell)$. Each component is equipped with a *position* attribute, named loc, which is always yielding the current position (i.e. point) in space of the component and is the only attribute of the component. Note that, given the abstract nature of the bi-dimensional Regular GRID, such a "point" could be a physical point is space, but also a specific region (or patch) in a patched representation of space. We will implicitly refer to the second interpretation in the sequel. In the model, given in Fig. 1, the purpose of auxiliary function Jump is twofold: (i) it defines a function from positions to discrete probability distributions which, given position ℓ, characterizes a probability distribution which assignes probability $p_N(\ell)$ to $N(\ell)$, probability $p_S(\ell)$ to $S(\ell)$, and so on and (ii) defines a random position generator which, given position ℓ,

$$S := h :: \texttt{inf}^*[\text{loc} = \textbf{my}.\text{loc}]()\{\textbf{my}.\text{loc} \leftarrow \text{Jump}(\textbf{my}.\text{loc})\}.E \; +$$
$$m_N :: \texttt{inf}^*[\text{loc} = \text{N}(\textbf{my}.\text{loc})]()\{\textbf{my}.\text{loc} \leftarrow \text{Jump}(\textbf{my}.\text{loc})\}.E \; +$$
$$m_S :: \texttt{inf}^*[\text{loc} = \text{S}(\textbf{my}.\text{loc})]()\{\textbf{my}.\text{loc} \leftarrow \text{Jump}(\textbf{my}.\text{loc})\}.E \; +$$
$$m_E :: \texttt{inf}^*[\text{loc} = \text{E}(\textbf{my}.\text{loc})]()\{\textbf{my}.\text{loc} \leftarrow \text{Jump}(\textbf{my}.\text{loc})\}.E \; +$$
$$m_W :: \texttt{inf}^*[\text{loc} = \text{W}(\textbf{my}.\text{loc})]()\{\textbf{my}.\text{loc} \leftarrow \text{Jump}(\textbf{my}.\text{loc})\}.E \; +$$
$$ext :: \texttt{ext}^*[\bot]\langle\rangle\{\textbf{my}.\text{loc} \leftarrow \text{Jump}(\textbf{my}.\text{loc})\}.E \; +$$
$$sr :: \texttt{rec}^*[\bot]\langle\rangle\{\textbf{my}.\text{loc} \leftarrow \text{Jump}(\textbf{my}.\text{loc})\}.R \; +$$
$$rest :: \texttt{nsc}^*[\bot]\langle\rangle\{\textbf{my}.\text{loc} \leftarrow \text{Jump}(\textbf{my}.\text{loc})\}.S$$

$$E := ei :: \texttt{act}^*[\bot]\langle\rangle\{\textbf{my}.\text{loc} \leftarrow \text{Jump}(\textbf{my}.\text{loc})\}.I \; +$$
$$er :: \texttt{rec}^*[\bot]\langle\rangle\{\textbf{my}.\text{loc} \leftarrow \text{Jump}(\textbf{my}.\text{loc})\}.R \; +$$
$$rest :: \texttt{nsc}^*[\bot]\langle\rangle\{\textbf{my}.\text{loc} \leftarrow \text{Jump}(\textbf{my}.\text{loc})\}.E$$

$$I := ii :: \texttt{inf}^*[\top]\langle\rangle\{\textbf{my}.\text{loc} \leftarrow \text{Jump}(\textbf{my}.\text{loc})\}.I \; +$$
$$ir :: \texttt{rec}^*[\bot]\langle\rangle\{\textbf{my}.\text{loc} \leftarrow \text{Jump}(\textbf{my}.\text{loc})\}.R \; +$$
$$rest :: \texttt{nsc}^*[\bot]\langle\rangle\{\textbf{my}.\text{loc} \leftarrow \text{Jump}(\textbf{my}.\text{loc})\}.I$$

$$R := rs :: \texttt{loss}^*[\bot]\langle\rangle\{\textbf{my}.\text{loc} \leftarrow \text{Jump}(\textbf{my}.\text{loc})\}.S$$
$$rest :: \texttt{nsc}^*[\bot]\langle\rangle\{\textbf{my}.\text{loc} \leftarrow \text{Jump}(\textbf{my}.\text{loc})\}.R$$

Fig. 1. A four state model: *susceptible* (S), *exposed* (E), *infected* (I), and *recover* (R).

randomly returns a new position according to the specified probabilities. Note that the probabilities are themselves functions of the position and they are assumed being declared as additional auxiliary functions. In the equation for S in Fig. 1, probability constants $h, m_N, \ldots, m_W$ are factors in $[0, 1]$ with cumulative value at most 1, each to be multiplied by the actual probability of the associated (input) action. The latter will be computed as the fraction of the local states which satisfy the required predicate. The resulting values, when taken all together, will characterize a probability *sub*-distribution; the residual probability will be associated to a **rest**-self-loop. Similar considerations apply to the probability constants in the definition of other states (e.g. i in the figure). We assume $h > m_N \approx m_S \approx m_E \approx m_W$. In other words, an agent has higher probability to get the infection from agents in the same place than from agents in adjacent places; the probability drops to zero in all other cases.

A system is modelled as a population of N instances of a component, so a *system specification* Υ is a triple $(\Delta, F, \Sigma_0)^{(N)}$ where (Δ, F) is a component specification and Σ_0 is the *initial (system) global state*, which will be discussed below. In the sequel we will often write Δ instead of (Δ, F).

2.2 Probabilistic Semantics

In order to model component interactions within a system, each component is equipped with a local outbox. The idea is that, whenever a component executes an output action, the related output will be available in the component's outbox *only during the next clock tick*; in the next state, (other) components will be able to get the message by means of corresponding input actions. After such a tick, the outbox will be empty or filled with the information generated by a subsequent output action of the component. Formally, let Λ_Δ^O be the set $\Lambda_\Delta^O = \{\alpha\langle\rangle | \alpha \in \mathcal{A}_\Delta\}$. An *outbox-state* $O \in \mathcal{O}_\Delta = \{\langle\rangle\} \cup (\Gamma_\Delta \times \Pi_\Delta \times \Lambda_\Delta^O)$ is either empty or a triple $(\gamma, \pi, \alpha\langle\rangle)$. A *component-state* Σ is a triple $\Sigma = (C, \gamma, O) \in \mathcal{S}_\Delta \times \Gamma_\Delta \times \mathcal{O}_\Delta = \Omega_\Delta$, where C, γ, O are the current state, store and outbox-state of the component, respectively. If the component-state is the target of a transition modelling the execution of an *output* action, then $O = (\gamma', \pi, \alpha\langle\rangle)$, where γ' is the store of the (component-state) source of the transition, π is the predicate used in the action—actualized with γ'—and $\alpha\langle\rangle$ the actual message sent by the action. If, instead, the component-state is the target of a transition for an *input* action, then $O = \langle\rangle$, i.e. the empty outbox. A *global state* is a tuple $\Sigma = ((C_1, \gamma_1, O_1), \ldots, (C_N, \gamma_N, O_N)) \in \Omega_\Delta^N$ where $\Sigma_{[j]} = (C_j, \gamma_j, O_j)$ is the component-state of the j-th instance in the population for $j = 1 \ldots N$. We say that N is the *population size* of the system. In the sequel, we will omit the explicit indication of the size N in $(\Delta, F, \Sigma_0)^{(N)}$, and elements thereof or related functions, writing simply (Δ, F, Σ_0), when this cannot cause confusion. In summary, a system specification can be thought of as process algebraic clock-synchronous parallel composition of N processes. The probabilistic behaviour of a system can be derived from its specification $(\Delta, F, \Sigma_0)^{(N)}$. We remind that Ω_Δ is finite, since so are sets $\mathcal{S}_\Delta, \Gamma_\Delta$ and $\mathcal{O}_\Delta$. Assume $\Omega_\Delta = \{\Sigma_1, \ldots, \Sigma_S\}$ and let $\mathcal{U}^S$ be the set $\{\mathbf{m} \in [0,1]^S | \sum_{i=1}^S \mathbf{m}_{[i]} = 1\}$; we can assume, w.l.o.g. that there is a total ordering on Ω_Δ so that we can unambiguously associate each component m_j of a vector $\mathbf{m} = (m_1, \ldots, m_S) \in \mathcal{U}^S$ with a distinct element Σ_j of $\{\Sigma_1, \ldots, \Sigma_S\}$. With each global state $\Sigma^{(N)}$ an *occupancy measure* vector $\mathbf{M}^{(N)}(\Sigma^{(N)}) \in \mathcal{U}^S$ is associated where $\mathbf{M}^{(N)}(\Sigma^{(N)}) = (M_1^{(N)}, \ldots, M_S^{(N)})$ with $M_i^{(N)} = \frac{1}{N} \sum_{n=1}^N \mathbf{1}_{\{\Sigma_{[n]}^{(N)} = \Sigma_i\}}$ for $i = 1, \ldots, S$ and the value of $\mathbf{1}_{\{\alpha = \beta\}}$ is 1, if $\alpha = \beta$, and 0 otherwise. So, for $\Sigma_i = (C_i, \gamma_i, O_i)$, $M_i^{(N)}$ is the *fraction*, in the current global state $\Sigma^{(N)}$, of the component instances which are in state C_i, have store γ_i and outbox O_i, over the total number N. We assume semantic interpretation functions $\mathbf{E_L}[\cdot]$ and $\mathbf{E_R}[\cdot]$ for the *local*, *remote* respectively, interpretation of expressions and predicates and a function $\mathbf{E_P}[\cdot]$ for the interpretation of probability expressions. $\mathbf{E_L}[e]$ ($\mathbf{E_R}[e]$, respectively) takes a local (remote, respectively) store γ as an argument, whereas $\mathbf{E_P}[p]$ takes an occupancy measure vector $\mathbf{m}$ as an argument. We note that $\mathbf{E_L}[a]_\gamma = a$, $\mathbf{E_L}[\text{my}.a]_\gamma = \gamma(a)$, $\mathbf{E_R}[a]_\gamma = \gamma(a)$, and $\mathbf{E_P}[\text{frc } C]_\mathbf{m} = \sum_{i=1}^S \{\mathbf{m}_{[i]} | \Sigma_i = (C, \gamma_i, O_i)\}$; moreover, $\mathbf{E_R}[\text{my}.a]_\gamma$, $\mathbf{E_P}[\text{tt}]_\mathbf{m}$, $\mathbf{E_P}[\text{ff}]_\mathbf{m}$, $\mathbf{E_L}[\text{frc } C]_\gamma$, and $\mathbf{E_R}[\text{frc } C]_\gamma$ are undefined as are, for the sake of simplicity, $\mathbf{E_P}[a]_\mathbf{m}$, $\mathbf{E_P}[\text{my}.a]_\mathbf{m}$. The definition of the above semantic interpretation functions on composition terms can be given recursively on the structure of the terms and is left out here. In particular, we assume them extended to tuples. Similarly, we assume standard techniques and machinery for auxiliary functions in store updates; the semantics of update σ in the current store γ will be denoted by $\mathbf{E}_{\mathbf{U}}[\![\sigma]\!]_\gamma$, that is a probability distribution over stores[7].

Let Λ_Δ be defined as $\Lambda_\Delta = \Lambda_\Delta^O \cup \Lambda_\Delta^I$, with Λ_Δ^O as above, and $\Lambda_\Delta^I = \{\alpha()|\alpha \in \mathcal{A}_\Delta\}$. A component specification (Δ, F) characterises the (component) transition probability matrix as a function of occupancy measure vectors $\mathbf{m}$, $\mathbf{K}^{(N)} \colon \mathcal{U}^S \times \Omega_\Delta \times \Omega_\Delta \to [0,1]$ such that $\mathbf{K}^{(N)}(\mathbf{m})_{\Sigma,\Sigma'}$ is the probability of a one step jump from component-state Σ to component-state Σ', given (that the global system state induces) occupancy measure vector $\mathbf{m}$. $\mathbf{K}^{(N)}(\mathbf{m})_{\Sigma,\Sigma'}$ is computed by making use of a transition relation $(C,\gamma,O) \xrightarrow{\lambda,p} (C',\gamma',O')$ over the space of component-states Ω_Δ, with transition labels drawn from $\Theta_\Delta \subset \Lambda_\Delta \times [0,1]$. More specifically, the transition relation is the relation $\to \, \subseteq \Omega_\Delta \times \Theta_\Delta \times \Omega_\Delta$ such that $(C,\gamma,O) \xrightarrow{\lambda,p} (C',\gamma',O')$ iff $C := \sum_{j\in J}[g_j]p_j :: act_j.C_j$ is the defining equation for C and $p = \sum_{k\in J}\{\bar{p}_k|(C,\gamma,O) \xrightarrow{\lambda,\bar{p}_k}_k (C',\gamma',O')\}$, where $\xrightarrow{\lambda,\bar{p}_k}_k$ is the least relation induced by the rules in Fig. 2. The component transition matrix function $\mathbf{K}^{(N)}(\mathbf{m})_{\Sigma,\Sigma'}$ is defined as follows: $\mathbf{K}^{(N)}(\mathbf{m})_{\Sigma,\Sigma'} = \sum_{(\lambda,p)\in\Theta_\Delta}\{p|\Sigma \xrightarrow{\lambda,p} \Sigma'\}$. Note that all the above summations are finite under our assumption that so is $\mathcal{V}_\Delta$. The behaviour of the system is the result of the parallel-synchronous execution of the N instances of the component. Thus, the probabilistic behaviour of the system is characterised by the DTMC $\mathbf{X}^{(N)}(t)$ with initial probability distribution δ_{Σ_0} and one step probability matrix $\mathbf{P}^{(N)}$ defined by the following product: $\mathbf{P}^{(N)}_{\Sigma,\Sigma'} = \Pi_{n=1}^N \mathbf{K}^{(N)}(\mathbf{M}^{(N)}(\Sigma))_{\Sigma_{[n]},\Sigma'_{[n]}}$. Of course, the 'occupancy measure' view of the evolution in time of stochastic process $\mathbf{X}^{(N)}(t)$ is again a DTMC, namely the *occupancy measure DTMC*, which is defined as expected: $\mathbf{M}^{(N)}(t) = \mathbf{M}^{(N)}(\mathbf{X}^{(N)}(t))$.

$$\frac{C := \sum_{j\in J}[g_j]p_j :: act_j.C_j \quad k \in J \quad \mathbf{E}_{\mathbf{L}}[\![g_k]\!]_\gamma = \mathtt{tt}}{act_k = \alpha^*[\pi]\langle\rangle\sigma \quad p = \mathbf{E}_{\mathbf{U}}[\![\sigma]\!]_\gamma(\gamma')}{(C,\gamma,O) \xrightarrow{\alpha\langle\rangle,p\cdot\mathbf{E}_{\mathbf{P}}[\![p_k]\!]\mathbf{m}}_k (C_k,\gamma',(\gamma,\mathbf{E}_{\mathbf{L}}[\![\pi]\!]_\gamma,\alpha\langle\rangle))} \tag{1}$$

$$\frac{C := \sum_{j\in J}[g_j]p_j :: act_j.C_j \quad k \in J \quad [g_k]p_k = \mathtt{rest}}{act_k = \alpha^*[\pi]\langle\rangle\sigma \quad p = \mathbf{E}_{\mathbf{U}}[\![\sigma]\!]_\gamma(\gamma')}{(C,\gamma,O) \xrightarrow{\alpha\langle\rangle,p\cdot(1-\sum_{j\in(J\setminus\{k\})}\mathbf{E}_{\mathbf{P}}[\![p_j]\!]\mathbf{m})}_k (C_k,\gamma',(\gamma,\mathbf{E}_{\mathbf{L}}[\![\pi]\!]_\gamma,\alpha\langle\rangle))} \tag{2}$$

$$\frac{C := \sum_{j\in J}[g_j]p_j :: act_j.C_j \quad k \in J \quad \mathbf{E}_{\mathbf{L}}[\![g_k]\!] = \mathtt{tt}}{act_k = \alpha^*[\pi]()\sigma \quad p = \mathbf{E}_{\mathbf{U}}[\![\sigma]\!]_\gamma(\gamma')}{f = \sum_{i=1}^S\{\mathbf{m}_{[i]}|\Sigma_i = (C_i',\gamma_i',(\gamma_i'',\pi_i',\alpha\langle\rangle)) \wedge \mathbf{E}_{\mathbf{R}}[\![\pi_i']\!]_\gamma = \mathbf{E}_{\mathbf{R}}[\![\mathbf{E}_{\mathbf{L}}[\![\pi]\!]_\gamma]\!]_{\gamma_i''} = \mathtt{tt}\}}{(C,\gamma,O) \xrightarrow{\alpha(),p\cdot\mathbf{E}_{\mathbf{P}}[\![p_k]\!]\mathbf{m}\cdot f}_k (C_k,\gamma',\langle\rangle)} \tag{3}$$

Fig. 2. Probabilistic Semantics Rules

---

[7] In this paper, for the sake of simplicity, updates do not depend on the current occupancy measure vector, i.e. the frc operator cannot occur in their specification.

2.3   Bounded PCTL

We recall that, given a set $\mathscr{P}$ of atomic propositions, the syntax of PCTL *state formulas* Φ and *path formulas* φ is defined as follows, where $\mathsf{ap} \in \mathscr{P}$ and $k \geq 0$ $:\Phi ::= \mathsf{ap} \mid \neg\Phi \mid \Phi \wedge \Phi \mid \mathcal{P}_{\bowtie p}(\varphi)$ where $\varphi ::= \mathcal{X}\Phi \mid \Phi\mathcal{U}^{\leq k}\Phi$. PCTL formulas are interpreted over *state labelled* DTMCs, which are pairs $(\mathcal{M}, L)$ where $\mathcal{M}$ is a DTMC and L is a mapping from the set of states of $\mathcal{M}$ to $2^{\mathscr{P}}$; for each state s, $L(s)$ is the set of atomic propositions true in s[8]. For the purposes of FlyFast bounded PCTL model-checking, our system specifications are enriched with the declaration of three different kinds of atomic propositions. A declaration of the form $\mathsf{ap}\,\mathsf{at}\,C$ associates atomic proposition ap to state $C \in \mathcal{S}_\Delta$. Thus ap must be included in the set $L(\Sigma)$ for each global state $\Sigma = ((C_1, \gamma_1, O_1), \ldots, (C_N, \gamma_N, O_N))$ such that $C_1 = C$ (recall here that FlyFast performs model-checking of *the first* object in the context of the global system). A declaration of the form $\mathsf{ap}\,\mathsf{def}\,(\mathbf{my}.a \bowtie v)$ associates atomic proposition ap to all component-states (C, γ, O) s.t. attribute a is $\bowtie v$. So, ap must be included in the set $L(\Sigma)$ for each global state $\Sigma = ((C_1, \gamma_1, O_1), \ldots, (C_N, \gamma_N, O_N))$ such that $\mathbf{E_L}[\![\mathbf{my}.a \bowtie v]\!]_{\gamma_1} = \mathsf{tt}$. Finally, a limited form of *global* atomic predicate is provided by means of a declaration of the form $\mathsf{ap}\,\mathsf{def}\,(\mathsf{frc}\,C \bowtie v)$; in this case, ap must be included in the set $L(\Sigma)$ for each global state Σ s.t. the fraction in Σ of the component states (C, γ, O), for any γ and O, is $\bowtie$ than $v \in [0, 1]$.

3   A Translation to FlyFast

In this section we define a translation $\mathcal{I}$ such that, given system specification $\Upsilon = (\Delta_\Upsilon, F_\Upsilon, \Sigma_0)^{(N)}$, $\mathcal{I}(\Upsilon) = \langle \Delta, A, \mathbf{C_0} \rangle^{(N)}$ is a FlyFast [15,17] system specification preserving probabilistic semantics. The attribute-based FlyFast front-end is then completed with a simple translation at the PCTL level, also provided in this section. We map every component state of Υ to a distinct state of $\mathcal{I}(\Upsilon)$ by means of a total injection $\mathcal{I}_{\mathcal{S}}:\Omega_{\Delta_\Upsilon} \rightarrow \mathcal{S}$. The mapping of actions is a bit more delicate because we have to respect FlyFast static constraints and, in particular, we have to avoid multiple probability function definitions for the same action. To that purpose, we could distinguish different occurrences of the same action in different transitions, characterized by their source and target states in Ω_{Δ_Υ}. In practice, since an action of a component cannot be influenced by the current outbox of the component, it is sufficient to use a total injection $\mathcal{I}_\mathcal{A}$ of the following type $(\mathcal{S}_{\Delta_\Upsilon} \times \Gamma_{\Delta_\Upsilon}) \times \Lambda_{\Delta_\Upsilon} \times \Omega_{\Delta_\Upsilon} \rightarrow \mathcal{A}$ for the mapping of actions. In the sequel we show how to build $\mathcal{I}(\Upsilon) = \langle \Delta, A, \mathbf{C_0} \rangle^{(N)}$ from $\Upsilon = (\Delta_\Upsilon, F_\Upsilon, \Sigma_0)^{(N)}$. The translation algorithm is given in Fig. 3, where for action $act \in \{\alpha^*[\pi]\langle\rangle\sigma, \alpha^*[\pi]()\sigma\}$ we let $T(act) = \alpha$, $P(act) = \pi$, and $U(act) = \sigma$. $\mathsf{SUM}\{t|\mathsf{cond}(t)\}$ denotes the *syntactical* term representing the sum of terms $t \in \{t|\mathsf{cond}(t) = \mathsf{tt}\}$, i.e. $t_1 + \ldots + t_n$, if $\{t|\mathsf{cond}(t) = \mathsf{tt}\} = \{t_1, \ldots, t_n\} \neq \emptyset$ and 0 if $\{t|\mathsf{cond}(t) = \mathsf{tt}\}$ is the empty set. Finally, by $t * t'$ we mean the *syntactical* term representing the product of

---

[8] We refer to [11] for the formal definition of PCTL and to [15,17] for the details of its instantiation in FlyFast.

terms t and t'. Output actions are dealt with in step 1. Consider for example action $\text{ext}^*[\bot]\langle\rangle\{\mathbf{my}.\mathtt{loc} \leftarrow \text{Jump}(\mathbf{my}.\mathtt{loc})\}$ in the definition of state S in Fig. 1. Suppose the possible values for locations are A, B, C, D, so that stores are functions in $\{\mathtt{loc}\} \rightarrow \{A, B, C, D\}$. The algorithm generates 12 actions (diagonal jumps are not contemplated in the example). Let us focus on the action ξ associated to local position A (i.e. $\gamma = [\mathtt{loc} \mapsto A]$) and possible next position B (i.e. $\gamma' = [\mathtt{loc} \mapsto B]$); the algorithm will generate probability function definition $\xi :: \mathsf{p_W}(A) * ext$ as well as a transition leading to (a state which is the encoding, via $\mathcal{I}_S$, of) the component state with E as (proper) state, store γ', and outbox $(\gamma, \bot, \text{ext}\langle\rangle)$. Since the action is not depending on the current outbox, in practice a copy of such a transition is generated *for each* component state sharing the same proper state S and the same store γ. In the general case, in a defining equation for a state C there might be multiple occurrences of the same action, bringing to the same next state C'; the algorithm takes care of this and collects them in order to generate a single transition; the appropriate probability is expressed by means of the $\text{SUM}\{\ldots\}$ term. The translation scheme for input actions is defined in case 2 and is similar, except that for each term p_j in the $\text{SUM}\{\ldots\}$ expression one has also to consider the sum Φ_j of the fractions of the possible partners. The translation of the **rest** case is straighforward.

Let $\mathbf{K}_{\mathcal{I}(\Upsilon)}^{(N)} : \mathcal{U}^S \times \mathcal{I}_S(\Omega_\Delta) \times \mathcal{I}_S(\Omega_\Delta) \rightarrow [0,1]$ be the step probability function associated to $\mathcal{I}(\Upsilon)$ by the FlyFast language probabilistic semantics definition (see [15,17] for details) and $\mathbf{K}_\Upsilon^{(N)} : \mathcal{U}^S \times \Omega_\Delta \times \Omega_\Delta \rightarrow [0,1]$ be the step probability function for Υ as defined in Sect. 2.2. It is easy to see that:

Theorem 1. *For all $N > 0$, occupancy measure vector $\mathbf{m} \in \mathcal{U}^S$ and $\Sigma, \Sigma' \in \Omega_\Delta$ the following holds: $\mathbf{K}_\Upsilon^{(N)}(\mathbf{m})_{\Sigma,\Sigma'} = \mathbf{K}_{\mathcal{I}(\Upsilon)}^{(N)}(\mathbf{m})_{\mathcal{I}_S(\Sigma),\mathcal{I}_S(\Sigma')}.$*

Proof (scketch). We first observe that, by definition, $\mathbf{K}_\Upsilon^{(N)}(\mathbf{m})_{(C,\gamma,O),(C',\gamma',O')} = \sum_{(\lambda,p)\in\Theta_\Delta}\{p | (C,\gamma,O) \xrightarrow{\lambda,p} (C',\gamma',O')\}$ which, by definition of $\longrightarrow$, is equal to

$$\sum_{(\lambda,p)\in\Theta_\Delta}\{p | p = \sum_{k\in J}\{\bar{p}_k | (C,\gamma,O) \xrightarrow{\lambda,\bar{p}_k}_k (C',\gamma',O')\} \ \wedge$$
$$C := \sum_{j\in J}[g_j]p_j :: act_j.C_j \text{ is the def. eq. of } C \text{ in } \Upsilon\}.$$

Consider the outer summation and suppose $(\alpha\langle\rangle, p)$ be the index of a summand. Without loss of generality, assume there is only one instance of such a summand and there is only one $k \in J$ such that the following transition is derived using the rules of Fig. 2: $(C,\gamma,O) \xrightarrow{\alpha\langle\rangle,\bar{p}_k}_k (C',\gamma',O')$. So, we have $\mathbf{K}_\Upsilon^{(N)}(\mathbf{m})_{(C,\gamma,O),(C',\gamma',O')} = \bar{p}_k$ such that $(C,\gamma,O) \xrightarrow{\alpha\langle\rangle,\bar{p}_k}_k (C',\gamma',O')$, where $C := \sum_{j\in J}[g_j]p_j :: act_j.C_j$ is the defining equation for C. Suppose $[g_k]p_k \neq$ **rest**, so that Rule (1) of Fig. 2 has been used for generating the transition. This implies that $\mathbf{E_L}[\![g_k]\!]_\gamma = \mathtt{tt}$, $\bar{p}_k = \mathbf{E_U}[\![\sigma]\!]_\gamma(\gamma') \cdot \mathbf{E_P}[\![p_k]\!]_\mathbf{m}$, $C' = C_k$, and $O' = (\gamma, \mathbf{E_L}[\![\pi]\!]_\gamma, \alpha\langle\rangle)$. Under the above conditions, by definition of the translation algorithm, the action $\xi = \mathcal{I}_\mathcal{A}((C,\gamma), \alpha\langle\rangle, (C',\gamma',O'))$ and related action probability function definition

For each state equation $C := \sum_{j \in J} [g_j] p_j :: act_j.C_j$ in Δ_Υ:

1. For each *output* action $\alpha^*[\pi]\langle\rangle\sigma = act_k$ with $k \in J$, and $\gamma \in \Gamma_{\Delta_\Upsilon}$, let $J_{\alpha,\sigma,\gamma}$ be the largest subset of J s.t. there is $C' \in S_\Delta$ s.t. for all $j \in J_{\alpha,\sigma,\gamma}$ $C_j = C'$, $T(act_j) = \alpha$, $\mathbf{E_L}[P(act_j)]_\gamma = \mathbf{E_L}[\pi]_\gamma$, and $\mathbf{E_U}[U(act_j)]_\gamma = \mathbf{E_U}[\sigma]_\gamma$. For each $\gamma' \in \Gamma_{\Delta_\Upsilon}$, with $\xi = \mathcal{I_A}((C,\gamma),\alpha\langle\rangle,(C',\gamma',(\gamma,\mathbf{E_L}[\pi]_\gamma,\alpha\langle\rangle)))$, the following action probability function definition is included in A: $\xi :: \mathbf{E_U}[\sigma]_\gamma(\gamma') *$ SUM$\{p_j | j \in \hat{J}_{\alpha,\sigma,\gamma}\}$, where $\hat{J}_{\alpha,\sigma,\gamma} = \{j \in J_{\alpha,\sigma,\gamma} | [g_j]p_j \neq \mathbf{rest} \wedge \mathbf{E_L}[g_j]_\gamma = $ tt$\}$. Moreover, for each outbox $O \in \mathcal{O}_{\Delta_\Upsilon}$, the following summand is added to the equation in Δ for state $\mathcal{I_S}(C,\gamma,O)$: $\xi.\mathcal{I_S}(C',\gamma',(\gamma,\mathbf{E_L}[\pi]_\gamma,\alpha\langle\rangle))$;

2. For each *input* action $\alpha^*[\pi]()\sigma = act_k$, with $k \in J$, and $\gamma \in \Gamma_{\Delta_\Upsilon}$, let $J_{\alpha,\sigma,\gamma}$ be the largest subset of J s.t. there is $C' \in S_\Delta$ s.t. for all $j \in J_{\alpha,\sigma,\gamma}$ $C_j = C'$, $T(act_j) = \alpha$ and $\mathbf{E_U}[U(act_j)]_\gamma = \mathbf{E_U}[\sigma]_\gamma$. For each $\gamma' \in \Gamma_{\Delta_\Upsilon}$, with $\xi = \mathcal{I_A}((C,\gamma),\alpha(),(C',\gamma',\langle\rangle))$, the following action probability function definition is included in A: $\xi :: \mathbf{E_U}[\sigma]_\gamma(\gamma') *$ SUM$\{(p_j * \Phi_j) | j \in \hat{J}_{\alpha,\sigma,\gamma}\}$, where $\hat{J}_{\alpha,\sigma,\gamma} = \{j \in J_{\alpha,\sigma,\gamma} | [g_j]p_j \neq \mathbf{rest} \wedge \mathbf{E_L}[g_j]_\gamma = $ tt$\}$ and term Φ_j is: SUM$\{$frc$\mathcal{I_S}((\tilde{C},\tilde{\gamma},(\bar{\gamma},\bar{\pi},\alpha\langle\rangle))) | \mathbf{E_R}[\bar{\pi}]_\gamma = \mathbf{E_R}[\mathbf{E_L}[\pi_j]_\gamma]_{\tilde{\gamma}} = $ tt$\}$. Moreover, for each outbox $O \in \mathcal{O}_{\Delta_\Upsilon}$, the following summand is added to the equation in Δ for state $\mathcal{I_S}(C,\gamma,O)$: $\xi.\mathcal{I_S}(C',\gamma',\langle\rangle)$;

3. If there exists $k \in J$ s.t. $[g_k]p_k = \mathbf{rest}$, and $act_k = \alpha^*[\pi]\langle\rangle\sigma$, let $\bar{A}$ be the set of probability function definitions which has been constructed in steps (1) and (2) above; note that for every $\zeta :: p * q \in \bar{A}$, q is either a probability constant p_j occurring in a branch $[g_j]p_j :: act_j.C_j$ of the defining equation for C, or it is a term of the form SUM$\{(p_h * \Phi_h) | h \in H\}$, for some index set H. We define $\bar{p} = (1 - $ SUM$\{q | \zeta :: p * q \in \bar{A}\})$ and, for all $\gamma' \in \Gamma_{\Delta_\Upsilon}$, with $\xi = \mathcal{I_A}((C,\gamma),\alpha\langle\rangle,(C_k,\gamma',(\gamma,\mathbf{E_L}[\pi]_\gamma,\alpha\langle\rangle)))$, the following action probability function definition is included in A: $\xi :: \mathbf{E_U}[\sigma]_\gamma(\gamma') * \bar{p}$. Moreover, for each outbox $O \in \mathcal{O}_{\Delta_\Upsilon}$, the following summand is added to the equation in Δ for state $\mathcal{I_S}(C,\gamma,O)$: $\xi.\mathcal{I_S}(C_k,\gamma',(\gamma,\mathbf{E_L}[\pi]_\gamma,\alpha\langle\rangle))$;

4. No other action probability function definition and transition is included and the initial state $\mathbf{C_0}$ of $\mathcal{I}(\Upsilon)$ is defined as $\mathbf{C_0} = \mathcal{I_S}(\Sigma_0)$.

Fig. 3. The translation algorithm

$\xi :: \mathbf{E_U}[\sigma]_\gamma(\gamma') *$ SUM$\{p_k\}$ are included in the FlyFast model. Moreover, the summand $\xi.\mathcal{I_S}(C',\gamma',O')$ is added in the equation for state $\mathcal{I_S}(C,\gamma,O)$ in the FlyFast model. Using the semantics definition of the FlyFast language [15,17], we get that the probability assigned to ξ is $\mathbf{E_U}[\sigma]_\gamma(\gamma') \cdot \mathbf{E_P}[p_k]_m$, that is, exactly $\bar{p}_k$. Thus $\mathbf{K}_\Upsilon^{(N)}(m)_{\Sigma,\Sigma'} = \mathbf{K}_{\mathcal{I}(\Upsilon)}^{(N)}(m)_{\mathcal{I_S}(\Sigma),\mathcal{I_S}(\Sigma')}$. The proof for all the other cases is similar. $\bullet$

The translation of atomic proposition declarations into FlyFast formula declarations is the obvious one and is shown in Fig. 4 where OR$\{e|$cond$(e)\}$ denotes the *syntactical* term representing the disjunction of expressions $e \in \{e|$cond$(e) = $ tt$\}$, i.e. $e_1 | \ldots | e_n$, if $\{e|$cond$(e) = $ tt$\} = \{e_1, \ldots, e_n\} \neq \emptyset$ and ff, if $\{e|$cond$(e) = $ tt$\}$ is the empty set.

atomic prop. decl.	FlyFast formula declaration
ap at C	ap : OR$\{\mathcal{I}_S((C',\gamma,O))|(C',\gamma,O) \in \Omega_{\Delta_r} \wedge C' = C\}$
ap def (my.$a \bowtie v$)	ap : OR$\{\mathcal{I}_S((C,\gamma,O))|(C,\gamma,O) \in \Omega_{\Delta_r} \wedge \gamma(a) \bowtie v\}$
ap def (frc $C \bowtie v$)	ap : SUM$\{$frc $\mathcal{I}_S((C',\gamma,O))|(C',\gamma,O) \in \Omega_{\Delta_r} \wedge C' = C\} \bowtie v$

Fig. 4. Translation of atomic proposition declarations. The translation is not defined whenever OR$\{t|$cond$(t)\} =$ ff or SUM$\{t|$cond$(t)\} = 0$.

4 Epidemic Example Revisited

We return to the distributed Epidemic example of Fig. 1 where, for the sake of simplicity, we consider a simple patched space, consisting of the usual four quadrants A, B, C, D in the Cartesian Plane, as in Fig. 5 (left). We model a 'flow' from quadrant C to quadrant A by defining the jump probabilities as in the table in Fig. 5 (right)[9], where $l = 0.6$ and $s = 1 - l$, so that $l > s$.

We consider a model in which initially there are 10.000 components in state S in quadrant C and 100 in state S in quadrant A. The non-zero values of the parameters are the same for each quadrant, defined as follows: $h = 0.2, ext = 0.1, ei = 0.4, ii = 0.8, ir = 0.2, rs = 0.1, m_N = m_S = m_E = m_W = 0.05$.

Figure 6 shows the fast-simulation results[10] for the model for each of the four quadrants. This functionality is built-in in the FlyFast tool. In the figure, the fractions of numbers of the components in each of the four states at each of the four locations are shown. Note that these fractions correspond to appropriate predicates on standard atomic propositions; for instance the fraction of components in state S at quandrant A is captured by s $\wedge$ a, assuming the following declarations: s at S and a def (my.loc $= A$). The simulation of single elements, taken as the average over 10 runs shows a very good correspondence with the fast-simulation results. The results also show good correspondence to the original SEIR model [5] when the probability to move between quadrants is set to zero and in the initial state the total population is in state S and in one specific quadrant in the former model. Besides fast simulation, that gives an idea of the average global behaviour of the system, we can also analyse the behaviour of a single component in the context

			p_H	p_N	p_S	p_E	p_W
B	A	A	l	0	$s/2$	0	$s/2$
		B	$s/2$	0	$s/2$	l	0
C	D	C	s	$l/2$	0	$l/2$	0
		D	$s/2$	l	0	0	$s/2$

Fig. 5. The Cartesian quadrants (left) and the jump probabilities (right).

---

[9] We assume: N(A) = N(B) = S(C) = S(D) = E(A) = E(D) = W(B) = W(C) = undefined, with [loc = undefined] = $\perp$ for all loc..

[10] Experiments have been performed using the FlyFast on-the-fly mean field model checker on a PC with an Intel Core i7 1.7 GHz, RAM 8 Gb.

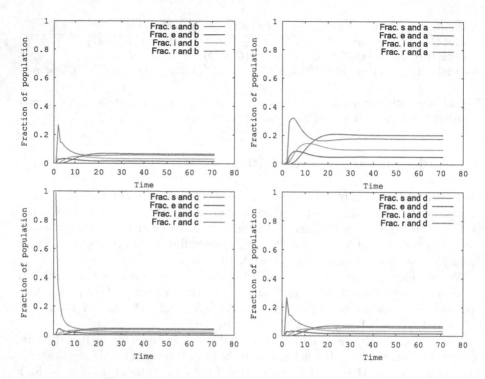

Fig. 6. Fast simulation for each of the four quadrants.

of the overall behaviour. We consider two example properties as illustration. Let us first consider a component initially in state S and located in A and let atomic propositions i and c be declared as follows: i at I and c def $(\mathbf{my}.\mathrm{loc} = C)$. The following formula (P1) states that the probability is greater than p that the component ends up infected in quadrant C by time t: $\mathcal{P}_{>p}(\mathrm{tt}\,\mathcal{U}^{\leq t}\,(i \wedge c))$. FlyFast allows one to study the dynamics of the actual probability as a function of t, by means of the notation $\mathcal{P}_{=?}(\mathrm{tt}\,\mathcal{U}^{\leq t}\,(i \wedge c))$ and the resulting graph, for the above initial conditions and for the first 70 time units is shown in Fig. 7 (left). For comparison, the formula for an agent starting in C and ending up in A and being infected is shown as well in the same figure. The results for a more complicated, nested, formula (P2) are shown in Fig. 7 (right). P2 expresses the probability, over time, of a component reaching a situation in which it is neither infected nor exposed, and from which it can reach a state in which it has a probability higher than 0.15 to be infected and located in C within the next 10 time units; formula P2 is given below, where i is assumed defined by i at I: $\mathcal{P}_{=?}(\mathrm{tt}\,\mathcal{U}^{\leq t}\,(\neg(i \vee e) \wedge \mathcal{P}_{>0.15}(\mathrm{tt}\,\mathcal{U}^{\leq 10}\,(i \wedge c))))$. The formula has been considered for a component which is initially in A and in state S; the figure shows also a similar formula, where the role of A and C is exchanged and a probability higher than 0.45 instead of 0.15 is considered.

For both types of properties a considerable difference in the probabilities can be observed for an agent that is initially located in A or in C, due to the flow of

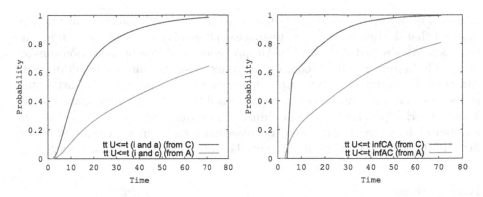

Fig. 7. Model checking results for properties P1 (left) and P2 (right).

movement that has been introduced. This illustrates a clear dependence of the results on the dynamically changing spatial distribution of components. The total number of states, actions and transitions for the resulting FlyFast *object specification* is 52, 114 and 468 respectively, while the number of states of the global *approximated* model which have been generated for the analysis of formula P2 is 2.323 (2.185 when A and C are swapped). The model checking time for the more complicated nested formula P2 and for all values of t (70) is 10.343 (9.921 when A and C are swapped) ms, ≈ 148 (141) ms per checking session, for a model with a total population of 10.100 objects. A well-known feature of mean-field model checking is that the model checking time is independent of the size of the population, however, further experimentation with more extended spatial models and more attributes, that do effect this time, is planned as future work.

5   Conclusions

The attribute-based interaction paradigm is deemed fundamental for agent interaction in the context of Autonomic or Collective Adaptive Systems [1,3,9,12,20]. In this paper we have presented a attribute-based coordination modelling language as a front-end for FlyFast, an on-the-fly mean-field model-checker for bounded PCTL. The language extends the original FlyFast modelling language by replacing its actions with input (output, respectively) actions where senders (receivers, respectively) are specified by means of predicates on dynamic attributes on system components, where a component is a process/attribute-store pair. A translation to the standard FlyFast language has been presented, its correctness has been showed as well as an example of its application to a simple case study. It should be noted that the introduction of attributes in a process model is an *intrinsic* source of complexity in terms of component state-space size. Such an increase, in the worst case, goes with $|\mathcal{V}_\Delta|^{|Att_\Delta|} \cdot (|\mathcal{A}_\Delta^O| + 1)$, where Att_Δ is the set of attributes of the component, $\mathcal{V}_\Delta$ is the set of values they can take, and $\mathcal{A}_\Delta^O$ is the set of output actions occurring in the component specification (which may appear in its outbox). The obvious consequence of this is that one has to carefully ponder the importance and necessity of each and every new attribute used in a model, although, it must be kept in mind that the real source of state-space explosion is the size of the system, and this issue is addressed by Mean-Field approximation. A first optimisation consists in considering only reachable component states as well as eliminating actions with constant zero probability and simplifying boolean combinations of FlyFast atomic propositions in the translation. A possible additional line of investigation is the study of techniques for DTMC minimization to Mean-field analysis, so that the number of difference equations can decrease as a consequence, in a similar way as for CTMCs and the number of differential equations in fluid flow analysis [24].

References

1. Alrahman, Y.A., De Nicola, R., Loreti, M., Tiezzi, F., Vigo, R.: A calculus for attribute-based communication. In: ACM SAC 2015, pp. 1840–1845 (2015)
2. Baier, C., Haverkort, B., Hermanns, H., Katoen, J.P.: Model-checking algorithms for continuous-time Markov chains. IEEE TSE **29**(6), 524–541 (2003)
3. Bortolussi, L., De Nicola, R., Galpin, V., Gilmore, S., Hillston, J., Latella, D., Loreti, M., Massink, M.: CARMA: collective adaptive resource-sharing markovian agents. In: QAPL 2015, EPTCS, vol. 194, pp. 16–31 (2015)
4. Bortolussi, L., Hillston, J.: Fluid model checking. In: Koutny, M., Ulidowski, I. (eds.) CONCUR 2012. LNCS, vol. 7454, pp. 333–347. Springer, Heidelberg (2012)
5. Bortolussi, L., Hillston, J., Latella, D., Massink, M.: Continuous approximation of collective systems behaviour: a tutorial. Perform. Eval. **70**, 317–349 (2013). Elsevier
6. Bortolussi, L., Latella, D., Massink, M.: Stochastic process algebra and stability analysis of collective systems. In: De Nicola, R., Julien, C. (eds.) COORDINATION 2013. LNCS, vol. 7890, pp. 1–15. Springer, Heidelberg (2013)
7. Ciancia, V., Latella, D., Massink, M.: On Space in CARMA. Technical Report TR-QC-01-2015, QUANTICOL (2015)
8. Ciancia, V., Latella, D., Massink, M.: An Attribute-based Front-end for FlyFast. Technical Report CNR-ISTI 2015-TR-041 (2015)
9. De Nicola, R., et al.: The SCEL language: design, implementation, verification. Software Engineering for Collective Autonomic Systems - The ASCENS Approach. LNCS, vol. 8998, pp. 3–71. Springer, Heidelberg (2015)
10. Feng, C., Hillston, J.: PALOMA: a process algebra for located Markovian agents. In: Norman, G., Sanders, W. (eds.) QEST 2014. LNCS, vol. 8657, pp. 265–280. Springer, Heidelberg (2014)
11. Hansson, H., Jonsson, B.: A logic for reasoning about time and reliability. Formal Aspects Comput. **6**(5), 512–535 (1994)
12. Hillston, J., Loreti, M.: Specification and analysis of open-ended systems with CARMA. In: Weyns, D., Michel, F. (eds.) E4MAS 2014– 10 years later. LNCS, vol. 9068, pp. 95–116. Springer, Heidelberg (2015). doi:10.1007/978-3-319-23850-0_7
13. John, M., Lhoussaine, C., Niehren, J.: Dynamic compartments in the imperative π-calculus. In: Degano, P., Gorrieri, R. (eds.) CMSB 2009. LNCS, vol. 5688, pp. 235–250. Springer, Heidelberg (2009)
14. John, M., Lhoussaine, C., Niehren, J., Uhrmacher, A.M.: The attributed Pi calculus. In: Heiner, M., Uhrmacher, A.M. (eds.) CMSB 2008. LNCS (LNBI), vol. 5307, pp. 83–102. Springer, Heidelberg (2008)

15. Latella, D., Loreti, M., Massink, M.: On-the-fly fast mean-field model-checking. In: Abadi, M., Lluch Lafuente, A. (eds.) TGC 2013. LNCS, vol. 8358, pp. 297–314. Springer, Heidelberg (2014)
16. Latella, D., Loreti, M., Massink, M.: On-the-fly probabilistic model checking. In: ICE 2014. EPTCS, vol. 166, pp. 45–59 (2014). ISSN: 2075–2180
17. Latella, D., Loreti, M., Massink, M.: On-the-fly PCTL fast mean-field approximated model-checking for self-organising coordination. Sci. Comput. Program. **110**, 23–50 (2015)
18. Latella, D., Loreti, M., Massink, M.: Investigating fluid-flow semantics of asynchronous tuple-based process languages for collective adaptive systems. In: Holvoet, T., Viroli, M. (eds.) Coordination Models and Languages. LNCS, vol. 9037, pp. 19–34. Springer, Heidelberg (2015)
19. Latella, D.: Comunicazione basata su proprietà nei sistemi decentralizzati [Property-based inter-process communication in decentralized systems] , graduation Thesis. Istituto di Scienze dell'Informazione. Univ. of Pisa (in italian), December 1983
20. Latella, D., Loreti, M., Massink, M., Senni, V.: On StocS: a stochastic extension of SCEL. In: De Nicola, R., Hennicker, R. (eds.) Wirsing Festschrift. LNCS, vol. 8950, pp. 619–640. Springer, Heidelberg (2015)
21. Le Boudec, J.Y., McDonald, D., Mundinger, J.: A generic mean field convergence result for systems of interacting objects. In: QEST 2007, pp. 3–18. IEEE (2007)
22. Lesser, V.R., Corkill, D.D.: Functionally accurate, cooperative distributed systems. IEEE Trans. Syst. Man Cybern. **11**(1), 81–96 (1981)
23. Massink, M., Latella, D.: Fluid analysis of foraging ants. In: Sirjani, M. (ed.) COORDINATION 2012. LNCS, vol. 7274, pp. 152–165. Springer, Heidelberg (2012)
24. Tschaikowski, M., Tribastone, M.: A unified framework for differential aggregations in Markovian process algebra. J. Log. Algebr. Meth. Program. **84**(2), 238–258 (2015)

Scheduling Games for Concurrent Systems

Kasper Dokter[1]([✉]), Sung-Shik Jongmans[2,3], and Farhad Arbab[1]

[1] Centrum Wiskunde and Informatica, Amsterdam, The Netherlands
{dokter,farhad}@cwi.nl
[2] Open University of the Netherlands, Heerlen, The Netherlands
ssj@ou.nl
[3] Radboud University Nijmegen, Nijmegen, The Netherlands

Abstract. A scheduler is an algorithm that assigns at any time a set of processes to a set of processors. Processes usually interact with each other, which introduces dependencies amongst them. Typically, such dependencies induce extra delays that the scheduler needs to avoid. Specific types of applications, like streaming applications, synthesize a scheduler from a formal model that is aware of these interactions. However, such interaction-specific information is not available for general types of applications. In this paper, we propose an interaction aware scheduling framework for generic concurrent applications. We formalize the amount of work performed by an application as constraints. We use these constraints to generate a graph, and view scheduler synthesis as solving a game on this graph that is played between the scheduler and the application. We illustrate that our framework is expressive enough to subsume an established scheduling framework for streaming programs.

Keywords: Scheduling · Game theory · Synthesis · Constraint automata

1 Introduction

A scheduler of a concurrent application is an algorithm that assigns at any time *processes* of the application to a set of *processors* to execute them. The processes in a concurrent application interact with each other, which introduces dependencies amongst them. For example, a consumer process cannot execute if it requires data not yet provided by a producer process. Typically, such dependencies induce extra delays that the scheduler needs to avoid. For specific types of applications, like streaming applications [18], formal models exist that are aware of the interactions among their processes. Such models are then used to synthesize schedulers that optimize the execution of their applications with respect to a scheduling goal, such as latency or power consumption [4,15]. For general types of applications, like web servers [10], no a priori detailed information about the interactions among their constituent processes is available to the scheduler. In such cases, a general-purpose round-robin scheduler is typically used to execute the application on the available processors. However, we cannot expect such

A. Lluch Lafuente and J. Proença (Eds.): COORDINATION 2016, LNCS 9686, pp. 84–100, 2016.
DOI: 10.1007/978-3-319-39519-7_6

schedulers to optimize our scheduling goals, because they cannot anticipate the dependencies among application processes.

In this paper, we propose an interaction-aware scheduling framework that enables scheduler synthesis for *generic* concurrent applications, by explicitly modelling interactions among processes. In particular, this framework consists of two elements: a novel formal model of concurrent applications and a scheduler synthesis approach built on top of this formal model.

We base our formal model of concurrent applications on *constraint automata* [3], a general model of concurrency developed by Baier et al. (originally as a formal semantics for the coordination language Reo [2]). Basically, the idea is to model a concurrent application as a set of constraint automata, one for every process in the application. In this approach, every constraint automaton models the behaviour of a process at the level of its interactions with its environment (i.e., other processes). Using a special *composition operator*, we obtain a interaction-aware model for the entire concurrent application.

The existing theory of constraint automata focuses on processes and their interactions; it does not yet facilitate modelling the amount of work that processes need to carry out. However, such information is essential for scheduling. In this paper, we therefore extend transition labels in constraint automata with a declarative constraint that describes the work that needs to be done as part of a transition. These *job constraints* essentially generalize simple *weights* as in *weighted automata* [11], primarily to support true concurrency in composition. We call the resulting extension of constraint automata *work automata*, and we extend the composition operator on constraint automata to work automata accordingly. Work automata, then, constitute a formal model of concurrent applications in which both interaction among processes and work inside processes can be expressed, in a compositional *and* general manner.

Next, we use work automata in our interaction-aware scheduler synthesis. Given a formal model of a concurrent application as a set of work automata, our interaction-aware scheduler synthesis approach consists of two steps. In the first step, we use our composition operator on work automata to construct a work automaton for the entire concurrent application. The resulting work automaton models exactly the work of each process and the dependencies between the work. In the second step, we model the scheduler synthesis problem as a token *game* on a graph played between the scheduler and the application. The scheduler assigns the processes of the application to a heterogeneous set of processors, and the application non-deterministically selects a possible execution of the application. We apply results about the existence and quality of optimal strategies in *mean payoff games* [7,12] to find schedules that minimize the use of context-switches. Finally, we illustrate that our framework is expressive enough to subsume an established scheduling framework for streaming applications.

The structure of the paper is as follows: In Sect. 2, we introduce job constraints and define work automata. In Sect. 3, we define the graph on which a scheduling game is played. In Sect. 4, we apply our scheduling framework to streaming applications. In Sect. 5, we conclude and discuss future work.

2   Concurrent Applications

As a starting point, we use a system of communicating automata to model interaction among processes in a concurrent application. To define the scheduling problem for this system of automata, we annotate each transition with an expression that models the workload of that transition. In Sect. 2.1, we recall the definition of constraint automata. In Sect. 2.2, we introduce job constraints, which model the work of the processes in a concurrent application. In Sect. 2.3, we define work automata by adding job constraints to constraint automata. In Sect. 2.4, we informally discuss the semantics of work automata. In Sect. 2.5, we extend constraint automata composition to work automata.

2.1   Preliminaries on Constraint Automata

Baier et al. proposed constraint automata to model interaction amongst processes in a concurrent application [3]. A constraint automaton is a tuple $\mathcal{A} = (Q, \mathcal{P}, \rightarrow)$, where Q is a set of states, $\mathcal{P}$ is a set of ports, called the interface, and $\rightarrow \subseteq Q \times 2^{\mathcal{P}} \times Q$ is a transition relation. Informally, $\mathcal{A}$ is a labeled transition system with labels, called *synchronization constraints*, consisting of subsets $N \subseteq \mathcal{P}$. A synchronization constraint $N \subseteq \mathcal{P}$ describes the interaction of $\mathcal{A}$ with its environment: ports in N synchronize, while ports outside of N block. Note that $\emptyset \subseteq \mathcal{P}$ models an internal action of the automaton. Originally, in addition to a synchronization constraint, every transition in a constraint automaton carries also a *data constraint*. Data constraints are logical assertions that specify which particular data items may be observed on the ports that participate in a transition. Because data constraints do not matter in what follows—they address an orthogonal concern—we omit them from the definition for simplicity (technically, thus, we consider *port automata* [16]); the work presented in this paper straightforwardly extends to constraint automata with data constraints.

The constraint automaton of an entire application can be obtained by parallel composition of the constraint automata of its processes. For $i \in \{0, 1\}$, let $\mathcal{A}_i = (Q_i, \mathcal{P}_i, \rightarrow_i)$ be a constraint automaton. The composition $\mathcal{A}_0 \bowtie \mathcal{A}_1$ is defined by $(Q_0 \times Q_1, \mathcal{P}_0 \cup \mathcal{P}_1, \rightarrow)$, where $\rightarrow$ is the smallest relation that satisfies the following rule: if $i \in \{0, 1\}$, $\tau_i = (q_i, N_i, q_i') \in \rightarrow_i$, $\tau_{1-i} = (q_{1-i}, N_{1-i}, q_{1-i}') \in \rightarrow_{1-i} \cup \{(q, \emptyset, q) \mid q \in Q_{1-i}\}$ and $N_0 \cap \mathcal{P}_1 = N_1 \cap \mathcal{P}_0$, then $\tau_0 \mid \tau_1 = ((q_0, q_1), N_0 \cup N_1, (q_0', q_1')) \in \rightarrow$ (cf., Definition 3.2 in [3]). In other words, a transition $\tau = ((q_0, q_1), N, (q_0', q_1')) \in \rightarrow$ of the composition is possible if either (1) both restrictions $\tau|_{\mathcal{P}_0} = (q_0, N \cap \mathcal{P}_0, q_0')$ and $\tau|_{\mathcal{P}_1} = (q_1, N \cap \mathcal{P}_1, q_1')$ are transitions in $\mathcal{A}_0$ and $\mathcal{A}_1$, or (2) for some $i \in \{0, 1\}$, the restriction $\tau|_{\mathcal{P}_i}$ is a transition in $\mathcal{A}_i$ that is independent of $\mathcal{A}_{1-i}$, i.e., $N \cap \mathcal{P}_{1-i} = \emptyset$.

2.2   Job Constraints

A system of constraint automata describes only interaction, while the workload of each process remains unspecified. Therefore, we extend transition labels in constraint automata with a *work expression* that models the amount of work that needs to be done before a transitions fires.

In the simplest of cases, a transition in a constraint automaton models an atomic piece of work, belonging to a single process. In that case, we can straight-forwardly model this amount of work as a natural number $n \in \mathbb{N}_0$. However, through (parallel) composition, a transition in a constraint automaton may also model the synchronous firing of *multiple* transitions (originating from different constraint automata for different processes). In that case, a single natural number fails to express that the work involved by each of these multiple transitions may actually be done in parallel. For instance, for $i \in \{0, 1\}$, let $\mathcal{A}_i = (Q_i, \mathcal{P}_i, \rightarrow_i)$ be a work automaton and $\tau_i = (q_i, N_i, q_i') \in \rightarrow_i$ a transition that requires $n_i \in \mathbb{N}_0$ units of work. Suppose that τ_0 and τ_1 synchronize, i.e., $N_0 \cap \mathcal{P}_1 = N_1 \cap \mathcal{P}_0$. Intuitively, $\tau_0 \mid \tau_1$ then requires $n_0 + n_1$ units of work, which may seem to define the composition of work. However, this composition loses the information that $\mathcal{A}_0$ and $\mathcal{A}_1$ may run in parallel and that the n_0 and n_1 units of work are independent of each other. To avoid this loss, we keep the values n_0 and n_1 separate by associating τ_i with a *job* x_i that requires n_i units of work. We represent the work of τ_i as the *job constraint* $x_i = n_i$, and the work of $\tau_0 \mid \tau_1$ as $x_0 = n_0 \wedge x_1 = n_1$.

Although job constraints with equalities (as introduced above) enable us to express parallelism of work between *synchronizing* transitions, they do not enable us to express parallelism of work between *independent* transitions (i.e., transitions that do not share any ports). The issue here is that if a transition τ_0 in automaton $\mathcal{A}_0$ fires *before* an independent transition τ_1 in automaton $\mathcal{A}_1$ fires, $\mathcal{A}_1$ is free to already perform (some) work *while* τ_0 fires, *in anticipation of* later firing τ_1. To model this, we should associate τ_0 with a job constraint that specifies that the work associated with τ_1 can be performed *partially*. We do this by allowing inequalities in job constraints. For instance, if the job constraint of τ_0 is $x_0 = n_0$, while the job constraint of τ_1 is $x_1 = n_1$, we define the job constraint of $\tau_0 \mid \epsilon$ (i.e., the incarnation of τ_0 in the composition of $\mathcal{A}_0$ and $\mathcal{A}_1$, where ϵ denotes an internal action of $\mathcal{A}_1$) as $x_0 = n_0 \wedge x_1 \leq n_1$.

We define the set of job constraints w over a set of jobs $\mathcal{J}$ by the grammar

$$w ::= \top \mid x = n \mid x \leq n \mid w_0 \wedge w_1, \tag{1}$$

with $x \in \mathcal{J}$ and $n \in \mathbb{N}_0$. The need for inequalities in w, precludes using weights on transitions in weighted automata [11] to represent work.

For notational convenience, we introduce the following terminology regarding a job constraint w over a set of jobs $\mathcal{J}$. Let $F, G \subseteq \mathcal{J}$ and $n_x, m_y \in \mathbb{N}_0$, for all $x \in F$ and $y \in G$, such that w is equivalent to $\bigwedge_{x \in F} x = n_x \wedge \bigwedge_{y \in G} y \leq m_y$. We call w *saturated*, whenever $F \cup G = \mathcal{J}$. We call w *satisfiable*, whenever $n_x \leq m_x$, for all $x \in F \cap G$. If w is satisfiable and $x \in \mathcal{J}$, then we define the *available work* $w_x \in \mathbb{N}_0 \cup \{\infty\}$ for job x by $w_x = n_x$, if $x \in F$, $w_x = m_x$, if $x \in G \setminus F$, and $w_x = \infty$ otherwise. Finally, we define the set of *required jobs* $\rho_w \subseteq \mathcal{J}$ by $\rho_w = F$.

2.3   Work Automata

We now extend the transition labels of constraint automata from Sect. 2.1 with the job constraints from Sect. 2.2.

Definition 1. *A* work automaton *is a tuple* $(Q, \mathcal{P}, \mathcal{J}, \rightarrow)$ *that consists of a set of states* Q, *a set of ports* $\mathcal{P}$, *a set of jobs* $\mathcal{J}$, *and a transition relation* $\rightarrow \subseteq Q \times 2^{\mathcal{P}} \times \Omega_{\mathcal{J}} \times Q$, *where* $\Omega_{\mathcal{J}}$ *is the set of all satisfiable job constraints over* $\mathcal{J}$.

Example 1. One of the simplest non-trivial examples of concurrent systems is the producer-consumer system, shown in Fig. 1(a). The producer generates data and puts them into its buffer. The consumer takes these data from the buffer and processes them. We assume that the buffer has capacity 2. We split the system into a buffered producer and a consumer. Figure 1(b) and (c) show their respective work automata. States 0, 1 and 2 in Fig. 1(b) indicate the amount of data in the buffer. In state 0 or 1, the producer can produce a new datum by finishing 2 units of work of job x. In state 1 or 2, the consumer can take a datum from the buffer by synchronizing on port a, which requires no work on job x. In state 0 in Fig. 1(c), the consumer waits for a datum d at port a. When d arrives, the consumer takes it from the buffer, requiring 1 unit of work on job y. In state 1, the consumer processes datum d, requiring 3 units on job z.

2.4   Job Execution

Let $\mathcal{A} = (Q, \mathcal{P}, \mathcal{J}, \rightarrow)$ be some fixed work automaton. In this section, we informally introduce the semantics of $\mathcal{A}$. The jobs in a work automaton are executed by a *parallel machine* $\mathcal{M}$, which consists of a heterogeneous set of processors and a map that represents the execution speed of jobs on processors.

Definition 2. *A* parallel machine *is a tuple* $(M, \mathcal{J}, v)$, *where* M *is a set of processors,* $\mathcal{J}$ *is a set of jobs and* $v : \mathcal{J} \times M \rightarrow \mathbb{N}_0$ *is a map that models the speeds of jobs on processors.*

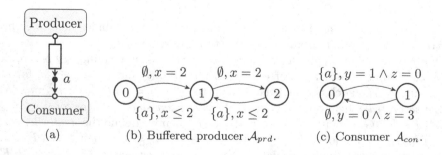

(a)   (b) Buffered producer $\mathcal{A}_{prd}$.   (c) Consumer $\mathcal{A}_{con}$.

Fig. 1. Producer-consumer application (a), and its corresponding system of work automata (b) and (c) with $\{a\}$ as their interface $\{x\}$ and $\{y, z\}$ as their respective job sets.

It is the task of a scheduler to assign jobs from a set $\mathcal{J}$ to processors in a parallel machine $(M, \mathcal{J}, v)$ over $\mathcal{J}$. We model this assignment of jobs to processors by an injective partial map $s : M \rightharpoonup \mathcal{J}$ that represents the *scheduled jobs*, i.e., $s(i) = s(j)$ implies $i = j$, for all $i, j \in M$. We write $S(M, \mathcal{J})$ for the set of all injective partial maps $s : M \rightharpoonup \mathcal{J}$.

We represent the *speeds of jobs* in $\mathcal{J}$ subject to the scheduled jobs $s \in S(M, \mathcal{J})$ by the map $v_s : \mathcal{J} \to \mathbb{N}_0$, given by $v_s(x) = v(x, s^{-1}(x))$ if $x \in \mathrm{im}(s)$ and $v_s(x) = 0$ otherwise. Here, $\mathrm{im}(s) = \{s(m) \in \mathcal{J} \mid m \in M\}$ is the image of s.

We represent the current *progress* of jobs by a map $p : \mathcal{J} \to \mathbb{Q}_{\geq 0}$, where $\mathbb{Q}_{\geq 0}$ is the set of non-negative rational numbers. After executing the scheduled jobs $s \in S(M, \mathcal{J})$ for $t \in \mathbb{Q}_{\geq 0}$ time, the progress of jobs in $\mathcal{J}$ equals $p' = p + v_s \cdot t$, where $+$ is pointwise addition and $\cdot$ is multiplication by a scalar, i.e., $p'(x) = p(x) + v(x, s^{-1}(x)) \cdot t$ if $x \in \mathrm{im}(s)$ and $p'(x) = p(x)$ otherwise.

Example 2. Let $k > 0$ be a positive integer and $\mathcal{J}$ a set of jobs. Then, $\mathcal{M}_k = (\{1, \ldots, k\}, \mathcal{J}, v)$, with $v(x, i) = 1$ for all $x \in \mathcal{J}$ and $1 \leq i \leq k$, models a parallel machine that consists of k identical processors. Any two processors are identical and interchangeable. Therefore, the scheduled jobs $s \in S(M, \mathcal{J})$ depend solely on the image $\mathrm{im}(s)$. If $s, s' \in S(\{1, \ldots, k\}, \mathcal{J})$ and $\mathrm{im}(s) = \mathrm{im}(s')$, then $v_s = v_{s'}$. Hence, we represent scheduled jobs as a subset $J \subseteq \mathcal{J}$.

Let $\tau = (q, N, w, q')$ be a transition in $\mathcal{A}$ and $p : \mathcal{J} \to \mathbb{Q}_{\geq 0}$ be the current progress of jobs. Recall the notation regarding job constraints from Sect. 2.2. We call a job x *finished* whenever its progress $p(x)$ equals $w_x \in \mathbb{N}_0 \cup \{\infty\}$. We demand that all required jobs $x \in \rho_w$ finish their available work w_x. The automaton $\mathcal{A}$ may take a transition τ if the progress of jobs p satisfies the job constraint w (notation: $p \models w$), i.e., $p(x) \leq w_x$ for all jobs $x \in \mathcal{J}$ and $p(x) = w_x$ for required jobs $x \in \rho_w$. Note that for $\rho_w = \emptyset$, transition τ requires no work, and τ then represents for example the arrival of input data.

Suppose that $p \models w$ and $\mathcal{A}$ takes transition τ. Then, the current state of $\mathcal{A}$ becomes q' and the progress of required jobs resets to zero. Formally, the progress becomes $p' = \overline{\rho_w}(p)$, where $\overline{\rho_w} : \mathbb{N}_0^{\mathcal{J}} \to \mathbb{N}_0^{\mathcal{J}}$ is the *reset operation* associated with ρ_w defined as $\overline{\rho_w}(p)(x) = p(x)$ if $x \notin \rho_w$ and $\overline{\rho_w}(p)(x) = 0$ otherwise.

2.5   Composition

In Sect. 2.3, we extended constraint automata to work automata. We now extend the composition of constraint automata from Sect. 2.1 to work automata.

Let $\mathcal{A}_0$ and $\mathcal{A}_1$ be two work automata. We want our composition of work automata to conservatively extend the composition of constraint automata. This means that the state space, interface and transition relation (up to job constraints) of the composition are already determined. Since a job x in $\mathcal{A}_i$, for $i \in \{0, 1\}$, is merely a name for a piece of work inside $\mathcal{A}_i$, we may rename x to (x, i). This allows us to define the set of jobs of the composition as the disjoint union $\mathcal{J}_0 + \mathcal{J}_1 = \mathcal{J}_0 \times \{0\} \cup \mathcal{J}_1 \times \{1\}$. For $i \in \{0, 1\}$, let $\tau_i = (q_i, N_i, w_i, q_i')$ be a transition in $\mathcal{A}_i$. If $N_0 \cap \mathcal{P}_1 = N_1 \cap \mathcal{P}_0$, then τ_0 and τ_1 synchronize and give rise to a transition $\tau_0 \mid \tau_1 = ((q_0, q_1), N_0 \cup N_1, w_0 \wedge w_1, (q_0', q_1'))$. If τ_0 and τ_1 are independent, i.e., $N_0 \cap P_1 = N_1 \cap P_0 = \emptyset$, then τ_0 and the relaxation $(q_1, \emptyset, w_1^{\leq}, q_1)$ of τ_1, give rise to a transition $\tau_0 \mid \tau_1^{\leq} = ((q_0, q_1), N_0, w_0 \wedge w_1^{\leq}, (q_0', q_1))$ in the composition, where $w_1^{\leq}$ is the job constraint derived from w_1 by substituting every $=$ with $\leq$. This substitution is well-defined, because, according to grammar (1), jobs exclusively appear on the left hand side of an equality. Transition $\tau_0 \mid \tau_1^{\leq}$ represents that τ_0 is taken, while jobs in τ_1 makes arbitrary progress bounded by w_1. We define the a lift $\tau_0^{\leq} \mid \tau_1$ of τ_1 analogously. Finally, if τ_0 is independent of $\mathcal{A}_1$ (i.e., $N_0 \cap P_1 = \emptyset$), then τ_0 gives rise to a transition $((q_0, q_1), N_0, w_0 \wedge \bigwedge_{x \in \mathcal{J}_1} x = 0, (q_0', q_1))$ in the composition, where τ_0 executes independently of $\mathcal{A}_1$ and all jobs in $\mathcal{A}_1$ block. This blocking means that $\mathcal{A}_1$ needs to wait, unless a transition τ_1 in $\mathcal{A}_1$ induces a synchronization $\tau_0 \mid \tau_1$ or $\tau_0 \mid \tau_1^{\leq}$.

Definition 3. *For $i \in \{0, 1\}$, let $\mathcal{A}_i = (Q_i, \mathcal{P}_i, \mathcal{J}_i, \rightarrow_i)$ be a work automaton. We define the composition $\mathcal{A}_0 \bowtie \mathcal{A}_1$ of $\mathcal{A}_0$ and $\mathcal{A}_1$ as the work automaton $(Q_0 \times Q_1, \mathcal{P}_0 \cup \mathcal{P}_1, \mathcal{J}_0 + \mathcal{J}_1, \rightarrow)$, where $\rightarrow$ is the smallest relation satisfying the following rule: if $i \in \{0, 1\}$, $\tau_i = (q_i, N_i, w_i, q_i') \in \rightarrow_i$, $\tau_{1-i} = (q_{1-i}, N_{1-i}, w_{1-i}, q_{1-i}') \in \rightarrow_{1-i} \cup \{(q, \emptyset, \bigwedge_{x \in \mathcal{J}_{1-i}} x = 0, q) \mid q \in Q_{1-i}\}$ and $I := N_0 \cap P_1 = N_1 \cap P_0$, then*

1. $\tau_0 \mid \tau_1 = ((q_0, q_1), N_0 \cup N_1, w_0 \wedge w_1, (q_0', q_1')) \in \rightarrow$; and
2. $I = \emptyset$ implies $\tau_0 \mid \tau_1^{\leq} \in \rightarrow$ and $\tau_0^{\leq} \mid \tau_1 \in \rightarrow$, where $\tau_i^{\leq} = (q_i, \emptyset, w_i^{\leq}, q_i)$.

Example 3. Fig. 2 shows the composition of the work automata from Fig. 1(b) and (c). A state ij indicates that the buffered producer is in state i and the consumer is in state j. In state 00, the consumer cannot retrieve a datum from the buffer. Hence, the consumer is not allowed to work on job y. The transition

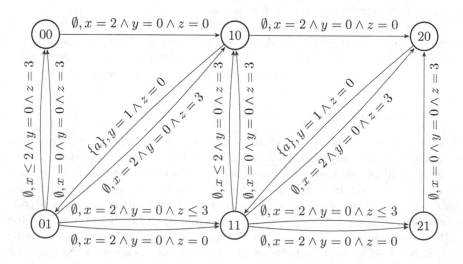

Fig. 2. Composition $\mathcal{A}_{prd} \bowtie \mathcal{A}_{con}$ of the work automata in Fig. 1(b) and (c).

from 01 to 11 with job constraint $x = 2 \wedge y = 0 \wedge z = 3$ is redundant, because the other transition from 01 to 11 has a weaker job constraint $x = 2 \wedge y = 0 \wedge z \leq 3$.

3 Scheduling Games

A work automaton can make non-deterministic internal choices, beyond the control of the scheduler. Therefore, we can view the scheduler synthesis problem over a work automaton and a parallel machine as a game that is played between the scheduler and the application modelled by a work automaton. The scheduler assigns jobs to processors and the application executes the running jobs and, whenever possible, makes a perhaps non-deterministically selected transition. We represent this game as a token game played on a graph that we derive from a work automaton and a parallel machine. Every play of this game (i.e., a path in this graph) corresponds to a run of the work automaton. Hence, a strategy in this game corresponds to a schedule of the corresponding concurrent application. In Sect. 3.1, we recall some basic terminology and known results for games played on graphs. In Sect. 3.2, we interpret the execution of jobs in a work automaton as a game played on a graph. In Sect. 3.3, we assign an execution time to every move in a scheduling game. In Sect. 3.4, we introduce a class of scheduling objectives for both terminating and non-terminating applications. In Sect. 3.5, we find schedules that minimize the number of context-switches.

3.1 Preliminaries on Games on Graphs

We view scheduler synthesis as a problem of finding optimal strategies in a game played on a graph. Therefore, we recall the basic definitions about these games.

A *game arena* is a finite directed bipartite leafless graph A. More formally, A is a triple (V, E, φ) that consists of a finite set of vertices V, a set of edges $\rightarrow \subseteq V \times V$ such that for all $a \in V$ there exists a $b \in V$ with $(a, b) \in E$, and a 2-colouring $\varphi : V \rightarrow \{0, 1\}$, i.e., $(a, b) \in E$ implies $\varphi(a) \neq \varphi(b)$, for all $a, b \in V$. Vertices and edges in this graph are called *positions* and *moves*. For every $a_0 \in V$, consider the following token game on A between Player 0 and Player 1. Let a_0 be the initial position of the token. Construct an infinite sequence $\pi = (a_i)_{i=0}^{\infty}$ as follows: for all $i \geq 0$, Player $\varphi(a_i)$ selects a successor position $a_{i+1} \in V$, with $(a_i, a_{i+1}) \in E$, and moves the token from a_i to a_{i+1}. The sequence π is called a *play* of this game, and plays$(A) \subseteq V^{\omega}$ is the set of all such plays in A. A *game* G is a triple (A, a_0, f), where $A = (V, E, \varphi)$ is a game arena, $a_0 \in V$ is the initial position, and $f : \text{plays}(A) \rightarrow D$ is a *payoff* function, where D is some partially ordered set. The goal of Player 0 is to maximize the value $f(\pi)$, while Player 1 tries to minimize $f(\pi)$. A *strategy* σ_k for Player $k \in \{0, 1\}$ in a game G is a map $\sigma_k : V^* \times V_k \rightarrow V_{1-k}$, such that $(v, \sigma_k(u, a)) \in E$ for all $u \in V^*$ and $a \in V_k$. Intuitively, a strategy σ_k determines the successor position $\sigma_k(u, a) \in V_{1-k}$ of Player k, based on the history u and the current position a. A strategy σ is called *memoryless* if and only if $\sigma(u, a) = \sigma(u', a)$, for all $u, u' \in V^*$ and $a \in V$. A play $\pi = a_0 a_1 \cdots$ is *consistent* with a strategy σ_k for Player k if and only if for all $i \geq 0$ we have that $\varphi(a_i) = k$ implies $a_{i+1} = \sigma_k(a_0 \cdots a_{i-1}, a_i)$.

Example 4 (Mean payoff games [12]). Let $A = (V, E, \varphi)$ be an arena, and let $c : E \to \mathbb{Z}$ be a *weight function*. In Sect. 3.3, we use these weights to represent the execution time of moves. A *mean payoff game* over A and c is a triple $G = (A, a_0, M_c)$, where $a_0 \in V$ is the starting position, and

$$M_c(a_0 a_1 a_2 \cdots) = \liminf_{n \to \infty} \frac{1}{n} \sum_{i=0}^{n-1} c(a_i, a_{i+1}).$$

Intuitively, M_c computes the 'smallest' average value of the play $a_0 a_1 a_2 \cdots$.

3.2 Scheduling Arena

We now formulate the problem of scheduling a concurrent application, represented as a work automaton $\mathcal{A} = (Q, \mathcal{P}, \mathcal{J}, \to)$, onto a set of heterogeneous processors, represented as a parallel machine $\mathcal{M} = (M, \mathcal{J}, v)$. The scheduling problem consists of finding an optimal strategy in a game on a graph played by the scheduler (Player 0) and the application (Player 1). Intuitively, the game is played by alternating moves by the scheduler and the application. A scheduler move selects a schedule $s \in S(M, \mathcal{J})$. Recall the notation for job constraints from Sect. 2.2. An application move selects a transition $\tau = (q, N, w, q')$ that allows scheduled jobs to progress, and then updates the progress $p : \mathcal{J} \to \mathbb{Q}_{\geq 0}$ of the jobs by executing the scheduled jobs s until one of the jobs $x \in \mathcal{J}$ finishes w_x units of work. If after the execution the job constraint w is satisfied, the application makes transition τ. Otherwise, the application makes the 'fictitious' idling transition $\epsilon_q := (q, \emptyset, \top, q)$, where $q \in Q$ is the current state of the automaton.

We now explain the construction of the game arena in more detail. We want every play of this game to correspond to an run of the associated work automaton. Therefore, we record, in every position of the game, the progress of the jobs and the state of the automaton. We define the positions of the scheduler as pairs (p, τ), where $p : \mathcal{J} \to \mathbb{Q}_{\geq 0}$ is the progress of jobs and $\tau = (q, N, w, q') \in \to \cup \{\epsilon_q \mid q \in Q\}$ is the transition that is previously taken by the application (i.e., q' is the current state of the work automaton). We define the positions of the application as triples $[p, q, s]$, where $p : \mathcal{J} \to \mathbb{Q}_{\geq 0}$ is the progress of jobs, $q \in Q$ is the current state of the work automaton and $s \in S(M, \mathcal{J})$ is the set of the scheduled jobs that are selected by the scheduler.

In a position (p, τ), the scheduler may select any assignment $s \in S(M, \mathcal{J})$ of jobs to processors, which corresponds to selecting a successor position $[p, q', s]$. For the definition of application moves, we first define *enabled* transitions. Intuitively, a transition is *enabled* in position $[p_b, q_b, s]$ if its source state is q_b, its job constraint is *potentially* satisfiable (i.e., $p_b(x) \leq w_x$, for all $x \in \mathcal{J}$) and all scheduled jobs s can execute (i.e., $v_s(x) > 0$ implies $p_b(x) < w_x$, for all $x \in \mathcal{J}$).

Definition 4. *We call a transition $\tau = (q, N, w, q')$ enabled at a position $b = [p_b, q_b, s]$ of the application if and only if for all $x \in \mathcal{J}$, we have that $q = q_b$, $p_b(x) \leq w_x$, and $v_s(x) > 0$ implies $p_b(x) < w_x$. We write $\mathcal{E}_b \subseteq \to$ for the set of all transitions that are enabled at b.*

If there is no enabled transition, then the application selects the successor position (p, ϵ_q). Otherwise, the application selects any enabled transition $\lambda = (q, N, w, q') \in \mathcal{E}_b$ and executes its scheduled jobs, until one of them finishes.

Definition 5. *The time to first completion $t_b(\lambda)$ of an enabled transition $\lambda \in \mathcal{E}_b$ at a position $b = [p, q, s]$ is*

$$t_b(\lambda) = \begin{cases} \min \ T_b(\lambda) & \text{if } T_b(\lambda) \neq \emptyset \\ 0 & \text{otherwise} \end{cases},$$

where $T_b(\lambda) = \{t \in \mathbb{Q}_{\geq 0} \mid \exists x \in \mathcal{J} : v_s(x) > 0 \ \text{and} \ p(x) + v_s(x) \cdot t = w_x\}$.

After executing the jobs for $t_b(\lambda)$ units of time, the progress of the jobs becomes $p + v_s \cdot t_b(\lambda)$, which is defined as $(p + v_s \cdot t_b(\lambda))(x) = p(x) + v_s(x) \cdot t_b(\lambda)$, for all $x \in \mathcal{J}$. If the job constraint of λ is satisfied ($p + v_s \cdot t_b(\lambda) \models w$), the application makes transition λ by selecting position $(\overline{\rho_w}(p + v_s \cdot t_b(\lambda)), \lambda)$, where $\overline{\rho_w}$ resets the progress of all finished jobs ρ_w to zero. If the job constraint of λ is not satisfied ($p + v_s \cdot t_b(\lambda) \not\models w$), the application selects position $(p + v_s \cdot t_b(\lambda), \epsilon_q)$.

Definition 6. *A scheduling arena A over a work automaton $(Q, \mathcal{P}, \mathcal{J}, \to)$ and a parallel machine $(M, \mathcal{J}, v)$ is a tuple $A = (V, E, \varphi)$, where $V = V_0 \cup V_1$,*

$$V_0 = \{(p, \tau) \mid p : \mathcal{J} \to \mathbb{Q}_{\geq 0} \ \text{and} \ \tau \in \to \cup \ \{\epsilon_q \mid q \in Q\}\},$$
$$V_1 = \{[p, q, s] \mid p : \mathcal{J} \to \mathbb{Q}_{\geq 0}, \ q \in Q \ \text{and} \ s \in S(M, \mathcal{J})\}$$

are the sets of positions of the scheduler and the application, $\varphi(a) = 0$ if and only if $a \in V_0$, and $E \subseteq V \times V$ is the largest relation that satisfies the following rule: for all $a = (p, \tau) \in V_0$ and $b = [p, q, s] \in V_1$ we have

1. *if $\tau = (-, -, -, q'_\tau)$, then $(a, [p, q'_\tau, s]) \in E$; and*
2. *if $\mathcal{E}_b = \emptyset$, then $(b, (p, \epsilon_q)) \in E$; and*
3. *if $\lambda = (q, N, w, q') \in \mathcal{E}_b$, then*
   (a) *$p + v_s \cdot t_a(\lambda) \models w$ implies $(b, (\overline{\rho_w}(p + v_s \cdot t_a(\lambda)), \lambda)) \in E$; and*
   (b) *$p + v_s \cdot t_a(\lambda) \not\models w$ implies $(b, (p + v_s \cdot t_a(\lambda), \epsilon_q)) \in E$.*

As a scheduling arena A is infinite, it is not an arena as in Sect. 3.1. The following lemma provides a sufficient condition ensuring that A is *locally finite*, i.e., only finitely many positions in the A are reachable from any given position.

Lemma 1. *Let A be a scheduling arena over a work automaton $\mathcal{A}$ and a parallel machine $(M, \mathcal{J}, v)$. If A has finitely many transitions, all job constraints in $\mathcal{A}$ are saturated and all speeds $v(x, i)$ are either zero or u, for some $u \in \mathbb{N}_0$, then only finitely many positions in A are reachable from any given position $a \in A$.*

Proof. For every job $x \in \mathcal{J}$, define $m_x = \max \{w_x \mid w$ is a job constraint in $\mathcal{A}\}$. Since all job constraints are saturated, we have that $|\mathcal{J}| < \infty$ and $m_x < \infty$, for all $x \in \mathcal{J}$. Hence, we find $\alpha \in \mathbb{N}_0$ such that for every job $x \in \mathcal{J}$ the progress $p_a(x)$ of x at a satisfies $\alpha p_a(x) \in \mathbb{N}_0$. Using Definitions 4, 5 and 6, it follows that for every job $x \in \mathcal{J}$ the progress $p_b(x)$ of x at a position $b \in A$ reachable from a satisfies $p_b(x) \in \{p_a(x), 0, \frac{1}{\alpha}, \ldots, \frac{\alpha m_x - 1}{\alpha}, m_x\}$, for all $x \in \mathcal{J}$. We conclude that only finitely many positions in A are reachable from any given position $a \in A$.

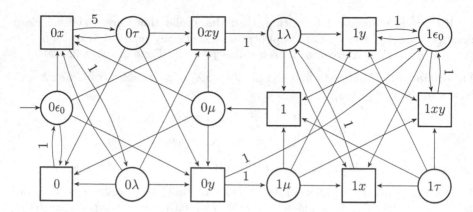

Fig. 3. Scheduling arena over a work automaton $\mathcal{A}$ from Example 5. Circular positions belong to the scheduler position and square positions belong to the application.

Example 5. Consider the work automaton $\mathcal{A} = (\{0\}, \emptyset, \{x, y\}, \{\lambda, \tau, \mu\})$ and parallel machine $\mathcal{M}_2$, where $\lambda = (0, \emptyset, x = 1 \wedge y \leq 1, 0)$, $\tau = (0, \emptyset, x = 5 \wedge y = 0, 0)$ and $\mu = (0, \emptyset, x = 0 \wedge y = 1, 0)$. Figure 3 shows the scheduling arena over $\mathcal{A}$ and $\mathcal{M}_2$ from Example 2 according to Definition 6. A circular position labelled by $k\alpha$, with $k \in \{0, 1\}$ and $\alpha \in \{\epsilon_0, \lambda, \tau, \mu\}$, corresponds to $(p, \alpha) \in V_0$, with $p(x) = 0$ and $p(y) = k$. For $k \in \{0, 1\}$, a square position labeled by k, kx, ky or kxy corresponds to a position $(p, 0, s) \in V_1$ with $p(x) = 0$, $p(y) = k$ and $\mathrm{im}(s) = \emptyset$, $\mathrm{im}(s) = \{x\}$, $\mathrm{im}(s) = \{y\}$ or $\mathrm{im}(s) = \{x, y\}$, respectively.

3.3   Strategies and Classical Schedules

From a given work automaton $\mathcal{A}$ and parallel machine $\mathcal{M}$, we constructed in Sect. 3.2 a scheduling arena A. Suppose that the non-deterministic behaviour of $\mathcal{A}$ is fully controlled by the scheduler, i.e., there is only one move possible at every position $a \in V_1$ of the application. We now argue that strategies in A naturally correspond to classical schedules of concurrent applications.

Since the application has a unique strategy, every strategy σ_0 of the scheduler induces a play π in A. The following definition assigns an execution time to every move in π, which allows us to represent π as a Gantt chart [13].

Definition 7. *The execution time $t(a, b)$ of a move $(a, b) \in E$ in a scheduling arena $A = (V, E, \varphi)$ is*

$$t(a, b) = \begin{cases} t_a(\lambda) & \text{if } (a, b) \in V_1 \times V_0 \text{ comes from } \lambda \in \mathcal{E}_a \\ 1 & \text{if } a = [p, q, s] \in V_1 \text{ and } \mathcal{E}_{[p,q,s']} \neq \emptyset = \mathcal{E}_a \text{ for some } s' \text{.} \\ 0 & \text{otherwise} \end{cases}$$

The case for $t(a, b) = 1$ can be seen as a time penalty for selecting $s \in S(M, \mathcal{J})$ that unnecessarily blocks the execution ($\mathcal{E}_{[p,q,s]} = \emptyset$).

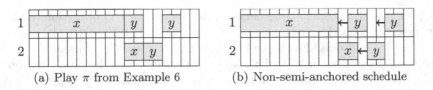

(a) Play π from Example 6   (b) Non-semi-anchored schedule

Fig. 4. Play π from Example 6 (a), and a schedule that is not semi-anchored (b).

Example 6. In the scheduling arena in Fig. 3, consider the play π that is given by $0\epsilon_0, 0x, 0\tau, 0xy, 1\lambda, 1, 0\mu, 0y, 1\mu, 1, 0\mu, 0y, 1\mu, 1y, 1\epsilon_0, 1y, \ldots$. All zeros on the move labels are omitted in this arena. Figure 4(a) shows a Gantt chart representation of π. Note that, since x and y are executed on identical processors $\mathcal{M}_2$, it is not important on which processor x and y are scheduled.

We conclude that every strategy in A naturally induces a classical schedule of the concurrent application. Conversely, not every classical schedule comes from a strategy in such an arena A. According to Definition 6, scheduling strategies induce only *semi-anchored* schedules, i.e., a job can start at time $t + n$, with $t \in \mathbb{Q}_{\geq 0}$ and $1 \leq n \in \mathbb{N}$, only if $t = 0$ or t is a time that some job finishes, and all processors are idle between t and $t + n$. Figure 4(b) shows a schedule that cannot be represented by a strategy in A. However, shifting the executions of all jobs y to the left transforms Fig. 4(b) into an anchored schedule.

We now show that this shifting always produces a valid schedule for A. Let S be a (non-semi-anchored) classical schedule, and $T \subseteq \mathbb{Q}_{\geq 0}$ be the set of all finish times of jobs in S including zero. Let t_s be the start time of a job x with $t_s \notin T$, and $t_f = \max \{t \in T \mid t \leq t_s\}$ the last time a job in S finishes before t_s. Every transition taken by A after t_f was already enabled at time t_f. Thus, shifting the execution of job x from t_s to t_f produces a valid schedule.

We call a scheduling objective *regular*, whenever this shifting operation produces a schedule that is at least as good as the initial schedule. For example, minimizing total execution time is a regular scheduling objective, while scheduling objectives that penalize for jobs that finish 'too early' are not regular.

3.4   Scheduling Games

In this section, we define payoff functions for games played on scheduling graphs that naturally correspond to regular scheduling objectives.

Let $\pi = a_0 a_1 \cdots$ be a play in a scheduling arena $A = (V, E, \varphi)$. Using Definition 7, we associate with every initial prefix $\pi_n = a_0 \cdots a_n$, $n \geq 0$, the total execution time $t_n = \sum_{i=0}^{n-1} t(a_i, a_{i+1})$. If our application terminates, then for every play $\pi = a_0 a_1 \cdots$, the sequence $t_0, t_1, \ldots$ eventually stabilizes, i.e., $t_n = t_m$, for some n and all $m \geq n$. Then, t_n represents the total execution time of π. If our application does not always terminate, then we cannot associate with every play π its total execution time. An example of such an application is a streaming application (cf., Sect. 4). A natural scheduling objective in a streaming application is latency minimization at some output port $o \in \mathcal{P}$. We define the latency at a port o as the average time between two successive I/O operations on o. To keep track of these I/O operations, we use a map $\theta_o : E \rightarrow \{0,1\}$, such that $\theta_o(a,b) = 1$ if and only if $b = (p,\tau) \in V_0$, where $\tau = (q,N,w,q')$ and $o \in N$. For a prefix $\pi_n = a_0 \cdots a_n$, $n \geq 0$, of π, we define the *latency* as the ratio between the total execution time t_n and the number of I/O operations $1 + \sum_{i=0}^{n-1} \theta_o(a_i, a_{i+1})$.

By varying $\theta : E \rightarrow \{0,1\}$, we define the following class of scheduling games, called *latency games*, wherein Player k maximizes the 'smallest limiting ratio'. Recall the definition of locally finite scheduling arena's from Sect. 3.2.

Definition 8. *Let $A = (V, E, \varphi)$ be a locally finite scheduling arena, $\theta : E \rightarrow \{0,1\}$ a map, and $k \in \{0,1\}$. A latency game G for Player k over A and θ is a tuple $G = (A, a_0, T_\theta^k)$, where a_0 is an initial position and*

$$T_\theta^k(a_0 a_1 \cdots) = \liminf_{n \to \infty} \frac{(-1)^k}{1 + \sum_{i=0}^{n-1} \theta(a_i, a_{i+1})} \sum_{i=0}^{n-1} t(a_i, a_{i+1}), \qquad (2)$$

where $t : E \rightarrow \mathbb{N}_0$ is the execution time from Definition 7.

Example 7 (Makespan games: T_0^1). Let θ be the map $0 : E \rightarrow \{0,1\}$, given by $0(a,b) = 0$, for all $(a,b) \in E$, and $k = 1$. The scheduling objective in the latency game over θ and k is given by $T_0^1 = \liminf_{n\to\infty} -\sum_{i=0}^{n-1} t(a_i, a_{i+1})$. Recall from Sect. 3.1 that Player 0 wants to maximize T_0^1, which corresponds to minimizing the total execution time $-T_0^1 = \limsup_{n\to\infty} \sum_{i=0}^{n-1} t(a_i, a_{i+1})$.

Example 8 (Context-switches: T_1^0). Due to changes in the assignment of jobs to processors, context-switches may occur. Typically, context-switches inflict substantial overhead and their occurrences should be avoided. This scheduling objective can be seen as a latency game, where $k = 0$ and θ is the map $1 : E \rightarrow \{0,1\}$, given by $1(a,b) = 1$, for all $(a,b) \in E$. Then, the scheduling objective becomes $T_1^0 = \liminf_{n\to\infty} \frac{1}{n+1} \sum_{i=0}^{n-1} t(a_i, a_{i+1})$, which can be interpreted as maximizing the average time between two consecutive context-switches. Indeed, every move by the application executes all scheduled jobs until at least one of them finishes. The job that finishes should subsequently be descheduled (context-switch), to avoid suboptimal use of compute resources (i.e., idling).

Note that $\lim_{n\to\infty} \frac{n+1}{n} = 1$ implies that the scheduling objective T_1^0 coincides with the payoff function of the mean payoff games in Example 4.

Example 9 (Latency at o: $T_{\theta_o}^1$). Let $\mathcal{A}$ be a work automaton with a port $o \in \mathcal{P}$, and let $A = (V, E, \varphi)$ be a scheduling arena over $\mathcal{A}$ and some parallel machine. Using Definition 6, we can identify the moves in the scheduling arena that come from a transition that requires an I/O operation on port o. Thus, let $\theta_o : E \rightarrow \{0,1\}$ be given by $\theta_o(a,b) = 1$ if and only if $b = (p,\tau) \in V_0$, where $\tau = (q,N,w,q')$ and $o \in N$. The scheduling objective $T_{\theta_o}^1$ corresponds to maximizing the production rate at port o.

3.5   Optimal Strategies

In Sect. 3.4, we viewed the scheduling problem as a game played on a graph. We now take advantage of the fact that these games have been extensively studied in the literature. To do this, we need some terminology about games on graphs. Let G be a game over an arena A, with initial position $a_0 \in A$, and payoff function $f : \text{plays}(A) \to D$, for some partially ordered set D of values. A strategy σ_k for Player $k \in \{0, 1\}$ *secures* a value $v \in D$ whenever $(-1)^k f(\pi) \geq (-1)^k v$, for every play $\pi \in \text{plays}(A)$ consistent with σ_k. Intuitively, this means that if Player k uses strategy σ_k then the value $f(\pi)$ of any resulting play is not worse than v. Now, there exists an optimal strategy for Player k, whenever the maximum value $v_k(G) = \max\{(-1)^k v \mid \text{some } \sigma_k \text{ secures } v\}$ exists. The game G is *determined*, whenever $v_0(G)$ and $v_1(G)$ exist and are equal.

Theorem 1. *The latency game for $\theta = 1$ is memorylessly determined, and a memoryless optimal strategy can be found for it in $\mathcal{O}(|V|^2 \cdot |E| \cdot \log(|V| \cdot T) \cdot T)$ time, with $T = \max_{(a,b) \in E} u \cdot t(a,b)$ and u the speed of the processors.*

Proof. For $\theta = 1$, a latency game coincides with a mean payoff game (cf., Example 8). Ehrenfeucht and Mycielski show that mean payoff games are memorylessly determined [12]. Brim et al. provide a pseudopolynomial time algorithm for finding an optimal memoryless strategy [7].

In view of Example 8, the result of Theorem 1 shows that there exists an optimal strategy (determinacy) of good quality (memoryless) for maximizing the average time between two consecutive context-switches. For optimal play, the scheduler need not remember earlier scheduling decisions. Moreover, such an optimal strategy can be efficiently computed from the scheduling arena.

4   Cyclo-Static Dataflow

In a streaming application, a network of filters transforms an input stream of data into an output stream. Examples of such applications range from video decoding to sorting algorithms. A streaming application can be formally represented by a *cyclo-static dataflow* (CSDF) graph. Bamakhrama and Stefanov proposed a framework for scheduling CSDF graphs that are annotated with worst-case execution times [4]. In this section, we argue that our proposed scheduling framework of Sect. 3 subsumes this scheduling framework for CSDF graphs.

Consider the CSDF graph in Fig. 5(a), wherein four filter processes A_1, A_2, A_3 and A_4, called *actors*, are connected by FIFO buffers. The behaviour of an actor consists of a periodic sequence of execution steps, whose worst-case execution time is represented the value (μ_i) at A_i, for $i \in \{1, 2, 3, 4\}$. In each step, an actor atomically consumes tokens from its input buffers and produces tokens for its output buffers. The production and consumption rates of an actor A_i with period n are determined by vectors $[x_1, \ldots, x_n]$ (Sect. 3.1 in [4]).

Bamakhrama and Stefanov generate from a CSDF graph with worst-case execution times a strictly periodic task set (Example 3 in [4]), by determining

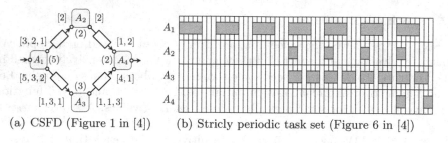

(a) CSFD (Figure 1 in [4])   (b) Stricly periodic task set (Figure 6 in [4])

Fig. 5. Cyclo-static dataflow model (a) and strictly periodic task set (b).

for every filter A_i, a starting time $S_i \in \mathbb{N}_0$ and a period $T_i \in \mathbb{N}_0$ such that all required input tokens are available for all execution steps of all actors and all buffers need only a finite capacity throughout the execution. Figure 5(b) shows the strictly periodic task-set of the CSDF graph in Fig. 5(a). Bamakhrama and Stefanov then use standard scheduling algorithms for strictly periodic task set to compute a schedule S for this CSDF graph (cf., Sect. 3.2.2 in [4]).

Every actor A_i, with $i \in \{1, 2, 3, 4\}$, can be represented as a work automaton over a single job x_i, and every buffer can be represented as a work automaton without jobs. Using the composition operator from Sect. 2.5, we find a work automaton $\mathcal{A}$ that describes the behaviour of the CSFD graph in Fig. 5(a). The behaviour of $\mathcal{A}$ is fully under the control of the scheduler. Hence, Sect. 3.3 shows that, for regular scheduling objectives, the schedule S obtained in [4] induces a strategy in the scheduling arena A over $\mathcal{A}$ and $\mathcal{M}_4$.

We conclude that, for regular scheduling objectives, a schedule induced by an optimal scheduling strategy in a scheduling game is not worse than any schedule found by the scheduling framework proposed by Bamakhrama and Stefanov.

5 Discussion

We extended constraint automata with job constraints to model the work of processes in a concurrent application. We recognize that scheduling decisions do not completely determine the execution of a concurrent application, and therefore view scheduler synthesis as playing a game on a graph between a scheduler and the application. We introduced a class of natural scheduling objectives, and applied game-theoretic results for mean payoff games to find a scheduling strategy that maximizes the time between subsequent context-switches.

Work automata are similar to timed automata [1]. Clock constraints and clock valuations correspond to job constraints and progress of jobs. Still, there are two main differences between them. First, we reset only required jobs in work automata, while in timed automata clocks can reset at any time. Second, we allow jobs to make progress at different speeds, while clocks in timed automata increment uniformly. Using this clock-speed relaxation, the scheduler controls the execution rate of each job by selecting which jobs to schedule. Using our notion of jobs, it seems possible to represent the execution of a concurrent application on a set of processors by means of hybrid automata [14] or hybrid constraint automata [9]. However, since such a representation convolutes the specification of the application with the specification of the parallel machine, hybrid (constraint) automata are unsuitable for our purpose.

Scheduler synthesis for concurrent applications is similar to controller synthesis for real-time systems [5,6,8,17], because the non-deterministic behaviour of a real-time system, modeled as a timed automaton [1], is not fully determined by its controller. Therefore, the controller synthesis problem is formulated as a game on the automaton that is played between the controller and an adversary. However, our problem differs from controller synthesis in that scheduler synthesis requires a strong relation between processes and processors.

The size of a composed work automaton for a whole application very quickly becomes too large. Moreover, the size of a scheduling arena is again much larger than that of the work automaton. Nevertheless, an optimal strategy in such an immense game may indeed have a very simple form (like balancing production and consumption rates in buffers). One direction for our future work is to investigate under what conditions it is possible to bypass these exponential blow-ups. The existence of efficient solutions for more restricted scheduling problems (e.g., CSDF programs [4]) leads us to believe that it is possible to find such conditions.

References

1. Alur, R., Dill, D.L.: A theory of timed automata. Theor. Comput. Sci. **126**, 183–235 (1994)
2. Arbab, F.: Puff, the magic protocol. In: Agha, G., Danvy, O., Meseguer, J. (eds.) Formal Modeling: Actors, Open Systems, Biological Systems. LNCS, vol. 7000, pp. 169–206. Springer, Heidelberg (2011)
3. Baier, C., Sirjani, M., Arbab, F., Rutten, J.: Modeling component connectors in Reo by constraint automata. Sci. Comput. Programming **61**(2), 75–113 (2006)
4. Bamakhrama, M.A., Stefanov, T.P.: On the hard-real-time scheduling of embedded streaming applications. Des. Autom. Embed. Syst. **17**(2), 221–249 (2013)
5. Bouyer, P., Cassez, F., Fleury, E., Larsen, K.G.: Optimal strategies in priced timed game automata. In: Lodaya, K., Mahajan, M. (eds.) FSTTCS 2004. LNCS, vol. 3328, pp. 148–160. Springer, Heidelberg (2004)
6. Bouyer, P., Cassez, F., Fleury, E., Larsen, K.G.: Synthesis of optimal strategies using hytech. Electron. Notes Theor. Comput. Sci. **119**(1), 11–31 (2005)
7. Brim, L., Chaloupka, J., Doyen, L., Gentilini, R., Raskin, J.F.: Faster algorithms for mean-payoff games. Form. Method. Syst. Des. **38**(2), 97–118 (2011)
8. Cassez, F., David, A., Fleury, E., Larsen, K.G., Lime, D.: Efficient on-the-fly algorithms for the analysis of timed games. In: Abadi, M., de Alfaro, L. (eds.) CONCUR 2005. LNCS, vol. 3653, pp. 66–80. Springer, Heidelberg (2005)
9. Chen, X., Sun, J., Sun, M.: A hybrid model of connectors in cyber-physical systems. In: Merz, S., Pang, J. (eds.) ICFEM 2014. LNCS, vol. 8829, pp. 59–74. Springer, Heidelberg (2014)
10. Crovella, M., Frangioso, R., Harchol-Balter, M.: Connection scheduling in web servers. Proc. USITS **10**, 243–254 (1999)

11. Droste, M., Kuich, W., Vogler, H. (eds.): Handbook of Weighted Automata. Monographs in Theoretical Computer Science. An EATCS Series. Springer Science & Business Media, Heidelberg (2009)
12. Ehrenfeucht, A., Mycielski, J.: Positional strategies for mean payoff games. Int. J. Game Theory **8**(2), 109–113 (1979)
13. Gantt, H.L.: Work, Wages, and Profits. Engineering Magazine Co., New York (1913)
14. Henzinge, T.A.: The theory of hybrid automata. Verification of Digital and Hybrid Systems. NATO ASI Series. Springer, Heidelberg (2000)
15. Jha, N.K.: Low power system scheduling and synthesis. In: Proceedings of ICCAD, pp. 259–263. IEEE (2001)
16. Koehler, C., Clarke, D.: Decomposing port automata. In: Proceedings of SAC, pp. 1369–1373. ACM (2009)
17. Maler, O., Pnueli, A., Sifakis, J.: On the synthesis of discrete controllers for timed systems. In: Mayr, Ernst W., Puech, C. (eds.) STACS 1995. LNCS, vol. 900, pp. 229–242. Springer, Heidelberg (1995)
18. Thies, W., Karczmarek, M., Amarasinghe, S.: StreamIt: a language for streaming applications. In: Nigel Horspool, R. (ed.) CC 2002. LNCS, vol. 2304, pp. 179–196. Springer, Heidelberg (2002)

ParT: An Asynchronous Parallel Abstraction for Speculative Pipeline Computations

Kiko Fernandez-Reyes[(✉)], Dave Clarke, and Daniel S. McCain

Department of Information Technology, Uppsala University, Uppsala, Sweden
kiko.fernandez@it.uu.se

Abstract. The ubiquity of multicore computers has forced programming language designers to rethink how languages express parallelism and concurrency. This has resulted in new language constructs and new combinations or revisions of existing constructs. In this line, we extended the programming languages Encore (actor-based), and Clojure (functional) with an asynchronous parallel abstraction called ParT, a data structure that can dually be seen as a collection of asynchronous values (integrating with futures) or a handle to a parallel computation, plus a collection of combinators for manipulating the data structure. The combinators can express parallel pipelines and speculative parallelism. This paper presents a typed calculus capturing the essence of ParT, abstracting away from details of the Encore and Clojure programming languages. The calculus includes tasks, futures, and combinators similar to those of Orc but implemented in a non-blocking fashion. Furthermore, the calculus strongly mimics how ParT is implemented, and it can serve as the basis for adaptation of ParT into different languages and for further extensions.

1 Introduction

The ubiquity of multicore computers has forced programming language designers to rethink how languages express parallelism and concurrency. This has resulted in new language constructs that, for instance, increase the degree of asynchrony while exploiting parallelism. A promising direction is programming languages with constructs for tasks and actors, such as Clojure and Scala [8,16], due to the lightweight overhead of spawning parallel computations. These languages offer coarse-grained parallelism at the task and actor level, where futures act as synchronisation points. However, these languages are lacking in high-level coordination constructs over these asynchronous computations. For instance, it is not easy to express dependence on the first result returned via a bunch of futures and to safely terminate the computations associated with the other futures. The task of terminating speculative parallelism is quite delicate, as the futures

---

Partly funded by the EU project FP7-612985 UPSCALE: From Inherent Concurrency to Massive Parallelism through Type-based Optimisations.

A. Lluch Lafuente and J. Proença (Eds.): COORDINATION 2016, LNCS 9686, pp. 101–120, 2016.
DOI: 10.1007/978-3-319-39519-7_7

may have attached parallel computations that depend on other futures, creating complex dependency patterns that need to be tracked down and terminated.

To address this need, this paper presents the design and implementation of ParT, a non-blocking abstraction that asynchronously exploits futures and enables the developer to build complex, data parallel coordination workflows using high-level constructs. These high-level constructs are derived from the combinators of the orchestration language Orc [11,12]. ParT is formally expressed in terms of a calculus that, rather than being at a high level of abstraction, strongly mimics how this asynchronous abstraction is implemented and is general enough to be applied to programming languages with notions of futures.

The contributions of the paper are as follows: the design of an asynchronous parallel data abstraction to coordinate complex workflows, including pipeline and speculative parallelism, *and* a typed, non-blocking calculus modelling this abstraction, which integrates futures, tasks and Orc-like combinators, supports the separation of the realisation of parallelism (via tasks) from its specification, and offers a novel approach to terminating speculative parallelism.

2   Overview

To set the scene for this paper, we begin with a brief overview to asynchronous computations with futures and provide an informal description of the ParT abstraction and its combinators. A SAT solver example is used as an illustration.

In languages with notions of tasks and active objects [2,8,16], asynchronous computations are created by spawning tasks or calling methods on active objects. These computations can exploit parallelism by decoupling the execution of the caller and the callee [7]. The result of a spawn or method call is immediately a future, a container that will eventually hold the result of the asynchronous computation. A future that has received a value is said to be *fulfilled*. Operations on futures may be blocking, such as getting the result from a future, or may be asynchronous, such as attaching a callback to a future. This second operation, called *future chaining* and represented by $f \leadsto callback$, immediately returns a new future, which will contain the result of applying the callback function *callback* to the contents of the original future after it has been fulfilled. A future can also be thought of as a handle to an asynchronous computation that can be extended via future chaining or even terminated. This is an useful perspective that we will further develop in this work. In languages with notions of actors, such as Clojure and Encore [2], asynchrony is the rule and blocking on futures suffers a large performance penalty. But creating complex coordination patterns based on a collection of asynchronous computations without blocking threads (to maintain the throughput of the system) is no easy task.

To address this need, we have designed an abstraction, called ParT, which can be thought of as a handle to an ongoing parallel computation, allowing the parallel computation to be manipulated, extended, and terminated. A ParT is a functional data structure, represented by type $Par\ t$, that can be empty $\{\} :: Par\ t$, contain a single expression $\{-\} :: t \rightarrow Par\ t$, or futures attached to computations producing values, using $(-)^\circ :: Fut\ t \to Par\ t$, or computations producing ParTs, embedded using $(-)^\dagger :: Fut\ (Par\ t) \to Par\ t$. Multiple ParTs can be combined using the par constructor, $\| :: Par\ t \to Par\ t \to Par\ t$. This constructor does not necessarily create new parallel threads of control, as this would likely have a negative impact on performance, but rather specifies that parallelism is available. The scheduler in the ParT implementation can choose to spawn new tasks as it sees fit — this is modelled in the calculus as a single rule that nondeterministically spawns a task from a par (rule RED-SCHEDULE).

The combinators can express complex coordination patterns and operate on them in a non-blocking manner, and safely terminate speculative parallelism even in the presence of complex workflows. These combinators will be illustrated using an example, then explained in more detail.

Illustrative Example. Consider a portfolio-based SAT solver (Fig. 1), which creates numerous strategies, of which each finds an assignment of variables to Boolean values for a given proposition, runs them in parallel, and accepts the first solution found. Each strategy tries to find a solution by selecting a variable and creating two instances of the formula, one where the variable is assigned true, the other where it is assigned false (called splitting) — strategies differ in the order they select variables for splitting. These new instances can potentially be solved in parallel.

The example starts in function **process** (line 20) which receives an array of strategies and the formula to solve. Strategies do not interact with each other and can be lifted to a ParT, creating a parallel pipeline (line 21) using the **each**

```
1    def fut2Par(f: Fut(Maybe a)): Par a
2      (f ~> \(m: Maybe a) ->
3            match m with Nothing => {}; Just val => {val})†
4
5    def evaluateFormula(form: Formula, a: Assignment): (Maybe bool, Assignment)
6      ...
7
8    def sat(st: Strategy, fml: Formula, a: Assignment): Par Assignment
9      let variable = st.getVariable(fml, a)
10         a1 = a.extendAssignment(variable, true)
11         a2 = a.extendAssignment(variable, false)
12     in
13         ({evaluateFormula(fml, a1)} || {evaluateFormula(fml, a2)}) >>=
14             \(result: (Maybe bool, Assignment)) ->
15                 match result with
16                     (Nothing, ar) => sat(st, fml, ar);
17                     (Just true, ar) => {ar};
18                     (Just false, ar) => {};
19
20   def process(sts: [Strategy], fml: Formula): Par Assignment
21     fut2Par << (each(sts) >>= \(s: Strategy) ->
22                 (async sat(s, fml, new Assignment())))†
```

Fig. 1. A SAT solver in Encore.

and bind ($\ggeq$) combinators. As soon as one strategy finds an assignment, the remaining computations are terminated via the prune ($\ll$) combinator.

For each strategy, a call to the sat function (line 8) is made in parallel using a call to async, which in this case returns a value of type $Fut\ (Par\ \mathtt{Assignment})$. Function sat takes three arguments: a strategy, a formula and an assignment object containing the current mapping from variables to values. This function uses the strategy object to determine which variable to split next, extends the assignment with new valuations (lines 9–11), recursively solves the formula (by again calling sat), and returns an assignment object if successful. The evaluation of the formula, evaluateFormula returns, firstly, an optional Boolean to indicate whether evaluation has completed, and if it has completed, whether the formula is satisfiable, and secondly, the current (partial) variable assignment. The two calls to evaluateFormula are grouped into a new ParT collection (using ||) and, with the use of the $\ggeq$ combinator, a new asynchronous pipeline is created to either further evaluate the formula by calling sat, to return the assignment in the case that a formula is satisfiable as a singleton ParT, or {} when the assignment does not satisfy the formula (lines 14–18).

Finally, returning back to process, the prune combinator ($\ll$) (line 21) is used to select the first result returned by the recursive calls to sat, if there is one. This result is converted from an option type to an empty or singleton ParT collection (again asynchronously), which can then be used in a larger parallel operation, if so desired. The prune combinator will begin poisoning and safely terminating the no longer needed parallel computations, which in this case will be an ongoing parallel pipeline of calls to sat and evaluateFormula.

ParT Combinators. The combinators are now described in detail. The combinators manipulate ParT collections and were derived from Orc [11,12], although in our setting, they are typed and redefined to be completely asynchronous, never blocking the thread. Primitive combinators express coordination patterns such as pipeline and speculative parallelism, and more complex patterns can be expressed based on these primitives.

Pipeline parallelism is expressed in ParT with the sequence and bind combinators. The sequence combinator, $\gg\ ::\ Par\ t \to (t \to t') \to Par\ t'$, takes a ParT collection and applies the function to each element in the collection, potentially in parallel, returning a new ParT collection. The bind combinator (derived from other combinators) $\ggeq\ ::\ Par\ t \to (t \to Par\ t') \to Par\ t'$ is similar to the sequence combinator, except that the function returns a ParT collection and the resulting nested ParT collection is flattened. (Par is a monad![1]) In the presence of futures inside a ParT collection, these combinators use the future chaining operation to create independent and asynchronous pipelines of work.

Speculative parallelism is realised by the peek combinator, $\mathtt{peek}\ ::\ Par\ t \to Fut\ (Maybe\ t)$, which sets up a speculative computation, asynchronously waits for a single result to be produced, and then safely terminates the speculative work. To terminate speculative work the ParT abstraction poison these specu-

---

[1] The monad operations on Par are essentially the same as for lists but parallelised.

lative computations, which may have long parallel pipelines to which the poison spreads recursively, producing a pandemic infection among futures, tasks and pipelines of computations. Afterwards, poisoned computations that are no longer needed can safely be terminated. Metaphorically, this is analogous to a tracing garbage collector.

The value produced by peek is a future to an option type. The option type is used to capture whether the parallel collection was empty or not. The empty collection {} results in Nothing, and a non-empty collection results in a Just v, where v is the first value produced. The conversion to option type is required because ParTs cannot be tested for emptiness without blocking. The peek combinator is an internal combinator, i.e., it is not available to the developer and is used by the prune ≪ combinator (explained below).

Built on top of peek is the prune combinator, ≪ :: $(Fut\ (Maybe\ t) \rightarrow Par\ t') \rightarrow Par\ t \rightarrow Par\ t'$, which applies a function in parallel to the future produced by peek, and returns a parallel computation.

Powerful combinators can be derived from the ones mentioned above. An example of a derived combinator, which is a primitive in Orc, is the otherwise combinator, ⋉ :: $Par\ t \rightarrow Par\ t \rightarrow Par\ t$ (derivation is shown in Sect. 3.1). Expression $e_1 ⋉ e_2$ results in e_1 unless it is an empty ParT, in which case it results in e_2.

Other ParT combinators are available. For instance, each :: $[t] \rightarrow Par\ t$ and extract :: $Par\ t \rightarrow [t]$ convert between sequential (arrays) and ParTs. The latter potentially requires a lot of synchronisation, as all the values in the collection need to be realised. Both have been omitted from the formalism, because neither presents any real technical challenge — the key properties of the formalism, namely, deadlock-freedom, type preservation and task safety (Sect. 3.5), still hold with these extensions in place.

3   A Typed ParT Calculus

This section presents the operational semantics and type system of a task-based language containing the ParT abstraction. The formal model is roughly based on the Encore formal semantics [2,5], with many irrelevant details omitted.

3.1   Syntax

The core language (Fig. 2) contains expressions e and values v. Values include constants c, variables, futures f, lambda abstractions, and ParT collections of values. Expressions include values v, function application $(e\ e)$, task creation, future chaining, and parallel combinators. Tasks are created via the async expression, which returns a future. The parallel combinators are those covered in Sect. 2 (||, ≫, peek and ≪), plus some derived combinators, together with the low-level combinator join that flattens nested ParT collections. Recall that peek is used under-the-hood in the implementation of ≪. Status π controls how peek behaves: when π is ⊘ and the result in peek is an empty ParT collection, the value is discarded and not written to the corresponding future. This status helps to ensure that precisely one speculative computation writes into the future and that a speculative computation fails to produce a value only when all relevant tasks fail to produce a value.

$$e ::= v \mid e\; e \mid \textbf{async}\; e \mid e \rightsquigarrow e \mid \{e\} \mid e \,\|\, e$$
$$\mid\; e \gg e \mid e \ll e \mid e^{\circ} \mid e^{\dagger} \mid \textbf{join}\; e \mid \textbf{peek}^{\pi}\; e$$
$$v ::= c \mid f \mid x \mid \lambda x.e \mid \{\} \mid \{v\} \mid f^{\circ} \mid f^{\dagger} \mid v \,\|\, v$$
$$\pi ::= \_ \mid \oslash$$

Fig. 2. Syntax of the language.

ParT collections are monoids, meaning that the composition operation $e \,\|\, e$ is associative and has $\{\}$ as its unit. As such, ParT collections are sequences, though no operations such as getting the first element are available to access them sequentially. As an alternative, adding in commutativity of $\|$ would give multiset semantics to the ParT collections — the operational semantics is otherwise unchanged. Two for one!

A number of the constructs are defined by translation into other constructs.

$$\textbf{let}\; x = e \;\textbf{in}\; e' \; \hat{=} \; (\lambda x.e')\; e$$
$$e_1 \times e_2 \; \hat{=} \; \textbf{let}\; x = e_1 \;\textbf{in}$$
$$(\lambda y.(y \rightsquigarrow (\lambda z.\texttt{match}\; z \;\texttt{with}\; \texttt{Nothing} \rightarrow e_2;\; \_ \rightarrow x))^{\dagger}) \ll x$$
$$e_1 \ggg e_2 \; \hat{=} \; \textbf{join}\; (e_1 \gg e_2)$$
$$\texttt{maybe2par} \; \hat{=} \; \lambda x.\texttt{match}\; x \;\texttt{with}\; \texttt{Nothing} \rightarrow \{\};\; \texttt{Just}\; y \rightarrow \{y\}$$

The encoding of $\texttt{let}$ is standard. In $e_1 \times e_2$, pruning $\ll$ is used to test the emptyness of e_1. If it is not empty, the result of e_1 is returned, otherwise the result is e_2. The definition of $\ggg$ is a standard definition of monadic bind in terms of map ($\gg$) and join. We assume for convenience a Maybe type and pattern matching on it.

3.2   Configurations

Running programs are represented by configurations (Fig. 3). Configurations can refer to the global system or a partial view of the system. A global configuration $\{config\}$ captures the complete global state, e.g., $\{(\texttt{fut}_f)\; (\texttt{task}_f\; e)\}$ shows a global system containing a single task running expression e. Local configurations, written as $config$, show a partial view of the state of the program. These are multisets of tasks, futures, poison and future chains. The empty configuration is represented by ϵ. Future configurations, $(\texttt{fut}_f)$ and $(\texttt{fut}_f\; v)$, represent unfulfilled and fulfilled futures, respectively. Poison is the configuration $(\texttt{poison}\; f)$ that will eventually terminate tasks and chains writing to future f and their dependencies. A running task $(\texttt{task}_f^{\alpha}\; e)$ has a body e and will write its result to future f. The chain configuration ($\mathtt{chain}_f^\alpha\ g\ e$) depends on future g that, when fulfilled, will then run expression e on the value stored in g, and write its value into future f. Concatenation of configurations, *config config'*, is associative and commutative with the empty configuration ϵ as its unit (Fig. 12).

$$gconfig ::= \{config\}$$
$$config ::= \epsilon \mid (\mathtt{fut}_f) \mid (\mathtt{fut}_f\ v) \mid (\mathtt{poison}\ f) \mid (\mathtt{task}_f^\alpha\ e) \mid (\mathtt{chain}_f^\alpha\ g\ e) \mid config\ config$$
$$\alpha ::= {}_{\llcorner} \mid \text{⋔}$$

Fig. 3. Runtime configurations.

Tasks and chains have a flag α that indicates the poisoned state of the computation. Whitespace '$_{\llcorner}$' indicates that the computation has not been poisoned, and ⋔ indicates that the computation has been poisoned and can be safely terminated, if it is not needed (see Rule RED-TERMINATE of Fig. 10).

The initial configuration to evaluate expression e is $\{(\mathtt{task}_f\ e)\ (\mathtt{fut}_f)\}$, where the value written into future f is the result of the expression.

3.3 Reduction Rules

The operational semantics is based on a small-step, reduction-context based rules for evaluation within tasks, and parallel reduction rules for evaluation across configurations. Evaluation is captured by expression-level evaluation context E containing a hole • that marks where the next step of the reduction will occur (Fig. 4). Plugging an expression e into an evaluation context E, denoted $E[e]$, represents both the subexpression to be evaluated next and the result of reducing that subexpression in context, in the standard fashion [21].

$$E ::= \bullet \mid E\ e \mid v\ E \mid E \rightsquigarrow e \mid v \rightsquigarrow E \mid \{E\} \mid E \| e \mid v \| E \mid E \gg e \mid v \gg E$$
$$\mid E \ll e \mid E^\circ \mid E^\dagger \mid \mathtt{join}\ E \mid \mathtt{peek}^\pi E$$

Fig. 4. Expression-level evaluation contexts.

Reduction of configurations is denoted *config* → *config'*, which states that *config* reduces in a single step to *config'*.

Core Expressions. The core reduction rules (Fig. 5) for functions, tasks and futures are well-known or derived from earlier work [5]. Together, the rules RED-CHAIN and RED-CHAINV describe how future chaining works, initially attaching a closure to a future (via the chain configuration), then evaluating the closure in a new task after the future has been fulfilled.

$$(\text{Red-}\beta\text{-Red})$$
$$(\text{task}_g^\alpha \ E[(\lambda x.e)\ v]) \to (\text{task}_g^\alpha \ E[e[v/x]])$$

$$(\text{Red-Async})$$
$$\textit{fresh } f$$
$$(\text{task}_g^\alpha \ E[\text{async } e]) \to (\text{fut}_f)\ (\text{task}_f^\alpha \ e)\ (\text{task}_g^\alpha \ E[f])$$

$$(\text{Red-FutV})$$
$$(\text{task}_f^\alpha \ v)\ (\text{fut}_f) \to (\text{fut}_f \ v)$$

$$(\text{Red-Chain})$$
$$\textit{fresh } h$$
$$(\text{task}_g^\alpha \ E[f \rightsquigarrow v]) \to (\text{fut}_h)\ (\text{chain}_h^\alpha \ f\ v)\ (\text{task}_g^\alpha \ E[h])$$

$$(\text{Red-ChainV})$$
$$(\text{chain}_g^\alpha \ f\ e)\ (\text{fut}_f \ v) \to (\text{task}_g^\alpha \ (e\ v))\ (\text{fut}_f \ v)$$

Fig. 5. Core reduction rules.

$$(\text{Red-SeqS})$$
$$(\text{task}_g^\alpha \ E[\{\} \gg v]) \to (\text{task}_g^\alpha \ E[\{\}])$$

$$(\text{Red-SeqV})$$
$$(\text{task}_g^\alpha \ E[\{v\} \gg v']) \to (\text{task}_g^\alpha \ E[\{v'\ v\}])$$

$$(\text{Red-SeqF})$$
$$(\text{task}_g^\alpha \ E[f^\circ \gg v]) \to (\text{task}_g^\alpha \ E[(f \rightsquigarrow v)^\circ])$$

$$(\text{Red-SeqFP})$$
$$(\text{task}_g^\alpha \ E[f^\dagger \gg v]) \to (\text{task}_g^\alpha \ E[(f \rightsquigarrow (\lambda x.x \gg v))^\dagger])$$

$$(\text{Red-SeqP})$$
$$(\text{task}_g^\alpha \ E[(v_1 \mathbin{||} v_2) \gg v]) \to (\text{task}_g^\alpha \ E[(v_1 \gg v) \mathbin{||} (v_2 \gg v)])$$

Fig. 6. Reduction rules for the sequence $\gg$ combinator.

Sequencing. The sequencing combinator $\gg$ creates pipeline parallelism. Its semantics are defined inductively on the structure of ParT collections (Fig. 6). The second argument must be a function (tested in function application, but guaranteed by the type system). In Red-SeqS, sequencing an empty ParT results in another empty ParT. A ParT with a value applies the function immediately (Red-SeqV). A lifted future is asynchronously accessed by chaining the function onto it (Red-SeqF). Rule Red-SeqP recursively applies $\gg v$ to the two sub-collections. A future whose content is a ParT collection chains a recursive call to $\gg v$ onto the future and lifts the result back into a ParT collection (Red-SeqFP).

Join. The `join` combinator flattens nested ParT collections of type $Par\ (Par\ t)$ (Fig. 7). Empty collections flatten to empty collections (Red-JoinS). Rule Red-JoinV extracts the singleton value from a collection. A lifted future that contains a ParT (type $Fut\ (Par\ t)$) is simply lifted to a ParT collection (Red-JoinF). In Red-JoinFP, a future containing a nested ParT collection (type $Fut\ (Par\ (Par\ t)))$, chains a call to `join` to flatten the inner structure. Rule Red-JoinP applies the `join` combinator recursively to the values in the ParT collection.

Prune and Peek. Pruning is the most complicated part of the calculus, though most of the work is done using the `peek` combinator (Fig. 8). Firstly, rule Red-Prune spawns a new task that will peek the collection v', and passes this new task's future to the function v. The essence of the `peek` rules is to set up a

(RED-JOINS)

$(\text{task}_g^\alpha \ E[\text{join} \ \{\}]) \rightarrow (\text{task}_g^\alpha \ E[\{\}])$

(RED-JOINV)

$(\text{task}_g^\alpha \ E[\text{join} \ \{v\}]) \rightarrow (\text{task}_g^\alpha \ E[v])$

(RED-JOINF)

$(\text{task}_g^\alpha \ E[\text{join} \ f^\circ]) \rightarrow (\text{task}_g^\alpha \ E[f^\dagger])$

(RED-JOINFP)

$(\text{task}_g^\alpha \ E[\text{join} \ f^\dagger]) \rightarrow (\text{task}_g^\alpha \ E[(f \rightsquigarrow (\lambda x.\text{join} \ x))^\dagger])$

(RED-JOINP)

$(\text{task}_g^\alpha \ E[\text{join} \ (v_1 \,||\, v_2)]) \rightarrow (\text{task}_g^\alpha \ E[(\text{join} \ v_1) \,||\, (\text{join} \ v_2)])$

Fig. 7. Reduction rules for the `join` combinator.

(RED-PRUNE)

fresh f

$$(\text{task}_g^\alpha \ E[v \lll v']) \rightarrow (\text{fut}_f) \ (\text{task}_f^\alpha \ (\text{peek} \ v')) \ (\text{task}_g^\alpha \ E[v \ f])$$

(RED-PEEKS$^\oslash$)

$(\text{task}_g^\alpha \ E[\text{peek}^\oslash \ \{\}]) \rightarrow \epsilon$

(RED-PEEKS)

$(\text{task}_g^\alpha \ E[\text{peek} \ \{\}]) \ (\text{fut}_g) \rightarrow (\text{fut}_g \ \text{Nothing}) \ (\text{poison} \ g)$

(RED-PEEKV)

$(\text{task}_g^\alpha \ E[\text{peek}^\pi \ (\{v\} \,||\, v')]) \ (\text{fut}_g) \rightarrow (\text{fut}_g \ (\text{Just} \ v)) \ (\text{poison} \ g) \bigcup_{h \in deps(v')} (\text{poison} \ h)$

(RED-PEEKF)

$(\text{task}_g^\alpha \ E[\text{peek}^\pi \ (f^\circ \,||\, v)]) \rightarrow (\text{chain}_g^\alpha \ f \ (\lambda x.\text{peek}^\pi \ \{x\})) \ (\text{task}_g^\alpha \ (\text{peek}^\oslash \ v))$

(RED-PEEKFP)

fresh h

$(\text{task}_g^\alpha \ E[\text{peek}^\pi \ (f^\dagger \,||\, v)]) \rightarrow$
$(\text{chain}_g^\alpha \ f \ (\lambda x.\text{peek}^\pi \ (x \,||\, (h \rightsquigarrow \text{maybe2par})^\dagger)))$
$(\text{fut}_h) \ (\text{task}_h^\alpha \ (\text{peek} \ v)) \ (\text{chain}_g^\alpha \ h \ (\lambda x.\text{peek}^\oslash(\text{maybe2par} \ x)))$

Fig. 8. Reduction rules for pruning. For singleton collections are handled via equality $v = v \,||\, \{\}$.

bunch of computations that compete to write into a single future, with the strict requirement that `Nothing` is written only when all competing tasks cannot produce a value—that is, when the ParT being peeked is empty. This is challenging due to the lifted future ParTs (type *Fut (Par t)*) within a collection, because such a future may be empty, but this fact cannot easily be seen in a non-blocking way. Another challenge is to avoid introducing sequential dependencies between entities that can potentially run in parallel, to avoid, for instance, a non-terminating computation blocking one that will produce a result.

A task that produces a ParT containing a value (rule RED-PEEKV) writes the value, wrapped in an option type, into the future and poisons all computations writing into that future, recursively poisoning direct dependencies. The $\oslash$ status on `peek` prevents certain `peek` invocations from writing a final empty result, as in rule RED-PEEKS$^\oslash$. Contrast with RED-PEEKS, in which a task resulting in an empty ParT writes `Nothing` into the future — in this case it is guaranteed that no other `peek` exists writing to the future.

$$\frac{(\text{Red-Schedule})}{\textit{fresh } f}$$
$$(\texttt{task}_g^\alpha \ E[e_1 \ || \ e_2]) \rightarrow (\texttt{task}_g^\alpha \ E[e_1 \ || \ f^\dagger]) \ (\texttt{fut}_f) \ (\texttt{task}_f^\alpha \ e_2)$$

Fig. 9. Spawning of tasks inside a ParT.

A lifted future f is guaranteed to produce a result, though it may not produce it in a timely fashion. This case is handled (rule Red-PeekF) by chaining a function onto it that will ultimately write into future g when the value is produced, if it wins the race. Otherwise, the result of peeking into v is written into g, unless the value produced is $\{\}$ (which is controlled by $\oslash$).

A lifted future to a ParT is not necessarily guaranteed to produce a result, and neither is any ParT that runs in parallel with it. Thus, extra care needs to be taken to ensure that Nothing is written if and only if both are actually empty. This is handled in rule Red-PeekFP. Firstly, a function is chained onto the lifted future to get access to the eventual ParT collection. This is combined with future h that is used to peek into v via a new task.

In all cases, computations propagate the poison state α to new configurations.

Scheduling. Rule Red-Schedule (Fig. 9) models the non-deterministic scheduling of parallelism within a task, converting some of the parallelism latent in a ParT collection into a new task. Apart from this rule, expressions within tasks are evaluated sequentially.

$$(\text{Red-Poison})$$
$$(\texttt{poison } f) \ (PC_f \ e) \rightarrow (\texttt{poison } f) \ (PC_f^\uparrow \ e) \bigcup_{g \in deps((PC_f \ e))} (\texttt{poison } g)$$

$$\frac{(\text{Red-Terminate})}{\neg(\textit{config} \vdash \textit{needed}(f))}$$
$$\{(PC_f^\uparrow \ e) \ \textit{config}\} \rightarrow \{\textit{config}\}$$

Fig. 10. Poisoning reduction rules.

Poisoning and Termination. The rules for poisoning and termination (Fig. 10) are based on a *poisoned carrier configuration* defined as $(PC_f^\alpha \ e) ::= (\texttt{task}_f^\alpha \ e) \ | \ (\texttt{chain}_f^\alpha \ g \ e)$; these rules rely on the definition of when a future is needed (Definition 2), which in turn is defined in terms of the futures on which a task depends to produce a value (Definition 1).

Definition 1. *The dependencies of an expression e, $deps(e)$, is the set of the futures upon which the computation of e depends in order to produce a value:*

$$deps(f) = \{f\}$$
$$deps(c) = deps(\{\}) = deps(x) = \varnothing$$

$$deps(\{e\}) = deps(\lambda x.e) = deps(\texttt{async } e) = deps(e^\circ) = deps(e^\dagger) =$$
$$deps(\texttt{peek}^\pi \ e) = deps(\texttt{join } e) = deps(e)$$
$$deps(e \parallel e') = deps(e \ e') = deps(e \gg e') = deps(e \ggg e') =$$
$$deps(e \times e') = deps(e \rightsquigarrow e') = deps(e \ll e') = deps(e) \cup deps(e')$$
$$deps((\texttt{task}^\alpha_f \ e)) = deps(e)$$
$$deps((\texttt{chain}^\alpha_f \ g \ e)) = \{g\} \cup deps(e).$$

Definition 2. *A future f is needed in configuration config, denoted config $\vdash$ needed(f), whenever some other element of the configuration depends on it:*

$$config \vdash needed(f) \ \textit{iff} \ (PC^\alpha_g \ e) \in config \wedge f \in deps((PC^\alpha_g \ e)) \wedge (\texttt{fut}_f) \in config.$$

Configurations go through a two step process before being terminated. In the first step (rule RED-POISON) the poisoning of future f poisons any task or chain writing to f, marks it with ⋔, and the poison is transmitted to the direct dependencies of the expression e in the task or chain. In the second step (RED-TERMINATE), a poisoned configuration is terminated when there is no other configuration relying on its result — that is, a poisoned task or chain is terminated if there is no expression around to keep it alive. This rule is global, referring to the entire configuration. Termination can be implemented using tracing garbage collection, though in the semantics a more global specification of dependency is used.

An example (Fig. 11) illustrates how poisoning and termination work to prevent a task that is still needed from being terminated. Initially, there is a bunch of tasks (squares) and futures (circles) (Fig. 11A), where one of the tasks completes and writes a value to future f. This causes all of the other tasks writing to f to be poisoned, via Rule RED-PEEKV (Fig. 11B). After application of rule RED-POISON, the dependent tasks and futures are recursively poisoned (Fig. 11C). Finally, the application of rule RED-TERMINATE terminates tasks that are not needed (Fig. 11D). Task e_1 is not terminated, as future g is required by the task computing $e \ g$.

Configurations. The concatenation operation on configurations is commutative and associative and has the empty configuration as its unit (Fig. 12). We assume that these equivalences, along with the monoid axioms for $\parallel$, can be applied at any time during reduction.

The reduction rules for configurations (Fig. 13) have the individual configuration reduction rules at their heart, along with standard rules for parallel evaluation of non-conflicting sub-configurations, as is standard in rewriting logic [14].

3.4   Type System

The type system (Fig. 14) assigns the following types to terms:

$$\tau ::= K \mid Fut \ \tau \mid Par \ \tau \mid Maybe \ \tau \mid \tau \rightarrow \tau$$

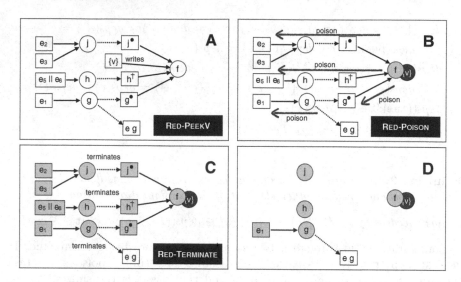

Fig. 11. Safely poisoning and terminating a configuration. The letter in the top right corner indicates the order. Tasks are represented by squares, contain a body and have an arrow to the future they write to. Futures (circles) have dotted arrows to tasks that use them. Grey represents poisoned configurations. Terminated configurations are removed (Color figure online).

$$\epsilon\ config \equiv config\ \epsilon \equiv config \qquad config\ config' \equiv config'\ config$$

$$config\ (config'\ config'') \equiv (config\ config')\ config'' \qquad \frac{config \equiv config'}{\{config\} \equiv \{config'\}}$$

Fig. 12. Configuration equivalence modulo associativity and commutativity.

$$\frac{config \to config'}{config\ config'' \to config'\ config''} \qquad \frac{config_0 \to config'_0 \quad config_1 \to config'_1}{config_0\ config_1 \to config'_0\ config'_1}$$

$$\frac{config_0\ config'' \to config'_0\ config'' \quad config_1\ config'' \to config'_1\ config''}{config_0\ config_1\ config'' \to config'_0\ config'_1\ config''}$$

$$\frac{config \to config'}{\{config\} \to \{config'\}}$$

Fig. 13. Configuration reduction rules

where K represents the basic types, *Fut* τ is the type of a future containing a value of type τ, *Par* τ is the type of a ParT collection of type τ, *Maybe* τ represents an option type, and $\tau \to \tau$ represents function types. We also let ρ range over types.

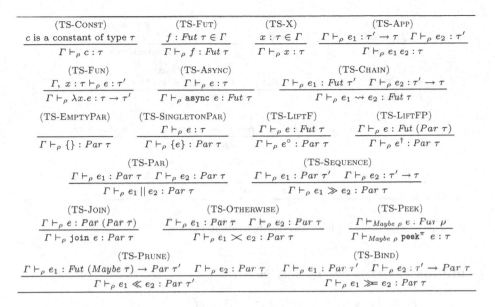

Fig. 14. Expression Typing.

The key judgement in the type system is $\Gamma \vdash_\rho e : \tau$ which asserts that, in typing context Γ, the expression e is a well-formed term with type τ, where ρ is the expected return type of the task in which this expression appears — ρ is required to type **peek**. The typing context contains the types of both free variables and futures.

Rule TS-ASYNC gives the type for task creation and rule TS-CHAIN shows how to operate on such values — future chaining has the type of map for the *Fut* constructor. Rules TS-EMPTYPAR, TS-SINGLETONPAR, TS-LIFTF, TS-LIFTFP, and TS-PAR give the typings for constructing ParT collections. Rule TS-SEQUENCE implies that sequencing has the type of map for the *Par* constructor. TS-BIND and TS-JOIN give $\ggg$ and **join** the types of the monadic bind and join operators for the *Par* constructor, respectively. Rule TS-PRUNE captures the communication between the two parameters via the future passed as an argument to the first parameter — the future will contain the first value of the second parameter if there is one, captured by the *Maybe* type. Rule TS-PEEK captures the conversion of the singleton or empty argument of **peek** from *Par* ρ to *Maybe* ρ, the expected result type of the surrounding task. Because **peek** terminates the task and does not return locally, its return type can be any type.

Well-formed configurations (Fig. 15) are expressed by the judgement $\Gamma \vdash$ *config* ok, where Γ is the assumptions about the future types in *config*. Rules T-TASK and T-CHAIN propagate the eventual expected result type on the turnstyle $\vdash$ when typing the enclosed expression. Rule T-CONFIG depends upon the following definition, a function that collects all futures defined in a configuration:

$$\frac{(\text{T-Fut})}{f \in dom(\Gamma)} \qquad \frac{(\text{T-FutV})}{\Gamma \vdash (\texttt{fut}_f) \text{ ok}} \qquad \frac{f : Fut\ \tau \in \Gamma \quad \Gamma \vdash_\tau v : \tau}{\Gamma \vdash (\texttt{fut}_f\ v) \text{ ok}} \qquad \frac{(\text{T-Poison})}{f : Fut\ \tau \in \Gamma}{\Gamma \vdash (\texttt{poison}\ f) \text{ ok}}$$

$$\frac{(\text{T-Task})}{f : Fut\ \tau \in \Gamma \quad \Gamma \vdash_\tau e : \tau}{\Gamma \vdash (\texttt{task}_f^\alpha\ e) \text{ ok}} \qquad \frac{(\text{T-Chain})}{f_1 : Fut\ \tau_1 \in \Gamma \quad f_2 : Fut\ \tau_2 \in \Gamma \quad \Gamma \vdash_{\tau_2} e : \tau_1 \to \tau_2}{\Gamma \vdash (\texttt{chain}_{f_2}^\alpha\ f_1\ e) \text{ ok}}$$

$$\frac{(\text{T-Config})}{\Gamma \vdash config_1 \text{ ok} \quad \Gamma \vdash config_2 \text{ ok} \quad futset(config_1) \cap futset(config_2) = \varnothing}{\Gamma \vdash config_1\ config_2 \text{ ok}}$$

$$\frac{(\text{T-GConfig})}{\Gamma \vdash config \text{ ok} \quad dom(\Gamma) = futset(config) \quad \textsc{TaskSafe}(config) \quad \textsc{AcyclicDep}(config)}{\Gamma \vdash \{config\} \text{ ok}}$$

Fig. 15. Configuration Typing.

Definition 3. *Define futset(config) as:*

$$futset((\texttt{fut}_f)) = futset((\texttt{fut}_f\ v)) = \{f\}$$
$$futset((config_1\ config_2)) = futset(config_1) \cup futset(config_2)$$
$$futset(\_) = \varnothing.$$

Rule T-GCONFIG defines the well-formedness of global configurations, judgement $\Gamma \vdash \{config\}$ ok. This rule depends on a number of definitions that capture properties on futures and tasks and on the dependency between futures. The invariance of these properties is ultimately used to proof type soundness and other safety properties of the system.

Definition 4. *Define the following functions for collecting the different kinds of tasks and chains of a configuration:*

$$regular_f(config) = \{(\texttt{task}_f\ e) \in config \mid e \neq \texttt{peek}^\pi\ e'\}$$
$$\cup \{(\texttt{chain}_f\ g\ e) \in config \mid e \neq \lambda\_.\texttt{peek}^\pi\ e'\}$$
$$peeker_f(config) = \{(\texttt{task}_f\ (\texttt{peek}\ e)) \in config\}$$
$$\cup \{(\texttt{chain}_f\ g\ (\lambda\_.\texttt{peek}\ e)) \in config\}$$
$$peeker_f^\varnothing(config) = \{(\texttt{task}_f\ (\texttt{peek}^\varnothing\ e)) \in config\}$$
$$\cup \{((\texttt{chain}_f\ g\ (\lambda\_.\texttt{peek}^\varnothing\ e)) \in config\}$$

Tasks with no **peek** expression are called *regular tasks*, while *peeker tasks* have the **peek** expression — there are both $\varnothing$- and non-$\varnothing$-peeker tasks. These functions can be used to partition the tasks and chains in a configuration into these three kinds of tasks and chains. These definitions consider **peek** expressions only at the top level of a task, although the syntax allows them to be anywhere. Based on the reduction rules, one can prove that **peek** only appears at the top level of a task or chain, so no task or chain is excluded by these definitions.

Definition 5. *Define predicate* TASKSAFE(*config*) *as follows:*

TASKSAFE(*config*) iff for all $f \in futset(config)$
$|regular_f(config) \cup peeker_f(config)| \leq 1$
$\wedge$ $(\textbf{fut}_f) \in config \wedge (\textbf{poison } f) \notin config \Rightarrow$
$\qquad\qquad\qquad |regular_f(config) \cup peeker_f(config)| = 1$
$\wedge$ $|regular_f(config)| = 1 \Rightarrow peeker_f(config) \cup peeker_f^\oslash(config) = \emptyset$
$\wedge$ $(\textbf{task}_f^\alpha \ (\textbf{peek } \{\})) \in config \Rightarrow (\textbf{fut}_f) \in config \wedge peeker_f^\oslash(config) = \emptyset$

Predicate TASKSAFE(*config*) (Definition 5) describes the structure of the configuration *config*. It states that:

- there is at most one regular or non-$\oslash$-peeker task per future;
- if a future has not yet been fulfilled and it is not poisoned, then there exists exactly one regular task or non-$\oslash$-peeker task that fulfils it;
- regular tasks and peeker tasks do not write to the same futures; and
- if a peeker task that is about to fulfil a future with Nothing, then the future is unfulfilled and no $\oslash$-peeker task fulfilling the same future exists.

The following definition establishes dependencies between futures. Predicate $config \vdash f \lhd g$ holds for all future g whose eventual value could influence the result stored in future f.

Definition 6. *Define the predicate* $config \vdash f \lhd g$ *as the least transitive relation satisfying the following rules:*

$$\frac{(\textbf{task}_f^\alpha \ e) \in config \quad g \in deps(e)}{config \vdash f \lhd g} \qquad \frac{(\textbf{chain}_f^\alpha \ h \ e) \in config \quad g \in deps(e) \cup \{h\}}{config \vdash f \lhd g}$$

$$\frac{(\textbf{fut}_f \ v) \in config \quad g \in deps(v)}{config \vdash f \lhd g}$$

Definition 7. *Predicate* ACYCLICDEP(*config*) *holds iff relation* $\lhd$ *is acyclic, where* $\lhd$ *is defined for config in Definition 6.*

Rule T-GCONFIG for well-formed global configurations requires that precisely the futures that appear in the typing environment Γ appear in the configuration, that the configuration is well-formed, and that it satisfies the properties TASKSAFE and ACYCLICDEP. By including these properties as a part of the well-formedness rule for global configurations, type preservation (Lemma 1) makes these invariants. These invariants on the structure of tasks and the dependency relation together ensure that well-typed configurations are deadlock-free, as we explore next.

3.5   Formal Properties

The calculus is sound and deadlock-free. These results extend previous work [15] to address the pruning combinator.

Lemma 1 (Type Preservation). *If $\Gamma \vdash \{config\}$ ok and $\{config\} \rightarrow \{config'\}$, then there exists a Γ' such that $\Gamma' \supseteq \Gamma$ and $\Gamma' \vdash \{config'\}$ ok.*

Proof. By induction on derivation $\{config\} \rightarrow \{config'\}$. In particular, the invariance of ACYCLICDEP is shown by considering the changes to the dependencies caused by each reduction rule. The only place where new dependencies are introduced is when new futures are created. Adding a future to the dependency relation cannot introduce cycles.   □

The following lemma states that the notion of *needed*, which determines whether or not to garbage collect a poisoned task or chain, is anti-monotonic, meaning that after a future is no longer needed according to the definitions, it does not subsequently become needed.

Lemma 2 (Safe Task Kill). *If $\Gamma \vdash \{config\}$ ok and $\{config\} \rightarrow \{config'\}$, then $\neg(config \vdash needed(f))$ implies $\neg(config' \vdash needed(f))$.*

Proof. A future is initially created in a configuration where it is needed. If ever a future disappears from $deps(e)$, if can never reappear.   □

This lemma rules out the situation where a task is poisoned and garbage collected, but is subsequently needed. For instance, the application of rule RED-TERMINATE in Fig. 11C kills tasks e_2, e_3, e_5 and e_6 (shown in Fig. 11D). If the future into which these tasks were going to write is needed afterwards, there would be a deadlock as a new task could chain on that future but never be fulfilled.

Definition 8 (Terminal Configuration). *A global configuration $\{config\}$ is terminal iff every element of config has one of the following shapes: $(\mathtt{fut}_f)$, $(\mathtt{fut}_f\ v)$ or $(\mathtt{poison}\ f)$.*

Lemma 3 (Deadlock-Freedom/Progress). *If $\Gamma \vdash \{config\}$ ok, then config is a terminal configuration, or there exists a config' such that $\{config\} \rightarrow \{config'\}$.*

Proof. By induction on a derivation of $\{config\} \rightarrow \{config'\}$, relying on the invariance of ACYCLICDEP and Lemma 2.   □

Deadlock-freedom guarantees that some reduction rule can be applied to a well-typed, non terminal, global configuration — this is essentially the progress property required to prove type safety. It implies further that there are no local deadlocks, such as a deadlocked configuration like $(\mathtt{chain}_f\ g\ e)\ (\mathtt{chain}_g\ f\ e')$. Such a configuration fails to satisfy the ACYCLICDEP invariant, thus cannot exist. If mutable state is added to the calculus, deadlock-freedom is lost.

Implementations. There are two prototypes of the ParT abstraction. In the first prototype,[2] ParT has been written as an extension to the Encore compiler (written in Haskell) and runtime (written in C) but, it can be implemented in well-established languages with notions of tasks and futures. This prototype integrates futures produced by tasks and active objects with the ParT abstraction. The other prototype has been written in Clojure,[3] which is not statically typed. Both prototypes follow the semantics to guide the implementation. In practice, this means that the semantic rules are written in such a way that they can be easily mimicked in a library or in a language runtime.

4   Related Work

Our combinators have been adapted from those of the Orc [11,12] programming language. In ParT, these combinators are completely asynchronous and are integrated with futures. ParTs are first class citizens and can be nested *Par* (*Par t*), neither of which is possible in Orc, which sits on top of the expression being coordinated and a flat collection of values.

Meseguer et al. [1] used rewriting logic semantics and Maude to provide a distributed implementation of Orc. Their focus on the semantic model allows them to model check Orc programs. In this paper, our semantics is more fine-grained, and guides the implementation in a multicore setting.

ParT uses a monad to encapsulate asynchronous computations, which is not a new idea [3,13,20]. For instance, F# expresses asynchronous workflows using a continuation monad [20] but cannot create more parallelism within the monad, making the model better suited for event-based programming. In contrast, our approach can spawn parallel computations and include them within ParTs.

Other work implements Orc combinators in terms of a monad within the pure functional language Haskell [3,13]. One of these approaches [3] relies on threads and channels and implements the prune ≪ combinator using sequential composition, losing potential parallelism. The other approach [13] uses Haskell threads and continuations to model parallel computations and re-designs the prune ≪ combinator in terms of a *cut* combinator thats sparks off parallel computations, waits until there is a value available and terminates, in bulk, the remaining computations. In contrast, the ParT abstraction relies on more lightweight tasks instead of threads, has fully asynchronous combinators, which maintain the throughput of the system, and terminates speculative work by recursively poisoning dependencies and terminating computations that are not needed.

An approach to increase parallelism is to create parallel versions of existing collections. For instance, Haskell [10] adds parallel operations to its collections, and the Scala parallel collections [18] adds new methods to their collection, **par** and **seq**, that return a parallel and a sequential version of the collection. However these approaches cannot coordinate complex workflows, which is possible with the ParT abstraction.

---

[2] Encore ParT prototype: http://52.50.101.143/kompile/encore/.

[3] Clojure ParT prototype: https://github.com/kikofernandez/ParT.

Recent approaches to creating pipeline parallelism are the Flowpool [19] and FlumeJava [4] abstractions. In the former, functions are attached to Flowpool and, with the `foreach` combinator, the attached functions are applied to items asynchronously added to the Flowpool thereby creating parallel pipelines of computations. The latter, FlumeJava, is a library extending the MapReduce framework; it provides high-level constructs to create efficient data-parallel pipelines of MapReduce jobs, via an optimisation phase. The ParT abstraction can create data-parallel pipelines with the sequence ≫ and bind ≫= combinators (at the moment there is no optimisation phase) and further can terminate speculative work.

Existing approaches to safely terminating speculative parallelism [6,9,17] did not integrate well with the ParT abstraction. For instance, the Cilk programming language provides the `abort` keyword to terminate all speculative work generated by a procedure [6]. The termination does not happen immediately, instead, computations are marked as not-runnable; already running computations would get marked as non-runnable but do not stop execution until their work is finished. In other approaches, the developer specifies termination checkpoints at which a task may be terminated [9,17]. This solves the previous problem and improves responsiveness but, adds an extra overhead (for the checking) and puts the responsibility on the developer, who specifies the location of the checkpoints. In our design, the developer does not need to specify these checkpoints and speculative work is terminated as soon as there are no dependencies. No other approach considers that the results of tasks may be needed elsewhere.

5   Conclusion and Future Work

This paper presented the ParT asynchronous, parallel collection abstraction, and a collection of combinators that operate over it. ParT was formalised as a typed calculus of tasks, futures and Orc-like combinators. A primary characteristic of the calculus is that it captures the non-blocking implementation of the combinators, including an algorithm for pruning that tracks down dependencies and is safe with respect to shared futures. The ParT abstraction has prototypes in the Encore (statically typed) and Clojure (dynamically typed) programming languages.

Currently, the calculus does not support side-effects. These are challenging to deal with, due to potential race conditions and terminated computations leaving objects in an inconsistent state. We expect that Encore's capability type system [2] can be used to avoid data races, and a run-time, transactional mechanism can deal with the inconsistent state. At the start of the paper we mentioned that ParT was integrated into an actor-based language, but the formalism included no actors. This work abstracted away the actors, replacing them by tasks and futures—message sends in the Encore programming language return results via futures—which were crucial for tying together the asynchronous computations underlying a ParT. Actors can easily be re-added as soon as the issues of shared mutable state have been addressed. The distribution aspect of actors has not yet been considered in Encore or in the ParT abstraction. This would be an interesting topic for future work. Beyond these extensions, we also plan to extend the range of combinators supporting the ParT abstraction.

References

1. AlTurki, M., Meseguer, J.: Dist-Orc: A rewriting-based distributed implementation of Orc with formal analysis. In: Ölveczky, P.C., (ed.) Proceedings First International Workshop on Rewriting Techniques for Real-Time Systems, RTRTS 2010, 6–9 April, 2010, vol. 36 of EPTCS, pp. 26–45. Longyearbyen, Norway (2010)
2. Brandauer, S., et al.: Parallel objects for multicores: a glimpse at the parallel language encore. In: Bernardo, M., Johnsen, E.B. (eds.) Formal Methods for Multicore Programming. LNCS, pp. 1–56. Springer, Switzerland (2015)
3. Campos, M.D., Barbosa, L.S.: BarbosaImplementation of an orchestration language as a haskell domain specific language. Electr. Notes Theor. Comput. Sci. **255**, 45–64 (2009)
4. Chambers, C., Raniwala, A., Perry, F., Adams, S., Henry, R.R., Bradshaw, R., Weizenbaum, N.: Flumejava: Easy, efficient data-parallel pipelines. In: Proceedings of the 31st ACM SIGPLAN Conference on Programming Language Design and Implementation, PLDI 2010, pp. 363–375, New York, NY, USA. ACM (2010)
5. Clarke, D., Wrigstad, T.: Vats: a safe, reactive storage abstraction. In: Ábrahám, E., Bonsangue, M., Johnsen, E.B. (eds.) Theory and Practice of Formal Methods. LNCS, vol. 9660, pp. 140–154. Springer, Switzerland (2016)
6. Frigo, M., Leiserson, C.E., Randall, K.H.: The implementation of the Cilk-5 multithreaded language. In: Davidson, J.W., Cooper, K.D., Berman, A.M., (eds.) Proceedings of the ACM SIGPLAN 1998 Conference on Programming Language Design and Implementation (PLDI), pp. 212–223. ACM, Montreal, 17–19 June 1998
7. Robert Jr., R.H.: Multilisp: A language for concurrent symbolic computation. ACM Trans. Program. Lang. Syst. **7**(4), 501–538 (1985)
8. Hickey, R.: The clojure programming language. In: Brichau, J. (ed.) Proceedings of the 2008 Symposium on Dynamic Languages, DLS 2008, p. 1. ACM, Paphos, Cyprus (2008)
9. Imam, S., Sarkar, V.: The Eureka programming model for speculative task parallelism. In: Boyland, J.T. (ed.) 29th European Conference on Object-Oriented Programming, ECOOP 2015, vol. 37 of LIPIcs, pp. 421–444, Schloss Dagstuhl - Leibniz-Zentrum fuer Informatik. Prague, Czech Republic, 5–10 July 2015
10. Peyton Jones, S.: Harnessing the multicores: nested data parallelism in haskell. In: Ramalingam, G. (ed.) APLAS 2008. LNCS, vol. 5356, p. 138. Springer, Heidelberg (2008)
11. Kitchin, D.E., Cook, W.R., Misra, J.: A language for task orchestration and its semantic properties. In: Baier, C., Hermanns, H. (eds.) CONCUR 2006. LNCS, vol. 4137, pp. 477–491. Springer, Heidelberg (2006)
12. Kitchin, D., Quark, A., Cook, W., Misra, J.: The Orc programming language. In: Lee, D., Lopes, A., Poetzsch-Heffter, A. (eds.) FMOODS 2009. LNCS, vol. 5522, pp. 1–25. Springer, Heidelberg (2009)
13. Launchbury, J., Elliott, T.: Concurrent orchestration in haskell. In: Gibbons, J., (ed.) Proceedings of the 3rd ACM SIGPLAN Symposium on Haskell, Haskell 2010, pp. 79–90. ACM, Baltimore, MD, USA, 30 September 2010

14. Martí-Oliet, N., Meseguer, J.: Rewriting logic: roadmap and bibliography. Theor. Comput. Sci. **285**(2), 121–154 (2002)
15. McCain, D.: Parallel combinators for the Encore programming language. Master's thesis, Uppsala University (2016)
16. Odersky, M., Spoon, L., Venners, B.: Programming in Scala: A Comprehensive Step-by-step Guide, 1st edn. Artima Incorporation, USA (2008)
17. Peierls, T., Goetz, B., Bloch, J., Bowbeer, J., Lea, D., Holmes, D.: Java Concurrency in Practice. Addison-Wesley Professional, Boston (2005)
18. Prokopec, A., Bagwell, P., Rompf, T., Odersky, M.: A generic parallel collection framework. In: Jeannot, E., Namyst, R., Roman, J. (eds.) Euro-Par 2011, Part II. LNCS, vol. 6853, pp. 136–147. Springer, Heidelberg (2011)
19. Prokopec, A., Miller, H., Schlatter, T., Haller, P., Odersky, M.: FlowPools: a lock-free deterministic concurrent dataflow abstraction. In: Kasahara, H., Kimura, K. (eds.) LCPC 2012. LNCS, vol. 7760, pp. 158–173. Springer, Heidelberg (2013)
20. Syme, D., Petricek, T., Lomov, D.: The F# asynchronous programming model. In: Rocha, R., Launchbury, J. (eds.) PADL 2011. LNCS, vol. 6539, pp. 175–189. Springer, Heidelberg (2011)
21. Wright, A.K., Felleisen, M.: A syntactic approach to type soundness. Inf. Comput. **115**(1), 38–94 (1994)

Modelling Ambulance Deployment with CARMA

Vashti Galpin[✉]

Laboratory for Foundations of Computer Science, School of Informatics,
University of Edinburgh, Edinburgh, UK
Vashti.Galpin@ed.ac.uk

Abstract. CARMA is a process-algebra influenced language for the quantitative modelling of collective adaptive systems which involve collaboration and coordination. These systems consist of multiple components that interact to achieve certain goals and that adapt to changes in the environment. As a case study for the application of CARMA, this paper presents an ambulance deployment system where ambulances go to medical incidents and either treat patients at the scene or transfer them to hospital. The Eclipse CARMA Plug-in is used to simulate the system, and demonstrate its behaviour in different circumstances.

1 Introduction

Creating formal dynamic models of systems that can be simulated and subjected to other forms of quantitative analysis is one way in which formal methods can be used in the development and evaluation of these systems. Frequently, it is not possible to experiment with the system itself, because of the cost or disruption involved. Hence development of models that can be used for experimentation is important. This paper applies a language that has been developed to model collective adaptive systems (CAS) to an existing ambulance deployment scenario.

CAS feature frequently in modern information systems. Multiple components interact (and sometimes compete) to achieve various outcomes. The components can be individual pieces of software or different physical devices, and such systems are often characterised by local information and local action which therefore, requires a notion of space. Coordination and collaboration are features of these models because of the components communicate to achieve their aims. The language CARMA and its associated software tool the Eclipse CARMA Plug-in have been developed for the quantitative modelling of CAS allowing for an understanding of both functional and nonfunctional properties of models [3,5]. Important aspects of CARMA include attribute-based communication, in the sense that the possibility of a component taking part in an interaction depends on the current values in the store of the component, thus allowing for a rich representation of state. Both unicast and broadcast modes of communication are supported. Furthermore, CARMA allows the environment within which the model components interact to be defined separately from the components. The development of CARMA has been influenced by a number of previous process algebra including

© IFIP International Federation for Information Processing 2016
Published by Springer International Publishing Switzerland 2016. All Rights Reserved
A. Lluch Lafuente and J. Proença (Eds.): COORDINATION 2016, LNCS 9686, pp. 121–137, 2016.
DOI: 10.1007/978-3-319-39519-7_8

the Markovian process algebra PEPA [12], the location-focussed PALOMA [9] and SCEL [8] which uses attribute-based communication. Attribute-based communication is explored further in the process calculus AbC [2].

In this paper, the modelling and analysis of a particular system using CARMA is considered. Jagtenberg et al. have proposed a new approach to ambulance deployment [14]. The general goal of such systems is to minimise the time it takes to respond to medical incidents by ensuring good base locations for ambulances together with a distribution of ambulances over bases that leads to fast response. Traditionally, deciding how to deploy ambulances across a region has been done statically, in the sense that once an ambulance has completed its current task, it returns to a predefined base, and moreover determining the best bases is done in advance of deployment. In the dynamic approach, depending on the locations of the other ambulances, an ambulance that is no longer busy can be requested to go to a specific location in a set of base locations to wait for its next task, thus allowing the system to adapt to the current circumstances. The ambulance system is modelled as a graph of locations with edges representing roads, annotated with information about how long it takes to traverse the edge, as shown in Fig. 5. Locations may be cities, towns, road junctions or other points of interest. Each location has an incident probability, and some locations have ambulances bases or hospitals. There has been much research into different aspects of ambulance response time that use a graph to represent the road network. These have considered how many ambulances to use, the best locations for bases and how to distribute vehicles over bases [1,4,6,10,15,16]. The specific system modelled here has been chosen because of its time-based performance evaluation aspects and straightforward heuristic function. The developed model could be modified to investigate other aspects of ambulance deployment.

This paper presents a CARMA model of such an ambulance system. As CARMA is a new modelling language, it is necessary to evaluate it by developing interesting and complex models, and the ambulance deployment system fulfils these requirements. First, the ambulance scenario is introduced after which details of CARMA are presented, followed by the ambulance model expressed in CARMA. Finally results of simulation of the model are presented and a discussion of further research relating to the model discussed.

2   An Ambulance Deployment Scenario

This section describes the mathematical model that Jagtenberg et al. [14] propose, together with their heuristic for best real-time redeployment of ambulances. This model considers a scenario where there is a fairly sparse network of roads between cities and towns (as shown in Fig. 5), and hence is slightly more appropriate for a non-urban situation, where there are not many routes between each point of interest. An urban map can be transformed into a similar sparse network by focussing on major routes.

Let $N = (V, E)$ be a graph where $E \subseteq V \times V$. Four functions are associated with this graph.

- $r : E \rightarrow \mathbb{R}_{>0}$ describes the time it takes to traverse an edge (when using sirens and lights – this figure increases for travel without lights and sirens).
- $h : V \rightarrow \{0, 1\}$ defines the presence of a hospital at a vertex.
- $b : V \rightarrow \{0, 1\}$ defines whether a vertex is an ambulance base.
- $d : V \rightarrow [0, 1]$ with $\sum_{v \in V} d(v) = 1$, defines the distribution of incidences over the vertices of the graph.

There is also a set of ambulances A labelled $\{1, \ldots, n\}$ and two functions $l : A \rightarrow V$ describing the current location of an ambulance and $w : A \rightarrow \{0, 1\}$ describing whether an ambulance is currently allocated to an incident. Furthermore, a function $s : A \rightarrow V$ which describes the home station of an ambulance in the static case. There are three rates that describe how long it takes for an ambulance to treat a patient at the scene, λ_p, how long it takes for an ambulance to load up a patient at the scene for transportation to hospital, λ_t and how long it takes to offload a patient at hospital, λ_d. It is assumed that patients are either treated at the scene or uploaded to be taken to hospital but not both. Furthermore, there is a probability m that determines whether an incident is severe, requiring the patient to be transported to hospital, or minor, meaning that the patient only needs to be treated at the scene. The operation of the system is now described.

1. An incident occurs at a vertex based on the distribution defined by d and its level of severity is determined using the probability m.
2. An ambulance is identified to go to the incident location based on distance from the incident.
3. The ambulance uses the shortest route to get to the scene. Since distances are deterministic and unchanging, shortest routes can be determined in advance from the network, and hence are static in the model.
4. The ambulance treats the patient at the scene and then proceeds with item 7, or the ambulance uploads the patient to take them to hospital.
5. The ambulance uses the shortest route to the hospital using sirens and lights.
6. The ambulance drops the patient off at the hospital.
7. The ambulances uses the shortest route to go to a base but taking longer as it is not using sirens and lights. In the static case, this is the base defined by s. In the dynamic case, the base is determined by the heuristic.

Once an ambulance has been allocated to an incident, it must complete the journey to the incident, and to the hospital, if necessary, and cannot be diverted. However, once an ambulance has started to return to base, it can be immediately allocated to a new incident. An ambulance that is involved in items 2 to 6 is considered to be busy, otherwise it is idle. When it is idle, it is associated either with the base it has reached or the base to which it is travelling.

2.1   Evaluation of Base Heuristic

The reason to model such systems is to investigate the performance of different deployment approaches. The proportion of ambulances that do not reach the incident within a fixed time period (denoted T) after being allocated to that incident, is often used [14] and will be used here.

In the case of static deployment where each ambulance has a fixed base, simulation can be used to assess the best distribution of ambulances, in the planning stages of a system. Different variants of the maximum expected covering location problem (MEXCLP) [6] have been used to tackle this task. The disadvantage of the static approach is that it ignores real-time information that can be used to provide better coverage [14]. Coverage describes the number of ambulances that can provide service at a specific location within the time limit. Increasing coverage means that there is a higher probability that an ambulance will be available if one is needed.

Dynamic deployment approaches can be divided into two main techniques. The first, based on lookup tables, requires dispatchers to steer the system to these optimal configurations. A better approach is based on real-time approximation. However, even using approximate dynamic programming and post-decision state is time-consuming and requires an expert to implement and choose base functions [14]. By contrast, the approach taken in [14] is moderately coarse-grained and needs little real-time information, and takes a marginal cover approach based on MEXCLP.

Consider a set of ambulances A with behaviour as described above. Also let $B = \{u \in V | b(u) = 1\}$ be the set of vertices that are bases. It is assumed that there is a probability q which is the same for all ambulances and represents the fraction of time that the ambulance is busy. It can be determined by dividing the load of the system by the number of ambulances [14]. The expected coverage at vertex v when v is in the range of k ambulances is $E_k(v) = d(v)(1 - q^k)$ and as shown in [6], the marginal coverage is $E_k(v) - E_{k-1}(v) = d(v)(1 - q)q^{k-1}$. This figure can be used to determine to which base to send an ambulance once it has completed its task, by finding $u \in B$ such that the increase in coverage is maximised, and hence the maximum coverage overall is obtained. Let $\rho(v, w)$ be the time taken for the shortest route between vertices v and w, calculated from the values of individual hops given by the function r. Let n_u represent the number of ambulances at $u \in B$, or moving towards $u \in B$ after completing their allocated task, and let $N = \{n_u \mid u \in B\}$ represent the current number of idle ambulances for each possible base location. The function p captures the heuristic for determining ambulance base and is defined by[1]

$$p(N) = \arg \max_{w \in B} \sum_{v \in V} d(v)(1 - q)q^{k(v,w,N)-1} \cdot \mathbf{1}(\rho(w,v) \leq T) \qquad \text{where}$$

$$k(v,w,N) = \sum_{u \in B} n_u \cdot \mathbf{1}(\rho(u,v) \leq T) + \mathbf{1}(\rho(w,v) \leq T).$$

---

[1] This function differs from that in [14] due to the additional term $\mathbf{1}(\rho(u,v) \leq T$ in the first part of the definition. It does, however, match the algorithm that was used in that paper [13].

Here $\mathbf{1}$ is the indicator function. This function can also be simplified to

$$p(N) = arg\ \underset{w \in B}{max} \sum_{v \in V} d(v)(1-q)q^{c(v,N)} \cdot \mathbf{1}(\rho(w,v) \leq T) \qquad \text{where}$$

$$c(v,N) = \sum_{u \in B} n_u \cdot \mathbf{1}(\rho(u,v) \leq T)$$

For each possible base of the ambulance that has just completed its task, the increased coverage is calculated for every location in the graph whenever addition of the base would increase coverage at that location, and summed. The function c counts the number of ambulances that are already in the range of each base (reachable within the limit of T time units) as defined by the set N. If it is the case that both $|A|$, the number of idle ambulances, and $|B|$, the number of bases, are small compared to the number of vertices $|V|$, then the algorithm is linear in $|V|$ [14].

It is important to note that some aspects of the model are generic such as the ambulance behaviour but others are specific to the system under consideration such as the graph of locations, the functions relating to these locations, and the heuristic function p. This distinction will be used when deciding how to build the CARMA model. The next section introduces CARMA, after which the CARMA model of the system is presented.

3   CARMA

CARMA is a powerful language, influenced by process algebra, for describing systems consisting of different interacting components which allows for an explicit definition of environment. Its semantics are time-inhomogeneous continuous-time Markov chains [5] thus permitting both simulation and other analysis techniques. It is embodied in software in the CARMA Eclipse Plug-in tool which implements the basic language and supports features such as function definition, enumerated types, and measures which enable quantitative behaviour of a model to be calculated and recorded.

A CARMA model consists of a number of different elements. At the highest level, there is a collective that consists of different components that interact, together with an environment that contains information about the global state, as well as information about how components interact. Thus SYS is the set of CARMA *systems* S defined by

$$S ::= N \text{ in } \mathcal{E}$$

where N is a *collective* and $\mathcal{E}$ is an *environment*. The set of collectives COL is defined by

$$N ::= C \mid N \parallel N$$

A collective N is either a *component* C or the parallel composition of two collectives $(N \parallel N)$. The syntax of components is

$$C ::= \mathbf{0} \mid (P, \gamma)$$

where **0** is the null component, P is a process that describes the behaviour of the component and γ is the store for the component. COMP is defined to be the set of components. A store maps from *attribute names* to *basic values* where

- ATTR is the set of *attribute names* a, a', $a_1, \ldots$, b, b', $b_1, \ldots$;
- VAL is the set of *basic values* v, v', $v_1, \ldots$; and
- Γ is the set of *stores* $\gamma, \gamma_1, \gamma', \ldots$, are functions from ATTR to VAL.

PROC is the set of processes that define the behaviour of components and they are specified by

$$
\begin{array}{ll}
P, Q ::= \textbf{nil} & act ::= \alpha^\star[\pi]\langle \overrightarrow{e} \rangle \sigma \\
\quad | \quad \textbf{kill} & \quad | \quad \alpha[\pi]\langle \overrightarrow{e} \rangle \sigma \\
\quad | \quad act.P & \quad | \quad \alpha^\star[\pi](\overrightarrow{x}) \sigma \\
\quad | \quad P + Q & \quad | \quad \alpha[\pi](\overrightarrow{x}) \sigma \\
\quad | \quad P \mid Q & e ::= a \mid \mathsf{my}.a \mid x \mid v \mid \mathsf{now} \mid \cdots \\
\quad | \quad [\pi]P & \pi ::= \top \mid \bot \mid e_1 \bowtie e_2 \mid \neg\pi \mid \pi \wedge \pi \mid \cdots \\
\quad | \quad A \quad (A \stackrel{\triangle}{=} P) &
\end{array}
$$

In CARMA processes can have different prefixes relating to four types of actions which are *broadcast output* $(\alpha^\star[\pi]\langle \overrightarrow{e} \rangle \sigma)$, *broadcast input* $(\alpha^\star[\pi](\overrightarrow{x}) \sigma)$, *output* $(\alpha[\pi]\langle \overrightarrow{e} \rangle \sigma)$, and *input* $(\alpha[\pi](\overrightarrow{x}) \sigma)$, where

- α is an *action type* in the set of action type ACTTYPE;
- π is a *predicate*;
- x is a *variable* in the set of variables VAR;
- e is an expression in the set of expressions EXP;
- $\overrightarrow{\cdot}$ indicates a sequence of elements;
- σ is an *update*, i.e. a function from Γ to $Dist(\Gamma)$ in the set of *updates* Σ; where $Dist(\Gamma)$ is the set of probability distributions over Γ.

A unicast communication involves two components where the sender and receiver attributes must satisfy any predicates in the prefixes, the expressions in the output prefix are assigned to the variables in the input prefix (and hence successful communication requires the two sequences are the same length), and updates are applied to both components to complete the interaction. Furthermore, there can be a probability describing whether the receiver does actually receive the communication. Unicast is blocking in that a sender cannot proceed until a receiver takes part in the interaction.

By contrast, broadcast is not blocking and the sender can proceed regardless of whether there are many, one or no suitable receivers. Again, the sender and potential receivers must satisfy the predicates in the prefixes, and additionally there is a probability that the receiver although suitable to take part in the interaction, does not receive it. Expressions from the output prefix are passed to variables in the input prefix and updates are applied to all participants on completion of their roles, in the same manner as unicast. For both unicast and broadcast, rates of actions and probabilities of receiving are defined in the environment part of the model.

Specific expressions of interest are now for the current simulation time and my.a which refers to the value of the attribute a in the current component.

Apart from the four different prefix types, there is choice between two processes, the parallel composition of two processes, a guarded process which requires satisfaction of its predicate before it can perform an action and definition of constant processes. There are two distinct operators for termination. The operator **nil** represents the process that can perform no further actions and it can be placed in parallel with other processes. The operator **kill**, on the other hand, indicates termination of the whole component so that all processes in the component stop, and the component is transformed into **0**, the null component which can do nothing and has no store.

CARMA collectives interact within an environment $\mathcal{E}$. The environment describes the rules that regulate the system such as rates of interaction and probabilities that interaction may occur. It also contains global information. The environment has two elements: a *global store* γ_g, that records the value of global attributes, and an *evolution rule* ρ. This is a function which, depending on the *current time* (using now), on the global store and on the current state of the collective returns a tuple of functions $\varepsilon = \langle \mu_p, \mu_r, \mu_u \rangle$ known as the *evaluation context* where $\text{ACT} = \text{ACTTYPE} \cup \{\alpha^* | \alpha \in \text{ACTTYPE}\}$ and

- $\mu_p : \Gamma \times \Gamma \times \text{ACT} \to [0, 1]$, $\mu_p(\gamma_s, \gamma_r, \alpha)$ determines is the probability that a component with store γ_r can receive a message from a component with store γ_s when α is executed;
- $\mu_r : \Gamma \times \text{ACT} \to \mathbb{R}_{\geq 0}$, $\mu_r(\gamma, \alpha)$ determines the execution rate of action α executed at a component with store γ;
- $\mu_u : \Gamma \times \text{ACT} \to \Sigma \times \text{COL}$, $\mu_u(\gamma, \alpha)$ determines the updates on the environment (global store and collective) induced by the execution of action α at a component with store γ. The execution of an action can modify the values of global variables and also add new components to the collective.

In each of the rules, the notation sender.a is used to refer to the value of the attribute a in the store of the acting or sending component, and receiver.a refers to the value of the attribute a in the store of the receiving component.

Operational semantics of CARMA specifications are defined in three stages using the following transition relations. For reasons of space, the rules are not presented here, but can be found in [5].

1. The relation $\longrightarrow$ describes the behaviour of a single component.
2. The relation $\longrightarrow$ builds on the first relation to describe the behaviour of collectives.
3. The relation $\longmapsto$ describes how CARMA systems evolve.

All relations are defined in the FuTS style [7] and are described using a triple $(N, \ell, \mathcal{N})$ where the first element is a component, or a collective, or a system. The second element is a transition label. The third element is a function associating each component, collective, or system with a non-negative number. A non-zero value represents the rate of the exponential distribution characterising the time needed for the execution of the action represented by ℓ. The zero value is associated with unreachable terms. FUTS style semantics are used because it makes explicit an underlying (time-inhomogeneous) Action Labelled Markov Chain, which can be simulated with standard algorithms [11].

4   Ambulance Model

The CARMA model is presented in Figs. 1, 2, 3 and 4. Each component consists of the attributes that form its local store, its behaviour defined by processes and its initial state. Additionally, the attributes of the global store are defined in Fig. 4 together with the evolution rule functions over actions (one function for the rates, one for the probabilities and one for the updates of global attributes and additions to the collective). There are four actions with non-negligible rates, and the remainder are zero or fast (since CARMA does not currently support instantaneous actions). Figure 4 also includes the initial collective definition as the last item.

Th symbols $\top$ and $\perp$ as used for true and false, respectively. A broadcast action of the form $\alpha^\star[\perp]\langle\rangle$ is an action that cannot be received (because no component can satisfy the predicate false) and hence is local to the component that executes it, although it may also update the global store or add components to the collective.

As mentioned previously, some aspects of the model are generic and some are specific to the network of roads and places. These two concerns have been separated in the model. The components are generic, and functions (indicated in bold in the figures) embody the knowledge of the network[2]. The CARMA Eclipse Plug-in supports function definitions, hence this separation is both possible and sensible, and also supports the design of a tool for ambulance modelling, as discussed in the further work section.

These functions comprise of one to provide the distributions over location and type of incidents respectively, **IncidentLocation**(), **IncidentType**(); information about routes in the network, **RouteLength**(., .), **NextHop**(., ., .) and **MoveTime**(., ., .); location of the closest hospital to an incident, **HospitalLocation**(.); location of the closest idle ambulances to an incident location, **ClosestIdleLoc**(., N); and the base to which an ambulance should go, **GetBase**(., ., N) which can be defined statically or dynamically. Note that both **ClosestIdleLoc** and **GetBase** take N, the set of the counts of idle ambulances at each base or on their way to each base as an argument. For the former, N is used to find the closest location to the incident where there are idle ambulances, so that a request can be sent to ambulances in that location. For the latter, the counts of idle ambulances are required to calculate p.

---

[2] A different approach is to use components to embody the knowledge of the network and for the generic components to communicate with these components to obtain this information, but this leads to increase complexity of interaction. Alternatively, the environment could contain this knowledge.

Store of *Incident_Queue* **component:**

inum   number of incidents generated

rnum   next incident to be dealt with

Behaviour of *Incident_Queue* **component:**

$IG \overset{\text{def}}{=} \text{incident}^*[\bot]\langle\rangle\{inum \leftarrow inum + 1\}.IG$

$RN \overset{\text{def}}{=} \text{release}[\top]\langle rnum\rangle.RN'$

$RN' \overset{\text{def}}{=} \text{confirm}^*[\top](an, al)\{rnum \leftarrow rnum + 1\}.RN$

Initial state of *Incident_Queue* **component:** $IG \mid RN$

Store of *Incident_Queue_Item* **component:**

qnum   number of incident

itime   time of incident

Behaviour of *Incident_Queue Item* **component:**

$IQI \overset{\text{def}}{=} \text{release}[\text{my}.qnum == n](n).IQI'$

$IQI' \overset{\text{def}}{=} \text{new\_handler}^*[\bot]\langle\rangle.\textbf{kill}$

Initial state of *Incident_Queue_Item* **component:** IQI

Store of *Incident_Handler* **component:**

loc   location of incident or hospital

anum   id of ambulance assigned to incident

aloc   current location of ambulance assigned to incident

dest   current destination type and incident type

itime   time of incident

atime   arrival time at incident

Behaviour of *Incident_Handler* **component:**

$IH \overset{\text{def}}{=} \text{request\_ambulance}^*[\top]\langle loc\rangle.IH_C$

$IH_C \overset{\text{def}}{=} \text{confirm}^*[an, al](\{anum \leftarrow an, aloc \leftarrow al\}).IH_I$

$IH_I \overset{\text{def}}{=} \text{makeroute}^*[\bot]\langle\rangle.IH_S$

$IH_S \overset{\text{def}}{=} \text{arrive}^*[an == \text{my}.anum](an).IH_T$

$IH_T \overset{\text{def}}{=} \text{timecheck}^*[\bot]\langle\rangle\{atime \leftarrow \text{now}\}.IH_P$

$IH_P \overset{\text{def}}{=} \text{pickup}^*[an == \text{my}.anum](an)\{aloc \leftarrow \text{my}.loc,$

$\qquad\qquad loc \leftarrow \textbf{HospitalLocation}(\text{my}.loc), dest \leftarrow ToHosp\}.IH_H +$

$\qquad\quad \text{treat}^*[an == \text{my}.anum](an)\{aloc \leftarrow \text{my}.loc, dest \leftarrow ToBase\}.IH_F$

$IH_H \overset{\text{def}}{=} \text{makeroute}^*[\bot]\langle\rangle.IH_D$

$IH_D \overset{\text{def}}{=} \text{dropoff}^*[an == \text{my}.anum](an)\{aloc \leftarrow \text{my}.loc, dest \leftarrow ToBase\}.IH_F$

$IH_F \overset{\text{def}}{=} \text{tobase}^*[\bot]\langle\rangle.\textbf{kill}$

Initial state of *Incident_Handler* **component:** IH

Fig. 1. Incident queue, incident queue item and incident handler components

There are seven generic components in the model. The *Incident_Queue* generates *Incident_Queue_Items* using the action incident* which has the side-effect of adding a new *Incident_Queue_Item* to the collective (as specified by the function μ_u appearing in the environment in Fig. 4). Each item has a unique number, and in turn generates an *Incident_Handler* using the action new_handler*. The first action of the *Incident_Handler* is to request an ambulance from another

Store of *Return_Handler* **component:**

anum   id of ambulance assigned

 aloc   current location of ambulance

 dest   current destination and incident type

  loc   location of base of ambulance

Behaviour of *Return_Handler* **component:**

$RH \overset{\text{def}}{=} \text{tell\_base}[\top]\langle loc \rangle.RH'$

$RH' \overset{\text{def}}{=} \text{makeroute}^*[\bot]\langle\rangle.RH'' + \text{kill\_handler}^*[\text{my}.anum == an](an).\textbf{kill}$

$RH'' \overset{\text{def}}{=} \text{atbase}^*[\text{my}.anum == an](an).\textbf{kill} + \text{kill\_handler}^*[\text{my}.anum == an](an).\textbf{kill}$

Initial state of *Return_Handler* **component:** RH

Store of *Closest_Idle_Ambulance* **component:**

 iloc   location of incident

 dloc   location of idle ambulances

   t   timer variable for timeout

Behaviour of *Closest_Idle_Ambulance* **component:**

$CIA \overset{\text{def}}{=} \text{request\_ambulance}[\top](l)\{iloc \leftarrow l, dloc \leftarrow \textbf{ClosestIdleLoc}(iloc, N), t \leftarrow \text{now}\}.CIA'$

$CIA' \overset{\text{def}}{=} \text{request}[\top]\langle dloc \rangle.CIA'' +$

$\qquad\quad \text{pause}^*[\bot]\langle\rangle\{dloc \leftarrow \textbf{ClosestIdleLoc}(iloc, N), t \leftarrow \text{now}\}.CIA'$

$CIA'' \overset{\text{def}}{=} \text{confirm}^*[\top](an, al).CIA$

Initial state of *Return_Handler* **component:** CIA

Fig. 2. Return handler and idle ambulance components

component *Closest_Idle_Ambulance*. This is a separate component for clarity of structure. On receiving a request for a specific location, it calls the function to find the location with idle ambulances that is closest to that location, and take note of the current time. It then tries to communicate (via unicast) with any ambulance in that location. If that succeeds, then it, the *Incident_Handler* and the *Incident_Queue* receive a confirm* message from the ambulance that has responded. If there is no response, which is possible because there may be no idle ambulances, a timeout occurs. The timeout is defined by the rate for pause* in the environment in Fig. 4 where if insufficient time has passed the rate is zero (otherwise, it is λ_{fast}). If the timeout happens, it calls the function again and send out another request to the location that the function returns.

The *Incident_Queue* interacts with each *Incident_Queue_Item* and its associated *Incident_Handler* to ensure that at most one *Incident_Handler* at a time is contacting the closest idle ambulance (because two incidents may have the same closest idle ambulance). The use of queue numbers ensures fairness in the sense that an *Incident_Handler* cannot be starved of access to an *Ambulance* by later incidents and their associated *Incident_Handlers*. A queue item cannot be released and hence cannot execute new_handler*, until the *Incident_Handler* associated with the previous *Incident_Queue_Item* and its interaction with *Closest_Idle_Ambulance* has successfully concluded negotiations with the closest idle ambulance via communication on the confirm* action.

Store of *Ambulance* **component:**

anum	ambulance id
aloc	current location of ambulance
abase	current base of ambulance
idle	whether ambulance is idle or not

Behaviour of *Ambulance* **component:**

$Idle \stackrel{\text{def}}{=} \text{request}[al == \text{my}.aloc](al)\{idle \leftarrow \perp\}.Respond$

$Respond \stackrel{\text{def}}{=} \text{confirm}^\star[\top]\langle anum, aloc \rangle.Busy$

$Busy \stackrel{\text{def}}{=} \text{end\_move}[an == \text{my}.anum \wedge now >= t + d](an, al, t, d)\{aloc \leftarrow al\}.Busy +$
$\quad\quad \text{arrive}^\star[an == \text{my}.anum](an).AtScene +$
$\quad\quad \text{drop\_off}^{\wedge}[an == \text{my}.anum](an)\{idle \leftarrow \top\}.AskBase$

$AtScene \stackrel{\text{def}}{=} \text{pickup}^\star[an == \text{my}.anum](an).Busy +$
$\quad\quad \text{treat}^\star[an == \text{my}.anum](an)\{idle \leftarrow \top\}.AskBase$

$AskBase \stackrel{\text{def}}{=} \text{tell\_base}[an == \text{my}.anum](an, ab)\{abase \leftarrow ab\}.GoToBase$

$GoToBase \stackrel{\text{def}}{=} \text{end\_move}[an == \text{my}.anum \wedge now >= t + d](an, al, t, d)\{aloc \leftarrow al\}.GoToBase +$
$\quad\quad \text{atbase}^\star[an == \text{my}.anum](an).Idle +$
$\quad\quad \text{request}[an == \text{my}.anum](an).CleanUp1$

$CleanUp1 \stackrel{\text{def}}{=} \text{kill\_handler}^\star[\top]\langle anum \rangle.CleanUp2$

$CleanUp2 \stackrel{\text{def}}{=} \text{kill\_route}^\star[\top]\langle anum \rangle.Respond$

Initial state of *Ambulance* **component:**   *Idle*

Store of *Route* **component:**

anum	number of ambulance
dest	current destination type and incident type
start	start of route
end	end of route
nexts	start of next hop
nexte	end of next hop
h	number of hops in route
i	hop counter
t	timer variable for deterministic movement

Behaviour of *Route* **component:**

$R \stackrel{\text{def}}{=} [i < h]\text{start\_move}^\star[\perp]\langle\rangle\{i \leftarrow i+1, t \leftarrow now\}.RC +$
$\quad\quad [i = h \wedge (\text{my}.dest == ToSevere \vee \text{my}.dest == ToMinor)]$
$\quad\quad\quad\quad\quad\quad\quad\quad\quad\quad \text{arrive}^\star[\top]\langle anum \rangle.RS +$
$\quad\quad [i = h \wedge \text{my}.dest == ToHosp]\text{dropoff}^\star[\top]\langle anum \rangle.\textbf{kill} +$
$\quad\quad [i = h \wedge \text{my}.dest == ToBase]\text{atbase}^\star[\top]\langle anum \rangle.\textbf{kill} +$

$RS \stackrel{\text{def}}{=} [i = h \wedge \text{my}.dest == ToSevere]\text{pickup}^\star[\top]\langle anum \rangle.\textbf{kill} +$
$\quad\quad [i = h \wedge \text{my}.dest == ToMinor]\text{treat}^\star[\top]\langle anum \rangle.\textbf{kill}$

$RC \stackrel{\text{def}}{=} \text{end\_move}[\top]\langle anum, nexte, t, \textbf{MoveTime}(nexts, nexte, dest)\rangle$
$\quad\quad\quad\quad \{nexts \leftarrow \text{my}.nexte, nexte \leftarrow \textbf{NextHop}(i, \text{my}.start, \text{my}.end)\}.R$

$KR = \text{kill\_route}[\text{my}.anum == an](an).\textbf{kill}$

Fig. 3. Ambulance and route components

Constants:

T limit for response time

timeout   time to wait for a response for a request

Measures:

N set containing the number of idle ambulances at each possible base

Global store:

ontime   number of ontime ambulances

late   number of late ambulances

Evolution rule functions:

$$\mu_p(\gamma_s, \gamma_r, \alpha) = 1$$

$$\mu_r(\gamma_s, \alpha) = \begin{cases} 1/r & \alpha = \mathsf{incident}^\star \quad \text{(where } r \text{ is the mean time between incidents)} \\ \lambda_p & \alpha = \mathsf{pickup}^\star \\ \lambda_t & \alpha = \mathsf{treat}^\star \\ \lambda_d & \alpha = \mathsf{dropoff}^\star \\ 0 & \alpha = \mathsf{pause}^\star \wedge now < sender.t + timeout \\ \lambda_{fast} & \text{otherwise} \end{cases}$$

$$\mu_u(\gamma_s, \alpha) = \begin{cases} \{ontime \leftarrow ontime + 1\}, 0 & \alpha = \mathsf{timecheck}^\star \wedge now <= sender.itime + T \\ \{late \leftarrow late + 1\}, 0 & \alpha = \mathsf{timecheck}^\star \wedge now > sender.itime + T \\ \{\}, (Incident\_Queue\_Item, \{qnum \leftarrow sender.inum, itime \leftarrow now\}) \\ \qquad\qquad\qquad\qquad\qquad \alpha = \mathsf{incident}^\star \\ \{\}, (Incident\_Handler, \{loc \leftarrow \mathbf{IncidentLocation}(), dest \leftarrow \mathbf{IncidentType}(), \\ \qquad\qquad\qquad itime \leftarrow sender.itime\}) \\ \qquad\qquad\qquad\qquad\qquad \alpha = \mathsf{new\_handler}^\star \\ \{\}, (Return\_Handler, \{anum \leftarrow sender.anum, aloc \leftarrow sender.aloc, \\ \qquad\qquad\qquad dest \leftarrow sender.dest, \\ \qquad\qquad\qquad loc \leftarrow \mathbf{GetBase}(sender.anum, sender.aloc, N)\}) \\ \qquad\qquad\qquad\qquad\qquad \alpha = \mathsf{tobase}^\star \\ \{\}, (Route, \{anum \leftarrow sender.anum, dest \leftarrow sender.dest, \\ \qquad\qquad start \leftarrow sender.aloc, end \leftarrow sender.loc \\ \qquad\qquad nexts \leftarrow sender.aloc, nexte \leftarrow \mathbf{NextHop}(1, sender.aloc, sender.loc), \\ \qquad\qquad h \leftarrow \mathbf{RouteLength}(sender.aloc, sender.loc), \}) \\ \qquad\qquad\qquad\qquad\qquad \alpha = \mathsf{makeroute}^\star \\ \{\}, 0 & \text{otherwise} \end{cases}$$

Collective:

$$EMS \overset{\text{def}}{=} (Incident\_Queue, \{inum \mapsto 0, rnum \mapsto 1) \parallel$$
$$(ClosestIdleAmbulance, \{dloc \mapsto nullLoc, iloc \mapsto nullLoc, t \mapsto 0) \parallel) \parallel$$
$$(Ambulance, \{anum \mapsto 1, aloc \mapsto l_1, abase \mapsto l_1, idle \mapsto \top\}) \parallel \ldots \parallel$$
$$(Ambulance, \{anum \mapsto n, aloc \mapsto l_n, abase \mapsto l_n, idle \mapsto \top\})$$

Fig. 4. Constants, environment and collective

Each *Incident_Handler* has an assigned ambulance and interacts with the ambulance and generates *Routes* to move the ambulance to the location of the incident and then to the nearest hospital, if required. After this a *Return_Handler* is created using tobase*. The two handlers are separate components because an ambulance cannot be diverted once it has been assigned to an incident but once it is returning to a base position, it can be called to a new incident, so *Return_Handler* has behaviour to allow it to remove itself from the collective if this happens, and it is no longer needed in the collective.

Once an *Incident_Handler* and an *Ambulance* have been matched, the ambulance number is used in all communication between the *Incident_Handler*, *Ambulance* and *Route* components to limit broadcast communication to these three components. The queue number could also have been used for these purposes but ambulance number is sufficient. Since broadcast is not blocking, the model must be constructed so that *Incident_Handler* and *Ambulance* are in a state to receive the message from *Route*.

The *Route* component works through the route hops. It is initialised with the start and end of the route, and after obtaining the length of route from **RouteLength**, it works through each hop of the route[3] using the function **NextHop** until the end of the route when the appropriate action occurs depending on the destination type. For pickup and treatment at the scene, an arrive* action is required followed by a timecheck* action for the global count of late and on-time ambulances to be updated, based on the time the timecheck* action happens and the time the incident was generated.

The *Ambulance* and *Route* components assume that travel times are deterministic rather than stochastic (although it is straightforward to modify the model to use stochastic durations). The *Route* component performs a local start_move* action and notes the time of the action. The ambulance component responds to an end_move action once sufficient time has elapsed. Since *Route* components can also be generated by *Return_Handlers*, they can remove themselves from the collective on receipt of a kill command from the associated *Ambulance* when it receives an incident request during going to a base location.

After a simulation completes, the performance measure of the proportion of late ambulances can be calculated from the two global variables *ontime* and *late*. The model describes a system where ambulances behave in the manner described by the seven points in Sect. 2. The next section considers results of experiments with this model.

Table 1. Parameters for model

λ_p	1/12	rate of pickup* action	q	0.45	busy fraction
λ_t	1/12	rate of treat* action	m	1	proportion of serious incidents
λ_d	1/15	rate of dropoff* action	r	25	mean time between incidents
λ_{fast}	100	rate of fast actions	*timeout*	1	timeout period in minutes

---

[3] For the calculation of the performance measure, this detailed level of movement is not necessary but if one wanted to create an animation from a simulation then this detail is required.

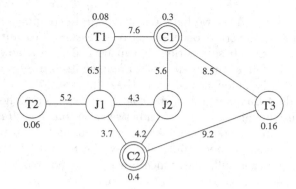

Fig. 5. Network configuration for experiments

5 Results

To explore the behaviour of the model and the heuristic, the network shown in Fig. 5 is used (which by contrast with [14] is a compact network rather than long and narrow). and is somewhat simpler than a real scenario. The number annotating the edges of the network gives the time in minutes that it takes to traverse the edge at the faster speed (with sirens and lights on). Locations with hospitals are indicated by double circles at vertices. The number annotating a vertex is the proportion of incidents at that location.

The parameters chosen for the model are given in Table 1. The parameter T which is used as the limit in the calculation of the late rate varies across experiments. The busy fraction q which is used in the calculation of the heuristic function π is estimated by simulation, for the given network with three ambulances to be 0.65.

The experiments explore how the late rate varies for different values of the time limit, and furthermore, they consider how the hospital location can affect the late rate, and are illustrated in Fig. 6. The square nodes indicate the hospital locations in each case. Each combination of time limit and hospital location was simulated for 500 runs over 20 h of simulated time. The shaded circles indicate at which locations the idle ambulances were based, and all locations were considered as possible base locations. The area of the circle represents the proportion of simulations that idle ambulances are at a location (or on their way to that location as a base) at the time point of 1200 min (20 h). Since there are three ambulances, fewer than three circles indicate that multiple ambulances are idle at a location.

The results show that the heuristic does not appear to have monotonic behaviour since an increased time limit can lead to a different location with a worse late rate, and this requires further investigation. The heuristic does not use the hospital location but obviously distance from hospital back to base will impact availability, and hence late rate. The lowest late rates occur when there are two hospitals at the two cities, and an ambulance goes to the closest hospital. This

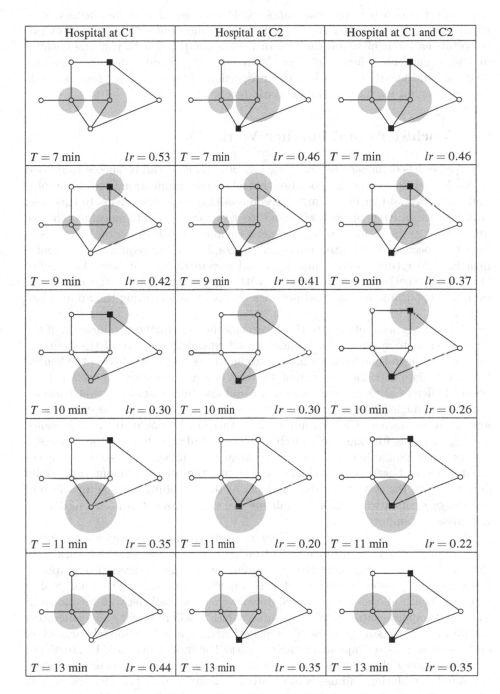

Fig. 6. Idle ambulances and proportions of late arrivals for time limits and hospital locations

experiment shows how the late rates would be affected if it was necessary to close one of the hospitals. However, for some time limits, the presence of two hospitals has little effect on the late rate when compared with just one hospital at the second city, where for others it makes a significant difference. The fact that hospital location can affect the proportion of late arrivals suggests a role for the hospital location in the heuristic function.

6   Conclusions and Further Work

This paper has demonstrated how the language CARMA can be successfully used to model a system involving coordination where communication is often complex and multiway, and various components interaction to achieve goals. In this case, this is identification of an ambulance to go to an incident, movement of the ambulance to the incident using a generic component that draws on functions to give the specifics of a route, movement to hospital where required, then choice of a base to return to on completion and movement to that base. Because of the use of generic functions together with generic components, the model can be made applicable to any road network simply by substituting the appropriate functions.

Further research relating to this case study include further exploration of the parameter state space, in particular to understand the nature of the heuristic function as mean time between incidents change, as well as modifying the heuristic to take into account the current location of idle ambulances as well as their bases. Different performance measures could also be investigated that consider not just a single deadline but how late the ambulance is, in the case of late arrival at the scence. Clearly, many variations can be made to the ambulance model, including for example, switching to an ambulance closer to the incident if one becomes available when another is already on the way; investigating movement between bases as an incident occurs; and the use of different time limits depending on the severity of the incident. At the modelling level, comparison of the use of CARMA with other formalisms and an assessment of its strengths and weaknesses is important.

As often is the case in modelling for performance assessment, the users who are interested in the measure often do not have the skills to work with the modelling language directly. A ongoing project is to develop a graphical front-end for general modelling of this ambulance scenario. The final goal is software which allows a user to graphically create a road network as shown in Fig. 5 with appropriate annotations, after which it will automatically generate a CARMA model consisting of the seven generic components, the model parameters and the functions to implement the network. The model can then be simulated in the CARMA Eclipse Plug-in. An additional step would be to take the output of a single simulation and use it to create an animation over the network, to give users an insight to what is happening during the simulation. This gives more information about the model over and above the performance measure.

Acknowledgements. This work is supported by the EU project QUANTICOL, 600708. The author thanks Jane Hillston and Yehia Abd Alrahman for their useful comments.

References

1. Alanis, R., Ingolfsson, A., Kolfal, B.: A Markov chain model for an EMS system with repositioning. Prod. Oper. Manag. **22**, 216–231 (2013)
2. Alrahman, Y.A., De Nicola, R., Loreti, M., Tiezzi, F., Vigo, R.: A calculus for attribute-based communication. In: Proceedings of SAC, pp. 1840–1845 (2015)
3. Bortolussi, L., De Nicola, R., Galpin, V., Gilmore, S., Hillston, J., Latella, D., Loreti, M., Massink, M.: CARMA: collective adaptive resource-sharing markovian agents. In: Proceedings of QAPL 2015. EPTCS, vol. 194, pp. 16–31 (2015)
4. Church, R., Velle, C.: The maximal covering location problem. Pap. Reg. Sci. Assoc. **32**, 101–118 (1974)
5. Ciancia, V., De Nicola, R., Hillston, J., Latella, D., Loreti, M., Massink, M.: CAS-SCEL semantics and implementation. QUANTICOL Deliverable D4.2 (2015)
6. Daskin, M.: A maximum expected covering location model: formulation, properties and heuristic solution. Transp. Sci. **17**, 48–70 (1983)
7. De Nicola, R., Latella, D., Loreti, M., Massink, M.: A uniform definition of stochastic process calculi. ACM Comput. Surv. **46**, 5 (2013)
8. De Nicola, R., Loreti, M., Pugliese, R., Tiezzi, F.: A formal approach to autonomic systems programming: the SCEL language. ACM TAAS **9**, 7:1–7:29 (2014)
9. Feng, C., Hillston, J.: PALOMA: a process algebra for located Markovian agents. In: Norman, G., Sanders, W. (eds.) QEST 2014. LNCS, vol. 8657, pp. 265–280. Springer, Heidelberg (2014)
10. Gendreau, M., Laporte, G., Semet, F.: A dynamic model and parallel tabu search heuristic for real-time ambulance relocation. Parallel Comput. **27**, 1641–1653 (2001)
11. Gillespie, D.: A general method for numerically simulating the stochastic time evolution of coupled chemical reactions. J. Comput. Phys. **22**, 403–434 (1976)
12. Hillston, J.: A Compositional Approach to Performance Modelling. CUP. Cambridge University Press, New York (1996)
13. Jagtenberg, C.: Personal communication (2016)
14. Jagtenberg, C., Bhulai, S., van der Mei, R.: An efficient heuristic for real-time ambulance redeployment. Oper. Res. Health Care **4**, 27–35 (2015)
15. Maxwell, M., Henderson, S., Topaloglu, H.: Tuning approximate dynamic programming policies for ambulance redeployment via direct search. Stoch. Syst. **3**, 322–361 (2013)
16. Toregas, C., Swain, R., ReVelle, C., Bergman, L.: The location of emergency service facilities. Oper. Res. **19**, 1363–1373 (1971)

On Synchronous and Asynchronous Compatibility of Communicating Components

Rolf Hennicker[1]([✉]), Michel Bidoit[2], and Thanh-Son Dang[1]

[1] Ludwig-Maximilians-Universität, Munich, Germany
hennicker@ifi.lmu.de
[2] LSV, CNRS and ENS de Cachan, Cachan, France

Abstract. We study interacting components and their compatibility with respect to synchronous and asynchronous composition. The behavior of components is formalized by I/O-transition systems. Synchronous composition is based on simultaneous execution of shared output and input actions of two components while asynchronous composition uses unbounded FIFO-buffers for message transfer. In both contexts we study compatibility notions based on the idea that any output issued by one component should be accepted as an input by the other. We distinguish between strong and weak versions of compatibility, the latter allowing the execution of internal actions before a message is accepted. We consider open systems and study conditions under which (strong/weak) synchronous compatibility is sufficient and necessary to get (strong/weak) asynchronous compatibility. We show that these conditions characterize half-duplex systems. Then we focus on the verification of weak asynchronous compatibility for possibly non half-duplex systems and provide a decidable criterion that ensures weak asynchronous compatibility.

1 Introduction

Structuring software systems by interconnected components is a standard technique in software engineering. In this work we consider active components with a well defined behavior which work together by message exchange. Each single component has a life cycle during which it sends and receives messages and it can also perform internal actions in between. For the correct functioning of the overall system it is essential that no communication errors occur during component interactions. There are different types of communication errors which are influenced by the communication style and system architecture. In our study we focus on bidirectional, peer to peer communication and we discuss synchronous and asynchronous message exchange. The former is based on a rendezvous mechanism such that two components must execute shared output and input actions together. The latter uses unbounded FIFO-buffers which hold the messages sent by one component and received by the other. In this context two prominent types of communication errors can be distinguished. The first one concerns situations, in which an output of one component is not accepted as an input by the other,

A. Lluch Lafuente and J. Proença (Eds.): COORDINATION 2016, LNCS 9686, pp. 138–156, 2016.
DOI: 10.1007/978-3-319-39519-7_9

the second one occurs if a component waits for an input which is never delivered. Inspired by the work of de Alfaro and Henzinger [11] on compatibility of interface automata, we focus on the former kind of communication error which itself gives rise to several variations.

De Alfaro and Henzinger deal with open systems and synchronous communication. They consider two interface automata to be compatible if there exists a "helpful" environment such that the interacting components can never reach an error state where "one of the automata may produce an output action that is in the input alphabet of the other automaton, but is not accepted". We allow open systems as well but follow the "pessimistic" approach where components should be compatible in any environment. For the formalization of component behaviors we use I/O-transition systems (IOTSes) and call two IOTSes *strongly synchronously compatible* if the compatibility requirement from above holds. In many practical examples it turns out that before interacting with the sending component the receiving component should still be able to perform some internal actions in between. This leads to our notion of *weak synchronous compatibility* (which works well with weak bisimulation and refinement [4]).

In this work we study also asynchronous compatibility of components communicating via unbounded message queues. Asynchronous compatibility requires that whenever a message queue is not empty, the receiver component must be able to take the next element of the queue; a property called *specified reception* in [6]. We distinguish again between strong and weak versions of asynchronous compatibility. In the asynchronous context the weak compatibility notion is particularly powerful since it allows a component, before it inputs a message waiting in the queue, still to put itself messages in its output queue (since we consider such enqueue actions as internal). We have shown in [3] that also weak asynchronous compatibility works well with weak bisimulation and refinement.

An obvious question is to what extent synchronous and asynchronous compatibility notions can be related to each other and, if this is not possible, which proof techniques can be used to verify asynchronous compatibility. We contribute to this issues with the following results:

1. We establish a relationship between strong/weak synchronous and asynchronous compatibility of two components (Sects. 4.1 and 4.2) and formulate three equivalent (and decidable) conditions such that strong/weak synchronous compatibility is sufficient, and even necessary, for strong/weak asynchronous compatibility. One of the three conditions is the half-duplex property: at any time at most one message queue is not empty; see, e.g., [5,9].
2. In the second part of this work (Sect. 5), we consider general, possibly non half-duplex systems, and study the verification of weak asynchronous compatibility in such cases. Due to the unboundedness of the FIFO-buffers the problem is not decidable [6]. We investigate, however, decidable and powerful criteria which allow us to prove weak asynchronous compatibility.

Related Work. In our study we focus on asynchronous message exchange via FIFO-buffers. Of course, other kinds of asynchronous communication using, e.g., event pools for modeling the composition of state machines in UML, or communication channels storing messages as bags are often considered. For instance, in [12], we have studied (modal) asynchronous I/O-transition systems and Petri nets where communication is realized by unbounded, but unordered, channel places. We have shown that in this case various compatibility problems are decidable. Systems of finite automata which contain both FIFO-buffers and bag channels are studied in [10] where topologies are investigated in which the reachability problem is decidable.

Compatibility notions are mostly considered for synchronous systems, since in this case compatibility checking is easier manageable and even decidable if the behaviors of local components have finitely many states. Some approaches use process algebras to study compatibility, like [7] using the π-calculus, others investigate interface theories with binary compatibility relations preserved by refinement, see, e.g., [14,16] for modal interfaces, or consider n-ary compatibility in multi-component systems like, e.g., team automata in [8]. A prominent example of multi-component systems with asynchronous communication via unbounded FIFO-buffers are CFSMs [6], for which many problems, like unspecified reception, are undecidable. The situation is different, if half-duplex systems of two CFSMs are considered. Cécé and Finkel have shown in [9] that then the set of reachable configurations is recognizable and several problems, including unspecified reception, are decidable. The approach in [5] even suggests to built in the half-duplex property in the system semantics to facilitate desynchronization.

There is, however, not much work on relationships between synchronous and asynchronous compatibility. An exception are the approaches of Basu, Bultan, Ouederni, and Salaün; see [1,2] for language-based and [15] for LTS-based semantics. Their crucial assumption is usually *synchronizability* which requires, for LTSes, a branching bisimulation between the synchronous and the asynchronous versions of a system (with message consumption from buffers considered internal). Under this hypothesis [15] proposes methods to prove compatibility of asynchronously communicating peers by checking synchronous compatibility. Their central notion is UR compatibility which is close to our weak compatibility concept but requires additionally deadlock-freeness. Obvious differences to our work are that [15] considers multi-component systems while we study binary compatibility relations. On the other hand, [15] considers closed systems while we allow open systems which can be incrementally extended to larger ones. Also our method for checking asynchronous compatibility is very different. In the first part of our work we rely on half-duplex systems (instead of synchronizability) and we show that for such systems synchronous and asynchronous compatibility are even equivalent. In the second part of our work we drop any assumptions and investigate powerful and decidable criteria for asynchronous compatibility of systems which are neither half-duplex nor synchronizable.

Quite close to the first part of our work is the study of half-duplex systems by Cécé and Finkel [9]. Due to their decidability result for unspecified reception (for two communicating CFSMs) it is not really surprising that we get an effective characterization of asynchronous compatibility and a way to decide it for components with finitely many states. A main difference to [9] is that we consider also synchronous systems and relate their compatibility properties to the asynchronous versions. Moreover, we deal with open systems as well and consider a weak variant of asynchronous compatibility, which we believe adds much power to the strong version. Finally, as explained above, a significant part of our work deals also with systems which are not necessarily half-duplex.

2   I/O-Transition Systems and Their Compositions

We start with the definitions of I/O-transition systems and their synchronous and asynchronous compositions which are the basis of the subsequent study.

Definition 1 (IOTS). *An* I/O-transition system *is a quadruple* $A = (states_A, start_A, act_A, \longrightarrow_A)$ *consisting of a set of states* $states_A$, *an initial state* $start_A \in states_A$, *a set* $act_A = in_A \cup out_A \cup int_A$ *of actions being the disjoint union of sets* in_A, out_A *and* int_A *of input, output and internal actions resp., and a transition relation* $\longrightarrow_A \subseteq states_A \times act_A \times states_A$.

We write $s\xrightarrow{a}_A s'$ instead of $(s, a, s') \in \longrightarrow_A$. For $X \subseteq act_A$ we write $s\xrightarrow{X}_A^* s'$ if there exists a (possibly empty) sequence of transitions $s\xrightarrow{a_1}_A s_1 \ldots s_{n-1}\xrightarrow{a_n}_A s'$ involving only actions of X, i.e. $a_1, \ldots, a_n \in X$. A state $s \in states_A$ is *reachable* if $start_A\xrightarrow{act_A}_A^* s$. The set of reachable states of A is denoted by $\mathcal{R}(A)$.

Two IOTSes A and B are *(syntactically) composable* if their actions only overlap on complementary types, i.e. $act_A \cap act_B \subseteq (in_A \cap out_B) \cup (in_B \cap out_A)$. The *set of shared actions* $act_A \cap act_B$ is denoted by $shared(A, B)$. The *synchronous composition* of two IOTSes A and B is defined as the product of transition systems with synchronization on shared actions which become internal actions in the composition. Shared actions can only be executed together; they are blocked if the other component is not ready for communication. In contrast, internal actions and non-shared input and output actions can always be executed by a single component in the composition. These (non-shared) actions are called *free actions* in the following.

Definition 2 (Synchronous composition). *Let A and B be two composable IOTSes. The* synchronous composition *of A and B is the IOTS $A \otimes B = (states_A \times states_B, (start_A, start_B), act_{A\otimes B}, \longrightarrow_{A\otimes B})$ where $act_{A\otimes B}$ is the disjoint union of the input actions $in_{A\otimes B} = (in_A \cup in_B) \setminus shared(A, B)$, the output actions $out_{A\otimes B} = (out_A \cup out_B) \setminus shared(A, B)$, and the internal actions $int_{A\otimes B} = int_A \cup int_B \cup shared(A, B)$. The transition relation of $A \otimes B$ is the smallest relation such that*

- *for all $a \in act_A \setminus shared(A, B)$, if $s\xrightarrow{a}_A s'$, then $(s, t)\xrightarrow{a}_{A\otimes B}(s', t)$ for all $t \in states_B$,*
- *for all $a \in act_B \setminus shared(A, B)$, if $t\xrightarrow{a}_B t'$, then $(s, t)\xrightarrow{a}_{A\otimes B}(s, t')$ for all $s \in states_A$, and*
- *for all $a \in shared(A, B)$, if $s\xrightarrow{a}_A s'$ and $t\xrightarrow{a}_B t'$, then $(s, t)\xrightarrow{a}_{A\otimes B}(s', t')$.*

The synchronous composition of two IOTSes A and B yields a *closed* system if it has no input and output actions, i.e. $(in_A \cup in_B) \setminus shared(A, B) = \emptyset$ and $(out_A \cup out_B) \setminus shared(A, B) = \emptyset$, otherwise the system is *open*.

In distributed applications, implemented, e.g., with a message-passing middleware, usually an asynchronous communication pattern is used. In this paper, we consider asynchronous communication via unbounded message queues. In Fig. 1 two asynchronously communicating IOTSes A and B are depicted. A sends a message a to B by putting it, with action $a^\triangleright$, into a queue which stores the outputs of A. Then B can receive a by removing it, with action a, from the queue. In contrast to synchronous communication, there is a delay between sending and reception. Similarly, B can send a message b to A by using a second queue which stores the outputs of B. The system in Fig. 1 is open: A has an open output x to the environment and an open input y for messages coming from the environment. Similarly B has an open input u and an open output v. Additionally, A and B may have some internal actions.

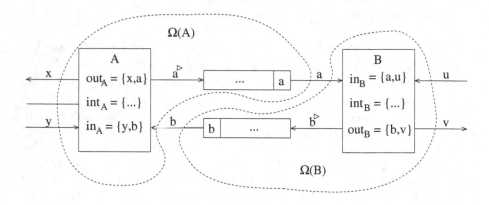

Fig. 1. Asynchronous communication

To formalize asynchronous communication, we equip each communicating IOTS with an "output queue", which leads to a new IOTS indicated in Fig. 1 by $\Omega(A)$ and $\Omega(B)$ respectively. For this construction, we represent an output queue as an (infinite) IOTS and then we compose it with a renamed version of A where all outputs a of A (to be stored in the queue) are renamed to enqueue actions of the form $a^\triangleright$.

Definition 3 (IOTS with output queue).

1. *Let M be a set of names and $M^\triangleright = \{a^\triangleright \mid a \in M\}$ be disjoint from M. The queue IOTS for M is $Q_M = (M^*, \epsilon, act_{Q_M}, \longrightarrow_{Q_M})$ where the set of states is the set M^* of all words over M, the initial state $\epsilon \in M^*$ is the empty word, and the set of actions act_{Q_M} is the disjoint union of input actions $in_{Q_M} = M^\triangleright$, output actions $out_{Q_M} = M$ and with no internal action. The transition relation $\longrightarrow_{Q_M}$ is the smallest relation such that*

– *for all $a^{\triangleright} \in M^{\triangleright}$ and states $q \in M^*$:* $q \xrightarrow{a^{\triangleright}}_{Q_M} qa$ *(enqueue on the right),*

– *for all $a \in M$ and states $q \in M^*$:* $aq \xrightarrow{a}_{Q_M} q$ *(dequeue on the left).*

2. *Let A be an IOTS such that $M \subseteq out_A$ and $M^{\triangleright} \cap act_A = \emptyset$. Let $A_M^{\triangleright}$ be the renamed version of A where all $a \in M$ are renamed to $a^{\triangleright}$. The IOTS A equipped with output queue for M is given by the synchronous composition $\Omega_M(A) = A_M^{\triangleright} \otimes Q_M$. (Note that $A_M^{\triangleright}$ and Q_M are composable.)*

The states of $\Omega_M(A)$ are pairs (s, q) where s is a state of A and q is a word over M. The initial state is $(start_A, \epsilon)$. For the actions we have $in_{\Omega_M(A)} = in_A$, $out_{\Omega_M(A)} = out_A$, and $int_{\Omega_M(A)} = int_A \cup M^{\triangleright}$. Transitions in $\Omega_M(A)$ are:

– if $a \in in_A$ and $s \xrightarrow{a}_A s'$ then $(s, q) \xrightarrow{a}_{\Omega_M(A)} (s', q)$,

– if $a \in out_A \setminus M$ and $s \xrightarrow{a}_A s'$ then $(s, q) \xrightarrow{a}_{\Omega_M(A)} (s', q)$,

– if $a \in M \subseteq out_A$ then $(s, aq) \xrightarrow{a}_{\Omega_M(A)} (s, q)$,

– if $a \in int_A$ and $s \xrightarrow{a}_A s'$ then $(s, q) \xrightarrow{a}_{\Omega_M(A)} (s', q)$,

– if $a^{\triangleright} \in M^{\triangleright}$ and $s \xrightarrow{a}_A s'$ (i.e. $s \xrightarrow{a^{\triangleright}}_{A_M^{\triangleright}} s'$) then $(s, q) \xrightarrow{a^{\triangleright}}_{\Omega_M(A)} (s', qa)$.

To define the asynchronous composition of two IOTSes A and B, we assume that A and B are *asynchronously composable* which means that A and B are composable (as before) and $shared(A, B)^{\triangleright} \cap (act_A \cup act_B) = \emptyset$. Then, we equip A with an output queue for those outputs shared with inputs of B, and, similarly, we equip B with an output queue for those outputs shared with inputs of A. The IOTSes $\Omega_{out_A \cap in_B}(A)$ and $\Omega_{out_B \cap in_A}(B)$ are then synchronously composed which gives the asynchronous composition of A and B.

Definition 4 (Asynchronous composition). *Let A, B be two asynchronously composable IOTSes. The asynchronous composition of A and B is defined by $A \otimes_{as} B = \Omega_{out_A \cap in_B}(A) \otimes \Omega_{out_B \cap in_A}(B)$.*[1]

In the sequel we will briefly write $\Omega(A)$ for $\Omega_{out_A \cap in_B}(A)$ and $\Omega(B)$ for $\Omega_{out_B \cap in_A}(B)$. The states of $\Omega(A) \otimes \Omega(B)$ are pairs $((s_A, q_A), (s_B, q_B))$ where s_A is a state of A, the queue q_A stores elements of $out_A \cap in_B$, s_B is a state of B, and the queue q_B stores elements of $out_B \cap in_A$. The initial state is $((start_A, \epsilon), (start_B, \epsilon))$. For the actions we have $in_{\Omega(A) \otimes \Omega(B)} = in_{A \otimes B}$, $out_{\Omega(A) \otimes \Omega(B)} = out_{A \otimes B}$, and $int_{\Omega(A) \otimes \Omega(B)} = int_{A \otimes B} \cup shared(A, B)^{\triangleright}$. For the transitions in $\Omega(A) \otimes \Omega(B)$ we have two main cases:

1. Transitions which can freely occur in A or in B without involving any output queue. These transitions change just the local state of A or of B. An example would be a transition $s_A \xrightarrow{a}_A s'_A$ with action $a \in out_A \setminus in_B$ which induces a transition $((s_A, q_A), (s_B, q_B)) \xrightarrow{a}_{\Omega(A) \otimes \Omega(B)} ((s'_A, q_A), (s_B, q_B))$.

2. Transitions which involve the output queue of A. There are two sub-cases concerning dequeue and enqueue actions which are internal actions in $\Omega(A) \otimes \Omega(B)$:

---

[1] Note that $\Omega_{out_A \cap in_B}(A)$ and $\Omega_{out_B \cap in_A}(B)$ are composable.

(a) $a \in out_A \cap in_B$ (hence $a \in out_{Q_{out_A \cap in_B}}$) and $s_B \xrightarrow{a}_B s'_B$

then $((s_A, aq_A), (s_B, q_B)) \xrightarrow{a}_{\Omega(A) \otimes \Omega(B)} ((s_A, q_A), (s'_B, q_B))$.

(b) $a^{\triangleright} \in (out_A \cap in_B)^{\triangleright}$ (hence $a \in in_{Q_{out_A \cap in_B}}$) and $s_A \xrightarrow{a}_A s'_A$

then $((s_A, q_A), (s_B, q_B)) \xrightarrow{a^{\triangleright}}_{\Omega(A) \otimes \Omega(B)} ((s'_A, q_A a), (s_B, q_B))$.

Transitions which involve the output queue of B are analogous.

3   Compatibility Notions

In this section we review our compatibility notions introduced in [4] for the synchronous and in [3] for the asynchronous case. For synchronous compatibility the idea is that whenever a component wants to issue an output a then its communication partner should be ready to accept a as an input.

Definition 5 (Strong synchronous compatibility). *Two IOTSes A and B are* strongly synchronously compatible, *denoted by $A \longleftrightarrow B$, if they are composable and if for all reachable states $(s_A, s_B) \in \mathcal{R}(A \otimes B)$,*

(1) $\forall a \in out_A \cap in_B : \ s_A \xrightarrow{a}_A s'_A \implies \exists \ s_B \xrightarrow{a}_B s'_B$,

(2) $\forall a \in out_B \cap in_A : \ s_B \xrightarrow{a}_B s'_B \implies \exists \ s_A \xrightarrow{a}_A s'_A$.

This definition requires that IOTSes should work properly together in *any* environment, in contrast to the "optimistic" approach of [11] in which the existence of a "helpful" environment to avoid error states is sufficient. For closed systems this makes no difference. In [4] we have introduced a weak version of compatibility such that a component can delay an expected input and perform some internal actions before. (This works well with weak refinement; see [4].)

Definition 6 (Weak synchronous compatibility). *Two IOTSes A and B are* weakly synchronously compatible, *denoted by $A \leftarrow\dashrightarrow B$, if they are composable and if for all reachable states $(s_A, s_B) \in \mathcal{R}(A \otimes B)$,*

(1) $\forall a \in out_A \cap in_B : \ s_A \xrightarrow{a}_A s'_A \implies \exists \ s_B \xrightarrow{int_B}^{*}_B \bar{s}_B \xrightarrow{a}_B s'_B$,

(2) $\forall a \in out_B \cap in_A : \ s_B \xrightarrow{a}_B s'_B \implies \exists \ s_A \xrightarrow{int_A}^{*}_A \bar{s}_A \xrightarrow{a}_A s'_A$,

Now we turn to compatibility of asynchronously communicating components. In this case outputs of a component are stored in a queue from which they can be consumed by the receiver component. Therefore, in the asynchronous context, compatibility means that if a queue is not empty, the receiver component must be ready to take (i.e. input) the next removable element from the queue. This idea can be easily formalized by requiring synchronous compatibility between the communicating IOTSes which are enhanced by their output queues. We distinguish again between strong and weak compatibility versions.

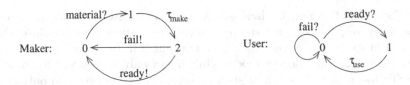

Fig. 2. Maker and User

Definition 7 (Strong and weak asynchronous compatibility). *Let A and B be two asynchronously composable I/O-transition systems. A and B are* strongly asynchronously compatible, *denoted by $A \overset{a}{\longleftrightarrow} B$, if $\Omega(A) \longleftrightarrow \Omega(B)$. A and B are* weakly asynchronously compatible, *denoted by $A \overset{a}{\leftarrow\dashrightarrow} B$, if $\Omega(A) \leftarrow\dashrightarrow \Omega(B)$.*

Example 1. Figure 2 shows the behavior of a Maker and a User process. Here and in the subsequent drawings we use the following notations: Initial states are denoted by 0, input actions a are indicated by a?, output actions a by a!, and internal actions a by τ_a. The maker expects some material from the environment (input action material), constructs some item (internal action make), and then it signals either that the item is ready (output action ready) or that the production did fail (output action fail). Both actions are shared with input actions of the user. When the user has received the ready signal it uses the item (internal action use). Maker and User are weakly synchronously compatible but not strongly synchronously compatible. The critical state in the synchronous product Maker $\otimes$ User is (2,1) which can be reached with the transitions $(0,0) \xrightarrow{\text{material}} (1,0) \xrightarrow{\text{make}} (2,0) \xrightarrow{\text{ready}} (0,1) \xrightarrow{\text{material}} (1,1) \xrightarrow{\text{make}} (2,1)$.
In this state the maker wants to send ready or fail but the user must first perform its internal use action before it can receive the corresponding input. The asynchronous composition Maker $\otimes_{as}$ User has infinitely many states since the maker can be faster then the user. We will see, as an application of the forthcoming results, that Maker and User are also weakly asynchronously compatible.

4 Relating Synchronous and Asynchronous Compatibility

We are now interested in possible relationships between synchronous and asynchronous compatibility. This is particularly motivated by the fact that for finite IOTSes reachability, and therefore synchronous (strong and weak) compatibility, are decidable which is in general not the case for asynchronous communication with unbounded FIFO-buffers.

4.1 From Synchronous to Asynchronous Compatibility

In this section we study conditions under which it is sufficient to check strong (weak) synchronous compatibility to ensure strong (weak) asynchronous compatibility. In general this implication does not hold. As an example consider the two IOTSes A and B in Fig. 3. Obviously, A and B are strongly synchronously compatible. They are, however, not strongly asynchronously compatible since A may first put a in its output queue, then B can output b in its queue and then both are blocked (A can only accept ack_a while B can only accept ack_b). In Fig. 3 each IOTS has a state (the initial state) where a choice between an output and an input action is possible. We will see (Corollary 1) that if such situations are avoided synchronous compatibility implies asynchronous compatibility, and we will even get more general criteria (Theorem 1) for which the following property $\mathcal{P}$ is important.

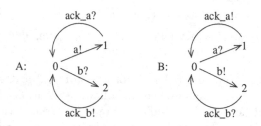

Fig. 3. A $\longleftrightarrow$ B but <u>not</u> A $\overset{a}{\longleftrightarrow}$ B

Property $\mathcal{P}$: Let A and B be two asynchronously composable IOTSes. The asynchronous system $A \otimes_{as} B$ satisfies property $\mathcal{P}$ if for each reachable state $((s_A, q_A), (s_B, q_B)) \in \mathcal{R}(\Omega(A) \otimes \Omega(B))$ one of the following conditions holds:

(i) $q_A = q_B = \epsilon$ and $(s_A, s_B) \in \mathcal{R}(A \otimes B)$.
(ii) $q_A = a_1 \ldots a_m \neq \epsilon$ and $q_B = \epsilon$ and there exists $r_A \in states_A$ such that: $(r_A, s_B) \in \mathcal{R}(A \otimes B)$ and $r_A \overset{a_1}{\Longrightarrow}_A \ldots \overset{a_m}{\Longrightarrow}_A s_A$.
(iii) $q_A = \epsilon$ and $q_B = b_1 \ldots b_m \neq \epsilon$ and there exists $r_B \in states_B$ such that: $(s_A, r_B) \in \mathcal{R}(A \otimes B)$ and $r_B \overset{b_1}{\Longrightarrow}_B \ldots \overset{b_m}{\Longrightarrow}_B s_B$.

To explain the notation $\Longrightarrow_A$, let $a \in out_A \cap in_B$ and $F_A = act_A \setminus shared(A, B)$ be the set of the free actions of A. Then $s \overset{a}{\Longrightarrow}_A s'$ stands for a sequence of transitions $s \overset{F_A *}{\longrightarrow}_A \bar{s} \overset{a}{\longrightarrow}_A \bar{s}' \overset{F_A *}{\longrightarrow}_A s'$ such that the transition with $a \in out_A \cap in_B$ is surrounded by arbitrary transitions in A involving only free actions of A. The notation $\Longrightarrow_B$ is defined analogously.

Property $\mathcal{P}$ expresses that (a) in each reachable state of the asynchronous composition at least one of the two queues is empty and (b) the state of the component where the output queue is not empty can be reached from a reachable state in the *synchronous product* by outputting the actions stored in the queue, possibly interleaved with free actions. Part (a) specifies half-duplex systems; see, e.g., [9].

Definition 8. *Let A and B be two asynchronously composable IOTSes. The asynchronous system $A \otimes_{as} B$ is half-duplex, if for all reachable states $((s_A, q_A), (s_B, q_B)) \in \mathcal{R}(\Omega(A) \otimes \Omega(B))$ it holds that $q_A = \epsilon$ or $q_B = \epsilon$.*

It turns out that also part (b) explained above holds for half-duplex systems, i.e. property $\mathcal{P}$ characterizes this class of systems as stated in Lemma 1, (1) and (2). In [9] it is shown that membership is decidable for half-duplex systems. This corresponds to condition (3) of Lemma 1 which says that in the synchronous product of A and B there is no reachable state where at the same time an output from A to B and an output from B to A is enabled. Obviously this is decidable for finite A and B.

Lemma 1. *Let A and B be two asynchronously composable IOTSes. The following conditions are equivalent:*

1. *The asynchronous system $A \otimes_{as} B$ satisfies property $\mathcal{P}$.*
2. *The asynchronous system $A \otimes_{as} B$ is half-duplex.*
3. *For each reachable state $(s_A, s_B) \in \mathcal{R}(A \otimes B)$ and each transitions $s_A \xrightarrow{a}_A s'_A$ and $s_B \xrightarrow{b}_B s'_B$ either $a \notin out_A \cap in_B$ or $b \notin out_B \cap in_A$.*

Proof. (1) $\Rightarrow$ (2) is trivial. (2) $\Rightarrow$ (3) is straightforward by contradiction. The direction (3) $\Rightarrow$ (1) is non-trivial. It involves a complex case distinction on the form of the transitions in the asynchronous composition. Interestingly only the case of transitions with enqueue actions needs the assumption (3). $\qquad \square$

Theorem 1. *Let A and B be two asynchronously composable IOTSes such that one (and hence all) of the conditions in Lemma 1 are satisfied. Then the following holds:*

1. $A \longleftrightarrow B \Longrightarrow A \xleftarrow{a} B.$
2. $A \leftarrow\text{-}\rightarrow B \Longrightarrow A \leftarrow\underline{a}\rightarrow B.$

Proof. The proof uses Lemma 1 for both cases. (1) Assume $A \longleftrightarrow B$. We have to show $\Omega(A) \longleftrightarrow \Omega(B)$. We prove condition (1) of Definition 5. Condition (2) is proved analogously. Let $((s_A, q_A), (s_B, q_B)) \in \mathcal{R}(\Omega(A) \otimes \Omega(B))$, $a \in out_{\Omega(A)} \cap in_{\Omega(B)}$ and $(s_A, q_A) \xrightarrow{a}_{\Omega(A)} (s'_A, q'_A)$. Then q_A has the form $u a_2 \ldots a_m$. By assumption, $\Omega(A) \otimes \Omega(B)$ satisfies the property $\mathcal{P}$. Hence, there exists $r_A \in states_A$ such that $(r_A, s_B) \in \mathcal{R}(A \otimes B)$ and $r_A \xRightarrow{a}_A \bar{r}_A \xRightarrow{a_2} \ldots \xRightarrow{a_m}_A s_A$. Thereby $r_A \xRightarrow{a}_A \bar{r}_A$ is of the form $r_A \xrightarrow{F_A}{}^*_A s \xrightarrow{a}_A s' \xrightarrow{F_A}{}^*_A \bar{r}_A$. Since F_A involves only free actions of A (not shared with B), and since $(r_A, s_B) \in \mathcal{R}(A \otimes B)$ we have that $(s, s_B) \in \mathcal{R}(A \otimes B)$. Now we can use the assumption $A \longleftrightarrow B$ which says that there exists $s_B \xrightarrow{a}_B s'_B$. Since $a \in in_B$, we get a transition $(s_B, q_B) \xrightarrow{a}_{\Omega(B)} (s'_B, q_B)$ and we are done.

(2) The weak case is a slight generalization of the proof of (1). The first part of the proof is the same but then we use the assumption $A \leftarrow\text{-}\rightarrow B$ which says that there exists $s_B \xrightarrow{int_B}{}^*_B \bar{s}_B \xrightarrow{a}_B s'_B$ consisting of a sequence of internal transitions of B followed by $\bar{s}_B \xrightarrow{a}_B s'_B$ with $a \in in_B$. Therefore we get transitions $(s_B, q_B) \xrightarrow{int_B}{}^*_{\Omega(B)} (\bar{s}_B, q_B) \xrightarrow{a}_{\Omega(B)} (s'_B, q_B)$ and, since $int_B \subseteq int_{\Omega(B)}$ we are done. $\qquad \square$

We come back to our discussion at the beginning of this section where we have claimed that for I/O-transition systems which do not show states where input and output actions are both enabled, synchronous compatibility implies asynchronous compatibility. We must, however, be careful whether we consider the strong or the weak case which leads us to two versions of I/O-separation.

Definition 9 (I/O-separated transition systems). *Let A be an IOTS.*

1. *A is called* I/O-separated *if for all reachable states $s \in \mathcal{R}(A)$ it holds: If there exists a transition $s \xrightarrow{a}_A s'$ with $a \in out_A$ then there is no transition $s \xrightarrow{a'}_A s'$ with $a' \in in_A$.*
2. *A is called* observationally I/O-separated *if for all reachable states $s \in \mathcal{R}(A)$ it holds: If there exists a transition $s \xrightarrow{a}_A s'$ with $a \in out_A$ then there is no sequence of transitions $s \xrightarrow{int_A}_A^* \bar{s}_A \xrightarrow{a'}_A s'$ with $a' \in in_A$.*

Obviously, observational I/O-separation implies I/O-separation but not the other way round.

Lemma 2. *Let A and B be two asynchronously composable IOTSes.*

1. *If A and B are I/O-separated and $A \longleftrightarrow B$, then one (and hence all) of the conditions in Lemma 1 are satisfied.*
2. *If A and B are observationally I/O-separated and $A \leftarrow \dashrightarrow B$, then one (and hence all) of the conditions in Lemma 1 are satisfied.*

Proof. The proof of both cases is by contradiction.   □

The notion of I/O-separation appears in a more strict version, called *input-separation*, in [13] and similarly as *system without local mixed states* in [9]. Part (1) of Lemma 2 can be considered as a generalization of Lemma 4 in [13] which has shown that input-separated IOTSes which are strongly compatible and form a closed system are half-duplex. This result was in turn a generalization of Theorem 35 in [9]. Open systems and weak compatibility were not an issue in these approaches. With Theorem 1 and Lemma 2 we get:

Corollary 1. *Let A and B be two asynchronously composable IOTSes.*

1. *If A and B are I/O-separated and $A \longleftrightarrow B$, then $A \xleftrightarrow{a} B$.*
2. *If A and B are observationally I/O-separated and $A \leftarrow \dashrightarrow B$, then $A \xleftarrow{a}\dashrightarrow B$.*

Let us note that part (2) of Corollary 1 would not hold, if we would only assume I/O-separation. As an application of Corollary 1 we refer to Example 1. `Maker` and `User` are observationally I/O-separated, they are weakly synchronously compatible and therefore, by Corollary 1(2), they are also weakly asynchronously compatible.

4.2   From Asynchronous to Synchronous Compatibility

This section studies the other direction, i.e. whether asynchronous compatibility can imply synchronous compatibility. It turns out that for the strong case this is indeed true without any further assumptions while for the weak case this holds under the equivalent conditions of Lemma 1. In any case, we need for the proof the following lemma which shows that all reachable states in the synchronous product are reachable in the asynchronous product with empty output queues.

Lemma 3. *Let A and B be two asynchronously composable IOTSes. For any state $(s_A, s_B) \in \mathcal{R}(A \otimes B)$, the state $((s_A, \epsilon), (s_B, \epsilon))$ belongs to $\mathcal{R}(\Omega(A) \otimes \Omega(B))$.*

Proof. The proof is straightforward by induction on the length of the derivation of $(s_A, s_R) \in \mathcal{R}(A \otimes B)$. ☐

Theorem 2. *For asynchronously composable IOTSes A and B it holds:*

1. $A \overset{a}{\longleftrightarrow} B \Longrightarrow A \longleftrightarrow B$.
2. *If one (and hence all) of the conditions in Lemma 1 are satisfied, then $A \overset{a}{\leftarrow\!-\!\rightarrow} B \Longrightarrow A \leftarrow\!-\!\rightarrow B$.*

Proof. (1) Assume $A \overset{a}{\longleftrightarrow} B$, i.e. $\Omega(A) \longleftrightarrow \Omega(B)$. We have to show $A \longleftrightarrow B$. We prove condition (1) of Definition 5. Condition (2) is analogous.

Let $(s_A, s_B) \in \mathcal{R}(A \otimes B), a \in out_A \cap in_B$ and $s_A \overset{a}{\longrightarrow}_A s'_A$. By Lemma 3, $((s_A, \epsilon), (s_B, \epsilon)) \in \mathcal{R}(\Omega(A) \otimes \Omega(B))$. Since $s_A \overset{a}{\longrightarrow}_A s'_A$, we have a transition in $\Omega(A) \otimes \Omega(B)$ with enqueue action for a: $((s_A, \epsilon), (s_B, \epsilon)) \overset{a^{\triangleright}}{\longrightarrow}_{\Omega(A) \otimes \Omega(B)} ((s'_A, a), (s_B, \epsilon))$ and it holds $((s'_A, a), (s_B, \epsilon)) \in \mathcal{R}(\Omega(A) \otimes \Omega(B))$. Then, there is a transition $(s'_A, a) \overset{a}{\longrightarrow}_{\Omega(A)} (s'_A, \epsilon)$. Since $\Omega(A) \longleftrightarrow \Omega(B)$ there must be a transition $(s_B, \epsilon) \overset{a}{\longrightarrow}_{\Omega(B)} (s'_B, \epsilon)$. This transtion must be caused by a transition $s_B \overset{a}{\longrightarrow}_B s'_B$ and we are done.

(2) Assume $A \overset{a}{\leftarrow\!-\!\rightarrow} B$, i.e. $\Omega(A) \leftarrow\!-\!\rightarrow \Omega(B)$. We have to show $A \leftarrow\!-\!\rightarrow B$. We prove condition (1) of Definition 6. Condition (2) is proved analogously.

Let $(s_A, s_B) \in \mathcal{R}(A \otimes B), a \in out_A \cap in_B$ and $s_A \overset{a}{\longrightarrow}_A s'_A$. With the same reasoning as in case (1) we get $((s'_A, a), (s_B, \epsilon)) \in \mathcal{R}(\Omega(A) \otimes \Omega(B))$ and we get a transition $(s'_A, a) \overset{a}{\longrightarrow}_{\Omega(A)} (s'_A, \epsilon)$. Since $\Omega(A) \leftarrow\!-\!\rightarrow \Omega(B)$ there are transitions $(s_B, \epsilon) \overset{int_{\Omega(B)}}{\longrightarrow}{}^*_{\Omega(B)} (\overline{s}_B, \overline{q}_B) \overset{a}{\longrightarrow}_{\Omega(B)} (s'_B, \overline{q}_B)$. Since internal transitions of $\Omega(B)$ do not involve any steps of $\Omega(A)$, we have $((s'_A, a), (\overline{s}_B, \overline{q}_B)) \in \mathcal{R}(\Omega(A) \otimes \Omega(B))$. Due to the assumption that the conditions in Lemma 1 are satisfied, $\Omega(A) \otimes \Omega(B)$ is half-duplex and therefore $\overline{q}_B$ must be empty and the same holds for all intermediate queues reached by the transitions in $(s_B, \epsilon) \overset{int_{\Omega(B)}}{\longrightarrow}{}^*_{\Omega(B)} (\overline{s}_B, \overline{q}_B)$. Therefore no enqueue action can occur in these transitions. Noticing that $int_{\Omega(B)} = int_B \cup (out_B \cap in_A)^{\triangleright}$, we get $(s_B, \epsilon) \overset{int_B}{\longrightarrow}{}^*_{\Omega(B)} (\overline{s}_B, \epsilon) \overset{a}{\longrightarrow}_{\Omega(B)} (s'_B, \epsilon)$ and all these transtions must be induced by transitions $s_B \overset{int_B}{\longrightarrow}{}^*_B \overline{s}_B \overset{a}{\longrightarrow}_B s'_B$, i.e. we are done. ☐

As a consequence of Theorems 1, 2 we see that under the equivalent conditions of Lemma 1, in particular when the asynchronous system is half-duplex, (weak) synchronous compatibility is equivalent to (weak) asynchronous compatibility.

5   Weak Asynchronous Compatibility: The General Case

In this section we are interested in the verification of asynchronous compatibility in the general case, where at the same time both queues of the communicating IOTSes may be not empty. We focus here on weak asynchronous compatibility since non-half duplex systems are often weakly asynchronously compatible but not weakly synchronously compatible.[2] A simple example would be two components which both start to send a message to each other and after that each component takes the message addressed to it from the buffer.

Example 2. Figure 4 shows two IOTSes MA and MB which produce items for each other. After reception of some material from the environment, MA produces an item (internal action makeA) followed by either a signal that the item is ready for use (output readyA) or a signal that the production did fail (output failA). Whenever MA reaches its initial state it can also accept an input readyB and then use the item produced by MB (internal action useB) or it can accept a signal that the production of its partner did fail (input failB). The behavior of MB is analogous. The asynchronous composition of MA and MB is not half-duplex; both processes can produce and signal concurrently. Clearly, the system is not weakly synchronously compatible. For instance, the state (2,2) is reachable in the synchronous product and in this state each of the two processes wants to output an action which the other is not able to accept. The system is also not synchronizable in the sense of [15]. We will prove below that the system is weakly asynchronously compatible.

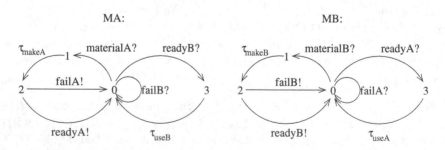

Fig. 4. MA ←ᵃ→ MB but not MA ← -→ MB .

In general, the problem of weak asynchronous compatibility is undecidable due to the unbounded message queues. We develop in the following a criterion,

---

[2] For the strong case this is not possible, see Theorem 2(1).

which is decidable if the underlying IOTSes are finite, which works for non half-duplex systems, and which ensures weak asynchronous compatibility. The idea is to use again synchronous products, but not the standard synchronous composition of two IOTSes A and B but variants of it. First we focus only on one direction of compatibility concerning the outputs of A which should be received by B. Due to the weak compatibility notion B can, before it takes an input message, execute internal actions. In particular, it can put outputs directed to A in its output queue. (Remember that enqueue actions are internal). To simulate this in a synchronous product we must artificially hide these outputs of B such that they become free actions in the synchronous product. Consequently also the corresponding inputs of A must be hidden. Then we require that outputs of A directed to B can be received by B possibly after some internal actions are executed, which now subsumes also the hidden outputs of B. A symmetric requirement is obtained when we consider compatibility in the direction from B to A. For the formalization of these ideas we first define hiding of actions.

Definition 10 (Hiding). *Let* $A = (states_A, start_A, act_A, \longrightarrow_A)$ *be an IOTS and* $H \subseteq in_A \cup out_A$. *The hiding of* H *in* A *yields the IOTS* $A \backslash H = (states_A, start_A, act_{A \backslash H}, \longrightarrow_A)$ *where* $act_{A \backslash H}$ *is the disjoint union of the input actions* $in_{A \backslash H} = in_A \smallsetminus H$, *the output actions* $out_{A \backslash H} = out_A \smallsetminus H$, *and the internal actions* $int_{A \backslash H} = int_A \cup int_B \cup H$.

Taking the synchronous compositions of IOTSes with hidden actions we can formulate our requirements explained above by the following (symmetric) conditions (a) and (b). Let A and B be two asynchronously composable IOTSes, let $out_{BA} = out_B \cap in_A$ and $out_{AB} = out_A \cap in_B$.

(a) For all reachable states $(s_A, s_B) \in \mathcal{R}(A \backslash out_{BA} \otimes B \backslash out_{BA})$, $\forall a \in out_A \cap in_B$:

$$s_A \xrightarrow{a}_A s'_A \implies \exists\, s_B \xrightarrow{int(B \backslash out_{BA})}_B{}^{*} \bar{s}_B \xrightarrow{a}_B s'_B.$$

(b) For all reachable states $(s_A, s_B) \in \mathcal{R}(A \backslash out_{AB} \otimes B \backslash out_{AB})$, $\forall b \in out_B \cap in_A$:

$$s_B \xrightarrow{b}_B s'_B \implies \exists\, s_A \xrightarrow{int(A \backslash out_{AB})}_A{}^{*} \bar{s}_A \xrightarrow{b}_A s'_A.$$

Notation: We write $A \backslash out_{BA} \dashrightarrow B \backslash out_{BA}$ if condition (a) holds and $B \backslash out_{AB} \dashrightarrow A \backslash out_{AB}$ if condition (b) holds.

Concerning (a), the essential difference between $A \otimes B$ and $A \backslash out_{BA} \otimes B \backslash out_{BA}$ is that shared actions belonging to $out_{BA} = out_B \cap in_A$ must synchronize in $A \otimes B$ while they can occur freely in $A \backslash out_{BA} \otimes B \backslash out_{BA}$ whenever A or B can perform one of them. Hence $A \backslash out_{BA} \otimes B \backslash out_{BA}$ can have significantly more reachable states than $A \otimes B$, in particular the ones reached by autonomous outputs of B directed to A. These states are often relevant in the asynchronous composition of A and B since outputs of B directed to A are internally put in the output queue of B. The same reasoning holds symmetrically for condition (b).

The following lemma, used for the proof of Theorem 3, establishes an important relationship between the reachable states considered in the synchronous products after hiding and those of the asynchronous composition of A and B.

The properties Q_A and Q_B stated in the lemma have a pattern similar to property $\mathcal{P}$ in Sect. 4.1. In contrast to property $\mathcal{P}$ they are generally valid.

Lemma 4. *For any two asynchronously composable IOTSes A and B both of the following two properties Q_A and Q_B are satisfied.*
Property Q_A: For each reachable state $((s_A, q_A), (s_B, q_B)) \in \mathcal{R}(\Omega(A) \otimes \Omega(B))$ one of the following two conditions holds:

(i) $q_A = \epsilon$ and $(s_A, s_B) \in \mathcal{R}(A \backslash out_{BA} \otimes B \backslash out_{BA})$,
(ii) $q_A = a_1 \ldots a_m \neq \epsilon$ and there exists $r_A \in states_A$ such that: $(r_A, s_B) \in \mathcal{R}(A \backslash out_{BA} \otimes B \backslash out_{BA})$ and $r_A \overset{a_1}{\Rightarrow}_A \ldots \overset{a_m}{\Rightarrow}_A s_A$.

The notation $s \overset{a}{\Rightarrow}_A s'$ stands for an arbitrary sequence of transitions in A which contains exactly one transition with an output action in $out_A \cap in_B$ and this output action is a.

Property Q_B: For each reachable state $((s_A, q_A), (s_B, q_B)) \in \mathcal{R}(\Omega(A) \otimes \Omega(B))$ one of the following two conditions holds:

(i) $q_B = \epsilon$ and $(s_A, s_B) \in \mathcal{R}(A \backslash out_{AB} \otimes B \backslash out_{AB})$,
(ii) $q_B = b_1 \ldots b_m \neq \epsilon$ and there exists $r_B \in states_B$ such that: $(s_A, r_B) \in \mathcal{R}(A \backslash out_{AB} \otimes B \backslash out_{AB})$ and $r_B \overset{b_1}{\Rightarrow}_B \ldots \overset{b_m}{\Rightarrow}_B s_B$. The notation $\overset{b}{\Rightarrow}_B$ is defined analogously to $\overset{a}{\Rightarrow}_A$.

Proof. The initial state $((start_A, \epsilon), (start_B, \epsilon))$ satisfies Q_A and Q_B. Then we consider transitions $((s_A, q_A), (s_B, q_B)) \overset{a}{\longrightarrow}_{\Omega(A) \otimes \Omega(B)} ((s'_A, q'_A), (s'_B, q'_B))$ and show that if $((s_A, q_A), (s_B, q_B))$ satisfies Q_A (Q_B resp.) then $((s'_A, q'_A), (s'_B, q'_B))$ satisfies Q_A (Q_B resp.). Then the result follows by induction on the length of the derivation to reach $((s_A, q_A), (s_B, q_B)) \in \mathcal{R}(\Omega(A) \otimes \Omega(B))$.   □

Property Q_A(ii) shows that a state of component A where the output queue is not empty can be reached from a state in the synchronous product of $A \backslash out_{BA}$ and $B \backslash out_{BA}$ by outputting the actions stored in the queue, possibly interleaved with arbitrary other actions of A which are not output actions directed to B. Property Q_B(ii) is the symmetric property concerning the output queue of B.

Theorem 3. *Let A and B be two asynchronously composable IOTSes such that $A \backslash out_{BA} \dashrightarrow B \backslash out_{BA}$ and $B \backslash out_{AB} \dashrightarrow A \backslash out_{AB}$ holds. Then A and B are weakly asynchronously compatible, i.e. $A \overset{a}{\leftrightarrow} B$.*

Proof. The proof relies on Lemma 4. We prove condition (1) of Definition 6. Condition (2) is proved analogously.
Let $((s_A, q_A), (s_B, q_B)) \in \mathcal{R}(\Omega(A) \otimes \Omega(B))$, $a \in out_{\Omega(A)} \cap in_{\Omega(B)}$ and $(s_A, q_A) \overset{a}{\longrightarrow}_{\Omega(A)} (s'_A, q'_A)$. Then q_A has the form $aa_2 \ldots a_m$. By Lemma 4, property Q_A(ii) holds. Hence, there exists $r_A \in states_A$ such that $(r_A, s_B) \in$

$\mathcal{R}(A\backslash out_{BA} \otimes B\backslash out_{BA})$ and $r_A \overset{a}{\Rightarrow}_A \overline{r}_A \overset{a_2}{\Rightarrow}_A \ldots \overset{a_m}{\Rightarrow}_A s_A$. Thereby $r_A \overset{a}{\Rightarrow}_A \overline{r}_A$ is of the form $r_A \overset{Y_A}{\longrightarrow}^*_A s \overset{a}{\longrightarrow}_A s' \overset{Y_A}{\longrightarrow}^*_A \overline{r}_A$ with $a \in out_A \cap in_B$ and Y_A involves no action in $out_{AB} = out_A \cap in_B$. Since out_{AB} are the only shared actions of $A\backslash out_{BA}$ and $B\backslash out_{BA}$, the transitions in $r_A \overset{Y_A}{\longrightarrow}^*_A s$ induce transitions in $A\backslash out_{BA} \otimes B\backslash out_{BA}$ without involving B. Therefore, since $(r_A, s_B) \in \mathcal{R}(A\backslash out_{BA} \otimes B\backslash out_{BA})$, we get $(s, s_B) \in \mathcal{R}(A\backslash out_{BA} \otimes B\backslash out_{BA})$. Now we can use the assumption $A\backslash out_{BA} \dashrightarrow B\backslash out_{BA}$ which says that there exists $s_B \xrightarrow{int_{(B\backslash out_{BA})}}^*_B \overline{s}_B \overset{a}{\longrightarrow}_B s'_B$ consisting of a sequence of internal transitions in $B\backslash out_{BA}$ followed by $\overline{s}_B \overset{a}{\longrightarrow}_B s'_B$ with $a \in in_B$. Now we notice that the internal actions of $B\backslash out_{BA}$ are either internal in B, and hence in $\Omega(B)$, or they are actions $b \in out_{BA} = out_B \cap in_A$, which induce internal enqueue actions $b^{\triangleright}$ in $\Omega(B)$. Thus we get transitions $(s_B, q_B) \xrightarrow{int_{\Omega(B)}}^*_{\Omega(B)} (\overline{s}_B, \overline{q}_B) \overset{a}{\longrightarrow}_{\Omega(B)} (s'_B, \overline{q}_B)$ (where $\overline{q}_B$ extends q_B according to the elements that have been enqueued with internal enqueue actions). Thus $\Omega(B)$ accepts a, possibly after some internal actions, and we are done. $\qquad\square$

Example 3. To apply Theorem 3 to Example 2 we have to prove MA $\backslash\{$readyB,failB$\}$ $\dashrightarrow$ MB$\backslash\{$readyB,failB$\}$ and MB$\backslash\{$readyA,failA$\}$ $\dashrightarrow$ MA$\backslash\{$readyA,failA$\}$. For the former case, Fig. 5 shows the IOTS MA after hiding its inputs readyB,failB shared with outputs of MB and the IOTS MB after hiding its outputs. We will check only this case, the other one is analogous. We have to consider the reachable states in the synchronous product MA$\backslash\{$readyB,failB$\} \otimes$ MB$\backslash\{$readyB,failB$\}$ and when an output readyA or failA is possible in MA$\backslash\{$readyB,failB$\}$. These states are (2,0), (2,1), (2,2) and also (2,3). In state (2,0) any output readyA or failA is immediately accepted. In all other states MB$\backslash\{$readyB,failB$\}$ can perform some internal actions first before it accepts readyA or failA. Hence, MA$\backslash\{$readyB,failB$\}$ $\dashrightarrow$ MB$\backslash\{$readyB,failB$\}$ holds. We want to point out particularly state (2,2). In this state MB$\backslash\{$readyB,failB$\}$ can perform the internal action $\tau_{\text{readyB!}}$ before accepting readyA or failA. The internal action $\tau_{\text{readyB!}}$ has been obtained from hiding the output action readyB in MB. In this way we have simulated in the synchro-

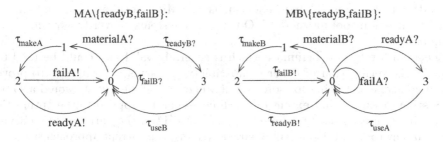

MA$\backslash\{$readyB,failB$\}$:   MB$\backslash\{$readyB,failB$\}$:

Fig. 5. Compatibility check: MA$\backslash\{$readyB,failB$\}$ $\dashrightarrow$ MB$\backslash\{$readyB,failB$\}$

nous product the (internal) enqueue action readyB$^{\triangleright}$ that would have happened by MB in the asynchronous composition.[3]

6   Conclusion

We have proposed techniques to verify asynchronous compatibility by using criteria that are based on synchronous composition. Our results lead to the following verification methodology: Assume given two asynchronously communicating components, each one having finitely many local states. First we check whether condition (3) of Lemma 1 holds (in the synchronous product) which is decidable. It characterizes half-duplex systems. If the answer is positive, then we can decide strong and weak asynchronous compatibility using Theorems 1 and 2. If the answer is negative, then our system is not half-duplex. In this case we check the decidable conditions formulated in Theorem 3. If they are satisfied then the system is weakly asynchronously compatible. If they are not satisfied then all examples we have considered so far were in fact not weakly asynchronously compatible; but since the problem is undecidable we cannot expect that this is always the case. To illustrate this issue we consider a simple example with two components A and B such that A has one input action a and one output action b, and B has one input action b and one output action a. A has three states and the following two transitions $start_A \xrightarrow{a?}_A s'_A \xrightarrow{b!}_A s''_A$. B has only the initial state $start_B$ and no transition. Then it is trivial that A and B are weakly asynchronously compatible, since in the asynchronous composition A will never receive a message from B and therefore A will never put b in its output buffer. However, our criterion $A \backslash out_{BA} \dashrightarrow B \backslash out_{BA}$ is not satisfied since $out_{BA} = \{a\}$ is hidden in $A \backslash out_{BA}$ and therefore the state $(s'_A, start_B)$ is reachable in $\mathcal{R}(A \backslash out_{BA} \otimes B \backslash out_{BA})$. Then $A \backslash out_{BA} \dashrightarrow B \backslash out_{BA}$ would require that $B \backslash out_{BA}$ is able to receive b in its initial state which is not the case. As a consequence of this discussion our conjecture is that the criterion of Theorem 3 may not work only if there are states in which one component has a transition with an output action which will never be executed in the composition due to missing input before.

The verification conditions studied in this paper involve only synchronous compatibility checking. Therefore we can use the MIO Workbench [4], an Eclipse-based verification tool for modal I/O-transition systems, to verify asynchronous compatibility.

Theorem 3 relies on Lemma 4 which is generally valid and could be used to support the verification of other compatibility problems as well, e.g., to prove that a component waiting for some input will eventually get it. It would also be interesting to see to what extent our techniques can be applied to the optimistic compatibility notion used for interface automata [11] if they are put in an asynchronous environment. Concerning larger systems, the current approach suggests

---

[3] Our technique would also work for the non synchronizable system in [15], Fig. 4.

to add incrementally one component after the other and to verify compatibility in each step. But we also want to extend our work and study asynchronous compatibility of multi-component ensembles.

Acknowledgement. We are very grateful to Alexander Knapp for his suggestion to use output queues (instead of input queues) for the formalization of asynchronous compatibility.

References

1. Basu, S., Bultan, T., Ouederni, M.: Deciding choreography realizability. In: Proceedings of ACM SIGPLAN-SIGACT Symposium on Principles of Programming Languages, POPL, pp. 191–202. ACM (2012)
2. Basu, S., Bultan, T., Ouederni, M.: Synchronizability for verification of asynchronously communicating systems. In: Kuncak, V., Rybalchenko, A. (eds.) VMCAI 2012. LNCS, vol. 7148, pp. 56–71. Springer, Heidelberg (2012)
3. Sebastian, S. B., Hennicker, R., Janisch, S.: Interface theories for (a)synchronously communicating modal I/O-transition systems. In: Proceedings of the Foundations for Interface Technologies, FIT, EPTCS 46, pp. 1–8 (2010)
4. Bauer, S.S., Mayer, P., Schroeder, A., Hennicker, R.: On weak modal compatibility, refinement, and the MIO workbench. In: Esparza, J., Majumdar, R. (eds.) TACAS 2010. LNCS, vol. 6015, pp. 175–189. Springer, Heidelberg (2010)
5. Beohar, H., Cuijpers, P.J.L.: Avoiding diamonds in desynchronisation. Sci. Comput. Program. **91**, 45–69 (2014)
6. Brand, D., Zafiropulo, P.: On communicating finite-state machines. J. ACM **30**(2), 323–342 (1983)
7. Canal, C., Pimentel, E., Troya, J.M.: Compatibility and inheritance in software architectures. Sci. Comput. Program. **41**(2), 105–138 (2001)
8. Carmona, J., Kleijn, J.: Compatibility in a multi-component environment. Theor. Comput. Sci. **484**, 1–15 (2013)
9. Cécé, G., Finkel, A.: Verification of programs with half-duplex communication. Inf. Comput. **202**(2), 166–190 (2005)
10. Clemente, L., Herbreteau, F., Sutre, G.: Decidable Topologies for communicating automata with FIFO and bag channels. In: Baldan, P., Gorla, D. (eds.) CONCUR 2014. LNCS, vol. 8704, pp. 281–296. Springer, Heidelberg (2014)
11. de Alfaro, L., Henzinger, T.A.: Interface automata. In: Proceedings of the 9th ACM SIGSOFT Annual Symposium Foundations of Software Engineering (FSE 2001), pp. 109–120. ACM Press, Wien (2001)
12. Haddad, S., Hennicker, R., Møller, M.H.: Channel properties of asynchronously composed Petri nets. In: Colom, J.-M., Desel, J. (eds.) PETRI NETS 2013. LNCS, vol. 7927, pp. 369–388. Springer, Heidelberg (2013)
13. Hennicker, R., Janisch, S., Knapp, A.: Refinement of components in connection-safe assemblies with synchronous and asynchronous communication. In: Choppy, C., Sokolsky, O. (eds.) Monterey Workshop 2008. LNCS, vol. 6028, pp. 154–180. Springer, Heidelberg (2010)
14. Larsen, K.G., Nyman, U., Wąsowski, A.: Modal I/O automata for interface and product line theories. In: De Nicola, R. (ed.) ESOP 2007. LNCS, vol. 4421, pp. 64–79. Springer, Heidelberg (2007)

15. Ouederni, M., Salaün, G., Bultan, T.: Compatibility checking for asynchronously communicating software. In: Fiadeiro, J.L., Liu, Z., Xue, J. (eds.) FACS 2013. LNCS, vol. 8348, pp. 310–328. Springer, Heidelberg (2014)
16. Raclet, J.-B., Badouel, E., Benveniste, A., Caillaud, B., Legay, A., Passerone, R.: A modal interface theory for component-based design. Fundam. Inform. **108**(1–2), 119–149 (2011)

A Semantic Theory of the Internet of Things
(Extended Abstract)

Ruggero Lanotte[1] and Massimo Merro[2]([⊠])

[1] Dipartimento di Scienza e Alta Tecnologia, Università dell'Insubria, Como, Italy
[2] Dipartimento di Informatica, Università degli Studi di Verona, Verona, Italy
massimo.merro@univr.it

Abstract. We propose a process calculus for modelling and reasoning on systems in the *Internet of Things* paradigm. Our systems interact both with the physical environment, via *sensors* and *actuators*, and with *smart devices*, via short-range and Internet channels. The calculus is equipped with a standard notion of labelled *bisimilarity* which represents a fully abstract characterisation of a well-known contextual equivalence. We use our semantic proof-methods to prove run-time properties of a non-trivial case study as well as system equalities.

1 Introduction

In the *Internet of Things* (IoT) paradigm, *smart devices*, such as smartphones, automatically collect information from shared resources (e.g. Internet access or physical devices) and aggregate them to provide new services to end users [13]. The "things" commonly deployed in IoT systems are: *RFID tags*, for unique identification, *sensors*, to detect physical changes in the environment, and *actuators*, to pass information to the environment.

The research on IoT is currently focusing on practical applications such as the development of enabling technologies, ad hoc architectures, semantic web technologies, and cloud computing [13]. However, as pointed out by Lanese et al. [16], there is a lack of research in formal methodologies to model the interactions among system components, and to verify the correctness of the network deployment before its implementation.

The main goal of this paper is to propose a process calculus with a clearly-defined semantic theory, for specifying and reasoning on IoT applications. Designing a calculus for modelling a new paradigm requires understanding and distilling, in a clean algebraic setting, the main features of the paradigm. Let us try to figure out what the main ingredients of IoT are, by means of an example.

Suppose a simple *smart home* (see Fig. 1) in which the user can use her smartphone to remotely control the heating boiler of her house, and automatically turn on lights when entering a room. The house consists of an entrance and a lounge, separated by a patio. Entrance and lounge have their own lights (actuators) which are governed by different light manager processes, *LightMng*. The

© IFIP International Federation for Information Processing 2016
Published by Springer International Publishing Switzerland 2016. All Rights Reserved
A. Lluch Lafuente and J. Proença (Eds.): COORDINATION 2016, LNCS 9686, pp. 157–174, 2016.
DOI: 10.1007/978-3-319-39519-7_10

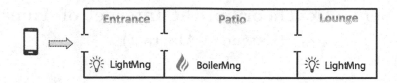

Fig. 1. A simple smart home

boiler is in the patio and is governed by a boiler manager process, *BoilerMng*. This process senses the local temperature (via a sensor) and decides whether to turn on/off the boiler, setting a proper actuator to signal the state of the boiler.

The smartphone executes two concurrent processes: *BoilerCtrl* and *LightCtr*. The first one reads user's commands, submitted via the phone touch-screen (a sensor), and forward them to the process *BoilerMng*, via an Internet channel. Whereas, the process *LightCtrl* interacts with the processes *LightMng*, via short-range wireless channels (e.g. Bluetooth), to automatically turn on lights when the smartphone physically enters either the entrance or the lounge.

The whole system is given by the parallel composition of the smartphone (a mobile device) and the smart home (a stationary entity).

On this kind of systems one may wish to prove interesting *run-time properties*. Think of a *fairness* property saying that the boiler will be eventually turned on/off whenever specific conditions are satisfied. Or consistency properties, saying the smartphone will never be in two rooms at the same time. Even more, one may be interested in understanding whether our system has the same *observable behaviour* of another system. Let us consider a variant of our smart home, where lights functionality depends on GPS coordinates of the smartphone (localisation is a common feature of today smartphones). Intuitively, the smartphone sends its GPS position to a centralised light manager, *CLightMng* (possibly placed in the patio), via an Internet channel. The process *CLightMng* will then interact with the two processes *LightMng*, via short-range channels, to switch on/off lights, depending on the position of the smartphone. Here comes an interesting question: Can these two implementations of the smart home, based on different light management mechanisms, be actually distinguished by an end user?

In the paper at hand we develop a fully abstract semantic theory for a process calculus of IoT systems, called CaIT. We provide a formal notion of when two systems in CaIT are indistinguishable, in all possible contexts, from the point of view of the end user. Formally, we adopt the approach of [15,24], often called *reduction (closed) barbed congruence*, which relies on two crucial concepts: a *reduction semantics* to describe system computations, and the *basic observables* to represent what the environment can directly observe of a system. In CaIT, there are at least two possible observables: the ability to transmit along channels, *logical observation*, and the capability to diffuse messages via actuators, *physical observation*. We have adopted the second form as our contextual equality remains invariant when adding logical observation. However, the right definition of physical observation is far from obvious as it involves some technical challenges in the definition of the reduction semantics (see the discussion in Sect. 2.3).

Our calculus is equipped with two *labelled transition semantics* (LTS) in the SOS style of Plotkin: an *intensional* semantics and an *extensional* semantics. The adjective intensional is used to stress the fact that the actions here correspond to activities which can be performed by a system in isolation, without any interaction with the external environment. While, the extensional semantics focuses on those activities which require a contribution of the environment. We prove that the reduction semantics coincides with the intensional semantics (Harmony Theorem), and that they satisfy some desirable time properties such as *time determinism*, *patience*, *maximal progress* and *well-timedness* [14].

However, the main result of the paper is that weak *bisimilarity* in the extensional LTS is *sound* and *complete* with respect to our contextual equivalence, reduction barbed congruence. This required a non-standard proof of the congruence theorem (Theorem 2). Finally, in order to show the effectiveness of our bisimulation proof method, we prove a number of non-trivial system equalities.

In this extended abstract proofs are omitted; full details can be found in [7].

Outline. Section 2 contains the calculus together with the reduction semantics, the contextual equivalence, and a discussion on design choices. Section 3 gives the details of our smart home example, and proves desirable run-time properties for it. Section 4 defines both the intensional and the extensional LTS. In Sect. 5 we define bisimilarity for IoT-systems, and prove the full abstraction result together with a number of non-trivial system equalities. Section 6 discusses related work.

2   The Calculus

The syntax of our *Calculus of the Internet of Things*, shortly CaIT, is given in a two-level structure: a lower one for *processes* and an upper one for *networks* of smart devices.

$$M, N ::= \mathbf{0} \mid n[\mathcal{I} \bowtie P]_l^\mu \mid M \mid N \mid (\nu c)M$$
$$P, Q ::= \mathsf{nil} \mid \rho.P \mid P \mid Q \mid \lfloor \pi.P \rfloor Q \mid \lfloor b \rfloor P; Q \mid X \mid \mathsf{fix}\, X.P$$

We use letters n, m to denote *nodes/devices*, c, g for *channels*, l, h, k for (physical) *locations*, s, s' for *sensors*, a, a' for *actuators* and x, y, z for *variables*. Our *values*, ranged over by v and w, are constituted by basic values, such as booleans and integers, sensor and actuator values, and coordinates of physical locations.

A network M is a pool of *distinct nodes* running in parallel and living in physical locations. We assume a discrete notion of *distance* between two locations h and k, i.e. $d(h, k) \in \mathbb{N}$. We write $\mathbf{0}$ to denote the empty network, while $M|N$ represents the parallel composition of two networks M and N. In $(\nu c)M$ channel c is private to the nodes of M. Each node is a term of the form $n[\mathcal{I} \bowtie P]_l^\mu$, where n is the device ID; $\mathcal{I}$ is the physical interface of n, represented as a partial mapping from sensor and actuator names to physical values; P is the process modelling the logics of n; l is the physical location of the device; $\mu \in \{s, m\}$ is a tag to distinguish between stationary and mobile nodes.

For security reasons, sensors in $\mathcal{I}$ can be read only by its *controller process P*. Similarly, actuators in $\mathcal{I}$ can be modified only by P. No other devices can access the physical interface of n. P is a timed concurrent processes which manages both the interaction with the physical interface $\mathcal{I}$ and channel communication. The communication paradigm is *point-to-point* via channels that may have different transmission ranges. We assume a global function rng() from channel names to $\mathbb{N} \cup \{-1, \infty\}$. A channel c can be used for: (i) *intra-node communications*, if $\mathrm{rng}(c) = -1$; (ii) *short-range inter-node communications* (such as Bluetooth, infrared, etc.) if $0 \le \mathrm{rng}(c) < \infty$; (iii) *Internet communications*, if $\mathrm{rng}(c) = \infty$.

Technically, our processes build on CCS with discrete time [14]. We write $\rho.P$, with $\rho \in \{\sigma, @(x), s?(x), a!v\}$, to denote intra-node actions. The process $\sigma.P$ sleeps for one time unit. The process $@(x).P$ gets the current location of the enclosing node. Process $s?(x).P$ reads a value v from sensor s. Process $a!v.P$ writes the value v on the actuator a. We write $\lfloor \pi.P \rfloor Q$, with $\pi \in \{\bar{c}\langle v \rangle, c(x)\}$, to denote channel communication with timeout. This process can communicate in the current time interval and then continues as P; otherwise, after one time unit, it evolves into Q. We write $[b]P; Q$ for conditional (here guard $[\![b]\!]$ is always *decidable*). In processes of the form $\sigma.Q$ and $\lfloor \pi.P \rfloor Q$ the occurrence of Q is said to be *time-guarded*. The process fix $X.P$ denotes *time-guarded recursion*, as all occurrences of the process variable X may only occur time-guarded in P. In processes $\lfloor c(x).P \rfloor Q$, $s?(x).P$ and $@(x).P$ the variable x is said to be bound. Similarly, in process fix $X.P$ the process variable X is bound. In the term $(\nu c)M$ the channel c is bound. This gives rise to the standard notions of *free/bound (process) variables*, *free/bound channels*, and *α-conversion*. A term is said to be *closed* if it does not contain free (process) variables, although it may contain free channels. We always work with closed networks: the absence of free variables is preserved at run-time. We write $T\{^v/_x\}$ for the substitution of the variable x with the value v in any expression T of our language. Similarly, $T\{^P/_X\}$ is the substitution of the process variable X with the process P in T.

Actuator names are metavariables for actuators like *display@n* or *alarm@n*. As node names are unique so are actuator names: different nodes have different actuators. The sensors embedded in a node can be of two kinds: *location-dependent* and *node-dependent*. The first ones sense data at the current location of the node, whereas the second ones sense data within the node, independently on the node's location. Thus, node-dependent sensor names are metavariables for sensors like *touchscreen@n* or *button@n*; whereas a sensor *temp@h*, for temperature, is a typical example of location-dependent sensor. Node-dependent sensor names are unique. This is not the case of location-dependent sensor names which may appear in different nodes. For simplicity, we use the same metavariables for both kind of sensors. When necessary we will specify the type of sensor in use.

We rule out ill-formed networks by means of the following definition.

Definition 1. *A network M is said to be* well-formed *if: (i) it does not contain two nodes with the same name; (ii) different nodes have different actuators and* *different node-dependent sensors; (iii) for each* $n[\mathcal{I} \bowtie P]_h^\mu$ *in* M, *with a prefix* $s?(x)$ *(resp.* $a!v$) *in* P, $\mathcal{I}(s)$ *(resp.* $\mathcal{I}(a)$) *is defined; (iv) for each* $n[\mathcal{I} \bowtie P]_h^\mu$ *in* M *with* $\mathcal{I}(s)$ *defined for some location-dependent sensor* s, *it holds that* $\mu = \mathsf{s}$.

Last condition says that location-dependent sensors may be used only in stationary nodes (see discussion in Sect. 2.3). Hereafter, we will always work with *well-formed networks*. It is easy to show that well-formedness is preserved at runtime.

We adopt the following notational conventions. $\prod_{i \in I} M_i$ denotes the parallel composition of all M_i, for $i \in I$. $\prod_{i \in I} M_i = \mathbf{0}$ and $\prod_{i \in I} P_i = \mathsf{nil}$, for $I = \emptyset$. We write $\prod_i M_i$ when I is not relevant. We write $\pi.P$ instead of $\mathsf{fix}\, X.\lfloor \pi.P \rfloor X$. We use $(\boldsymbol{\nu}\tilde{c})M$ as an abbreviation for $(\nu c_1) \ldots (\nu c_k)M$, with $\tilde{c} = c_1, \ldots, c_k$.

2.1 Reduction Semantics

The dynamics of the calculus is specified in terms of *reduction relations* over networks (see Table 1). As usual in process calculi, a reduction semantics [22] relies on an auxiliary standard relation, $\equiv$, called *structural congruence*, which brings the participants of a potential interaction into contiguous positions. For lack of space, we omit the formal definition of $\equiv$, as it is quite standard.

As CaIT is a timed calculus, with a discrete notion of time, it will be necessary to distinguish between *instantaneous reductions*, $M \rightarrow_i N$, and *timed reductions*, $M \rightarrow_\sigma N$. Relation $\rightarrow_i$ denotes activities which take place within one time interval, whereas $\rightarrow_\sigma$ represents the passage of one time unit. Instantaneous reductions are of two kinds: those which involve the change of the values associated to some actuator a, written $\rightarrow_a$, and the others, written $\rightarrow_\tau$. Intuitively, reductions of the form $M \rightarrow_a N$ denote *watchpoints* which cannot be ignored by the physical environment (in Example 2, and more extensively at the end of Sect. 2.3, we explain why this is important). Thus, we define the instantaneous reduction relation $\rightarrow_i = \rightarrow_\tau \cup \rightarrow_a$, for any actuator a. We also define the reduction $\rightarrow = \rightarrow_\tau \cup \rightarrow_\sigma$.

The first seven rules in Table 1 model intra-node activities. Rule (pos) serves to compute the current position of a node. Rule (sensread) represents the reading of the current data detected at some sensor s. Rules (actunchg) and (actchg) implement the writing of some data v on an actuator a, distinguishing whether the value of the actuator changes or not. Rule (loccom) models intra-node communications on a local channel c ($\mathsf{rng}(c) = -1$). Rule (timestat) models the passage of time within a stationary node. Notice that all untimed intra-node actions are considered urgent actions as they must occur before the next timed action. Rule (timemob) models the passage of time for mobile nodes. This rule also serves to model *node mobility*. Mobile nodes can nondeterministically move from one physical location h to a (possibly different) location k, at the end of a time interval. Node mobility respects the following time discipline: in one time unit a node can move from h to k provided that $\mathrm{d}(h, k) \le \delta$, for some fixed $\delta \in \mathbb{N}$ (if $h = k$ then $\mathrm{d}(h, k) = 0$). For the sake of simplicity, we fix the same constant δ for all nodes of our systems. Rule (glbcom) models inter-node communication

Table 1. Reduction semantics

$$(\text{pos}) \quad \frac{-}{n[\mathcal{I} \bowtie @(x).P]_h^\mu \to_\tau n[\mathcal{I} \bowtie P\{^h/_x\}]_h^\mu} \qquad (\text{sensread}) \quad \frac{\mathcal{I}(s) = v}{n[\mathcal{I} \bowtie s?(x).P]_h^\mu \to_\tau n[\mathcal{I} \bowtie P\{^v/_x\}]_h^\mu}$$

$$(\text{actunchg}) \quad \frac{\mathcal{I}(a) = v}{n[\mathcal{I} \bowtie a!v.P]_h^\mu \to_\tau n[\mathcal{I} \bowtie P]_h^\mu} \qquad (\text{actchg}) \quad \frac{\mathcal{I}(a) \neq v \quad \mathcal{I}' := \mathcal{I}[a \mapsto v]}{n[\mathcal{I} \bowtie a!v.P]_h^\mu \to_a n[\mathcal{I}' \bowtie P]_h^\mu}$$

$$(\text{loccom}) \quad \frac{\text{rng}(c) = -1}{n[\mathcal{I} \bowtie \lfloor \bar{c}\langle v \rangle.P \rfloor R \mid \lfloor c(x).Q \rfloor S]_h^\mu \to_\tau n[\mathcal{I} \bowtie P \mid Q\{^v/_x\}]_h^\mu}$$

$$(\text{timestat}) \quad \frac{n[\mathcal{I} \bowtie \prod_i \lfloor \pi_i.P_i \rfloor Q_i \mid \prod_j \sigma.R_j]_h^s \not\to_\tau}{n[\mathcal{I} \bowtie \prod_i \lfloor \pi_i.P_i \rfloor Q_i \mid \prod_j \sigma.R_j]_h^s \to_\sigma n[\mathcal{I} \bowtie \prod_i Q_i \mid \prod_j R_j]_h^s}$$

$$(\text{timemob}) \quad \frac{n[\mathcal{I} \bowtie \prod_i \lfloor \pi_i.P_i \rfloor Q_i \mid \prod_j \sigma.R_j]_h^m \not\to_\tau \quad d(h,k) \leq \delta}{n[\mathcal{I} \bowtie \prod_i \lfloor \pi_i.P_i \rfloor Q_i \mid \prod_j \sigma.R_j]_h^m \to_\sigma n[\mathcal{I} \bowtie \prod_i Q_i \mid \prod_j R_j]_k^m}$$

$$(\text{glbcom}) \quad \frac{d(h,k) \leq \text{rng}(c)}{n[\mathcal{I} \bowtie \lfloor \bar{c}\langle v \rangle.P \rfloor R]_h^{\mu_1} \mid m[\mathcal{J} \bowtie \lfloor c(x).Q \rfloor S]_k^{\mu_2} \to_\tau n[\mathcal{I} \bowtie P]_h^{\mu_1} \mid m[\mathcal{J} \bowtie Q\{^v/_x\}]_k^{\mu_2}}$$

$$(\text{parp}) \quad \frac{\prod_i n_i[\mathcal{I}_i \bowtie P_i]_{h_i}^{\mu_i} \to_\omega \prod_i n_i[\mathcal{I}_i' \bowtie P_i']_{h_i}^{\mu_i} \quad \omega \in \{\tau, a\}}{\prod_i n_i[\mathcal{I}_i \bowtie P_i \mid Q_i]_{h_i}^{\mu_i} \to_\omega \prod_i n_i[\mathcal{I}_i' \bowtie P_i' \mid Q_i]_{h_i}^{\mu_i}} \qquad (\text{parn}) \quad \frac{M \to_\omega M' \quad \omega \in \{\tau, a\}}{M \mid N \to_\omega M' \mid N}$$

$$(\text{timepar}) \quad \frac{M \to_\sigma M' \quad N \to_\sigma N' \quad M \mid N \not\to_\tau}{M \mid N \to_\sigma M' \mid N'} \qquad (\text{timezero}) \quad \frac{-}{0 \to_\sigma 0}$$

$$(\text{res}) \quad \frac{M \to_\omega N \quad \omega \in \{\tau, a, \sigma\}}{(\nu c)M \to_\omega (\nu c)N} \qquad (\text{struct}) \quad \frac{M \equiv N \quad N \to_\omega N' \quad \omega \in \{\tau, a, \sigma\} \quad N' \equiv M'}{M \to_\omega M'}$$

along a global channel c ($\text{rng}(c) \geq 0$). Intuitively, two nodes can communicate via a channel c only if they are within the transmission range of c. Rules (parp) and (parn) serve to propagate instantaneous reductions through parallel processes, and parallel networks, respectively. Rule (timepar) is for inter-node time synchronisation. The remaining rules are standard.

We write $\to_i^k$ to denote k consecutive reductions $\to_i$; $\to_i^*$ is the reflexive and transitive closure of $\to_i$. We use the same notation for the reduction relation $\to$.

Below we report a few standard time properties which hold in our calculus: *time determinism*, *maximal progress*, *patience* and *well-timedness*.

Proposition 1 (Time Properties).

- If $M \to_\sigma M'$ and $M \to_\sigma M''$, then $M' \equiv \prod_{i \in I} n_i[\mathcal{I}_i \bowtie P_i]_{h_i}^{\mu_i}$ and $M'' \equiv \prod_{i \in I} n_i[\mathcal{I}_i \bowtie P_i]_{k_i}^{\mu_i}$, with $d(h_i, k_i) \leq 2\delta$, for all $i \in I$.
- If $M \to_i M'$, then there is no M'' such that $M \to_\sigma M''$.
- If $M \to_i M'$ for no M', then there is N such that $M \to_\sigma N$.
- For any M there is a $z \in \mathbb{N}$ such that if $M \to_i^u N$ then $u \leq z$.

In its standard formulation, time determinism says that a system reaches at most one new state by executing a reduction step $\to_\sigma$. However, by an application of Rule (timemob), our mobile nodes may change location when executing a reduction $\to_\sigma$. *Well-timedness* ensures the absence of infinite instantaneous traces which would prevent the passage of time.

2.2 Behavioural Equivalence

Our contextual equivalence is *reduction barbed congruence* [15,24], a standard contextually defined process equivalence that crucially relies on the definition of *basic observables* to represent what the environment can directly observe of a system[1]. As already said in the Introduction, we choose to observe the capability to publish messages via actuators (physical observation).

Definition 2 (Barbs). *We write* $M \downarrow_{a@h!v}$ *if* $M \equiv (\nu\tilde{g})(n[\mathcal{I} \bowtie P]^\mu_h \mid M')$, *with* $\mathcal{I}(a) = v$. *We write* $M \Downarrow_{a@h!v}$ *if* $M \to^* M' \downarrow_{a@h!v}$.

The reader may wonder why our barb reports the location and not the node of the actuator. We also recall that actuator names are unique, so they somehow codify the name of their node. The location is then necessary because the environment is potentially aware of its position when observing an actuator: if every day at 6.00 AM your smartphone rings to wake you up, then you may react differently depending whether you are at home or on holidays in the Bahamas!

Definition 3. *A binary relation* $\mathcal{R}$ *over networks is* barb preserving *if* $M \mathcal{R} N$ *and* $M \downarrow_{a@h!v}$ *implies* $N \Downarrow_{a@h!v}$.

Definition 4. *A binary relation* $\mathcal{R}$ *over networks is* reduction closed *if whenever* $M \mathcal{R} N$ *the following conditions are satisfied:*

- $M \to M'$ *implies* $N \to^* N'$ *and* $M' \mathcal{R} N'$
- $M \to_a M'$ *implies* $N \to^* \to_a \to^* N'$ *and* $M' \mathcal{R} N'$.

Here, we require reduction closure of both $\to$ and $\to_a$, for any a. This is a *crucial design decision* in CaIT (see Example 2 and Sect. 2.3 for details).

In order to model *sensor updates* made by the physical environment on a sensor s, in a given location h, we define the operator $[s@h \mapsto v]$ on networks.

Definition 5. *Given a location* h, *a sensor* s, *and a value* v, *we define:*

$$n[\mathcal{I} \bowtie P]^\mu_h[s@h \mapsto v] \stackrel{\text{def}}{=} n[\mathcal{I}[s \mapsto v] \bowtie P]^\mu_h, \text{ if } \mathcal{I}(s) \text{ defined}$$
$$n[\mathcal{I} \bowtie P]^\mu_k[s@h \mapsto v] \stackrel{\text{def}}{=} n[\mathcal{I} \bowtie P]^\mu_k, \text{ if } \mathcal{I}(s) \text{ undef. or } h \neq k$$
$$(M|N)[s@h \mapsto v] \stackrel{\text{def}}{=} M[s@h \mapsto v] \mid N[s@h \mapsto v]$$
$$((\nu c)M)[s@h \mapsto v] \stackrel{\text{def}}{=} (\nu c)(M[s@h \mapsto v])$$
$$0[s@h \mapsto v] \stackrel{\text{def}}{=} 0.$$

---

[1] See [24] for a comparison between this approach and the original barbed congruence.

Notice that when updating a sensor we use its location, also for node-dependent sensors. This is because when changing a node-dependent sensor (e.g. touching a touchscreen of a smartphone) the environment is in general aware of its position.

Definition 6. *A binary relation $\mathcal{R}$ is* contextual *if $M \mathcal{R} N$ implies that*

- *for all networks O, $M \mid O \mathcal{R} N \mid O$*
- *for all channels c, $(\nu c)M \mathcal{R} (\nu c)N$*
- *for all s, h, and v in the domain of s, $M[s@h \mapsto v] \mathcal{R} N[s@h \mapsto v]$.*

The first two clauses requires closure under *logical contexts* (parallel systems), while the last clause involves *physical contexts*, which can *nondeterministically update* sensor values.

Finally, everything is in place to define our touchstone behavioural equality.

Definition 7. Reduction barbed congruence, $\cong$, *is the largest symmetric relation over networks which is reduction closed, barb preserving and contextual.*

Remark 1. Obviously, if $M \cong N$ then M and N will be still equivalent in any setting where sensor updates are governed by specific physical laws.

We recall that the reduction relation $\rightarrowtail$ ignores the passage of time, and therefore the reader might suspect that our reduction barbed congruence is impervious to the precise timing of activities. We show that this is not the case.

Example 1. Let $M = n[\emptyset \bowtie \sigma.\lfloor \overline{c}\langle\rangle \rfloor \text{nil}]_h^s$ and $N = n[\emptyset \bowtie \lfloor \overline{c}\langle\rangle \rfloor \text{nil}]_h^s$, with $\text{rng}(c) = \infty$. Then, $M \rightarrowtail_\sigma N$. As $\rightarrowtail$ does not distinguish instantaneous from timed reductions, one may suspect that $M \cong N$, and that a prompt transmission along channel c is equivalent to the same transmission delayed of one time unit. However, the test $T = \text{test}[\mathcal{J} \bowtie \sigma.a!1.\lfloor c().a!0 \rfloor \text{nil}]_l^s$, with $\mathcal{J}(a) = 0$, for some actuator a, can distinguish the two networks. In fact, if $M \mid T \rightarrowtail^* \rightarrowtail_a O = n[\emptyset \bowtie \lfloor \overline{c}\langle\rangle \rfloor \text{nil}]_h^s \mid \text{test}[\mathcal{J}' \bowtie \lfloor c().a!0 \rfloor \text{nil}]_l^s$, with $\mathcal{J}'(a) = 1$, then there is no O' such that $N \mid T \rightarrowtail^* \rightarrowtail_a \rightarrowtail^* O'$ with $O \cong O'$. This is because O can perform a reduction sequence $\rightarrowtail \rightarrowtail_a$ that cannot be matched by any O'.

Behind this example there is the general principle that reduction barbed congruence is sensitive to the passage of time.

Proposition 2. *If $M \cong N$ and $M \rightarrowtail_\sigma M'$ then there is N' such that $N \rightarrowtail_\tau^* \rightarrowtail_\sigma \rightarrowtail_\tau^* N'$ and $M' \cong N'$.*

Now, we provide some insights into the design decision of having two different instantaneous reductions $\rightarrowtail_\tau$ and $\rightarrowtail_a$.

Example 2. Let $M = n[\mathcal{I} \bowtie a!1 \mid a!0.a!1]_h^\mu$ and $N = n[\mathcal{I} \bowtie a!1.a!0.a!1]_h^\mu$, with $\mathcal{I}(a) = 0$ and undefined otherwise. Then, within one time unit, M may display on the actuator a either the sequence of values 01 or the sequence 0101, while N can only display the sequence 0101. As a consequence, for a physical observer, the behaviours of M and N are clearly different. Now, if $M \rightarrowtail_\tau \rightarrowtail_a M' = n[\mathcal{J} \bowtie a!1]_h^\mu$, with $\mathcal{J}(a) = 1$, the only possible reply of N respecting reduction closure is

$N \twoheadrightarrow^* \twoheadrightarrow_a N' = n[\mathcal{J} \bowtie a!0.a!1]_h^\mu$. However, it is evident that $M' \not\cong N'$ because N' can turn the actuator a to 0 while M' cannot. Thus, $M \not\cong N$.

Had we merged $\twoheadrightarrow_a$ with $\twoheadrightarrow_\tau$ then we would have $M \cong N$ because the capability to observe messages on actuators, given by the barb, would not be enough to observe changes on actuators within one time interval.

2.3   Design Choices

CaIT is a value-passing process calculus, à la CCS, which can be easily adapted to deal with the transmission of channel names, à la π-calculus [24].

The time model we adopt is known as the fictitious clock approach (see [14]): a global clock is supposed to be updated whenever all nodes agree on this, by globally synchronising on a special timing action σ. Thus, time synchronisation relies on some clock synchronisation protocol for mobile wireless systems [27].

In *cyber-physical systems* [25], sensor changes are usually modelled either using continuous models (differential equations) or through discrete models (difference equations)[2]. However, in this paper we aim at providing a behavioural semantics for IoT applications from the point of view of the end user. And the end user cannot directly observe changes on the sensors of an IoT application: she can only observe the effects of those changes via actuators and communication channels. Thus, in CaIT we do not represent sensor changes via specific models, but we rather abstract on them by supporting *nondeterministic sensor updates* (see Definitions 5 and 6). Actually, as said in Remark 1, behavioural equalities derived in our setting remains valid when adopting any specific model for sensor updates.

In CaIT the value associated to sensors and actuators can change more than once within the same time interval. At first sight this choice may appear weird as certain actuators may require some time to turn on. On the other hand, other actuators may have a very quick reaction. A similar argument applies to sensors. In this respect CaIT does not enforce a synchronisation of physical events as it happens for logical signals in synchronous languages [5]. In fact, actuator changes are under nodes' control: if an actuator is a slow device then it is under the responsibility of its controller to update the actuator with a proper delay. Similarly, a sensor should be read only when its value makes sense.

Unlike *mobile computations* [6], smart devices do not decide where to move to: an external agent moves them. Furthermore, Definition 1 imposes that location-dependent sensors can only occur in stationary nodes. This allows us a local, rather than a global, representation of those sensors. The representation of mobile location-dependent sensors would have the same technical challenges of *mobile wireless sensor networks* [27].

Finally, we would like to explain our choice of barb. As said in the Introduction there are other possible definitions. For instance, one could observe the capability to transmit along a channel c, by defining $M \downarrow_{\bar{c}@h}$ if $M \equiv (\nu\tilde{g})(n[\mathcal{I} \bowtie \lfloor \bar{c}\langle v \rangle.P \rfloor Q \mid R]_k^\mu \mid N)$ with $c \notin \tilde{g}$ and $d(h,k) \leq \mathrm{rng}(c)$. However, if

---

[2] Difference equations relate to differential equations as discrete math relate to continuous math.

Table 2. A smart home in CaIT

$$
\begin{aligned}
Sys &\stackrel{\text{def}}{=} Phone \mid Home \\
Phone &\stackrel{\text{def}}{=} n_P[\mathcal{I}_P \bowtie BoilerCtrl \mid LightCtrl]_{out}^{\mathtt{m}} \\
Home &\stackrel{\text{def}}{=} LM_1 \mid BM \mid LM_2 \\
LM_1 &\stackrel{\text{def}}{=} n_1[\mathcal{I}_1 \bowtie LightMng_1]_{loc_1}^{\mathtt{s}} \\
LM_2 &\stackrel{\text{def}}{=} n_2[\mathcal{I}_2 \bowtie LightMng_2]_{loc_4}^{\mathtt{s}} \\
BM &\stackrel{\text{def}}{=} n_B[\mathcal{I}_B \bowtie BoilerMng]_{loc_2}^{\mathtt{s}} \\
BoilerCtrl &\stackrel{\text{def}}{=} \text{fix}\, X.mode?(z).\lfloor \overline{b}\langle z\rangle.\sigma.X \rfloor X \\
LightCtrl &\stackrel{\text{def}}{=} \prod_{j=1}^{2} \text{fix}\, X.\lfloor \overline{c_j}\langle\rangle.\sigma.X \rfloor X \\
LightMng_j &\stackrel{\text{def}}{=} \text{fix}\, X.\lfloor c_j().light_j!\text{on}.\sigma.X \rfloor light_j!\text{off}.X \quad \text{for } j \in \{1,2\} \\
BoilerMng &\stackrel{\text{def}}{=} \text{fix}\, X.\lfloor b(x).[x = \mathsf{man}]\, boiler!\text{on}.\sigma.Manual; TempCtrl \rfloor TempCtrl \\
Manual &\stackrel{\text{def}}{=} \text{fix}\, Y.b(y).[y = \mathsf{auto}]X; \sigma.Y \\
TempCtrl &\stackrel{\text{def}}{=} temp?(t).[t < \Theta]\, boiler!\text{on}.\sigma.X; boiler!\text{off}.\sigma.X
\end{aligned}
$$

you consider the system $S = (\boldsymbol{\nu}c)(M \mid m[\mathcal{J} \bowtie \lfloor c(x).a!1 \rfloor \text{nil}]_h^{\mu})$, with $\mathcal{J}(a) = 0$, then it is easy to show that $M \downarrow_{\overline{c}@h}$ if and only if $S \twoheadrightarrow \twoheadrightarrow_a S' \downarrow_{a@h!1}$. Thus, the barb on channels can always be reformulated in terms of our barb. The vice versa is not possible. The reader may also wonder whether it is possible to turn the reduction $\twoheadrightarrow_a$ into $\twoheadrightarrow_\tau$ by introducing some special barb which would be capable to observe actuators changes. For instance, something like $M \downarrow_{a@h!v.w}$ if $M \equiv (\boldsymbol{\nu}\tilde{g})(n[\mathcal{I} \bowtie a!w.P \mid Q]_h^{\mu} \mid M')$, with $\mathcal{I}(a) = v$ and $v \neq w$. It should be easy to see that this extra barb would not help in distinguishing the terms proposed in Example 2. Actually, here there is something deeper that needs to be spelled out. In process calculi, the term β of a barb $\downarrow_\beta$ is a concise encoding of a context C_β expressible in the calculus and capable to observe the barb $\downarrow_\beta$. However, our barb $\downarrow_{a@h!v}$ does not have such a corresponding *physical context* in our language. Said with an example, in CaIT we do not represent the "eyes of a person" looking at the values appearing to some display. Technically speaking, in our calculus we don't have terms of the form $a?(x).P$ to read values on the actuator a, simply because such terms would not be part of an IoT system. The lack of this physical context, together with the persistent nature of actuators' state, explains why our barb $\downarrow_{a@h!v}$ must work together with the reduction relation $\twoheadrightarrow_a$ to provide the desired distinguishing power of $\cong$. Further discussions can be found in [7].

3   Case Study: A Smart Home

In Table 2, we model the smart home discussed in the Introduction, and represented in Fig. 1. Our house spans over 4 contiguous physical locations loc_i, for $i = [1..4]$, such that $\mathrm{d}(loc_i, loc_j) = |i - j|$. The entrance is in loc_1, the patio spans from loc_2 to loc_3 and the lounge is at loc_4. The house can only be accessed via its entrance.

Our system Sys consists of the parallel composition of the smartphone, $Phone$, and the smart home, $Home$. The smartphone is represented as a mobile node, with $\delta = 1$, initially placed outside the house: $out \neq loc_j$, for $j \in [1..4]$. As the phone can only access the house from its entrance, and $\delta = 1$, we have $d(l, loc_i) \geq i$, for any $l \notin \{loc_1, loc_2, loc_3, loc_4\}$ and $i \in [1..4]$. Its interface $\mathcal{I}_P$ contains only one sensor, called $mode$, representing the touchscreen to control the boiler. This is a node-dependent sensor. The process $BoilerCtrl$ reads sensor $mode$ and forwards its value to the boiler manager in the patio, $BoilerMng$, via the Internet channel b ($\mathrm{rng}(b) = \infty$). The domain of $mode$ is $\{\mathsf{man}, \mathsf{auto}\}$, where man stands for manual and auto for automatic; initially, $\mathcal{I}_P(mode) = \mathsf{auto}$.

In $Phone$ there is a second process, called $LightCtrl$, which allows the smartphone to switch on lights *only when* getting in touch with the light managers installed in the rooms. Here, channels c_1 and c_2 serve to control the lights of entrance and lounge, respectively; these are short-range channels: $\mathrm{rng}(c_1) = \mathrm{rng}(c_2) = 0$.

The smart home $Home$ consists of three stationary nodes: LM_1, BM, and LM_2. The light managers processes $LightMng_1$, $LightMng_2$, are placed in LM_1 and LM_2, respectively. They manage the corresponding lights via the actuators $light_j$, for $j \in \{1, 2\}$. The domain of these actuators is $\{\mathsf{on}, \mathsf{off}\}$; initially, $\mathcal{I}_j(light_j) = \mathsf{off}$, for $j \in \{1, 2\}$.

The boiler manager process $BoilerMng$ is placed in BM (node n_B). Here, the physical interface $\mathcal{I}_B$ contains a sensor named $temp$ and an actuator called $boiler$; $temp$ is a location-dependent temperature sensor, whose domain is $\mathbb{N}$, and $boiler$ is an actuator to display boiler functionality, whose domain is $\{\mathsf{on}, \mathsf{off}\}$. The boiler manager can work either in automatic or in manual mode. In automatic mode, sensor $temp$ is periodically checked: if the temperature is under a threshold Θ then the boiler will be switched on, otherwise it will be switched off. Conversely, in manual mode, the boiler is always switched on. Initially, the boiler is in automatic mode, $\mathcal{I}_B(temp) = \Theta$, and $\mathcal{I}_B(boiler) = \mathsf{off}$.

Our system Sys enjoys a number of desirable *run-time properties*. For instance, if the boiler is in manual mode or its temperature is under the threshold Θ then the boiler will get switched on, within one time unit. Conversely, if the boiler is in automatic mode and its temperature is higher than or equal to the threshold Θ, then the boiler will get switched off within one time unit. These three *fairness* properties can be easily proved because our calculus is well-timed. In general, similar properties cannot be expressed in untimed calculi. Finally, our last property states the phone cannot act on the lights of the two rooms at the same time, manifesting a kind of "ubiquity". For the sake of simplicity, in the following proposition we omit location names both in barbs and in sensor updates, writing $\downarrow_{a!v}$ instead of $\downarrow_{a@h!v}$, and $[s \mapsto v]$ instead of $[s@h \mapsto v]$. The system Sys' denotes an arbitrary (stable) derivative of Sys.

Proposition 3 (Run-time Properties). *Let* $Sys \ (\rightarrow_i^* \rightarrow_\sigma)^* \ Sys'$.

- *If* $Sys'[mode \mapsto \mathsf{man}] \rightarrow_i^* Sys'' \rightarrow_\sigma$ *then* $Sys'' \downarrow_{boiler!on}$
- *If* $Sys'[temp \mapsto t] \rightarrow_i^* Sys'' \rightarrow_\sigma$, *with* $t < \Theta$, *then* $Sys'' \downarrow_{boiler!on}$

Table 3. Smart home: a position based light management

$$\overline{Sys} \stackrel{\text{def}}{=} \overline{Phone} \mid \overline{Home}$$

$$\overline{Phone} \stackrel{\text{def}}{=} n_P[\mathcal{I}_P \bowtie BoilerCtrl \mid \overline{LightCtrl}]_{out}^{\text{m}}$$

$$\overline{Home} \stackrel{\text{def}}{=} Home \mid \overline{CLM}$$

$$\overline{CLM} \stackrel{\text{def}}{=} n_C[\emptyset \bowtie \overline{CLightMng}]_{loc_3}^{\text{s}}$$

$$\overline{LightCtrl} \stackrel{\text{def}}{=} \text{fix}\, X.@(x).\lfloor \overline{g}\langle x\rangle.\sigma.X \rfloor X$$

$$\overline{CLightMng} \stackrel{\text{def}}{=} \text{fix}\, X.\lfloor g(y).[y = loc_1]\lfloor \overline{c_1}\langle\rangle.\sigma.X \rfloor X; [y = loc_4]\lfloor \overline{c_2}\langle\rangle.\sigma.X \rfloor X; \sigma.X \rfloor X$$

- If $Sys'[temp \mapsto t] \to_{\text{i}}^* Sys'' \to_\sigma$, with $t \geq \Theta$, then $Sys'' \downarrow_{boiler!off}$
- If $Sys' \to_{\text{i}}^* Sys'' \downarrow_{light_1!on}$ then $Sys'' \downarrow_{light_2!off}$, and vice versa.

Finally, we propose a variant of our system, where lights functionality depends on the position of the smartphone. Intuitively, the smartphone detects is current GPS position, via the process $@(x).P$, and then sends it to a centralised light manager process, $\overline{CLightMng}$, via an Internet channel g. This process will interact with the local light managers to switch on/off lights, depending on the position of the smartphone. In Table 3, new components have been overlined. Channels c_1 and c_2 have different range now, as they serve to communicate with the centralised light manager: $rng(c_1) = 2$ and $rng(c_2) = 1$.

Proposition 3 holds for $\overline{Sys}$ as well. Actually, the two systems are closely related.

Proposition 4. *For $\delta = 1$, $(\boldsymbol{\nu}\tilde{c})Sys \cong (\boldsymbol{\nu}\tilde{c})(\boldsymbol{\nu}g)\overline{Sys}$.*

The bisimulation proof technique developed in the remainder of the paper will be very useful to prove equalities between systems of such size.

We end this section with a comment. While reading this case study the reader should have noticed that our reduction semantics does not model sensor updates. This is because sensor changes depend on the physical environment, and a reduction semantics models the evolution of a system in isolation. Interactions with the external environment will be treated in our *extensional semantics*.

4   Labelled Transition Semantics

In this section we provide two labelled semantic models in the SOS style of Plotkin: the *intensional semantics* and the *extensional semantics*.

Intensional Semantics. Since our syntax distinguishes between networks and processes, we have two different kinds of transitions:

- $P \xrightarrow{\lambda} Q$, with $\lambda \in \{\sigma, \tau, \overline{c}v, cv, @h, s?v, a!v\}$, for *process transitions*
- $M \xrightarrow{\nu} N$, with $\nu \in \{\sigma, \tau, a, \overline{c}v@h, cv@h\}$, for *network transitions*

Table 4. Intensional semantics for processes

$$(\text{SndP}) \ \frac{-}{\lfloor \overline{c}\langle v\rangle.P\rfloor Q \xrightarrow{\overline{c}v} P} \qquad (\text{RcvP}) \ \frac{-}{\lfloor c(x).P\rfloor Q \xrightarrow{cv} P\{v/x\}}$$

$$(\text{PosP}) \ \frac{-}{@(x).P \xrightarrow{@h} P\{h/x\}} \qquad (\text{Com}) \ \frac{P \xrightarrow{\overline{c}v} P' \quad Q \xrightarrow{cv} Q' \quad \text{rng}(c) = -1}{P \mid Q \xrightarrow{\tau} P' \mid Q'}$$

$$(\text{Sensor}) \ \frac{-}{s?(x).P \xrightarrow{s?v} P\{v/x\}} \qquad (\text{Actuator}) \ \frac{-}{a!v.P \xrightarrow{a!v} P}$$

$$(\text{ParP}) \ \frac{P \xrightarrow{\lambda} P' \quad \lambda \neq \sigma}{P \mid Q \xrightarrow{\lambda} P' \mid Q} \qquad (\text{Fix}) \ \frac{P\{\text{fix}\,X.P/x\} \xrightarrow{\lambda} Q}{\text{fix}\,X.P \xrightarrow{\lambda} Q}$$

$$(\text{TimeNil}) \ \frac{-}{\text{nil} \xrightarrow{\sigma} \text{nil}} \qquad (\text{Delay}) \ \frac{-}{\sigma.P \xrightarrow{\sigma} P}$$

$$(\text{Timeout}) \ \frac{-}{\lfloor \pi.P\rfloor Q \xrightarrow{\sigma} Q} \qquad (\text{TimeParP}) \ \frac{P \xrightarrow{\sigma} P' \quad Q \xrightarrow{\sigma} Q' \quad P \mid Q \xrightarrow{\tau}\!\!\!\!\!/}{P \mid Q \xrightarrow{\sigma} P' \mid Q'}$$

In Table 4 we report transition rules for processes, very much in the style of [14]. As in CCS, we assume $[b]P; Q = P$ if $[\![b]\!] = \text{true}$, and $[b]P; Q = Q$ if $[\![b]\!] = \text{false}$. Rules (SndP), (RcvP) and (Com) model communications along a channel c. Rule (PosP) is for extracting the physical position of the embedding node. Rules (Sensor) and (Actuator) serve to read sensors, and to write on actuators, respectively. Rules (ParP) and (Fix) are straightforward. The remaining rules allow us the derive the timed action σ. In Rule (Delay) a timed prefix is consumed. Rule (Timeout) models timeouts when channel communications are not possible in the current time interval. Rule (TimeParP) is for time synchronisation of parallel processes. The symmetric counterparts of Rules (ParP) and (Com) are omitted.

In Table 5 we report the rules for networks. Rule (Pos) extracts the position of a node. Rule (SensRead) models the reading of a sensor of the enclosing node. Rules (ActUnChg) and (ActChg) describes the writing of a value v on an actuator a of the node, distinguishing whether the value of the actuator is changed or not. Rule (LocCom) models intra-node communications. Rule (TimeStat) models the passage of time for a stationary node. Rule (TimeMob) models both time passing and node mobility at the end of a time interval. Rules (Snd) and (Rcv) model transmission and reception along a global channel. Rule (GlbCom) models inter-node communications. The remaining rules are straightforward. The symmetric counterparts of Rules (ParN) and (GlobCom) are omitted.

The reduction semantics and the labelled intensional semantics coincide.

Table 5. Intensional semantics for networks

$$\text{(Pos)} \quad \frac{P \xrightarrow{@h} P'}{n[\mathcal{I} \Join P]_h^\mu \xrightarrow{\tau} n[\mathcal{I} \Join P']_h^\mu} \qquad \text{(SensRead)} \quad \frac{\mathcal{I}(s) = v \quad P \xrightarrow{s?v} P'}{n[\mathcal{I} \Join P]_h^\mu \xrightarrow{\tau} n[\mathcal{I} \Join P']_h^\mu}$$

$$\text{(ActUnChg)} \quad \frac{\mathcal{I}(a) = v \quad P \xrightarrow{a!v} P'}{n[\mathcal{I} \Join P]_h^\mu \xrightarrow{\tau} n[\mathcal{I} \Join P']_h^\mu} \qquad \text{(LocCom)} \quad \frac{P \xrightarrow{\tau} P'}{n[\mathcal{I} \Join P]_h^\mu \xrightarrow{\tau} n[\mathcal{I} \Join P']_h^\mu}$$

$$\text{(ActChg)} \quad \frac{\mathcal{I}(a) \neq v \quad P \xrightarrow{a!v} P' \quad \mathcal{I}' := \mathcal{I}[a \mapsto v]}{n[\mathcal{I} \Join P]_h^\mu \xrightarrow{a} n[\mathcal{I}' \Join P']_h^\mu}$$

$$\text{(TimeStat)} \quad \frac{P \xrightarrow{\sigma} P' \quad n[\mathcal{I} \Join P]_h^s \not\xrightarrow{\tau}}{n[\mathcal{I} \Join P]_h^s \xrightarrow{\sigma} n[\mathcal{I} \Join P']_h^s} \qquad \text{(TimeMob)} \quad \frac{P \xrightarrow{\sigma} P' \quad n[\mathcal{I} \Join P]_h^m \not\xrightarrow{\tau} \quad d(h,k) \leq \delta}{n[\mathcal{I} \Join P]_h^m \xrightarrow{\sigma} n[\mathcal{I} \Join P']_k^m}$$

$$\text{(Snd)} \quad \frac{P \xrightarrow{\bar{c}v} P' \quad \text{rng}(c) \geq 0}{n[\mathcal{I} \Join P]_h^\mu \xrightarrow{\bar{c}v@h} n[\mathcal{I} \Join P']_h^\mu} \qquad \text{(Rcv)} \quad \frac{P \xrightarrow{cv} P' \quad \text{rng}(c) \geq 0}{n[\mathcal{I} \Join P]_h^\mu \xrightarrow{cv@h} n[\mathcal{I} \Join P']_h^\mu}$$

$$\text{(GlbCom)} \quad \frac{M \xrightarrow{\bar{c}v@k} M' \quad N \xrightarrow{cv@h} N' \quad d(h,k) \leq \text{rng}(c)}{M \mid N \xrightarrow{\tau} M' \mid N'}$$

$$\text{(ParN)} \quad \frac{M \xrightarrow{\nu} M' \quad \nu \neq \sigma}{M \mid N \xrightarrow{\nu} M' \mid N} \qquad \text{(TimePar)} \quad \frac{M \xrightarrow{\sigma} M' \quad N \xrightarrow{\sigma} N' \quad M \mid N \not\xrightarrow{\tau}}{M \mid N \xrightarrow{\sigma} M' \mid N'}$$

$$\text{(TimeZero)} \quad \frac{-}{0 \xrightarrow{\sigma} 0} \qquad \text{(Res)} \quad \frac{M \xrightarrow{\nu} N \quad \nu \notin \{\bar{c}v@h, cv@h\}}{(\nu c)M \xrightarrow{\nu} (\nu c)N}$$

Theorem 1 (Harmony Theorem). *Let* $\omega \in \{\tau, a, \sigma\}$:

- $M \xrightarrow{\omega} M'$ *implies* $M \twoheadrightarrow_\omega M'$
- $M \twoheadrightarrow_\omega M'$ *implies* $M \xrightarrow{\omega} M''$, *for some* M'' *such that* $M' \equiv M''$.

Extensional Semantics. Here we redesign our LTS to focus on the interactions of our systems with the external environment. As the environment has a *logical part* (the parallel nodes) and a *physical part* (the physical world) our extensional semantics distinguishes two different kinds of transitions:

- $M \xrightarrow{\alpha} N$, *logical transitions*, for $\alpha \in \{\tau, \sigma, a, \bar{c}v \triangleright k, cv \triangleright k\}$, to denote the interaction with the *logical environment*; here, actuator changes, τ- and σ-actions are inherited from the intensional semantics, so we don't provide inference rules for them;
- $M \xrightarrow{\alpha} N$, *physical transitions*, for $\alpha \in \{s@h?v, a@h!v\}$, to denote the interaction with the *physical world*.

In Table 6 the extensional actions deriving from rules (SndObs) and (RcvObs) mention the location k of the logical environment which can *observe* the communication occurring at channel c. Rules (SensEnv) and (ActEnv) model the

Table 6. Extensional semantics: additional rules

$$(\text{SndObs}) \quad \frac{M \xrightarrow{\bar{c}v@h} M' \quad \text{d}(h,k) \leq \text{rng}(c)}{M \xrightarrow{\bar{c}v\triangleright k} M'} \qquad (\text{RcvObs}) \quad \frac{M \xrightarrow{cv@h} M' \quad \text{d}(k,h) \leq \text{rng}(c)}{M \xrightarrow{cv\triangleright k} M'}$$

$$(\text{SensEnv}) \quad \frac{v \text{ in the domain of } s}{M \xrightarrow{s@h?v} M[s@h \mapsto v]} \qquad (\text{ActEnv}) \quad \frac{M \downarrow_{a@h!v}}{M \xrightarrow{a@h!v} M}$$

interaction of a system M with the physical environment. The environment can *nondeterministically update* the current value of (location-dependent or node-dependent) sensors, and can read the information exposed on actuators.

Note that our LTSs are *image finite*. They are also *finitely branching*, and hence *mechanisable*, under the obvious assumption of finiteness of all domains of admissible values, and the set of physical locations.

5   Full Abstraction

Based on our extensional semantics, we are ready to define a notion of bisimilarity. We adopt a standard notation for weak transitions. We denote with $\Longrightarrow$ the reflexive and transitive closure of τ-actions, namely $(\xrightarrow{\tau})^*$, whereas $\xRightarrow{\alpha}$ means $\Longrightarrow \xrightarrow{\alpha} \Longrightarrow$, and finally $\xRightarrow{\hat{\alpha}}$ denotes $\Longrightarrow$ if $\alpha = \tau$ and $\xRightarrow{\hat{\alpha}}$ otherwise.

Definition 8 (Bisimulation). *A binary symmetric relation $\mathcal{R}$ over networks is a* bisimulation *if $M \mathcal{R} N$ and $M \xrightarrow{\alpha} M'$ imply there exists N' such that $N \xRightarrow{\hat{\alpha}} N'$ and $M' \mathcal{R} N'$. We say that M and N are bisimilar, written $M \approx N$, if $M \mathcal{R} N$ for some bisimulation $\mathcal{R}$.*

Later on, we will take into account the number of τ-actions performed by a process. The *expansion* relation [1], written $\lesssim$, is a well-known asymmetric variant of $\approx$ such that $P \lesssim Q$ holds if $P \approx Q$ and Q has at least as many τ-moves as P.

A main result is that our bisimilarity is a *congruence*.

Theorem 2 (Congruence Theorem). *The relation $\approx$ is contextual.*

The proof that $\approx$ is preserved by the sensor update operator $[s@h \mapsto v]$ is non-standard and *technically challenging*. It required a well-founded induction.

Theorem 2 is crucial to prove that our bisimilarity is sound with respect to reduction barbed congruence. Actually, our bisimilarity is both sound and complete.

Theorem 3 (Full abstraction). *$M \approx N$ iff $M \cong N$.*

Soundness follows from Theorems 1, 2, and the capability of extensional actions to capture barbs. As to completeness, for any extensional action α we exhibit an observing context C_α.

Remark 2. A consequence of Theorem 3 and Remark 1 is that our bisimulation proof-technique remains sound in a setting with more restricted contexts, where nondeterministic sensor updates are replaced by some specific model for sensors.

As testbed for our notion of bisimilarity, we prove a number of algebraic laws on well-formed networks.

Theorem 4 (Some Algebraic Laws).

1. $n[\mathcal{I} \bowtie a!v.P \mid R]_h^\mu \gtrsim n[\mathcal{I} \bowtie P \mid R]_h^\mu$, *if* $\mathcal{I}(a) = v$ *and* a *does not occur in* R
2. $n[\mathcal{I} \bowtie @(x).P \mid R]_h^\mu \gtrsim n[\mathcal{I} \bowtie \{^h/_x\}P \mid R]_h^\mu$
3. $n[\mathcal{I} \bowtie \lfloor \bar{c}\langle v \rangle.P \rfloor S \mid \lfloor c(x).Q \rfloor T \mid R]_h^\mu \gtrsim n[\mathcal{I} \bowtie P \mid Q\{^v/_x\} \mid R]_h^\mu$, c *not in* R *and* $\mathrm{rng}(c){=}{-}1$
4. $(\boldsymbol{\nu} c)(n[\mathcal{I} \bowtie \lfloor \bar{c}\langle v \rangle.P \rfloor S \mid R]_h^\mu \mid m[\mathcal{J} \bowtie \lfloor c(x).Q \rfloor T \mid U]_k^{\mu'})$
   $\gtrsim (\boldsymbol{\nu} c)(n[\mathcal{I} \bowtie P \mid R]_h^\mu \mid m[\mathcal{J} \bowtie Q\{^v/_x\} \mid U]_k^{\mu'})$, *if* $\mathrm{rng}(c) = \infty$ *and* c *does not occur in* R *and* U
5. $n[\mathcal{I} \bowtie P]_h^\mu \gtrsim n[\mathcal{I} \bowtie \mathsf{nil}]_h^\mu$, *if subterms* $\lfloor \pi.P_1 \rfloor P_2$ *or* $a!v.P_1$ *do not occur in* P
6. $n[\mathcal{I} \bowtie \mathsf{nil}]_h^\mu \approx \mathbf{0}$, *if* $\mathcal{I}(a)$ *is undefined for any actuator* a
7. $n[\emptyset \bowtie P]_h^\mathtt{m} \approx m[\emptyset \bowtie P]_k^\mathtt{s}$, *if* P *does not contain terms of the form* $@(x).Q$, *and for any channel* c *in* P *either* $\mathrm{rng}(c) = \infty$ *or* $\mathrm{rng}(c) = -1$.

Laws 1–4 are a sort of tau-laws. Laws 5 and 6 models garbage collection of processes and nodes, respectively. Law 7 gives a sufficient condition for node anonymity as well as for non-observable node mobility.

Finally, we show that our labelled bisimilarity can be used to deal with more complicated systems. Let us prove that the two variants of the smart home mentioned in Proposition 4 are actually bisimilar.

Proposition 5. *If* $\delta = 1$ *then* $(\boldsymbol{\nu}\tilde{c})Sys \approx (\boldsymbol{\nu}\tilde{c})(\boldsymbol{\nu} g)\overline{Sys}$.

Due to the size of the systems involved, the proof of the proposition above is quite challenging. In this respect, the first four laws of Theorem 4 are fundamentals to apply non-trivial up-to expansion proof-techniques [24].

6   Related Work

To our knowledge, the IoT-calculus [16] is the first (and only) process calculus for IoT systems. We report here the main differences between CaIT and the IoT-calculus. In CaIT, we can express desirable time and runtime properties (see Propositions 1 and 3). The nondeterministic link entailment of the IoT-calculus makes communication simpler than ours; on the other hand it does not allow to enforce that a smart device cannot be in two places at the same time. In CaIT, both sensors and actuators are under the control of a single entity, i.e. the process of the node where they were deployed. This was a security issue. CaIT has a finer control of inter-node communication: it takes into account both distance among nodes and transmission range of channels. Node mobility in CaIT is timed constrained: in one time unit at most a fixed distance δ may be covered.

Finally, Lanese et al. equip the IoT-calculus with an *end-user bisimilarity* which shares the same motivations of our bisimilarity. In the IoT-calculus, end users provide values to sensors and check actuators. Unlike us, they can also observe node mobility but they cannot observe channel communication. End-user bisimilarity is not preserved by parallel composition. Compositionality is recovered by strengthening its discriminating power.

Our calculus takes inspiration from algebraic models for wireless systems [3, 4, 8, 10–12, 17–21, 23, 26]. Most of these models adopt broadcast communication, while we consider point-to-point communication, as in [10, 16, 21]. We model network topology as in [17, 19]. Property 2 was inspired by [8]. Fully abstract observational theories for calculi of wireless systems appear in [8, 12, 19].

Vigo et al. [28] proposed a calculus for *wireless-based cyber-physical systems* endowed with a theory to model and reasoning on cryptographic primitives, together with explicit notions of communication failure and unwanted communication. However, as pointed out in [29], the calculus does not provide a notion of network topology, local broadcast and behavioural equivalence. It also lacks a clear distinction between physical components (sensor and actuators) and logical ones (processes). Compared to [28], paper [29] introduces a static network topology and enrich the theory with an harmony theorem.

CaIT shares some similarities with the *synchronous languages* of the Esterel family [5]. In synchronous languages, computations proceed in phases called instants, which have some similarity with our time intervals. For instance, our timed reduction semantics has some points in common with that of *CRL* [2].

Finally, CaIT is somehow reminiscent of the SCEL language [9]. A framework to model behaviour, knowledge, and data aggregation of Autonomic Systems.

Acknowledgements. We thank Ilaria Castellani and Matthew Hennessy for their precious comments, and Valentina Castiglioni for an early proof of the harmony theorem. The anonymous referees provided useful comments.

References

1. Arun-Kumar, S., Hennessy, M.: An efficiency preorder for processes. Acta Informatica **29**, 737–760 (1992)
2. Attar, P., Castellani, I.: Fine-grained and coarse-grained reactive noninterference. In: Abadi, M., Lluch Lafuente, A. (eds.) TGC 2013. LNCS, vol. 8358, pp. 159–179. Springer, Heidelberg (2014)
3. Benetti, D., Merro, M., Vigano, L.: Model checking ad hoc network routing protocols: Aran vs. endairA. In: Fiadeiro, J.L., Gnesi, S., Maggiolo-Schettini, M. (eds.) SEFM 2010. pp. 191–202. IEEE Computer Society (2010)
4. Borgström, J., Huang, S., Johansson, M., Raabjerg, P., Victor, B., Pohjola, J., Parrow, J.: Broadcast psi-calculi with an application to wireless protocols. Softw. Syst. Model. **14**(1), 201–216 (2015)
5. Boussinot, F., de Simone, R.: The SL synchronous language. IEEE Trans. Softw. Eng. **22**(4), 256–266 (1996)
6. Cardelli, L., Gordon, A.: Mobile ambients. TCS **240**(1), 177–213 (2000)
7. Castiglioni, V., Lanotte, R., Merro, M.: A Semantic Theory of the Internet of Things. CoRR abs/1510.04854 (2015)

8. Cerone, A., Hennessy, M., Merro, M.: Modelling mac-layer communications in wireless systems. Logical Methods Comput. Sci. **11**(1: 18), 1–59 (2015)
9. De Nicola, R., Loreti, M., Pugliese, R., Tiezzi, F.: A Formal Approach to Autonomic Systems Programming: The SCEL language. ACM TAAS **9**(2), 7: 1–7: 29 (2014)
10. Fehnker, A., van Glabbeek, R., Höfner, P., McIver, A., Portmann, M., Tan, W.L.: A process algebra for wireless mesh networks. In: Seidl, H. (ed.) Programming Languages and Systems. LNCS, vol. 7211, pp. 295–315. Springer, Heidelberg (2012)
11. Ghassemi, F., Fokkink, W., Movaghar, A.: Verification of mobile ad hoc networks: an algebraic approach. TCS **412**(28), 3262–3282 (2011)
12. Godskesen, J.C.: A calculus for mobile ad hoc networks. In: Murphy, A.L., Vitek, J. (eds.) COORDINATION 2007. LNCS, vol. 4467, pp. 132–150. Springer, Heidelberg (2007)
13. Gubbi, J., Palaniswami, M.: Internet of things (IoT): a vision, architectural elements, and future directions. Future Gener. Comput. Syst. **29**(7), 1645–1660 (2013)
14. Hennessy, M., Regan, T.: A process algebra for timed systems. Inf. Comput. **117**(2), 221–239 (1995)
15. Honda, K., Yoshida, N.: On reduction-based process semantics. TCS **151**(2), 437–486 (1995)
16. Lanese, I., Bedogni, L., Di Felice, M.: Internet of things: a process calculus approach. In: Shin, S.Y., Maldonado, J.C. (eds.) SAC 2013, pp. 1339–1346. ACM (2013)
17. Lanese, I., Sangiorgi, D.: An operational semantics for a calculus for wireless systems. TCS **411**, 1928–1948 (2010)
18. Lanotte, R., Merro, M.: Semantic analysis of gossip protocols for wireless sensor networks. In: Katoen, J.-P., König, B. (eds.) CONCUR 2011. LNCS, vol. 6901, pp. 156–170. Springer, Heidelberg (2011)
19. Merro, M.: An observational theory for mobile ad hoc networks (full version). Inf. Comput. **207**(2), 194–208 (2009)
20. Merro, M., Ballardin, F., Sibilio, E.: A timed calculus for wireless systems. TCS **412**(47), 6585–6611 (2011)
21. Merro, M., Sibilio, E.: A calculus of trustworthy ad hoc networks. Formal Aspects Comput. **25**(5), 801–832 (2013)
22. Milner, R.: The polyadic π-calculus: a tutorial. Technical report, LFCS (1991)
23. Nanz, S., Hankin, C.: A framework for security analysis of mobile wireless networks. TCS **367**(1–2), 203–227 (2006)
24. Sangiorgi, D., Walker, D.: The Pi-Calculus a Theory of Mobile Processes. Cambridge University Press, New York (2001)
25. Schaft, A., Schumacher, H.: An Introduction to Hybrid Dynamical Systems. Lecture Notes in Control and Information Science, vol. 251. Springer, Heidelberg (2000)
26. Singh, A., Ramakrishnan, C., Smolka, S.: A process calculus for Mobile Ad Hoc Networks. SCP **75**(6), 440–469 (2010)
27. Sundararaman, B., Buy, U., Kshemkalyani, A.D.: Clock synchronization for wireless sensor networks: a survey. Ad Hoc Netw. **3**(3), 281–323 (2005)
28. Vigo, R., Nielson, F., Nielson, H.R.: Broadcast, denial-of-service, and secure communication. In: Johnsen, E.B., Petre, L. (eds.) IFM 2013. LNCS, vol. 7940, pp. 412–427. Springer, Heidelberg (2013)
29. Wu, X., Zhu, H.: A calculus for wireless sensor networks from quality perspective. In: HASE 2015, pp. 223–231. IEEE Computer Society (2015)

A Formal Analysis of the Global Sequence Protocol

Hernán Melgratti[1,2] and Christian Roldán[1]([⊠])

[1] Departamento de Computación, FCEyN, Universidad de Buenos Aires,
Buenos Aires, Argentina
croldan@dc.uba.ar
[2] CONICET, Buenos Aires, Argentina

Abstract. The Global Sequence Protocol (GSP) is an operational
model for replicated data stores, in which updates propagate asynchronously. We introduce the GSP-calculus as a formal model for GSP. We
give a formal account for its proposed implementation, which addresses
communication failures and compact representation of data, and use
simulation to prove that the implementation is correct. Then, we use
the GSP-calculus to reason about execution histories and prove ordering guarantees, such as read my writes, monotonic reads, causality and
consistent prefix. We also prove that GSP extended with synchronous
updates provides strong consistency guarantees.

1 Introduction

Cloud infrastructures provide data storages that are virtually unlimited, elas-
tic (i.e., scalable at run time), highly available and partition tolerant. This is
achieved by replicating data over multiple servers. A client may perform update
and read operations over any of these replicas and the store is responsible for
keeping them synchronised. However, it is known (CAP theorem [7]) that any
system cannot simultaneously provide availability, partition tolerance, and consistency. Thus, one of these properties has to be discarded. Today's popular
data storages, such as Dynamo [6] and Cassandra [9], ensure availability and
offer weaker notions of consistency, called *eventual consistency*. Roughly, eventual consistency guarantees that all updates will be delivered to the different
replicas, which will eventually converge to the same state [1]. The storages adopt
different strategies to achieve eventual consistency, which impact on the guarantees provided by the system, i.e., on the kind of inconsistencies or anomalies that
are allowed to happen. For instance, a storage may resolve automatically conflicts introduced be concurrent updates (e.g., by using timestamps or causality)
or may leave the problem to applications that read the database (like in Cassandra). In this way, the consistency model supported by a data store becomes
crucial when writing applications.

Research partially supported by UBACyT project 2014-2017 20020130200092BA.

Consequently, there has been a growing interest on establishing programming abstractions to help developers to deal with eventual consistent stores. For instance, commutative replicated data types [10] and cloud types [3] provide programmers with suitable data type abstractions that encapsulate issues related to eventual consistency. Recent proposals advocate declarative approaches for programming with eventual consistency, e.g., to automatically select the consistency level required from a store provided with a consistency contract for the application [11] or to prove that a given consistency level is adequate for preserving some data invariant [8]. With similar aims, the Global Sequence Protocol (GSP) [5] proposes an operational model to reason about applications running on top of replicated stores. Basically, the state of a store is represented as the sequence of updates that have led to it. Clients have their own copy of the state which they operate upon: each read and write operation has immediate effect over the local state and the system propagates changes to make all replicas consistent using a reliable total order broadcast protocol (RTOB). The RTOB protocol guarantees that all messages are delivered in the same total order to all clients. Replicas rely on the order generated by RTOB to converge to the same state. In the very basic model, called core GSP, each client interacts with its local state by performing read and write operations. Albeit simple, this model introduces some subtleties when programming because it does not ensure read stability (i.e., two successive reads may return different values) nor atomicity of several updates (i.e., another client may partially observe the effects of a sequence of updates). To overcome these limitations, three synchronisation primitives, namely `pull`, `push` and `confirmed`, allow programmers to control the propagation of changes. It has been shown that this model can be implemented so to handle communication failures and to represent updates efficiently by using two type of objects: states and deltas. Both models, i.e. the idealised one and its implementation, have been defined in terms of a reference implementation.

In this paper, we propose a formal account for each model: the GSP and IGSP calculi (Sects. 2 and 3). We prove that the behaviour of a program running over IGSP can be observed over the idealised model. Technically, we show that each IGSP system can be simulated by the corresponding GSP system (Sect. 4). Then, we study and prove the consistency guarantees ensured by GSP. We rely on the characterisation of consistency guarantees in terms of abstract histories proposed in [2]. Abstract histories capture the visibility relation between actions and the arbitration order of updates in the system. Then, a wide-spectrum of consistency models can be characterised in terms of these two relations. In Sect. 5, we show how to operationally associate abstract histories to concrete computations and prove that GSP enjoys properties such as *Monotonic Read*, *Causal Visibility* and *Consistent prefix*, among others. Finally, in Sect. 6 we study the extension of GSP with synchronous write operations, which ensures strong consistency.

2   Global Sequence Protocol Calculus

2.1   Syntax

Clients interact with a store by performing operations in $\mathcal{U} \cup \mathcal{R}$: an element in $\mathcal{U}$ denotes an update operation, while one in $\mathcal{R}$ stands for a read operation.

No operation can simultaneously read and update a store, therefore we assume $\mathcal{U} \cap \mathcal{R} = \emptyset$. We write $u, u', u'', \ldots$ for updates and $r, r', r'', \ldots$ for reads.

The state of a store is represented by a sequence of updates. For technical convenience (particularly in Sect. 5), we distinguish different executions of the same operation. Formally, stores associate each update with a fresh event identifier. We assume a set $\mathbb{V}$ of event identifiers v, v_0, $\ldots$, v', $\ldots$ and write u^v for the update u associated with the event v.

We use u to denote sequences of decorated updates and $(\!|u|\!)$ for an atomic block of updates. We write b for a sequence of blocks. We denote the empty sequence with ϵ and use the usual operations on sequences such as $\mathsf{b}[i]$ to denote the i-th element of b, $\mathsf{b}[i..j]$ for the subsequence of b from position i to j, $|\mathsf{b}|$ for its length and $\mathsf{b} \setminus \mathsf{b}'$ for the relative complement of b in b'. Additionally, $\underline{\mathsf{b}}$ stands for the plain sequence of updates in b (i.e., without any separation in blocks).

We rely on the countable sets $\mathcal{X}$ of program variables $x, x', \ldots$ and $\mathcal{I}$ of client identifiers $i, i', \ldots, i_1, \ldots$.

Definition 2.1 (GSP Language). *The set of* GSP *terms is given by the grammar in Fig. 1.*

A GSP system N consists of a store and zero or more clients. The global store S is completely defined by its state, which consists of a sequence of blocks. The term $\langle P, \mathsf{u_T}, \mathsf{b_S}, \mathsf{b_P}, k, j \rangle_i$ stands for a client identified by i and engaged on the execution of the program P. The remaining elements are used to describe the state of the local replica: $\mathsf{u_T}$ contains the updates that have been made locally and are part of an unfinished block; b_S models the communication buffer, which keeps all blocks completed by the client but not received by the global store; b_P is the pending buffer, which contains all completed blocks that are unconfirmed by the global store. For simplicity, we do not have an explicit replica of the global store in each client; we use instead a natural number k to indicate the portion of the global state that is known to the client. Specifically, the client i knows the sequence $S[0..k - 1]$. Similarly, j indicates the number of updates received by the client that have not been added to the local replica, i.e., the client has received the updates contained in the segment $S[k..k + j - 1]$.

A program P is built as a sequence of operations that interacts with the store: $\mathtt{read}(r), \mathtt{update}(u), \mathtt{pull}, \mathtt{push}, \mathtt{confirmed}$ (we postpone their description

(NATURALS)	$j, k, n \in \mathbb{N}$		
(UPDATE)	$\mathcal{U} = \{u, u', \ldots, u_0, \ldots\}$	(UPD SEQ)	$\mathsf{u} ::= \epsilon \mid u^v \cdot \mathsf{u}$
(READ)	$\mathcal{R} = \{r, r', \ldots, r_0, \ldots\}$	(BLOCK SEQ)	$\mathsf{b} ::= \epsilon \mid (\!|u_T|\!) \cdot \mathsf{b}$
(EVENT)	$\mathbb{V} = \{v, v', \ldots, v_0, \ldots\}$	(SYSTEM)	$N ::= S \parallel C$
(VAR)	$\mathcal{X} = \{x, x', \ldots, x_0, \ldots\}$	(STORE)	$S ::= \mathsf{b}$
(IDS)	$\mathcal{I} = \{i, j, i', \ldots, i_0, \ldots\}$	(CLIENT)	$C ::= 0 \mid \langle P, \mathsf{u_T}, \mathsf{b}, \mathsf{b}, k, j \rangle_i \mid C \parallel C$

(PROGRAM) $P ::= \mathtt{update}(u); P \mid \mathtt{let}\ x = \mathtt{read}(r)\ \mathtt{in}\ P \mid \mathtt{pull}; P \mid$
$\qquad\qquad\ \mathtt{push}; P \mid \mathtt{let}\ x = \mathtt{confirmed}\ \mathtt{in}\ P$

Fig. 1. Syntax of the GSP calculus

until Sect. 2.2). A program let $x = \ldots$ in P introduces a bound variable whose scope is P. The definition of free variables of a program is standard. We say that a process P is *closed* when it does not contain free variables. We keep the language for programs simple. We remark that this choice does not affect the results presented in this paper. Actually, we could just have characterised the behaviour of programs as a labelled transition system, but we prefer to have a syntax throughout the presentation.

Definition 2.2 (Well-formedness). *A* GSP *system* $N = C_0 \| \ldots \| C_m \| S$ *where* $C_l = \langle P_l, \mathsf{u}_{Tl}, \mathsf{b}_{Sl}, \mathsf{b}_{\mathsf{p}l}, k_l, j_l \rangle_{\mathsf{i}_l}$ *for all* $l \in \{0, \ldots, m\}$ *is* well-formed *if the following conditions hold*

1. $\mathsf{i}_l \neq \mathsf{i}_{l'}$ *for all* $l \neq l'$;
2. $k_l + j_l \leq |S|$ *for all* l;
3. $\mathsf{b}_{Pl} = (\!|\mathsf{u}_1|\!) \cdots (\!|\mathsf{u}_p|\!) \cdot \mathsf{b}_{Sl}$ *and for all* $1 \leq x < y \leq \mathsf{p}$ *there exists* x', y' *s.t.* $S[x'] = (\!|\mathsf{u}_x|\!)$, $S[y'] = (\!|\mathsf{u}_y|\!)$ *and* $k_l \leq x' < y'$; *and*
4. $\mathsf{u} = S \cdot \mathsf{b}_{S0} \cdots \mathsf{b}_{Sm} \cdot \mathsf{u}_{T0} \cdots \mathsf{u}_{Tm}$, *if* $\mathsf{u}[x] = u^{\mathsf{v}}$, $\mathsf{u}[y] = u^{\mathsf{v}'}$ *and* $x \neq y$ *then* $\mathsf{v} \neq \mathsf{v}'$.

We require identifiers to univocally identify clients (1) and every local state to be consistent with the global store, i.e., a client can see at most every message in the store (2), all unconfirmed blocks in b_{Pl} are either in the communication buffer b_{Sl} or in the unseen part of the global store $(\!|\mathsf{u}_1|\!) \cdots (\!|\mathsf{u}_p|\!)$ (3). Moreover, an event identifier is associated with a unique update in the system (4). Hereafter, we assume every GSP system to be well-formed.

2.2 Operational Semantics

The operational semantics of GSP is given by a labelled transition system over well-formed terms, quotiented by the structural equivalence $\equiv$ defined as the least equivalence such that $\|$ is associative, commutative and has 0 as neutral element. The set of actions is given by the following grammar:

$$\lambda ::= \tau \mid rd(r) \mid wr(u^{\mathsf{v}}) \mid pull \mid push \mid cfm$$

As usual, τ stands for an internal, unobservable action, while the remaining ones correspond to the interaction of a client with the store. A label (λ, i) indicates that the client i performs the action λ. We write $\xrightarrow{\lambda}_{\mathsf{i}}$ instead of $\xrightarrow{(\lambda, \mathsf{i})}$.

We now comment on the inference rules in Fig. 2. When a client performs an update (rule UPDATE), the change has only local effects: the sequence of local updates u_T is extended with the operation u decorated with a globally fresh identifier v. We remark that decorations are used for technical reasons but they are operationally irrelevant (see Sect. 5).

A client propagates its local changes to the global store by executing push (rule PUSH): all local changes in u_T will be transmitted as a block $(\!|\mathsf{u}_T|\!)$, i.e., as an atomic unit. Nevertheless, these changes are not made available immediately at the global store because of the asynchronous communication model. In fact,

(UPDATE)

$$\text{v fresh}$$

$$\langle \mathtt{update}(u); P, \mathsf{u_T}, \mathsf{b_S}, \mathsf{b_P}, k, j \rangle_i \parallel N \xrightarrow{wr(u^{\mathsf{v}})}_i \langle P, \mathsf{u_T} \cdot u^{\mathsf{v}}, \mathsf{b_S}, \mathsf{b_P}, k, j \rangle_i \parallel N$$

(PUSH)

$$\langle \mathtt{push}; P, \mathsf{u_T}, \mathsf{b_S}, \mathsf{b_P}, k, j \rangle_i \parallel N \xrightarrow{push}_i \langle P, \epsilon, \mathsf{b_S} \cdot (\!|\mathsf{u_T}|\!), \mathsf{b_P} \cdot (\!|\mathsf{u_T}|\!), k, j \rangle_i \parallel N$$

(SEND)

$$\langle P, \mathsf{u_T}, (\!|\mathsf{u_T'}|\!) \cdot \mathsf{b_S}, \mathsf{b_P}, k, j \rangle_i \parallel C \parallel S \xrightarrow{\tau}_i \langle P, \mathsf{u_T}, \mathsf{b_S}, \mathsf{b_P}, k, j \rangle_i \parallel C \parallel S \cdot (\!|\mathsf{u_T'}|\!)$$

(RECEIVE)

$$k + j < |S|$$

$$\langle P, \mathsf{u_T}, \mathsf{b_S}, \mathsf{b_P}, k, j \rangle_i \parallel C \parallel S \xrightarrow{\tau}_i \langle P, \mathsf{u_T}, \mathsf{b_S}, \mathsf{b_P}, k, j+1 \rangle_i \parallel C \parallel S$$

(PULL)

$$\langle \mathtt{pull}; P, \mathsf{u_T}, \mathsf{b_S}, \mathsf{b_P}, k, j \rangle_i \parallel C \| S \xrightarrow{pull}_i \langle P, \mathsf{u_T}, \mathsf{b_S}, \mathsf{b_P} \setminus S[k..k+j-1], k+j, 0 \rangle_i \parallel C \| S$$

(READ)

$$rvalue(r, S[0..k-1] \cdot \mathsf{b_P} \cdot \mathsf{u_T}) = v$$

$$\langle \mathtt{let}\ x = \mathtt{read}(r)\ \mathtt{in}\ P, \mathsf{u_T}, \mathsf{b_S}, \mathsf{b_P}, k, j \rangle_i \parallel C \| S \xrightarrow{rd(r)}_i \langle P\{v/x\}, \mathsf{u_T}, \mathsf{b_S}, \mathsf{b_P}, k, j \rangle_i \parallel C \| S$$

(CONFIRM)

$$v = (\mathsf{b_P} \cdot \mathsf{u_T} == \epsilon)$$

$$\langle \mathtt{let}\ x = \mathtt{confirmed}\ \mathtt{in}\ P, \mathsf{u_T}, \mathsf{b_S}, \mathsf{b_P}, k, j \rangle_i \parallel N \xrightarrow{cfm}_i \langle P\{v/x\}, \mathsf{u_T}, \mathsf{b_S}, \mathsf{b_P}, k, j \rangle_i \parallel N$$

Fig. 2. Operational semantics for GSP

the new block $(\!|\mathsf{u_T}|\!)$ is added to the communication buffer $\mathsf{b_S}$, which contains all blocks that have not reached the global store. Also, $(\!|\mathsf{u_T}|\!)$ is added to the pending messages $\mathsf{b_P}$. Rule SEND stands for a block that finally reaches the global store. Conversely, rule RECEIVE models the reception of a new update. The received update is not immediately added to the local replica. Actually, each client explicitly refreshes its local view by executing pull (rule PULL). At this time, all previously received updates j are incorporated to the local copy (i.e., k is changed to $k + j$). Additionally, all pending updates in the new fragment $S[k..k+j-1]$ are remove from $\mathsf{b_P}$.

The semantics of operations is defined abstractly by the interpretation function $rvalue : \mathcal{R} \times \mathcal{U}^* \to \mathcal{V}$, i.e., a function that takes a read operation and a sequence of updates and returns a value in some domain $\mathcal{V}$. A read operation r is evaluated over the local state of the client (rule READ), i.e., the known prefix of the global store $S[0..k-1]$ and the local updates in $\mathsf{b_P}$ and $\mathsf{u_T}$. The value v is bound to the variable x, and hence all free occurrences of x in the continuation P are substituted by v. A client may perform confirmed to check whether its executed updates are already in the global store: this operation returns true only when the local buffers $\mathsf{b_P}$ and $\mathsf{u_T}$ are both empty (rule CONFIRM).

We remark that the operational semantics preserves well-formedness.

Lemma 2.1. *If N is well-formed and $N \xrightarrow{\lambda}_i N'$, then N' is well-formed.*

3   Implementation of GSP

The GSP model describes an idealised system that abstracts away from several implementation details, such as non-optimised representation of the state and unreliable communication. This section presents a formal model for the implementation proposed in [5].

3.1   Syntax

The implementation of GSP relies on a compact representation for states and updates. Their precise definition highly depends on the datatype of the values handled by the store, but they are characterised in terms of two abstract types: *State* and *Delta*, which provides the following operations [5]:

$$\delta_\emptyset \quad : Delta \qquad\qquad \emptyset \quad : State$$
$$append : Delta \times \mathcal{U} \to Delta \qquad apply : State \times Delta^* \to State$$
$$reduce \ : Delta^* \to Delta \qquad\qquad read \ : \mathcal{R} \times State \to \mathcal{V}$$

Constants $\delta_\emptyset$ and $\emptyset$ denote the empty elements in their respective types. An object $\delta \in Delta$ describes the effects of a sequence of updates and is built by either appending an update to an existing delta (*append*) or combining together several deltas (*reduce*). Operation *read* is the interpretation function for operations (i.e., the implementation counterpart of function $rvalue(\_, \_)$ used by the idealised model) and *apply* corresponds to state transformations.

Clients and the global store exchange δ objects to communicate changes. As each single δ may correspond to several update operations, clients send each δ accompanied by its own identifier and a sequence number n. Precisely, clients send rounds, i.e. triples $r = \langle i, n, \delta \rangle$. Differently, the global store sends segments $seg = \langle \delta, f \rangle$, in which δ is accompanied by a function $f \in \mathcal{I} \to \mathbb{N}$. In this way, the global store confirms all changes from client i until round $f(i)$. To deal with crashes and recovery, the server may send segments of the form $\langle s, f \rangle$, which communicates a complete state instead of a delta object.

Definition 3.1 (GSP Language). *The set of* IGSP *terms is given by the grammar in Fig. 3.*

As for GSP, a system is composed by a global store S and possibly many clients C. A global store is modelled by a tuple $\langle s, f, in_s, out_s \rangle$ containing a

(STATE)	$s, s', \ldots, s_1, \ldots \in State$	(SGMT SEQ)	$seg ::= \epsilon \mid seg \cdot seg$
(DELTA)	$\delta, \delta', \ldots, \delta_1, \ldots \in Delta$	(IN SRV)	$in_s \in \mathcal{I} \to r$
(ROUND)	$r ::= \langle i, n, \delta \rangle$	(OUT SRV)	$out_s \in \mathcal{I} \to seg$
(RND SEQ)	$\mathbf{r} ::= \epsilon \mid r \cdot r$	(SYSTEM)	$N ::= S \parallel C$
(MAX RND)	$f, f', \ldots, f_1, \ldots \in \mathcal{I} \to \mathbb{N}$	(SERVER)	$S ::= \langle s, f, in_s, out_s \rangle$
(SEGMENT)	$seg ::= \langle \delta, f \rangle \mid \langle s, f \rangle$	(CLIENTS)	$C ::= 0 \mid \langle P, s, \delta, \delta, n, \mathbf{r}, seg \rangle_i \mid C \parallel C$

Fig. 3. Syntax of the IGSP calculus

state s, a function f to keep track of processed rounds and the communication buffers in_s and out_s. There are two dedicated buffers for each client i: $in_s(i)$ contains the rounds received from i, and $out_s(i)$ the segments that have been sent to i.

A client is represented by a term $\langle P, s, \delta_T, \delta_P, n, r, in_c \rangle_i$. As for GSP, i is its identity and P is its program. Note that the language for programs remains unaltered. The component δ_T is analogous to u_T in the GSP model, i.e., it keeps all local updates until the client performs **push**. Differently, δ_P keeps all finished blocks that have not been sent. The number n identifies the current round. Buffer r keeps all sent rounds that have not been confirmed by the global store (similar to b_P in GSP), while in_c keeps all received segments (analogous to j).

We also impose the following well-formedness condition on systems.

Definition 3.2 (IGSP **well-formedness**). *A IGSP system* $N = C_0 \| \ldots \| C_m \| S$ *with* $S = \langle s, f, in_s, out_s \rangle$ *and* $C_l = \langle P_l, s_l, \delta_{Tl}, \delta_{Pl}, n_l, r_l, in_{cl} \rangle_{i_l}$ *for* $l \in \{0, \ldots, m\}$ *is* well-formed *if the following conditions hold*

1. $i_l \neq i_{l'}$ *for all* $l \neq l'$.
2. $dom(in_s) = dom(out_s) \subseteq \{0, \ldots, m\}$.
3. $i_l \notin dom(out_s)$ *implies* $in_{cl} = \epsilon$.
4. *if* $i_l \in dom(out_s)$ *and* $in_{cl} \cdot out_s(i_l) \neq \epsilon$ *then either*
   (i) $in_{cl} \cdot out_s(i_l) = \langle \delta_0, f_0 \rangle \cdots \langle \delta_h, f_h \rangle$; *or*
   (ii) $in_{cl} \cdot out_s(i_l) = \langle s, f_0 \rangle \cdot \langle \delta_1, f_1 \rangle \cdots \langle \delta_h, f_h \rangle$
   and $f_j(i_l) \leq f_k(i_l)$ *for all* $j < k \in \{0..h\}$ *and* $f_h = f$.
5. $r_l = \langle i_0, n_0, \delta_0 \rangle \cdots \langle i_r, n_r, \delta_r \rangle$, $n_j < n_k$ *for all* $j < k \in \{0..r\}$ *and either*
   (i) $\delta_{Pl} = \delta_\emptyset$, $n_r \leq n_l$ *and* $f(i_l) \leq n_l$; *or*
   (ii) $\delta_{Pl} \neq \delta_\emptyset$, $n_r < n_l$ *and* $f(i_l) < n_l$.
6. *either*
   (i) $r_l = \epsilon$, $f(i_l) \leq n_l$ *and if* $i_l \in dom(in_s)$ *then* $in_s(i_l) = \epsilon$;
   (ii) $r_l = in_s(i_l) = \langle i_l, n_{fst}, \delta_{fst} \rangle \cdot r_l'$ *and* $n_{fst} > f(i_l)$;
   (iii) $r_l = r_l'' \cdot \langle i_l, n_{lst}, \delta_{lst} \rangle \cdot in_s(i_l)$ *and* $in_{cl} \cdot out_s(i_l) = \langle \delta_0, f_0 \rangle \cdots \langle \delta'_{lst}, f_{lst} \rangle$
   with $f_{lst}(i_l) = n_{lst}$; *or*
   (iv) $in_s(i_l) = \epsilon$, $r_l = r_l'' \cdot \langle i_l, n_{lst}, \delta_{lst} \rangle$ *and either* $in_{cl} \cdot out_s(i_l) = \langle s, f' \rangle \cdot seg$
   with $f'(i_l) \leq n_{lst}$ *or* $in_{cl} \cdot out_s(i_l) = \epsilon$ *and* $f(i_l) \leq n_{lst}$.

We require all clients to have different identifiers (1). Communication channels in the implementation are bidirectional, hence $i_l \in dom(in_s)$ iff $i_l \in dom(out_s)$ (2). Moreover, the input buffer of a disconnected client is empty (3). Condition (4) states that $\langle s, f' \rangle$ can appear only as the first message in the flow from the store and that the store confirms processed rounds in a non-decreasing order. Similarly, clients send rounds with increasing round number (5). The last condition (6) states a coherence requirement between pending rounds and the segments sent by the store, which can only confirm rounds that are pending.

(I-UPDATE)

$$\langle \mathbf{update}(u); P, \mathbf{s}, \delta_T, \delta_P, n, \mathbf{r}, \mathbf{in}_c \rangle_i \parallel N \xrightarrow{wr(u^\vee)}_i \langle P, \mathbf{s}, append(\delta_T, u), \delta_P, n, \mathbf{r}, \mathbf{in}_c \rangle_i \parallel N$$

(I-PUSH)

$$\langle \mathbf{push}; P, \mathbf{s}, \delta_T, \delta_P, n, \mathbf{r}, \mathbf{in}_c \rangle_i \parallel N \xrightarrow{push}_i \langle P, \mathbf{s}, \delta_\emptyset, reduce(\delta_P \cdot \delta_T), n+1, \mathbf{r}, \mathbf{in}_c \rangle_i \parallel N$$

(I-SEND)

$$\dfrac{\delta_P \neq \delta_\emptyset \quad i \in dom(\mathbf{in}_s) \quad r = \langle i, n, \delta_P \rangle \quad \mathbf{in}_c \cdot \mathbf{out}_s(i) \neq \langle \mathbf{s}', \mathbf{f} \rangle \cdot \mathbf{seg}}{\begin{array}{l} \langle P, \mathbf{s}, \delta_T, \delta_P, n, \mathbf{r}, \mathbf{in}_c \rangle_i \parallel \langle \mathbf{s}', \mathbf{f}, \mathbf{in}_s, \mathbf{out}_s \rangle \parallel C \xrightarrow{\tau}_i \\ \qquad \langle P, \mathbf{s}, \delta_T, \delta_\emptyset, n, \mathbf{r} \cdot r, \mathbf{in}_c \rangle_i \parallel \langle \mathbf{s}', \mathbf{f}, \mathbf{in}_s[i \mapsto \mathbf{in}_s(i) \cdot r], \mathbf{out}_s \rangle \parallel C \end{array}}$$

(I-RECEIVE)

$$\dfrac{\mathbf{out}_s(i) = seg \cdot \mathbf{seg}}{\begin{array}{l} \langle P, \mathbf{s}, \delta_T, \delta_P, n, \mathbf{r}, \mathbf{in}_c \rangle_i \parallel \langle \mathbf{s}', \mathbf{f}, \mathbf{in}_s, \mathbf{out}_s \rangle \parallel C \xrightarrow{\tau}_i \\ \qquad \langle P, \mathbf{s}, \delta_T, \delta_P, n, \mathbf{r}, \mathbf{in}_c \cdot seg \rangle_i \parallel \langle \mathbf{s}', \mathbf{f}, \mathbf{in}_s, \mathbf{out}_s[i \mapsto \mathbf{seg}] \rangle \parallel C \end{array}}$$

(I-PULL₁)

$$\dfrac{\mathbf{r}' = filter(\mathbf{f}_k(i), \mathbf{r}) \quad \mathbf{in}_c = \langle \delta_1, \mathbf{f}_1 \rangle \ldots \langle \delta_k, \mathbf{f}_k \rangle}{\langle \mathbf{pull}; P, \mathbf{s}, \delta_T, \delta_P, n, \mathbf{r}, \mathbf{in}_c \rangle_i \parallel N \xrightarrow{pull}_i \langle P, apply(\mathbf{s}, reduce(\delta_1 \cdots \delta_k)), \delta_T, \delta_P, n, \mathbf{r}', \epsilon \rangle_i \parallel N}$$

(I-READ)

$$\dfrac{read(r, apply(\mathbf{s}, \Delta(\mathbf{r}) \cdot \delta_P \cdot \delta_T)) = v}{\langle \mathbf{let}\ x = \mathbf{read}(r)\ \mathbf{in}\ P, \mathbf{s}, \delta_T, \delta_P, n, \mathbf{r}, \mathbf{in}_c \rangle_i \parallel N \xrightarrow{rd(r)}_i \langle P\{v/x\}, \mathbf{s}, \delta_T, \delta_P, n, \mathbf{r}, \mathbf{in}_c \rangle_i \parallel N}$$

(I-CONFIRM)

$$\dfrac{v = (\mathbf{r} \cdot \delta_P \cdot \delta_T == \epsilon)}{\langle \mathbf{let}\ x = \mathbf{confirmed}\ \mathbf{in}\ P, \mathbf{s}, \delta_T, \delta_P, n, \mathbf{r}, \mathbf{in}_c \rangle_i \parallel N \xrightarrow{cfm}_i \langle P\{v/x\}, \mathbf{s}, \delta_T, \delta_P, n, \mathbf{r}, \mathbf{in}_c \rangle_i \parallel N}$$

(I-BATCH)

$$\dfrac{\langle \delta, \mathbf{f}' \rangle = rnds(\mathbf{in}_s) \quad \delta \neq \delta_\emptyset \quad \mathbf{s}' = apply(\mathbf{s}, \delta) \quad \forall i.(\mathbf{out}_s'(i) = \mathbf{out}_s(i) \cdot \langle \delta, \mathbf{f}[\mathbf{f}'] \rangle \wedge \mathbf{in}_s'(i) = \epsilon)}{\langle \mathbf{s}, \mathbf{f}, \mathbf{in}_s, \mathbf{out}_s \rangle \parallel C \xrightarrow{\tau} \langle \mathbf{s}', \mathbf{f}[\mathbf{f}'], \mathbf{in}_s', \mathbf{out}_s' \rangle \parallel C}$$

(I-DROP-CXN)

$$\dfrac{i \in \mathbf{in}_s \quad i \in \mathbf{out}_s}{\begin{array}{l} \langle P, \mathbf{s}, \delta_T, \delta_P, n, \mathbf{r}, \mathbf{in}_c \rangle_i \parallel \langle \mathbf{s}, \mathbf{f}, \mathbf{in}_s, \mathbf{out}_s \rangle \parallel C \xrightarrow{\tau} \\ \qquad \langle P, \mathbf{s}, \delta_T, \delta_P, n, \mathbf{r}, \epsilon \rangle_i \parallel \langle \mathbf{s}, \mathbf{f}, \mathbf{in}_s \setminus i, \mathbf{out}_s \setminus i \rangle \parallel C \end{array}}$$

(I-ACCEPT-CXN)

$$\dfrac{i \notin \mathbf{in}_s \quad i \notin \mathbf{out}_s}{\langle \mathbf{s}, \mathbf{f}, \mathbf{in}_s, \mathbf{out}_s \rangle \parallel C_i \parallel C \xrightarrow{\tau} \langle \mathbf{s}, \mathbf{f}, \mathbf{in}_s[i \mapsto \epsilon], \mathbf{out}_s[i \mapsto \langle \mathbf{s}, \mathbf{f} \rangle] \rangle \parallel C_i \parallel C}$$

(I-PULL₂)

$$\dfrac{\mathbf{in}_c = \langle \mathbf{s}''', \mathbf{f}_0 \rangle \cdot \langle \delta_1, \mathbf{f}_1 \rangle \ldots \langle \delta_k, \mathbf{f}_k \rangle \qquad \mathbf{s}'' = apply(\mathbf{s}''', reduce(\delta_\emptyset \cdot \delta_1 \cdots \delta_k)) \qquad \mathbf{r}' = filter(\mathbf{f}_k(i), \mathbf{r})}{\begin{array}{l} \langle \mathbf{pull}; P, \mathbf{s}, \delta_T, \delta_P, n, \mathbf{r}, \mathbf{in}_c \rangle_i \parallel \langle \mathbf{s}', \mathbf{f}, \mathbf{in}_s, \mathbf{out}_s \rangle \parallel C \xrightarrow{pull}_i \\ \qquad \langle P, \mathbf{s}'', \delta_T, \delta_P, n, \mathbf{r}', \epsilon \rangle_i \parallel \langle \mathbf{s}', \mathbf{f}, \mathbf{in}_s[i \mapsto \mathbf{in}_s(i) \cdot \mathbf{r}'], \mathbf{out}_s \rangle \parallel C \end{array}}$$

Fig. 4. Operational semantics of IGSP

3.2 Operational Semantics

As for the idealised model, the operational semantics is given by a labelled transition system over well-formed terms, up-to structural equivalence. We consider a new label τ without any client annotation for transitions associated with changes in the global store and communication failures. The inference rules are in Fig. 4.

Rule (I-UPDATE), which is analogous to rule (UPDATE), adds the operation u to the temporary block δ_T. The decoration v is irrelevant in this model, hence we do not impose any freshness requirement. A client terminates a block by executing push (I-PUSH). At this time, the block δ_T is appended to the already terminated blocks in δ_P, which will be sent on the next round. Additionally, the block counter n is incremented by 1. By rule (I-SEND), a client sends changes to the global store. This transition takes place whenever the client is connected (i.e., $i \in dom(in_s)$), there are finished blocks in δ_P (i.e., $\delta_P \neq \delta_\emptyset$) and there is no need for resynchronisation (i.e., $in_c \cdot out_s(i) \neq \langle s', f \rangle \cdot seg)^1$. The available blocks are sent within the same round $r = \langle i, n, \delta_P \rangle$, which contains the number n corresponding to the last finished block. The new round r is added to the corresponding input buffer in the store, i.e., $in_s(i)$ is updated to $in_s(i) \cdot r$ (where $\_[\_ \mapsto \_]$ is the update operator for functions). Additionally, r is added to the sequence of pending rounds r and the buffer δ_P is reset to $\delta_\emptyset$.

Symmetrically, the client i may receive an available segment at any time (I-RECEIVE). The new segment seg is removed from the buffer $out_s(i)$ of the global store and added to the input buffer of the client. As for the idealised model, all received changes are applied to the local replica when i performs pull. Rule (I-PULL$_1$) handles the case in which the connection with the global store has not been previously reset. In such case, all received segments are of the form $\langle \delta, f \rangle$. Therefore, the changes $\delta_1 \cdots \delta_k$ are applied to the local state s and all rounds confirmed by the received segments are removed from the pending list r. By well-formedness (Definition 3.2, 5), it suffices to consider the confirmation f_k, which has the greatest confirmation. Hence, all rounds up-to $f_k(i)$ are removed from r. This is done by the auxiliary function $filter(\_, \_)$, defined as follows

$$filter(n, \mathbf{r}) = \langle i, n_j, \delta_j \rangle \cdots \langle i, n_k, \delta_k \rangle \quad \text{if} \quad \mathbf{r} = \langle i, n_0, \delta_0 \rangle \cdots \langle i, n_j, \delta_j \rangle \cdots \langle i, n_k, \delta_k,$$
$$n_{j-1} \leq n \text{ and } n_j > n$$

Rules (I-READ) and (I-CONFIRM) are analogous the ones in the GSP calculus. We use $\Delta(\_)$ for the function that projects a sequence of rounds into the sequence that contains the corresponding δs. The global store changes its state as prescribed by rule (I-BATCH): it collects all received rounds in in_s by using the auxiliary function $rnds(\_)$, which builds a unique object δ by appending all available rounds, and a function f that associates each client with the number of the last received round. Let in_s be such that $dom(in_s) = \{i_0, \ldots, i_m\}$ and

---

[1] For simplicity we check re-synchronisation by inspecting buffers instead of explicitly adding the condition *channel established* used in the implementation.

$\forall i_l \in dom(\text{in}_s).\text{in}_s(i_l) = r_l \cdot \langle i_l, n_l^{k_l}, \delta_l^{k_l} \rangle$. Then, $rnds(\_)$ is defined as follows

$$rnds(\text{in}_s) = \langle \delta, f' \rangle \quad \text{with} \quad \delta = reduce(\Delta(\text{in}_s(i_0)) \cdots \Delta(\text{in}_s(i_m))),$$
$$dom(f') = \{i \mid i \in dom(\text{in}_s) \text{ and } \text{in}_s(i) \neq \epsilon\} \text{ and}$$
$$\forall i_l \in dom(\text{in}_s).f'(i_l) = n_l^{k_l}$$

The obtained δ is applied to the current state s and f is updated with f'. In addition, the new segment $\langle \delta, f[f'] \rangle$ is sent to every connected client, i.e., it is added at the end of every buffer $\text{out}_s(i)$. The input buffers $\text{in}_s(i_l)$ are emptied because all received rounds have been processed.

The remaining rules deal with connectivity issues: rule (I-DROP-CXN) models a disconnection: the buffers $\text{out}_s(i)$ and $\text{in}_s(i)$ are removed from the global store and also the input buffer of i is set to ϵ. When the client i (re-)establishes its connection (I-ACCEPT-CXN), the store creates the buffers for i and sends a segment containing the current state of the store. Rule (I-PULL$_2$) is analogous to (I-PULL$_1$), but handles the first pull after a reconnection. The first received segment $\langle s''', f_0 \rangle$ contains a state instead of a delta object. The client uses s''' instead of its local state to resynchronise. The application of successive segments is analogous to rule (I-PULL$_1$). Moreover, the client resends a round r' containing all pending segments lost by the server during the disconnection.

The proposed implementation allows for a server to crash, i.e., to close all communication buffers, but we do not model explicitly this behaviour because it can be obtained by applying rule (I-DROP-CXN) several times.

Lemma 3.1. *Let* N *be a well-formed* IGSP *system. If* $N \xrightarrow{\lambda}_i N'$, *then* N' *is well-formed.*

4 Correctness of the Implementation

We now prove that IGSP is a correct implementation of GSP. We recall in Fig. 5 the requirements stated in [5] for the operations provided by the data types State and Delta. Formally, the relation $\_ \lhd \_$ associates delta and state objects with sequences of updates: $\delta \lhd u$ (similarly, $s \lhd u$) means that δ (correspondingly, s) is a compact representation of u. Then, it is also assumed that $s \lhd u$ implies $read(r, s) = rvalue(r, u)$ for any r. Building on the above relation, we define under which conditions a IGSP system is an implementation of a GSP system.

Definition 4.1. *Let* $N = C_0 \parallel \ldots \parallel C_m \parallel S$ *be a* GSP *system such that* $C_l = \langle P_l, u_{Tl}, b_{Sl}, b_{Pl}, k_l, j_l \rangle_{i_l}$ *for all* $l \in \{0, \ldots, m\}$, *and* $N = C_0 \parallel \ldots \parallel C_m \parallel S$ *a* IGSP *system such that* $S = \langle s, f_s, \text{in}_s, \text{out}_s \rangle$ *and* $C_l = \langle P_l, s_l, \delta_{Tl}, \delta_{Pl}, n_l, r_l, \text{in}_{cl} \rangle_{i_l}$. *We say* N *implements* N *if the following conditions hold:*

1. $s \lhd \underline{S}$;
2. $s_l \lhd S[0..k_l - 1]$;
3. $\delta_{Tl} \lhd u_{Tl}$;
4. $reduce(\Delta(r_l) \cdot \delta_{Pl}) \lhd \underline{b_{Pl}}$;

$$(\triangleleft\text{-}\delta_{\emptyset}\ )\quad \overline{\delta_{\emptyset} \triangleleft \epsilon}$$

$$\frac{(\triangleleft\text{-}append)}{append(\delta, u) \triangleleft u \cdot u^{\mathsf{v}}} \quad \frac{(\triangleleft\text{-}read)}{read(r, \mathsf{s}) = rvalue(r, u)}$$

$$(\triangleleft\text{-}\emptyset\ )\quad \overline{\emptyset \triangleleft \epsilon}$$

$$\frac{(\triangleleft\text{-}apply)}{apply(\mathsf{s}, \delta_1 \cdots \delta_n) \triangleleft u \cdot u_1 \cdots u_n} \quad \frac{(\triangleleft\text{-}reduce)}{reduce(\delta_1 \cdots \delta_n) \triangleleft u_1 \cdots u_n}$$

Fig. 5. Coherence requirements for *Delta* and *State* operators

5. *if* $i_l \in dom(\mathsf{in_s})$ *and* $\mathsf{in_c} \cdot \mathsf{out_s}(i_l) \neq \langle \mathsf{s}', \mathbf{f} \rangle \cdot \mathbf{seg}$ *then*
   $reduce(\Delta(\mathsf{in_s}(i_l))) \cdot \delta_{Pl}) \triangleleft \underline{\mathsf{b}_{Sl}}$;
6. *if* $i_l \in dom(\mathsf{out_s})$ *then either*
   i. $\mathsf{in_{cl}} \cdot \mathsf{out_s}(i_l) = \epsilon$, $k_l = |S|$;
   ii. $\mathsf{in_{cl}} = \langle \delta', \mathbf{f} \rangle \cdot \mathbf{seg}$, $reduce(\Delta(\mathsf{in_{cl}})) \triangleleft S[k_l..k_l + j_l - 1]$, *and*
       $reduce(\Delta(\mathsf{out_s}(i_l))) \triangleleft S[k_l + j_l..|S| - 1]$;
   iii. $\mathsf{in_{cl}} = \langle \mathsf{s}', \mathbf{f_0} \rangle \cdot \mathbf{seg}$, *there exists* t *s.t.* $k_l \leq t \leq k_l + j_l$ *s.t.* $\mathsf{s}' \triangleleft S[0..t-1]$,
        $reduce(\Delta(\mathbf{seg})) \triangleleft S[t..k_l + j_l - 1]$ *and*
        $reduce(\Delta(\mathsf{out_s}(i_l))) \triangleleft S[k_l + j_l..|S| - 1]$; *or*
   iv. $\mathsf{in_{cl}} = \epsilon$, $\mathsf{out_s}(i_l) = \langle \mathsf{s}', \mathbf{f} \rangle \cdot \mathbf{seg}$ *there exists* $t \geq k_l + j_l$ *s.t.* $\mathsf{s}' \triangleleft S[0..t-1]$
        $reduce(\Delta(\mathbf{seg})) \triangleleft S[t..|S| - 1]$;
7. *for all* $\mathbf{f}$ *s.t* $\mathbf{f} = \mathbf{f}_s$ *or* $\langle \delta, \mathbf{f} \rangle \in \mathsf{in_{cl}} \cdot \mathsf{out_s}(i_l)$, *for all* $\langle i, n, \delta' \rangle \in \mathbf{r}_l$ *if* $n \leq \mathbf{f}(i_l)$
   then $\delta \triangleleft S[x..x']$ *and* $\delta' \triangleleft S[y..y']$ *with* $y' \leq x'$.

The first three conditions are self-explanatory. Condition (4) states that the pending blocks in $\underline{\mathsf{b}_{Pl}}$ correspond either to rounds in the pending list $\mathbf{r}_l$ or to blocks ready to be sent, i.e., in δ_{Pl}. By condition (5), if a client is synchronised with the store (i.e., $i_l \in dom(\mathsf{in_s})$ and $\mathsf{in_c} \cdot \mathsf{out_s}(i_l) \neq \langle \mathsf{s}', \mathbf{f} \rangle \cdot \mathbf{seg}$) then all blocks in the sending list b_{Sl} are either rounds that have been sent, i.e., in $\mathsf{in_s}(i_l)$, or ready blocks in δ_{Pl}. Condition (6) establishes the relation between the received messages in both models. Basically, the local replica is complete when there are no segments for the client (i). When the first received segment is a delta object (ii), the content in the input buffer $\mathsf{in_{cl}}$ corresponds to the received messages in $S[k_l..k_l + j_l - 1]$ and the output buffer $\mathsf{out_s}(i_l)$ contains the updates in the sequence $S[k_l + j_l..|S| - 1]$. In the remaining two cases, the first segment contains a state. When the segment is in the input buffer of the client (iii), the received state s' corresponds to a prefix of the sequence S whose length lies in between of the updates already received by the client in the idealised model, i.e., $S[0..t-1]$ with $k \leq t \leq k_l + j_l$, while the remaining conditions are analogous to the previous case. Differently, when the first segment is still on the output buffer of the store (iv), s' corresponds to a prefix that contains at least all updates in S already known to the client, i.e., $t \geq k_l + j_l$ because the store confirmations are monotonic.

Condition (7) states that in any segment $\langle \delta, \mathbf{f} \rangle$ sent by the store, δ corresponds to a contiguous sequence of updates in S, i.e., $S[x..x']$. Moreover, all confirmed rounds are also within the prefix $S[0..x']$.

We now show that IGSP is a correct implementation of GSP by proving that N weakly simulates N when N implements N. We use standard simulation but technically we take into account the fact that GSP associates a fresh event identifier to each update while IGSP does not. Take $\rightarrow = \xrightarrow{\tau} \bigcup_{i \in \mathcal{I}} \xrightarrow{\tau}_i$, $\Rightarrow$ as the reflexive and transitive closure of $\rightarrow$, i.e. $\Rightarrow = \rightarrow^*$, and $\xrightarrow{\lambda}_i = \Rightarrow; \xrightarrow{\lambda}_i; \Rightarrow$.

Definition 4.2. (Simulation). $\mathcal{R}$ *is an* implementation simulation *if for all* $(N, N) \in \mathcal{R}$ *we have:*

1. *If* N $\xrightarrow{wr(u^v)u}_i$ N′ *then* $\exists N′$, w *s.t.* N $\xrightarrow{wr(u^w)}_i N′$ *and* $(N′, N′) \in \mathcal{R}$;
2. *If* N $\xrightarrow{\lambda}_i$ N′ *and* $\lambda \neq wr(u^v)u, \tau$ *then* $\exists N′$ *s.t.* N $\xrightarrow{\lambda}_i N′$ *and* $(N′, N′) \in \mathcal{R}$;
3. *If* N $\rightarrow$ N′ *then* $\exists N′$ *s.t.* N $\Rightarrow N′$ *and* $(N′, N′) \in \mathcal{R}$;

As usual, we write N $\precsim N$ if there exists a simulation $\mathcal{R}$ s.t. $(N, N) \in \mathcal{R}$.

Theorem 4.1. *If* N *implements* N, *then* N $\precsim N$.

Proof. We show that $\mathcal{R} = \{(N, N) \mid N \text{ implements } N\}$ is a simulation.

We remark that $\mathcal{R}^{-1}$ is not a simulation because the implementation cannot mimic the behaviour in which a client have completed two consecutive blocks (i.e., two **push** commands) without sending the first block. In GSP it is still possible to interleave the two blocks with blocks sent by other clients but in IGSP they are treated as atomic because they will be sent as a unique δ object.

5   Consistency Guarantees

In this section we study the consistency properties offered by GSP. We rely on the characterisation of properties in terms of abstract executions [4], execution histories enriched with information about visibility and arbitration of actions.

Definition 5.1. *Let* N *be a well-formed* GSP *system, an abstract history for* N *is a tuple* $\mathbb{A} = \langle N, \text{OP}, \text{SS}, \text{SO}, \text{VIS}, \text{AR} \rangle$ *where:*

- OP : $\mathbb{V} \rightarrow \mathcal{R} \cup \mathcal{U}$ *maps events to operations;*
- SS : $\mathcal{I} \rightarrow \mathbb{V}$ *associates events with a session (i.e., a client);*
- SO $\subseteq \mathbb{V} \times \mathbb{V}$ *describes the order of operations within a session;*
- VIS $\subseteq \mathbb{V} \times \mathbb{V}$ *indicates whether the effects of an update are visible to a read;*
- AR $\subseteq \mathbb{V} \times \mathbb{V}$ *resolves concurrent update conflicts.*

We write $\_\downarrow\_$ for function/relation restriction. For a given abstract history $\mathbb{A}$, we write $\mathbb{U}$ (similarly, $\mathbb{R}$) for the codomain restriction of OP to $\mathcal{U}$ (correspondingly, $\mathcal{R}$), i.e., $\mathbb{U} = \{v \mid v \in \text{OP}, \text{OP}(v) \in \mathcal{U}\}$ ($\mathbb{R} = \{v \mid v \in \text{OP}, \text{OP}(v) \in \mathcal{R}\}$).

Definition 5.2 (Well-formed history). *Let* $N = C_0 \| \ldots \| C_m \| S$ *be a* GSP *system where* $C_l = \langle P_l, u_{\mathsf{T}l}, b_{\mathsf{S}l}, b_{\mathsf{P}l}, k_l, j_l \rangle_{i_l}$. *A history* $\mathbb{A} = \langle N, \text{OP}, \text{SS}, \text{SO}, \text{VIS}, \text{AR} \rangle$ *is well-formed if the following conditions hold:*

1. *for all* $i \in dom(\text{ss})$, $\text{ss}(i) \subseteq dom(\text{OP})$;
2. $(\mathsf{v}, \mathsf{w}) \in \text{SO}$ *then exist* $i \in dom(\text{ss})$ *s.t.* $\{\mathsf{v}, \mathsf{w}\} \in \text{ss}(i)$.
3. *for all* $i \in dom(\text{ss})$, $\text{SO} \downarrow_{\text{ss}(i)}$ *is a total order;*
4. $\text{VIS} \subseteq \mathbb{U} \times \mathbb{R}$;
5. $\text{AR} \subseteq \mathbb{U} \times \mathbb{U}$ *is a prefix order.*
6. $(\mathsf{v}, \mathsf{w}) \in \text{AR}$ *iff*
   - $\underline{S}[i] = u^{\mathsf{v}}$ *and* $\underline{S}[j] = u^{\mathsf{w}}$ *and* $i < j$; *or*
   - $u^{\mathsf{v}} \in \underline{S}$ *and* $u^{\mathsf{w}} \in \mathsf{b}_{Sl} \cdot \mathsf{u}_{Tl}$;
7. *if* $\mathsf{b}_{Sl} \cdot \mathsf{u}_{Tl}[i] = u^{\mathsf{v}}$ *and* $\mathsf{b}_{Sl} \cdot \mathsf{u}_{Tl}[j] = u^{\mathsf{w}}$ *and* $i < j$, *then* $(\mathsf{v}, \mathsf{w}) \in \text{SO}$ *and* $\{\mathsf{v}, \mathsf{w}\} \in \text{ss}(i_l)$.

The above conditions ensure that events in ss are associated with an operation by OP (1). Besides, SO only relates events belonging to the same session (2), which are totally ordered within each session (3). Differently from the definition in [2], we restrict visibility to keep track of dependencies between updates and read events(4). We do not require AR to be a total order but instead to be a prefix order (5). In this way the updates in different replicas are arbitrated when they reach the global store. The remaining two conditions require the abstract history to be consistent with the state of the system.

Rules in Fig. 6 provides an operational way to associate abstract executions with GSP computations. Rules (A-UPDATE) and (A-READ) add new events to the history and corresponds to the execution of a read or update operation by a client. In both cases OP is extended with a new event v (i.e., $\mathsf{v} \notin dom(\text{OP})$), which is associated with the corresponding operation (either r or u). The new event v is added to the corresponding session i, and SO is updated to make v the maximal event for the session i. Rule (A-UPDATE) amends AR by capturing the fact that all updates that are already in the global state took place before the new event. Rule (A-READ) instead augments VIS with the pairs associating the new event with all events that are seen by the read action, namely, the local view of the global state $S[0..k_i - 1]$ and the local buffers b_{Pi} and u_{Ti}. Rule (A-ARB) handles the changes in the state of the global store (due to a send transition in one client) and amends AR by arbitrating (i) the new events by respecting the relative order in which they are added to the store (i.e., $\{(\mathsf{v}_i, \mathsf{v}_j) \mid i, j \in \{0, \ldots, n\}, i < j\}$) and (ii) all updates in the local state of the clients after the new ones (i.e., $(\{\mathsf{v}_0, \ldots, \mathsf{v}_n\} \times \{\mathsf{w} \mid \mathsf{w} \in \mathbb{U} \; \forall u.u^{\mathsf{w}} \notin S \cdot u\})$). The remaining transitions of the system are considered as internal changes that do not affect the history and are handled by rule (A-INT).

Lemma 5.1. *Let* $\mathbb{A}$ *be a well-formed history. If* $\mathbb{A} \xrightarrow{\lambda}_i \mathbb{A}'$, *then* $\mathbb{A}'$ *is well-formed.*

We use histories to analyse the ordering guarantees offered by the GSP model. (Due to space limitation, we refer the interested reader to see the characterisations provided in [2, Ch.5]).

Theorem 5.1. *If* $\langle N, \emptyset, \emptyset, \emptyset, \emptyset, \emptyset \rangle \rightarrow^*_i \langle N', \text{OP}, \text{SS}, \text{SO}, \text{VIS}, \text{AR} \rangle$ *then*

(1) Read My Writes: $\text{SO} \downarrow_{\mathbb{U} \times \mathbb{R}} \subseteq \text{VIS}$

(A-UPDATE)

$$\dfrac{N \xrightarrow{wr(u^{\mathsf{v}})}_i N' \qquad \mathsf{v} \notin dom(\text{OP}) \qquad \text{OP}' = \text{OP}[\mathsf{v} \mapsto u] \qquad \text{SS}' = \text{SS}[i \mapsto \text{SS}(i) \cup \{\mathsf{v}\}]}{\text{SO}' = \text{SO} \cup (\text{SS}(i) \times \{\mathsf{v}\}) \qquad\qquad \text{AR}' = \text{AR} \cup (\{w \mid u^{\mathsf{w}} \in S\} \times \{\mathsf{v}\})}$$

$$\langle N, \text{OP}, \text{SS}, \text{SO}, \text{VIS}, \text{AR} \rangle \xrightarrow{wr(u^{\mathsf{v}})}_i \langle N', \text{OP}', \text{SS}, \text{SO}', \text{VIS}, \text{AR}' \rangle$$

(A-READ)

$$\dfrac{N \xrightarrow{rd(r)}_i N' \qquad \mathsf{v} \notin dom(\text{OP}) \qquad \text{OP}' = \text{OP}[\mathsf{v} \mapsto r] \qquad \text{SS}' = \text{SS}[i \mapsto \text{SS}(i) \cup \{\mathsf{v}\}]}{\text{SO}' = \text{SO} \cup (\text{SS}(i) \times \{\mathsf{v}\}) \qquad \text{VIS}' = \text{VIS} \cup (\{w \mid u^{\mathsf{w}} \in S[0..k_i - 1] \cdot \mathsf{b}_{\mathsf{P}i} \cdot \mathsf{u}_{\mathsf{T}i}\} \times \{\mathsf{v}\})}$$

$$\langle N, \text{OP}, \text{SS}, \text{SO}, \text{VIS}, \text{AR} \rangle \xrightarrow{rd(r^{\mathsf{v}})}_i \langle N', \text{OP}', \text{SS}', \text{SO}', \text{VIS}', \text{AR} \rangle$$

(A-ARB)

$$\dfrac{S \parallel C \xrightarrow{\lambda}_i S \cdot \mathsf{u} \parallel C' \qquad \lambda \neq wr(u^{\mathsf{v}}), rd(r) \qquad\qquad u = (\!|u_0{}^{\mathsf{v}_0} \cdots u_n{}^{\mathsf{v}_n}|\!)}{\substack{\text{AR}' = \text{AR} \cup \{(\mathsf{v}_i, \mathsf{v}_j) \mid i, j \in \{0, \ldots, n\}, i < j\} \\ \cup (\{\mathsf{v}_0, \ldots, \mathsf{v}_n\} \times \{w \mid w \in \mathbb{U}, \forall u. u^{\mathsf{w}} \notin S \cdot \mathsf{u}\})}}$$

$$\langle S \parallel C, \text{OP}, \text{SS}, \text{SO}, \text{VIS}, \text{AR} \rangle \xrightarrow{\lambda}_i \langle S \cdot \mathsf{u} \parallel C', \text{OP}, \text{SS}, \text{SO}, \text{VIS}, \text{AR}' \rangle$$

(A-INT)

$$\dfrac{S \| C \xrightarrow{\lambda}_i S \| C' \qquad \lambda \neq wr(u^{\mathsf{v}}), rd(r)}{\langle S \| C, \text{OP}, \text{SS}, \text{SO}, \text{VIS}, \text{AR} \rangle \xrightarrow{\lambda}_i \langle S \| C', \text{OP}, \text{SS}, \text{SO}, \text{VIS}, \text{AR} \rangle}$$

Fig. 6. Computation of abstract executions

(2) Monotonic Read: $\text{VIS}; \text{SO} \!\downarrow_{\mathbb{U} \times \mathbb{R}} \subseteq \text{VIS}$.
(3) No Circular Causality: $(\text{SO} \cup \text{VIS})^+$ *is acyclic.*
(4) Causal Visibility: $(\text{SO} \cup \text{VIS})^+ \!\downarrow_{\mathbb{U} \times \mathbb{R}} \subseteq \text{VIS}$.
(5) Causal Arbitration: $((\text{SO} \cup \text{VIS})^+ \setminus \text{SO}) \!\downarrow_{\mathbb{U} \times \mathbb{U}} \subseteq \text{AR}$.
(6) Consistent prefix: $\text{AR}; (\text{VIS} \setminus \text{SS}) \subseteq \text{VIS}$.

The following example shows that the GSP model exhibits the Dekker anomaly, hence it does not enjoy *sequential consistency* [2].

Example 5.1 (Dekker anomaly). Consider the following system consisting of two clients and the empty store $N = \epsilon \parallel C_1 \parallel C_2$ where

$$C_1 = \langle \mathtt{update}(u_1); \mathtt{let}\ y = \mathtt{read}(r_1)\ \mathtt{in}\ P, \epsilon, \epsilon, \epsilon, 0, 0 \rangle_{i_1}$$
$$C_2 = \langle \mathtt{update}(u_2); \mathtt{let}\ y = \mathtt{read}(r_2)\ \mathtt{in}\ Q, \epsilon, \epsilon, \epsilon, 0, 0 \rangle_{i_2}$$

Since the updates are made locally, none of the clients see the update performed by the other and this is the essence of the Dekker anomaly which is ruled out by strong consistency models like sequential consistency or linearizability.

6   GSP with atomic updates

In this section we study the atomic updates proposed in [5]. We extend the language of programs as follows:

$$(\text{PROGRAM}) \qquad P ::= \ldots \mid \mathtt{syncUpd}(u); P$$

The execution of a program $\mathtt{syncUpd}(u); P$ remains blocked until the update u is performed over the global store. This is achieved by continuously pulling (i.e., a busy-waiting) until the updates are confirmed by global store. In order to provide the formal semantics of the language, we consider the following runtime syntax for programs.

$$(\text{RUN-TIME-PROGRAM}) \qquad P ::= \ \ldots \ | \ \mathtt{wait}; P \ | \ e \triangleright (P); P$$

The operational semantics for the new primitives is given by the rules in Fig. 7. Rule (SYNC-UPD) rewrites each synchronous update as the sequence consisting of an asynchronous update followed by $\mathtt{pull}$ and $\mathtt{wait}$. Processes $\mathtt{wait}$ continuously checks whether local changes have been confirmed by the global store. As described by rule (WAIT), it is implemented as a busy-waiting loop that first checks the local buffers by executing $\mathtt{confirmed}$ and then performs the conditional jump $x \triangleright (\mathtt{pull}; \mathtt{wait}); P$. If the condition x is true, then it follows as P otherwise it continues as $\mathtt{pull}; \mathtt{wait}$, as described by rules (GUARD-TRUE) and (GUARD-FALSE).

Single order is characterised, essentially, by imposing arbitration and visibility to coincide [2]. Since our definition for AR and VIS makes them disjoint, we use an alternative characterisation of single order guarantee, which disregards the arbitration order of updates that are not observed. Hence, we use the following characterisation for single order:

$$\text{AR}; \text{VIS} \subseteq \text{VIS} \quad \text{and} \quad \text{AR}^{-1}; \neg\text{VIS} \subseteq \neg\text{VIS}$$

The following result shows that any well-formed GSP system, whose programs are free from asynchronous updates enjoy the single order guarantee.

Theorem 6.1 (Single Order). *Let N be a well-formed system s.t. $\mathtt{update}(u)$ does not appear in N. If $\langle N, \emptyset, \emptyset, \emptyset, \emptyset, \emptyset \rangle \rightarrow_i^* \langle N', \text{OP}, \text{SS}, \text{SO}, \text{VIS}, \text{AR} \rangle$ then* $\text{AR}; \text{VIS} \subseteq \text{VIS}$ *and* $\text{AR}^{-1}; \neg\text{VIS} \subseteq \neg\text{VIS}$.

(SYNC-UPD)
$$\langle \mathtt{syncUpd}(u); P, \mathsf{u_T}, \mathsf{b_S}, \mathsf{b_P}, k, j \rangle_i \parallel N \xrightarrow{\tau}_i$$
$$\langle \mathtt{update}(u); \mathtt{push}; \mathtt{wait}; P, \mathsf{u_T}, \mathsf{b_S}, \mathsf{b_P}, k, j \rangle_i \parallel N$$

(WAIT)
$$\langle \mathtt{wait}; P, \mathsf{u_T}, \mathsf{b_S}, \mathsf{b_P}, k, j \rangle_i \parallel N \xrightarrow{\tau}_i$$
$$\langle \mathtt{let} \ x = \mathtt{confirmed} \ \mathtt{in} \ x \triangleright (\mathtt{pull}; \mathtt{wait}; P); P, \mathsf{u_T}, \mathsf{b_S}, \mathsf{b_P}, k, j \rangle_i \parallel N$$

(GUARD-TRUE)
$$\frac{e \downarrow true}{\langle e \triangleright (P); Q, \mathsf{u_T}, \mathsf{b_S}, \mathsf{b_P}, k, j \rangle_i \parallel N \xrightarrow{\tau}_i \langle Q, \mathsf{u_T}, \mathsf{b_S}, \mathsf{b_P}, k, j \rangle_i \parallel N}$$

(GUARD-FALSE)
$$\frac{e \downarrow false}{\langle e \triangleright (P); Q, \mathsf{u_T}, \mathsf{b_S}, \mathsf{b_P}, k, j \rangle_i \parallel N \xrightarrow{\tau}_i \langle P, \mathsf{u_T}, \mathsf{b_S}, \mathsf{b_P}, k, j \rangle_i \parallel N}$$

Fig. 7. Semantics of GSP with atomic updates

7   Conclusions

We have proposed a formal model for the Global Sequence Protocol and its proposed implementation. We use our formal model to provide a simplified proof (that relies on standard simulation) that the proposed implementation is correct. We remark that our proof does not require to exhibit an auxiliary state for the simulation and that several invariants are trivially ensured by the definition of the model (e.g., the fact that clients have a consistent view of the global sequence) and the well-formed conditions imposed over systems. We have formally studied the consistency guarantees ensured by the model by relying on the operational semantics of the calculus to incrementally compute (a relaxed version of) abstract histories. We have also shown how GSP can be used to formally study programming patterns, like synchronous update operations, that provide stronger consistency guarantees at the expenses of efficiency and availability. We plan to use the GSP calculus as a formal basis for developing programming techniques to enable the fine-tuning of consistency levels in applications.

Acknowledgments. We thank the anonymous reviewers of Coordination 2016 for their careful reading of our paper and detailed comments.

References

1. Bailis, P., Ghodsi, A.: Eventual consistency today: limitations, extensions, and beyond. Commun. ACM **56**(5), 55–63 (2013)
2. Burckhardt, S.: Principles of eventual consistency. Found. Trends Program. Lang. **1**(1–2), 1–150 (2014)
3. Burckhardt, S., Fähndrich, M., Leijen, D., Wood, B.P.: Cloud types for eventual consistency. In: Noble, J. (ed.) ECOOP 2012. LNCS, vol. 7313, pp. 283–307. Springer, Heidelberg (2012)
4. Burckhardt, S., Leijen, D., Fähndrich, M., Sagiv, M.: Eventually consistent transactions. In: Seidl, H. (ed.) Programming Languages and Systems. LNCS, vol. 7211, pp. 67–86. Springer, Heidelberg (2012)
5. Burckhardt, S., Leijen, D., Protzenko, J., Fähndrich, M.: Global sequence protocol: a robust abstraction for replicated shared state. In: ECOOP 2015, pp. 568–590 (2015)
6. DeCandia, G., Hastorun, D., Jampani, M., Kakulapati, G., Lakshman, A., Pilchin, A., Sivasubramanian, S., Vosshall, P., Vogels, W.: Dynamo: amazon's highly available key-value store. In: SOSP 2007, pp. 205–220. ACM (2007)
7. Gilbert, S., Lynch, N.: Brewer's conjecture and the feasibility of consistent, available, partition-tolerant web services. SIGACT News **33**(2), 51–59 (2002)
8. Gotsman, A., Yang, H., Ferreira, C., Najafzadeh, M., Shapiro, M.: 'Cause i'm strong enough: reasoning about consistency choices in distributed systems. In: POPL 2016, pp. 371–384 (2016)
9. Lakshman, A., Malik, P.: Cassandra: a decentralized structured storage system. ACM SIGOPS Operating Syst. Rev. **44**(2), 35–40 (2010)

10. Shapiro, M., Preguiça, N., Baquero, C., Zawirski, M.: Conflict-free replicated data types. In: Défago, X., Petit, F., Villain, V. (eds.) SSS 2011. LNCS, vol. 6976, pp. 386–400. Springer, Heidelberg (2011)
11. Sivaramakrishnan, K., Kaki, G., Jagannathan, S.: Declarative programming over eventually consistent data stores. In: PLDI 2015, pp. 413–424. ACM (2015)

Improving Gossip Dynamics Through Overlapping Replicates

Danilo Pianini[1(✉)], Jacob Beal[2], and Mirko Viroli[1]

[1] ALMA MATER STUDIORUM–Università di Bologna, Cesena, Italy
{danilo.pianini,mirko.viroli}@unibo.it
[2] Raytheon BBN Technologies, Cambridge, USA
jakebeal@bbn.com

Abstract. Gossip protocols are a fast and effective strategy for computing a wide class of aggregate functions involving coordination of large sets of nodes. The monotonic nature of gossip protocols, however, mean that they can typically only adjust their estimate in one direction unless restarted, which disrupts the values being returned. We propose to improve the dynamical performance of gossip by running multiple replicates of a gossip algorithm, overlapping in time. We find that this approach can significantly reduce the error of aggregate function estimates compared to both typical gossip implementations and tree-based estimation functions.

1 Introduction

Gossip protocols are a coordination approach based on estimating a collective state by repeated propagation and aggregation of state estimates between neighboring devices [5,21]. They are widely used in the development of networked and distributed systems, as they can often provide a fast and effective means of enacting strategies for collective adaptation of large numbers of computing devices. This can be particularly important for emerging scenarios and the "internet of things," with the continued rapid increase in both the number of deployed mobile or embedded devices and the networking technologies for connecting them opportunistically. In theory, virtually any collective mechanism—sensing the environment, planning actions, information storage, physical actuation—can be realized by the resilient coordination of large sets of devices deployed in a given region of space [24], and gossip can play an important role as a composable "building block" algorithm for effective programming of such environments [3,22].

Unlike many scenarios where gossip has been deployed and studied, however, in pervasive and embedded environments network connections are typically strongly affected by physical proximity and the effective network diameter may be quite large. Overlay networks, which are often used to ensure that gossip estimates can be rapidly adapted to new circumstances (e.g., [11–13,23]), are often no longer applicable in these circumstances, and we need to find alternate strategies that can enable gossip estimates to adapt rapidly and smoothly to

Published by Springer International Publishing Switzerland 2016. All Rights Reserved
A. Lluch Lafuente and J. Proença (Eds.): COORDINATION 2016, LNCS 9686, pp. 192–207, 2016.
DOI: 10.1007/978-3-319-39519-7_12

changes in the values being aggregated. We address this challenge by defining a higher-order "time replication" coordination strategy that maintains a set of isolated replicas of a distributed process with staggered start times: applying this strategy to replicate gossip provides a significant improvement over prior approaches as well as an adjustable tradeoff between speed of adaptation and cost of replication.

Design, prototype implementation, and experiments, have been realized by exploiting the toolchain of *aggregate programming* [3], an approach aimed at simplifying the sound engineering of collective adaptive systems by shifting the programming focus from single devices to whole aggregates. This allowed us to smoothly express a formalized version of the proposed approach in terms of the Protelis programing language [20].

Following a brief review of gossip protocols in Sect. 2, we specify the proposed replication strategy in Sect. 3 and analyze the predicted performance of time-replicated gossip in Sect. 4. We then validate these predictions and compare performance against other methods for collective state estimation in Sect. 5, before summarizing contributions and future work in Sect. 6

2 Gossip Protocols

The term *gossip protocol* is used to cover a range of related algorithms and concepts [5,21]. For purposes of this paper, we will formalize gossip with the following generic algorithm, executed periodically on every participating device in unsynchronized rounds:

```
def gossip(f,x) {
    // Declare state variable v, initialized to current value of x
    rep(v <- x) {
        // Every round, merge v with neighbors' values of v and current value of x
        f.apply(x,hood((a,b) -> {f.apply(a,b)},x,nbr(v)));
    }
}
```

This algorithm begins with an input $x_{\delta,\tau}$ (the input x, potentially varying with device δ and time τ) and a fixed merging function f that takes two values of the type of x and returns another of the same type. The function f must be idempotent, meaning that $f(a, f(a,b)) = f(a,b)$, and commutative, meaning that $f(a,b) = f(b,a)$. This means that any number of copies of various values of $x_{\delta,\tau}$ can be combined in any order and yet always be guaranteed to eventually produce the same output value $v_{\delta',\tau'}$.

In particular, this algorithm realizes computation of $v_{\delta,\tau}$ by declaring v as a state variable (construct rep) initialized to $x_{\delta,\tau}$. In every round τ, $v_{\delta,\tau}$ is then updated by using f to combine it with the current value of $x_{\delta,\tau}$ (which may have changed), and with the latest values of $v_{\delta',\tau'}$ that have been shared by the device's current set of neighbors in the network (construct nbr, which also implies reciprocally sharing this device's value of $v_{\delta,\tau}$).

For all functions f that are both idempotent and commutative, repeated execution of this gossip algorithm on any connected network with stable inputs ($x_{\delta,\tau} = x_{\delta,\tau'}$) leads to all devices converging to the same value within *diameter* rounds. This algorithm can be optimized in various ways by optimizing the implementation of `rep`, `hood`, and `nbr` (e.g., sharing and computing only on differences), but the essence remains the same.

Gossip is thus a valuable tool for fast, distributed computation of aggregate functions of a network, for any function that can be mapped onto an appropriate f: examples include minimum value, union of sets, and mean value (the last being somewhat more subtle: see [16,21]). By contrast, other approaches to computing a consensus aggregate value are either slow (e.g., Laplacian averaging [9,17]), fragile (e.g., various exact consensus algorithms [10,15], PLD-consensus [1]), or both (e.g., Paxos [6,14]).

The idempotence property of gossip, however, also carries its own significant cost: it is asymmetric and information-destroying. Because a value can be merged in multiple times without affecting the value of the aggregate, it is not possible to know how many times this has actually taken place, and as such there is no inverse function that can be used to remove from the aggregate an input $x_{\delta,\tau}$ that is no longer valid. For example, with $f = \min(a, b)$ values can go down, but they cannot go up again. This means that removing obsolete values from the aggregate function can be difficult and costly. The two main strategies are:

– Values of $x_{\delta,\tau}$ may be in some way time-stamped and/or identified with their source, such that they can be superseded by new information from the same source or discarded if they are not periodically refreshed. Some form of this approach is often used for gossip algorithms that build indexing or routing data structures, such as in peer-to-peer systems (e.g., [11,23]), but has the drawback that either most devices know only a fragment of $v_{\delta,\tau}$ or else that the size of $v_{\delta,\tau}$ and of the updates that need to be shared between neighbors may become very large, since each value of $x_{\delta,\tau}$ needs to be tracked individually.
– The gossip algorithm can be periodically restarted, thus resetting v and effectively discarding all old values of $x_{\delta,\tau}$. This has the advantage of being very lightweight but can have significant lags before changes in $x_{\delta,\tau}$ are acknowledged and large transients in $v_{\delta,\tau}$ during the restart. Furthermore, care must be taken to ensure that no values of $v_{\delta,\tau}$ from the old algorithm instance can ever be shared with the new algorithm instance, or else the benefit of restarting will be lost.

In this paper, we focus on the periodic restart strategy, improving its dynamics through a refinement in which multiple overlapping replicates of gossip are run in parallel.

3   Time-Replicated Gossip

The approach we are investigating for improving gossip performance is a simple generalization of the periodic restart strategy for removing obsolete information

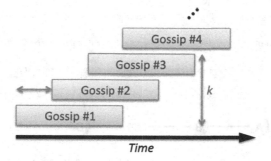

Fig. 1. Time-replicated gossip launches a new gossip process every p seconds, dropping the oldest replicate whenever there are more than k replicates.

from gossip. Rather than maintaining only a single instance of a gossip algorithm, each device will maintain up to k replicates with staggered launch times (Fig. 1). At a period of once every p seconds, a new replicate is launched, and if the full complement of replicates is already running then the oldest replicate will be dropped. This approach provides a compromise solution, avoiding the severe drawbacks of either of the prior methods: the amount of state communicated or stored cannot grow large as there are only k replicates, and large transients in v can be avoided by keeping the current replicate running while new replicates are still stabilizing.

We have implemented this strategy by means of a general time-replication algorithm, coded in Protelis [20] in order to take advantage of the mechanisms of its underlying computational model (the field calculus [7,8]) for succinct encapsulation and manipulation of distributed higher-order functions [3,8]:

```
def timeReplicated(process, default, p, k) {
  rep(state <- [[], 0]) { // [tuples of [replicate, value], oldest replicate ID]
    // Check whether p has elapsed without a new replicate beginning elsewhere
    let newRep = sharedTimer(p,state.get(0));
    // If so, create a new replicate and add it to the collection
    let newProc = if(newRep>0) { [[newRep, default]] } else { [] };
    let procs = state.get(0).mergeAfter(newProc);
    // Execute all processes from self and neighbors, aligning on ID using
    // alignedMap(argument, filter, function to run, default value)
    procs = alignedMap(nbr(processes),
      (replicate, value) -> { replicate >= state.get(1) }, // Ignore old
      (replicate, value) -> { process.apply() }, // Execute process
      default);
    // Prune to keep only the newest k and update the state
    procs = procs.subTupleEnd(max(0, procs.size() - k));
    [procs, procs.map((x) -> {x.get(0)}).fold(min)]
  }.get(0); // Return tuple of [replicate numbers, state] tuples
}
```

In essence, this maintains two pieces of state: the first is a set of running process replicates, each identified by its replicate number, i.e., the first is replicate 1,

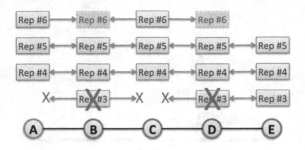

Fig. 2. Example of process replicates created by `timeReplicated`: here four replicates (purple boxes) are running on various subsets of a linear network of five devices (A-E) with $k = 3$, with communication between instances aligned by replicate number via `alignedMap` (purple arrows). Devices A and C have independently started replicate #6, and its instances are spreading new instances to other devices (greyed boxes), merging together as they go. Since $k = 3$, the arrival of replicate #6 also deletes replicate #3 and blocks its spread (red Xs). (Color figure online)

the second replicate 2, etc. The second piece of state is the oldest allowed replicate number, which rises over time as new replicates are created and old ones are discarded.

Every round, each device consults a "shared timer" function to determine whether it should locally launch a new replicate, and if the answer is yes (which happens somewhere in the network at least once every p seconds) then it appends the new replicate with its new, higher identifier, to the end of the current set of processes. This set of replicates are run across the network, using the `alignedMap` primitive to safely encapsulate each replicate, as well as to spread replicates to any other device where such replicates have not already been deemed too old and to merge replicates with other independently launched instances with the same replicate number (Fig. 2).

The `sharedTimer` function is implemented to coordinate with processes spreading via `alignedMap` as follows:

```
def sharedTimer(p,procs) {
  let newReplicate = 0;
  rep(state <- [0,0]) { // [top rep #, time remaining], start rep 1 immediately
    // Compare state replicate to maximum replicate number from elsewhere
    let maxID = max(state.get(0), procs.map((x)->{x.get(0)}).fold(max));
    // When advanced by extension of a process from elsewhere, reset timer.
    if(maxID > state.get(0)) { [maxID, p]
    // When timer expires, signal, advance replicate number, and reset timer.
    } else { if(state.get(1) <= 0) { newReplicate = maxID+1; [maxID+1, p]
    // Otherwise, count down toward timer expiring
    } else { [state.get(0), state.get(1) - self.dt()] }}
  };
  newReplicate // Return zero if nothing changes, otherwise new replicate number
}
```

In essence, this tracks the highest replicate number currently known and the time remaining until a new replicate should be launched. If a spreading process introduces a new replicate, then the replicate number is updated[1] and the timer is reset since a local launch has been pre-empted by an external launch. If, on the other hand, the timer runs out, then this device will launch a new replicate, possibly in parallel with other devices elsewhere.

Thus, a set of distributed timed replicates can be executed without any requirement for synchronization, effectively being launched in either one or many places at the same time, with faster-running devices pulling slower-running devices along after them, i.e., new replicates will tend to be initiated by the device(s) with the fastest clocks. It does not matter where or how many devices launch replicates, since all independent launches with the same number will end up merging in the `alignedMap`.

Whenever the addition of new processes (either locally or by spreading from neighbors) results in there being more than k processes, the oldest are discarded to reduce the number back down to k, and the oldest allowed replicate number updated accordingly. This prevents "old" processes from spreading back into devices where they have already been discarded and ratches the overlapping set of replicates forward incrementally over time.

Ultimately, the replication function returns a tuple of the replicate numbers and values of all currently running replicates. The time-replication algorithm may thus simply be applied to instantiate time-replicated gossip as follows:

```
timeReplicated(() -> gossip(f, x), x, p, k)
```

In other words, it replicates the distributed process $\mathrm{gossip}(f, x)$ with process default values taken from x, launch period p and number of replicates k.

In order to apply this approach to improving the dynamics of gossip algorithms, the following questions remain: what are the optimal values for p and k, and how should the values of v returned by each of the different replicates be combined in order to produce the best possible estimate of the true aggregate value v? In the next section, we will address these questions through analysis of the dynamics of gossip.

4   Analysis

The replication approach that we have proposed begins with the intuitive notion that we can avoid large transients and also bound algorithm state by keeping some replicates running while new replicates are started and come to stabilize. Now, let us analyze the process by which replicates launch and stabilize to new values in order to determine how many replicates to create, how frequently to

---

[1] Note that the algorithm is defined in terms of an unbounded integer; in implementations where there is a desired to use integers with few enough bits to make overflow a realistic possibility, strategies such as lollipop numbering [18] can be used to maintain ordering.

launch new replicates, and how to best make use of the values across multiple replicates.

For this analysis, let us consider an unchanging set of stationary devices, which thus form a fixed network graph of diameter d. Devices execute at the same rate but without any synchronization in phase, sending state updates of all of the values in nbr statements to one another once every t seconds. Given the simplicity of the algorithm, we will assume that there is no delay between the time when a device begins to execute a round and the time when its updated values arrive at its neighbors.[2]

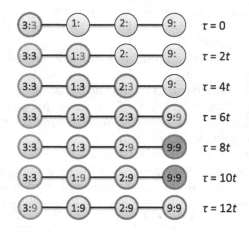

Fig. 3. Illustration of a case in which a new gossip replicate takes the maximum of $4td$ seconds for error from the initial transient to resolve, on a linear network of four devices. Here, gossip is computing the maximum value with $f = max(a, b)$, input x is shown as the left number in each device, and v the right number, which is only instantiated where the replicate is running (blue devices), and not where it has not yet launched (grey devices), and change in each round is indicated in red. The delay is caused by the new replicate launching only at the opposite end of the network from the highest value, and thus the value at this device cannot be correct until the replicate has had time to propagate its launch all the way to the right and for the maximum value to work its way back all the way to the left with, if devices are maximally desynchronized, a delay of $2t$ per hop. (Color figure online)

If devices are perfectly out of synchrony with one another, then it may take up to $2t$ seconds for a message from one device to affect the state of its neighbors. With the right arrangement of states, it may thus take up to $2td$ seconds for gossip replicates to be launched on all devices in the network, with the replicate starting at a single device and spreading to each other device just as its own launch timer expires.

---

[2] Our analysis may be generalized to devices with drifting clocks and non-trivial execution and transmission time by taking t to be the round length plus execution and transmission delay at the slowest device.

Likewise, the value of a gossip algorithm may have an unboundedly high error at any given device until there has been time enough for information to arrive at that device from every other device, another delay of $2td$ seconds. Consider, for example, gossiping $f = max(a, b)$ when one device has an input of $x = 1000$ and all other devices have value $x = 0$: every device would stay at $v = 0$ until the information from the one $x = 1000$ device reached it, at which point it would instantly leap to $v = 1000$.

Thus, for the first $4td$ seconds after a new gossip replicate begins (i.e., the maximum round-trip time for information to propagate across the network, as Fig. 3 points out), the value of v at any given device may have an unboundedly large "transient" error with respect to its converged value and should not be used.

This gives us a lower bound on when the value computed by a gossip replicate should be used; let us turn now to the opposite side, and consider when the information of a gossip replicate becomes redundant and can be discarded. Consider two sequential replicates of gossip, replicate i and replicate j, where $j = i + 1$. If $x_{\tau', \delta'}$ is the value of x at time τ' and device δ', then for any given device δ at time τ, we can partition the set of all values of $x_{\tau', \delta'}$ into three subsets:

- x_{IJ} are those values used by both replicate i and replicate j.
- x_I are those values used by replicate i but not by replicate j, i.e., those that appeared before replicate j launched.[3]
- x_0 are those values used by neither replicate.

Because the gossip function f is idempotent and commutative, we can thus reorganize the computation of the output values of the two replicates as:

$$v_{\tau,\delta,i} = f(f(x_I), f(x_{IJ})) \tag{1}$$
$$v_{\tau,\delta,j} = f(x_{IJ}) \tag{2}$$

abusing notation to consider $f(X)$ as f applied in arbitrary order to combine all members of set X. By the idempotence and property of f, it must be the case that $v_{\tau,\delta,i} = v_{\tau,\delta,j}$ unless there are values in x_I that are not in x_{IJ}.

Thus, we have that, once replicate j is past its initial transient (i.e., every device has been affected by the value of every other device) the outputs of replicate i and replicate j must be identical, except in the case where the value of replicate i is being affected by input values of $x_{\tau', \delta'}$ from before the launch of replicate j at δ'. Since ignoring such "obsolete" values is the entire point of replication, we thus see that as soon as a replicate has passed its initial transient, there is no reason to consider the output of any older replicate: the older replicate must be either identical or obsolete.

From these deductions, we now have answers to two of our questions about replication. First, only the output value v of the oldest replicate should be used.

---

[3] Note that no values can be used by replicate j but not replicate i, because replicate j cannot be launched on any device before replicate i is also launched at that device.

Second, replicates should be retained only until the next replicate has stabilized, at which point they are obsolete and may be discarded. More precisely, we may state this relationship in the form of an equation:

$$p = \frac{4dt}{(k-1)} \tag{3}$$

In other words, with one replicate providing the current "safe" estimate for v and $k-1$ later replicates maturing, with each replicate taking up to $4dt$ seconds to mature, replicated gossip can sustain a steady state in which one replicate matures every $\frac{4dt}{(k-1)}$ seconds.

What remains is the question of the size of k, or conversely of p. Unlike the other relations that we have considered, however, there is no optimal choice here, but rather a tradeoff between the speed with which obsolete information can be removed from a gossip and the number of replicates being maintained (with accompanying requirements for communication, computing, and memory resources). Thus, once a choice has been made for either k or p, the optimal value for the other parameter can be determined with the aid of any conservative estimate of the diameter of the network. Prioritizing the number of replicates, as diameter may often change dynamically over time, we can implement replicated gossip in Protelis as follows:

```
def tr_gossip(f, x, k, d) {
  // Compute p by Eq. 3
  let p = 4 * d * self.dt() / (k - 1);
  // Run replicated gossip and return the value from the oldest replicate (first tuple)
  timeReplicated(() -> gossip(f, x), x, p, k).get(0).get(1).
}
```

In terms of managing the tradeoff between number of replicates and speed of adaptation, from Eq. 3, we can see that the duration a replicate will persist (and thus potentially obsolete gossip inputs as well) will be $\frac{k+1}{k} \cdot 4dt$. Thus, if the minimum of two replicates is used, then obsolete information can persist for up to $8dt$ seconds, while if the number of replicates is allowed to grow without bound, the minimum time for obsolete information to persist is $4dt$. In between, a small handful of replicates is likely all that is necessary to get to a point where the diminishing returns on adaptation speed are not worth the additional cost in communication.

In practice, the better the estimate of diameter, the closer to optimal the tradeoff between adaptation speed and size can be made. Likewise, improvements in synchronization guarantees between devices may reduce the conservative $4dt$ closer toward the theoretical minimum of dt.

5   Experimental Validation of Performance

We now validate the performance of time-replicated gossip in simulation, comparing the performance for three representative gossip functions against several

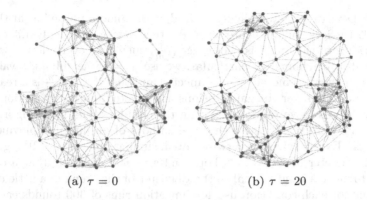

(a) $\tau = 0$ (b) $\tau = 20$

Fig. 4. Simulations are run on a unit disc graph over devices moving via Lévy walks from a random initial distribution: (a) shows a typical initial network and (b) the modified network after 20 rounds of simulation.

prior methods. All experiments have been performed using the Alchemist simulator [19] and Protelis algorithm implementations[4].

5.1   Experimental Setup

For our experiments, we compare the computation of three gossip functions, chosen as representative typical applications of gossip: The three gossip functions are minimum ($f = \min(a, b)$), logical AND ($f = and(a, b)$), and estimated mean (using the method presented in [16][5]). We compared the execution of time-replicated gossip (defaulting to $k = 5$) on these gossip functions with four representative prior methods for estimating aggregate functions, two gossip and two non-gossip:

1. **Gossip:** the baseline algorithm, as defined in Sect. 2, and never restarted.
2. **R-Gossip:** gossip restarted periodically, as discussed in Sect. 2, implemented by time-replicated gossip with $k = 1$.
3. **C+G:** estimate is computed over a spanning tree, then broadcast from the root; the name is taken from the particular implementation we use, which combines the C and G "aggregate building blocks" from [4].
4. **Laplacian-based consensus (mean only):** incrementally estimates mean $x_{\delta,\tau}$ by in each round adding to the current estimate α times the difference with the neighbor's estimates and the current $x_{\delta,\tau}$ (using $\alpha = 0.04$, which is expected to be fast yet stable per [17]).

All algorithms are executed in parallel on a simulated network of n devices distributed within a circular arena, each device uniquely identified by numbers

---

[4] Full code at: https://bitbucket.org/danysk/experiment-2016-coordination.

[5] Note that this method uses random numbers, so in order to ensure that replicates are identical except when given different inputs, we seed the pseudorandom generators identically for all replicates on a given device.

0 to $n - 1$. Devices execute unsynchronized, with random phase but at the same rate $t = 1$. Devices communicate with all other devices within 1 unit distance, and the radius of the arena is chosen as $\sqrt{\frac{n}{m}}$, such that every device will have an expected m neighbors. In particular, we use $m = 15$ neighbors, a value that ensures the network is mostly well-connected and that $d = 2\sqrt{\frac{n}{m}}$ is a reasonable estimate of its diameter. Initial positions are selected uniformly randomly, and thereafter devices move randomly within the circular arena following a speed s reactive Lévy walk [2]. Figure 4 shows snapshots of an initial deployment and its evolution. Except where otherwise noted, simulations use $n = 100$, giving an estimated diameter of just over 5 hops and $s = 0.05$, meaning that a device is expected to move a length equal to the diameter of the arena in a little over 100 rounds, and for each condition use 40 simulation runs of 300 rounds each.

Our experiments challenge adaptation dynamics by using a set of input values $x_{\delta,\tau}$ that are spatially correlated and have two large discontinuous changes across both space and time. For the mean and minimum functions $x_{\delta,\tau}$ is defined as:

- $\tau < 100$: Devices on the left half of the arena at $\tau = 0$ have $x_{\delta,\tau} = 2$, while those on the right have $x_{\delta,\tau} = 4$, except device 1 has $x_{\delta,\tau} = 1$
- $100 \leq \tau < 200$: Devices on the left half of the arena at $\tau = 100$ have $x_{\delta,\tau} = 6$, while those on the right have $x_{\delta,\tau} = 3$, except device 1 has $x_{\delta,\tau} = 50$
- $200 \leq \tau$: Devices on the left half of the arena at $\tau = 200$ have $x_{\delta,\tau} = 2$, while those on the right have $x_{\delta,\tau} = 4$, except device 1 has $x_{\delta,\tau} = 1$

For logical AND, all devices have $x_{\delta,\tau} = \text{true}$ except that device 0 is false for the first 100 rounds and device 1 is false for the final 100 rounds.

5.2   Convergence Dynamics

First, we examine a single simulation run in order to compare in detail the dynamics by which time-replicated gossip converges to a correct value against the convergence dynamics of the alternative algorithms. Figure 5 shows the evolution of mean value and mean root mean squared error (RMSE) across all devices for each function. As predicted, time-replicated gossip is safe from any unexpected transients, tracking to the correct value after a short delay. When the new value follows the monotonic direction of the function this is very fast (as in the second transition for minimum and logical AND); otherwise is must wait the full pk delay for all affected replicates to be discarded.

Non-restarted gossip, by contrast, can never discard old information, and thus cannot adapt during the 100–200 time interval, while non-replicated restarting gossip adapts quickly but experiences periodic sharp error transients at every restart. Laplacian consensus exhibits a smooth but very slow convergence, since values are not homogeneously distributed [9], and error never reaches zero, indicating that the apparently good mean value actually represents not correct values but balanced distribution of overestimates and underestimates. Finally, C+G continuously tries to converge to the correct value, but its tree structure continually gets disrupted by changes in the network structure, and therefore it shows a strong and variable error throughout the whole experiment.

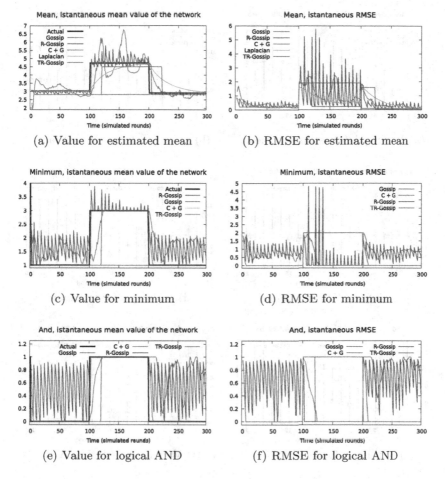

Fig. 5. Evolution of mean value across devices (a,c,e) and root mean squared error (RMSE) (b,d,f) for the three functions under test: estimated mean (a,b), minimum (c,d), and logical AND (e,f).

5.3 Effect of Varying of k and p

Our analysis in Sect. 4 identified an optimal conservative relationship between number of replicates k and replicate period p given a particular network diameter d. In practice, however, network diameter may frequently change and can be costly or difficult to estimate precisely, so it is important that estimation not be badly effected by the use of suboptimal parameters.

As the analysis was quite conservative, we should expect that as the duration covered by replicates is reduced (e.g., by reducing either k or p while holding the other fixed), error should gradually decrease as the delay to adapt is reduced. At some point, however, the transients of new replicates will not have had time to resolve and error will increase. Complementarily, increasing the duration covered

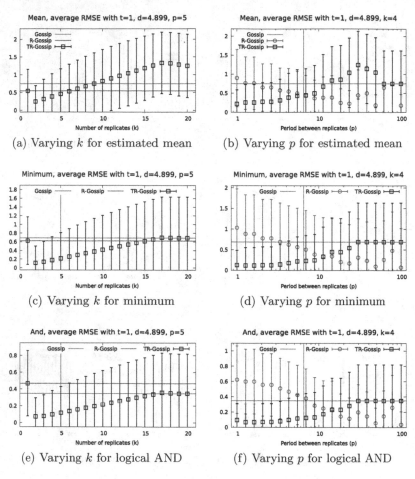

(a) Varying k for estimated mean

(b) Varying p for estimated mean

(c) Varying k for minimum

(d) Varying p for minimum

(e) Varying k for logical AND

(f) Varying p for logical AND

Fig. 6. Effect of varying number of replicates k (a,c,e) and replication period p (b,d,f) on mean RMSE. The red vertical line marks the value (for k and p respectively) that is suggested by our analysis. Non-restarted gossip and single-replicate restarting gossip (with restart time equal to p) are plotted for comparison. Error bars indicate the standard deviation of the average RMSE across the 40 simulation runs. (Color figure online)

by replicates will not expose transients but will increase error incrementally as the delay to adapt increases.

Figure 6 shows the results of testing these hypotheses against k varying from 1 to 20 and p varying geometrically from 1 to 100. As predicted our analysis is shown to be quite conservative: error in fact decreases with decreasing k and p until the very smallest values. Likewise, it increases smoothly with increasing k or p until it is so high that it saturates the experimental conditions and in some cases actually begins to decrease due to aliasing. As such, it appears that in practice the values for p can indeed be set significantly more aggressively than the bound computed in Sect. 4.

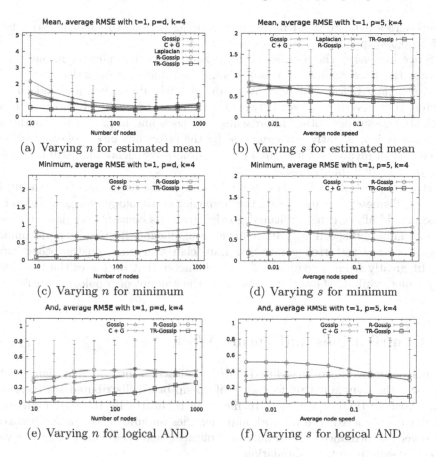

Fig. 7. Resilience of time-replicated gossip to changes in network size and volatility: its mean RMSE over time is not significantly degraded by varying number of devices n (a,c,e) or speed s (b,d,f), while other algorithms perform worse except under extreme conditions. Error bars indicate the standard deviation of the average RMSE across the 40 simulation runs.

Paradoxically, restarting gossip actually improves its performance as p increases, but due to the fact that less frequent restarts mean that its values are less often disrupted by transients. Thus, when the values of k and p are far from optimal, the mean error of replicated gossip is worse than restarting gossip and occasional transients may actually be less disruptive than overly long delays waiting for adaptation, depending on application.

5.4   Resilience to Network Size and Volatility

Finally, we tested how well time-replicated gossip scales to larger networks and adapts to differences in network volatility by changing the number of devices n and speed s. For each parameter, we evaluated a geometric distribution of nine values across two orders of magnitude, ranging n from 10 to 1000 and s from 0.05 to 0.5, respectively. Results are shown in Fig. 7.

Since increasing the number of devices increases the diameter in our experiments, the time-replicated gossip should degrade incrementally due to the increased time before old replicates can be safely discarded, and indeed this is what is observed. In larger networks, therefore, the mean advantage of time-replicated gossip over other approaches decreases, and in fact in the conditions we evaluate it is slightly outperformed by the faster but more volatile methods for estimated mean. In some circumstances, however, delay may still be preferable to unpredictable transients.

Higher speed of devices is expected to affect the network by decreasing its effective diameter but increasing the frequency of topology changes. Neither of these should affect time-replicated gossip, given its conservative diameter estimate, and indeed speed appears to have no significant effect on its performance. Single-replicate restarted gossip and Laplacian averaging, on the other hand, benefit greatly from a reduced effective diameter that decreases the transients they suffer, while C+G performs worse as the amount of topological disruption increases.

6   Contributions and Future Work

In this paper, we have introduced a time-replication method that significantly improves the dynamical performance of gossip-based distributed state estimation. Analysis bounds the time to maintain replicates by the round-trip time of information across the network and identifies an adjustable tradeoff between improved performance and number of replicates, and these conclusions are validated by experiments in simulation.

Future work can further improve performance by enabling tighter self-adjustment of parameters. In particular, a network diameter estimation algorithm, improved synchronization, and monitoring of transient length can all be employed to decrease the required replication interval, thereby allowing faster adaptation. Second, time-replicated gossip can be applied to any number of systems in which gossip is being used, in order to improve their performance. Finally, the generic nature of the time-replication algorithm we have introduced makes it a candidate for future studies to evaluate if and how time-replication can be used to improve other classes of distributed algorithms.

References

1. Beal, J.: Accelerating approximate consensus with self-organizing overlays. In: Spatial Computing Workshop, May 2013
2. Beal, J.: Superdiffusive dispersion and mixing of swarms. ACM Trans. Auton. Adapt. Syst. **10**(2), 1–24 (2015)
3. Beal, J., Pianini, D., Viroli, M.: Aggregate programming for the internet of things. IEEE Comput. **48**(9), 22–30 (2015)

4. Beal, J., Viroli, M.: Building blocks for aggregate programming of self-organising applications. In: IEEE SASO Workshops, pp. 8–13 (2014)
5. Birman, K.: The promise, and limitations, of gossip protocols. ACM SIGOPS Oper. Syst. Rev. **41**(5), 8–13 (2007)
6. Chandra, T.D., Griesemer, R., Redstone, J.: Paxos made live: an engineering perspective. In: Principles of Distributed Computing, pp. 398–407 (2007)
7. Damiani, F., Viroli, M., Beal, J.: A type-sound calculus of computational fields. Sci. Comput. Program. **117**, 17–44 (2016)
8. Damiani, F., Viroli, M., Pianini, D., Beal, J.: Code mobility meets self-organisation: a higher-order calculus of computational fields. In: Graf, S., Viswanathan, M. (eds.) Formal Techniques for Distributed Objects, Components, and Systems. LNCS, vol. 9039, pp. 113–128. Springer, Heidelberg (2015)
9. Elhage, N., Beal, J.: Laplacian-based consensus on spatial computers. In: International Conference on Autonomous Agents and Multiagent Systems, pp. 907–914 (2010)
10. Fischer, M.J., Lynch, N.A., Paterson, M.S.: Impossibility of distributed consensus with one faulty process. J. ACM (JACM) **32**(2), 374–382 (1985)
11. Gupta, I., Birman, K., Linga, P., Demers, A., van Renesse, R.: Kelips: building an efficient and stable P2P DHT through increased memory and background overhead. In: Kaashoek, M.F., Stoica, I. (eds.) Peer-to-Peer Systems II. LNCS, vol. 2735, pp. 160–169. Springer, Heidelberg (2003)
12. Jelasity, M., Montresor, A., Babaoglu, O.: Gossip-based aggregation in large dynamic networks. ACM Trans. Comput. Syst. (TOCS) **23**(3), 219–252 (2005)
13. Jelasity, M., Montresor, A., Babaoglu, O.: T-man: gossip-based fast overlay topology construction. Comput. Netw. **53**(13), 2321–2339 (2009)
14. Lamport, L.: The part-time parliament. ACM Trans. Comput. Syst. **16**(2), 133–169 (1998)
15. Lynch, N.: Distributed Algorithms. Morgan Kaufmann, San Francisco (1996)
16. Mosk-Aoyama, D., Shah, D.: Fast distributed algorithms for computing separable functions. IEEE Trans. Inf. Theor. **54**(7), 2997–3007 (2008)
17. Olfati-Saber, R., Fax, J.A., Murray, R.M.: Consensus and cooperation in networked multi-agent systems. Proc. IEEE **95**(1), 215–233 (2007)
18. Perlman, R.J.: Fault-tolerant broadcast of routing information. Comput. Netw. **7**, 395–405 (1983). http://dx.org/10.1016/0376-5075(83)90034-X
19. Pianini, D., Montagna, S., Viroli, M.: Chemical-oriented simulation of computational systems with ALCHEMIST. J. Simul. **7**(3), 202–215 (2013)
20. Pianini, D., Viroli, M., Beal, J.: Protelis: practical aggregate programming. In: ACM Symposium on Applied Computing, pp. 1846–1853 (2015)
21. Shah, D.: Gossip Algorithms. Now Publishers Inc, Norwell (2009)
22. Viroli, M., Beal, J., Damiani, F., Pianini, D.: Efficient engineering of complex self-organising systems by self-stabilising fields. In: IEEE SASO, pp. 81–90 (2015)
23. Voulgaris, S., van Steen, M.: An epidemic protocol for managing routing tables in very large peer-to-peer networks. In: Brunner, M., Keller, A. (eds.) DSOM 2003. LNCS, vol. 2867, pp. 41–54. Springer, Heidelberg (2003)
24. Zambonelli, F.: Toward sociotechnical urban superorganisms. IEEE Comput. **45**(8), 76–78 (2012)

From Modelling to Systematic Deployment of Distributed Active Objects

Ludovic Henrio and Justine Rochas[✉]

University Nice Sophia Antipolis, CNRS, I3S, UMR 7271,
06900 Sophia Antipolis, France
ludovic.henrio@cnrs.fr, justine.rochas@unice.fr

Abstract. In the context of the expansion of actors and active objects, we are still facing a gap between the safety guaranteed by modelling and verification languages and the efficiency of distributed middlewares. In this paper, we reconcile two active object-based languages, ABS and ProActive, that respectively target the aforementioned goals. We compile ABS programs into ProActive, making possible to benefit from the strengths of both languages, while requiring no modification on the source code. After introducing the translational semantics, we establish the properties and the correctness of the translation. Overall, this paper presents an approach to running different active object models in distributed environments, and more generally studies the implementation of programming languages based on active objects.

1 Introduction

Writing distributed and concurrent applications is a challenging task. In distributed environments, the absence of shared memory makes information sharing more difficult. In concurrent environments, data sharing is easy but shared data must be manipulated with caution. Several languages and tools have been developed to handle those two programming challenges and make distributed and concurrent systems safe by construction. Among them, the active object programming model [18] helps building safe multi-core applications in object-oriented programming languages. The active object model derives from the actor model [1] that is particularly regaining popularity with Scala [11] and Akka[1]. Such models are natively adapted to distribution because entities do not share memory and behave independently from each other.

There exist now several programming languages implementing and enhancing in various ways the active object and actor models. In particular, emerging active object languages, like the Abstract Behavioral Specification language [15] (hereafter ABS), provide various programming abstractions or static guarantees that help the developer designing and implementing robust distributed systems.

---

[1] http://akka.io.

© IFIP International Federation for Information Processing 2016
Published by Springer International Publishing Switzerland 2016. All Rights Reserved
A. Lluch Lafuente and J. Proença (Eds.): COORDINATION 2016, LNCS 9686, pp. 208–226, 2016.
DOI: 10.1007/978-3-319-39519-7_13

Among existing implementations of active objects, ProActive[2] is a Java middleware implementing multi-threaded active objects that provides a holistic support for deployment and execution of active objects on distributed infrastructures. This paper reconciles cooperative active object languages by translating their main concurrent paradigms into ProActive, thus benefiting from its support for deployment. We illustrate our approach on ABS, which has a wide support for modelling and verification. We translate all the concurrent object layer of ABS into ProActive. We also introduce in this paper MultiASP, a formal language that models ProActive, in order to verify the translation.

Beyond the generic high-level approach to cross-translating active object languages, the practical contribution of this paper is a ProActive backend for ABS, that automatically translates an ABS application into a distributed ProActive application. As a result, the programmer can design and verify his program using the powerful toolset of ABS, and then generate efficient distributed Java code that runs with ProActive. The proof of correctness of the translation ensures the equivalence of execution in terms of the operational semantics. Consequently, it guarantees that the verified properties dealing with the program behaviour (e.g. absence of deadlocks, typing properties) will still be valid. Our approach requires no change in the ABS code except the minimal (required) deployment information. Overall, our contribution can be summarised in four points:

- We analyse existing active object programming paradigms in Sect. 2.
- We provide MultiASP, a class-based semantics of the multi-threaded active objects featured in ProActive in Sect. 3.
- We present a systematic strategy to translate active objects with cooperative scheduling into ProActive, and present more specifically the ProActive backend for ABS in Sect. 4. The translation is formalised in Sect. 5.
- We prove translation equivalence in Sect. 6 and highlight similarities and differences between active object models. In particular the proof of equivalence reveals intrinsic differences between explicitly typed futures and transparent first-class futures.

2   Background and Related Works

The actor model was one of the first to schematically consider concurrent entities evolving independently and communicating via asynchronous messages. Later on, active objects have been designed as the object-oriented counterpart of the actor model. The principle of active objects is to have a thread associated to them. We call this notion *activity*: a thread together with the objects managed by this thread. Objects from different activities communicate with remote method invocations: when a method is invoked on a remote active object, this creates a *request* in the remote activity; the invoker continues its execution while the invoked active object serves the request asynchronously. Requests wait in a *request queue* until they are executed. In order to allow the invoker to continue

---

[2] http://proactive.inria.fr/.

execution, a placeholder for the expected result is created, known as *future* [9]: an empty object that will later be filled by the result of the request. When the value of a future is known, we say that it is *resolved*.

2.1 Design Choices for Active Object-Based Languages

Implementing active objects raises the three following questions:

How are Objects Associated to Activities? In uniform active object models, all objects are active and have their own execution thread (e.g. Creol [16]). This model is distinguished from non uniform active object models which feature active and passive objects (e.g. ASP [6]). Each passive object is a normal object not equipped with any thread nor request queue; there is no race condition on the access to passive object because each of them is accessible by a single active object. In practice, non uniform active object models are more scalable, but they are trickier to formalise than uniform active object models. A trade-off between those two models appeared with JCoBox [20] that introduced the active object group model, where all objects are accessible from any object, but where objects of the same group share the same execution thread.

How are Requests Scheduled? The way requests are executed in active objects depends on the threading model used. In the original programming model, active objects are mono-threaded. With cooperative scheduling like in Creol, requests in execution can be paused on some condition (e.g. awaiting on the resolution of a future), letting another request progress in the meantime. In all cooperative active object languages, while no data race is possible, interleaving of the different request services (triggered by the different release points) makes the behaviour more difficult to predict than for the mono-threaded model. Still, the previous models are inefficient on multi-cores and can lead to deadlocks due to reentrant calls and/or inadequately placed release points. Newest active object models like multiactive objects [12] and Encore [5] feature controlled multi-threading. Such active object models succeed in maximising local parallelism while avoiding communication overhead, thanks to shared memory between the different threads [12]. Also, controlled multi-threading prevents many deadlocks in active object executions.

Is the Programmer Aware of Distributed Aspects? Existing implementations of active objects either choose to hide asynchrony and distribution or, on the contrary to use an explicit syntax for handling asynchronous method calls and to use an explicit type for handling futures. This makes the programmer aware of where synchronisation occurs, but consequently requires more expertise. The choice of transparency also impacts the language possibilities, like future reference transmission: it is easier to transmit futures between active objects when no specific future type is used, and the programmer does not have to know how many future indirections have to be unfolded to get the final value.

$g ::= b \mid x? \mid g \wedge g'$ guard
$s ::= \textbf{skip} \mid x = z \mid \textbf{suspend} \mid \textbf{await } g$ statement
$\mid \textbf{return } e \mid \textbf{if } e \, \{s\} \textbf{ else } \{s\} \mid s \, ; \, s$
$z ::= e \mid e.m(\bar{e}) \mid e!m(\bar{e}) \mid \textbf{new } [cog]C(\bar{e}) \mid x.\textbf{get}$ expression with side effect
$e ::= v \mid x \mid \textbf{this} \mid arithmetic\text{-}bool\text{-}exp$ expression
$v ::= \textbf{null} \mid primitive\text{-}val$ value

Fig. 1. Class-based syntax of the concurrent object layer of ABS. Field access is restricted to current object (**this**).

2.2 Overview of Active Object-Based Languages

Creol [16] is a uniform active object language that features cooperative scheduling based on **await** operations that can release the execution thread. In this language, asynchronous invocations and futures are explicit, and futures are not transmitted between activities. De Boer et al. formalised such futures based on Creol in [4]. Overall, explicit future access, explicit release points, and explicit asynchronous calls make Creol rich and precise but also more difficult to program than the languages featuring more transparency.

JCoBox [20] is an active object programming model implemented in a language based on Java. It has an object group model, called CoBox, and also features cooperative scheduling. In each CoBox, a single thread is active at a time; it can be released using **await()**. JCoBox better addresses practical aspects than Creol: it is integrated with Java and the object group model improves thread scalability, however JCoBox does not support distributed execution. Thread interleaving is similar and has the same advantages and drawbacks as in Creol.

AmbientTalk [7] is an object-oriented distributed programming language that can execute on the JVM. One original aspect of AmbientTalk is that a future access is a non-blocking operation: it is an asynchronous call that returns another future; the call will be performed when the invoked future is resolved. The AmbientTalk future model forces two activities to coordinate only through callbacks. This inversion of control has the advantage to avoid deadlocks but also breaks the program into independent procedures where sequences of instructions are difficult to enforce.

ABS [15] is an active object-based language that targets modelling of distributed applications. The fragment of the ABS syntax regarding the concurrent object layer is shown on Fig. 1. ABS has an object group model, like JCoBox, based on the notion of concurrent object group (hereafter COG). Asynchronous method calls and futures are explicit:

```
Fut<V> future = object!method();
```

Figure 2 pictures an ABS configuration with a request sending between COGs. Requests are scheduled in a cooperative manner thanks to the **await** keyword, inspired from Creol and JCoBox and used as follows:

```
await future?;  await a > 2 && b < 3;
```

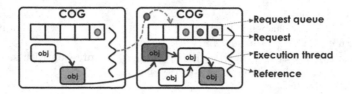

Fig. 2. An example of ABS program execution

In those examples, the execution thread is released if the future is not resolved or if the condition is not fulfilled. ABS also features a `get` accessor to retrieve a future's value; it blocks the execution thread until the future is resolved:

```
1  V v = future.get;
```

The ABS tool suite[3] provides a wide variety of static verification engines that help designing safe distributed and concurrent applications. Those engines include a deadlock analyser [10], resource, cost, and deployment analysers for cloud environments [2,17], and general program properties verification with the ABS-Key tool [8]. The ABS tool suite also includes a frontend compiler and several backend translators into various programming languages. The Java backend for ABS translates ABS programs into concurrent Java code that runs on a single machine. The Haskell backend for ABS [3] performs the translation into distributed Haskell code. The ABS semantics is preserved thanks to the thread continuation support of Haskell, which is not supported on the JVM.

ASP and ProActive. Asynchronous Sequential Processes (ASP) [6] is a mono-threaded active object programming language that has a non-uniform object model. In ASP, active objects are transparent to the programmer and futures are created and manipulated implicitly. A wait-by-necessity is triggered upon access to an unresolved future. Futures are first class: they are transparently passed and updated across activities. ProActive is the Java library that implements ASP. ProActive is a middleware that supports application deployment on distributed infrastructures such as clusters, grids and clouds. The program below creates explicitly an active object using **newActive** instead of **new**. The variable v stores an implicit future that is the result of a (transparent) asynchronous call.

```
1  T t = PAActiveObject.newActive(T.class, parameters, node);
2  V v = t.bar();
3  o.foo(v);   // does not block even if v is unresolved (o is any active or passive object)
4  v.foobar(); // blocks if v is unresolved
```

Recently, ProActive integrated multiactive objects [12] to enable multi-threaded request processing. MultiASP, presented in the next section, is an update of ASP and thus formalises the new version of ProActive. In practice, a programmer declares which requests of an active object can safely be executed in parallel, namely which requests are *compatible*, as shown in the following example:

---

[3] http://abs-models.org/.

```
1  @Group(name="group1", selfCompatible=true)
2  @Group(name={"group2", selfCompatible=false)
3  @Compatible({"group1", "group2"})
4  public class MyClass {
5    @MemberOf("group1")   public ... method1(...) { ... }
6    @MemberOf("group2")   public ... method2(...) { ... }
7  }
```

In this example, a request for `method1` can be executed at the same time as a request for `method2`, but two requests for `method2` cannot be executed at the same time. With similar annotations, it is also possible to set a limit on the number of threads running in parallel [13]. The limit can be applied in two ways: a hard limit restrains the overall number of threads whereas a soft limit only counts threads that are not in wait-by-necessity.

Encore. Encore [5] is an active object-based parallel language currently in development. Encore features active and passive objects but even if passive objects are private by default, they can be shared at different scales depending on qualifying keywords. Asynchronous calls are transparent for active objects (by default) but futures are explicit, using a dedicated type. Finally, an active object has a single thread of execution by default, but parallelism is automatically created by attaching callbacks to future updates and using parallel combinators.

2.3 Positioning of This Work

The reason why there are many different implementations of the active object programming model is to better fit particular objectives, from reasoning about programs to optimised program execution. Implementations that focus on the deployment of real-world systems comply to constraints related to existing execution platforms and languages. They are mostly used by programmers interested in the performance of the application. ProActive and Encore typically fit in this category. On the other side, some active object languages target verification and proof of programs, but have not been originally designed for efficient execution, like typically ABS and Creol. They are massively used and developed by academics and less constrained by existing execution platforms.

We give a proven translation of ABS programs into ProActive code in order to reconcile both domains: verified applications also have the right to be run efficiently. We also study the generalisation of our approach to other active object languages. Overall, our objective is to show that generic active object abstractions can be correctly encoded with different active object implementations.

3   Class-Based Semantics of MultiASP

We start by introducing the semantics of MultiASP[4], the calculus representing ProActive and multiactive objects. Unlike the preliminary formalisation of multiactive objects in [12], we present here a class-based formalisation and the formalisation of threading policies. MultiASP is an imperative programming language and its syntax is close to the one of ABS.

$$P ::= \overline{C} \; \{ \overline{x} \; ; \; s \} \qquad\qquad \text{program}$$
$$S ::= \texttt{m}(\overline{x}) \qquad\qquad \text{method signature}$$
$$C ::= \texttt{class } \texttt{C}(\overline{x}) \; \{ \overline{x} \; \overline{M} \} \qquad\qquad \text{class}$$
$$M ::= S\{ \overline{x} \; s \} \qquad\qquad \text{method definition}$$
$$s ::= \texttt{skip} \mid x = z \mid \texttt{return } e \mid s \; ; \; s \qquad \text{statement}$$
$$z ::= e \mid e.\texttt{m}(\overline{e}) \mid \texttt{new } \texttt{C}(\overline{e}) \mid \texttt{newActive } \texttt{C}(\overline{e}) \quad \text{expression with side effects}$$
$$e ::= v \mid x \mid \texttt{this} \mid \textit{arithmetic-bool-exp} \qquad \text{expression}$$
$$v ::= \texttt{null} \mid \textit{primitive-val} \qquad\qquad \text{value}$$

Fig. 3. Class-based static syntax of MultiASP

$$v ::= o \mid \alpha \mid \dots$$
$$elem ::= \textsc{fut}(f, v, \sigma) \mid \textsc{fut}(f, \bot) \mid \textsc{act}(\alpha, o, \sigma, p, Rq)$$
$$cn ::= \overline{elem}$$
$$E ::= \{\ell \mid s\}$$
$$F ::= E \mid E :: F$$
$$p ::= \overrightarrow{q \mapsto F}$$

$$Storable ::= [\overrightarrow{x \mapsto v}] \mid v \mid f$$
$$\sigma ::= \overrightarrow{o \mapsto Storable}$$
$$q ::= (f, m, \overline{v})$$
$$Rq ::= \varnothing \mid q :: Rq$$
$$\ell ::= \texttt{this} \mapsto v, \overrightarrow{x \mapsto v}$$
$$s ::= x = \bullet \mid \dots$$

Fig. 4. Runtime syntax of MultiASP

Syntax of MultiASP. Fig. 3 shows the static syntax of MultiASP. A program is made of classes and a main method. $\overline{x}$ denotes local variables in method bodies and object fields in class declarations. There are two ways to create an object: *new* creates a new object in the current activity, and *newActive* creates a new active object. $e.\texttt{m}(\overline{e})$ is the generic method invocation, there is no syntactic distinction between local and remote (asynchronous) invocations. Similarly, as synchronisation on futures is transparent and handled with wait-by-necessity, there is no particular syntax for interacting with a future. A special variable this exists for accessing the current object.

Semantics of MultiASP. MultiASP semantics is defined as a transition relation between configurations, noted cn, and for which the runtime syntax is displayed in Fig. 4. At runtime, the dynamic configuration of a MultiASP program consists of a set of activities and a set of futures. The transition relation uses three infinite sets: *object locations* in the local store, ranged over by o, o', $\cdots$; *active objects names*, ranged over by α, β, $\cdots$; and *future names*, ranged over by f, f', $\cdots$. *Activities* are of the form $\textsc{act}(\alpha, o, \sigma, p, Rq)$ where α is an activity name; o is the location of the active object in σ; σ is a *local store* mapping object locations to storable values; p is a set of *requests currently served* (a mapping from requests to their thread F); and Rq is a FIFO *request queue* of requests awaiting to be served. A thread is a stack of methods being executed, and each *method execution* E consists of *local variables* ℓ and *statement* s to execute. The first method of the stack is the one that is executing, the others have been put in the stack due to local synchronous method calls. ℓ is a mapping from local variables (including this) to runtime values. A configuration also contains *future*

---

[4] Formalised in Isabelle/HOL: www-sop.inria.fr/members/Ludovic.Henrio/misc.html.

binders. They are of two forms: FUT$(f, \perp)$, meaning that the value for the future has not been computed yet, and FUT(f, v, σ), when the *reply value* is known; if it is an object (and not a static value), then v will be its location in the store σ.

An object o is fresh if it does not exist in the store in which it is added. Similarly, a future or an activity name is fresh if it does not exist in the current configuration. *Runtime values* $(v, \cdots)$ can be either static values, object locations, or active object names. An object is a mapping from field names to their values, denoted $[\overrightarrow{x \mapsto v}]$. We denote mappings by $\_ \mapsto \_$, and use union $\cup$ (resp. disjoint union $\uplus$) over mappings. Mapping updates are of the form $\sigma[x \mapsto v]$. *dom* returns the domain of a mapping. *Storable values* are objects, futures, or runtime values.

The following auxiliary functions are used in the semantic rules: $[\![e]\!]_{(\sigma+\ell)}$ returns the value of e by computing the arithmetic and boolean expressions and by retrieving the values stored in σ or ℓ; the evaluation function is displayed in Fig. 6. If the value of e is a reference to a location in the store, it follows references recursively; it only returns a location if the location points to an object or a future. $[\![\overline{e}]\!]_{(\sigma+\ell)}$ returns the tuple of values of $\overline{e}$. *fields*(C) returns fields as defined in the class declaration C. *bind* initialises method execution: bind$(o, \mathtt{m}, \overrightarrow{v'}) = \{y \mapsto v', z \mapsto \mathtt{null}, \mathtt{this} \mapsto o \mid s\}$, where the arguments of method $\mathtt{m}$, typed in the class of o, are $\overline{y}$, and where the method body is $\{\overline{z}; s\}$. *ready* is a predicate deciding whether a request q in the queue Rq is ready to be served: *ready*(q, p, Rq) is *true* if q is compatible with all requests in p (requests currently served by the activity) and with older requests in Rq. Serialisation reflects the communication style happening in Java RMI; it ensures that each activity has a single entry point: the active object. Consequently, all references to passive objects are serialised when communicated between activities, so that they are always handled locally. *serialise*(o, σ) marks and copies the objects referenced from o to deeply serialise, recursively; it returns a new store made of all the objects that are referenced by o. *serialise* is defined as the mapping verifying the constraints of Fig. 5. *rename*$_\sigma(\overline{v}, \sigma')$ renames the object locations appearing in $\overline{v}$ and σ', making them disjoint from the object locations of σ; it returns a renamed set of values $\overline{v'}$ and a store σ''.

serialise$(o, \sigma) =$
  $(o \mapsto \sigma(o)) \cup$ serialise$(\sigma(o), \sigma)$
serialise$([\overrightarrow{x \mapsto v}], \sigma) =$
  $\bigcup_{v' \in \overline{v}}$ serialise(v', σ)
serialise$(f, \sigma) =$
  serialise$(\alpha, \sigma) =$
  serialise$(\mathtt{null}, \sigma) = \varnothing$
serialise$(primitive\text{-}val, \sigma) = \varnothing$

$[\![primitive\text{-}val]\!]_{(\sigma+\ell)} \triangleq primitive\text{-}val$
$[\![f]\!]_{(\sigma+\ell)} \triangleq \perp$
$[\![\alpha]\!]_{(\sigma+\ell)} \triangleq \alpha$
$[\![\mathtt{null}]\!]_{(\sigma+\ell)} \triangleq \mathtt{null}$
$[\![x]\!]_{(\sigma+\ell)} \triangleq [\![\ell(x)]\!]_{(\sigma+\ell)}$ if $x \in \mathrm{dom}(\ell)$
$[\![x]\!]_{(\sigma+\ell)} \triangleq [\![\ell(\mathtt{this})(x)]\!]_{(\sigma+\ell)}$ if $x \notin \mathrm{dom}(\ell)$
$[\![o]\!]_{(\sigma+\ell)} \triangleq o$ if $\sigma(o) = f$ or $\sigma(o) = [\overrightarrow{x \mapsto v}]$
$[\![o]\!]_{(\sigma+\ell)} \triangleq [\![\sigma(o)]\!]_{(\sigma+\ell)}$ else

Fig. 5. Serialisation   **Fig. 6.** Evaluation function

ASSIGN-LOCAL
$$\frac{x \in \mathrm{dom}(\ell) \qquad v = [\![e]\!]_{(\sigma+\ell)}}{\mathrm{ACT}(\alpha, o_\alpha, \sigma, \{q \mapsto \{\ell \mid x = e; s\} :: F\} \uplus p, Rq)}$$
$$\to \mathrm{ACT}(\alpha, o_\alpha, \sigma, \{q \mapsto \{\ell[x \mapsto v] \mid s\} :: F\} \uplus p, Rq)$$

SERVE
$$\frac{\mathrm{ready}(q, p, Rq) \qquad q = (f, m, \overline{v}) \qquad \mathrm{bind}(o_\alpha, m, \overline{v}) = \{\ell \mid s\}}{\mathrm{ACT}(\alpha, o_\alpha, \sigma, p, Rq :: q :: Rq') \to \mathrm{ACT}(\alpha, o_\alpha, \sigma, \{q \mapsto \{\ell|s\}\} \uplus p, Rq :: Rq')}$$

NEW-ACTIVE
$$\frac{\mathit{fields}(\mathtt{C}) = \overline{x} \qquad o, \gamma \ \mathrm{fresh} \qquad \sigma' = \{o \mapsto [\overline{x = \overrightarrow{v}}]\} \cup \mathrm{serialise}(\overline{v}, \sigma) \qquad [\![\overline{e}]\!]_{(\sigma+\ell)} = \overline{v}}{\mathrm{ACT}(\alpha, o_\alpha, \sigma, \{q \mapsto \{\ell \mid x = \mathtt{newActive}\ \mathtt{C}(\overline{e}); s\} :: F\} \uplus p, Rq)}$$
$$\to \mathrm{ACT}(\alpha, o_\alpha, \sigma, \{q \mapsto \{\ell \mid x = \gamma; s\} :: F\} \uplus p, Rq) \ \mathrm{ACT}(\gamma, o, \sigma', \varnothing, \varnothing)$$

INVK-ACTIVE
$$\frac{[\![e]\!]_{(\sigma+\ell)} = \beta \qquad [\![\overline{e}]\!]_{(\sigma+\ell)} = \overline{v}}{f, o \ \mathrm{fresh} \qquad \sigma_1 = \sigma \cup \{o \mapsto f\} \qquad (\overline{v_r}, \sigma_r) = \mathrm{rename}_{\sigma'}(\overline{v}, \mathrm{serialise}(\overline{v}, \sigma)) \qquad \sigma'' = \sigma' \cup \sigma_r}{\mathrm{ACT}(\alpha, o_\alpha, \sigma, \{q \mapsto \{\ell \mid x = e.\mathtt{m}(\overline{e}); s\} :: F\} \uplus p, Rq) \ \mathrm{ACT}(\beta, o_\beta, \sigma', p', Rq')}$$
$$\to \mathrm{ACT}(\alpha, o_\alpha, \sigma_1, \{q \mapsto \{\ell \mid x = o; s\} :: F\} \uplus p, Rq)$$
$$\mathrm{ACT}(\beta, o_\beta, \sigma'', p', Rq' :: (f, m, \overline{v_r})) \mathrm{FUT}(f, \bot)$$

UPDATE
$$\frac{\sigma(o) = f \qquad (v_r, \sigma_r) = \mathrm{rename}_\sigma(v, \sigma') \qquad \sigma'' = \sigma[o \mapsto v_r] \cup \sigma_r}{\mathrm{ACT}(\alpha, o_\alpha, \sigma, p, Rq) \ \mathrm{FUT}(f, v, \sigma') \to \mathrm{ACT}(\alpha, o_\alpha, \sigma'', p, Rq) \ \mathrm{FUT}(f, v, \sigma')}$$

RETURN
$$\frac{v = [\![e]\!]_{(o+\ell)}}{\mathrm{ACT}(\alpha, o_\alpha, \sigma, \{(f, m, \overline{v}) \mapsto \{\ell \mid \mathbf{return}\ e; s_r\}\} \uplus p, Rq) \ \mathrm{FUT}(f, \bot)}$$
$$\to \mathrm{ACT}(\alpha, o_\alpha, \sigma, p, Rq) \ \mathrm{FUT}(f, v, \mathrm{serialise}(v, \sigma))$$

Fig. 7. Semantics of MultiASP

Figure 7 shows the part of MultiASP semantics that regards active object execution. Rules involving classical objects, namely object creation, field assignment, passive invocation, and local return of method call have been removed due to space limitation. The full MultiASP semantics can be found in the extended version of this paper in [14]. In all cases, rules only show activities and futures involved in the current reduction. SERVE picks the first request that is ready in the queue (compatible with executing requests and with older requests in the queue) and allocates a new thread to serve it. It fetches the method body and creates the execution context. ASSIGN-LOCAL assigns a value to a local variable. If the statement to be executed is an assignment of an expression that can be reduced to a value, then the mapping of local variables is updated accordingly. NEW-ACTIVE creates a new activity that contains a new active object. It picks a fresh activity name, and assigns serialised object parameters: the initial local store of the activity is the piece of store referenced by the parameters. INVK-ACTIVE performs an asynchronous remote method invocation on an active object. It creates a fresh future with undefined value. The arguments of the invocation are serialised and put in the store of the invoked activity, possibly renaming locations to avoid clashes. The special case $\alpha = \beta$ requires a trivial adaptation of this rule (not shown here). RETURN is triggered when a request finishes. It stores the value computed by the request as a future value. Serialisation is necessary to pack the objects referenced by the future value. UPDATE updates a future reference with a resolved value. This is performed at any time when a future is referenced and the future value is resolved. Finally, the main effect of the missing rules is to modify the local store (NEW-OBJECT and ASSIGN-FIELD) and to affect the execution context (INVK-PASSIVE and RETURN-LOCAL).

Threading Policies. We extend the above semantics to specify the threading policies featured in multiactive objects (see Sect. 2.2). First, we extend the syntax of MultiASP so that the threading policy can be programmatically changed from a *soft limit*, i.e. a thread blocked in a wait-by-necessity is not counted in the limit, to a *hard limit*, i.e. all threads are counted in the limit:

$$s ::= \dots \mid \textbf{setLimitSoft} \mid \textbf{setLimitHard}$$

Each request q belongs to a group $group(q)$. The filter $p\big|_g$ gives, among the active threads p, only requests of group g. There is a thread limit $\mathcal{L}_g$ defined for each group. We tag each of the currently served request as either *active* or *passive*. p contains then two kinds of served requests: active ones, noted $q_A \mapsto F$, and passive ones, noted $q_P \mapsto F$. Active(p) returns the number of active requests in p. Finally, each activity is either in a *soft limit* state written $\text{ACT}(\dots)_S$ (by default at activity creation), or in a *hard limit* state written $\text{ACT}(\dots)_H$. *sh* is a variable ranging over S and H. MultiASP semantics is modified as follows:

- Each rule allowing a thread to progress requires now that the thread is active, i.e. q is replaced by q_A in all rules except SERVE and UPDATE.
- The rule SERVE is only triggered if the thread limit is not reached, i.e. if Active($p\big|_{group(q)}$) $< \mathcal{L}_g$. Similarly, a rule for activating a thread is added:

ACTIVATE-THREAD
$$\frac{Group(q) = g \qquad \text{Active}(p\big|_g) < \mathcal{L}_g}{\text{ACT}(\alpha, o_\alpha, \sigma, \{q_P \mapsto F\} \uplus p, Rq)_{sh} \;\rightarrow\; \text{ACT}(\alpha, o_\alpha, \sigma, \{q_A \mapsto F\} \uplus p, Rq)_{sh}}$$

- There are two additional rules for switching the kind of limit, we show one hereafter (SET-SOFT-LIMIT is the reverse):

SET-HARD-LIMIT
$$\text{ACT}(\alpha, o_\alpha, \sigma, \{q_A \mapsto \{\ell \mid \textbf{setLimitHard}; s\} :: F\} \uplus p, Rq)_{sh}$$
$$\rightarrow \text{ACT}(\alpha, o_\alpha, \sigma, \{q_A \mapsto \{\ell \mid s\} :: F\} \uplus p, Rq)_H$$

– If the kind of limit is a *soft limit*, a wait-by-necessity passivates the current thread[5]; a rule for method invocation on a future is added:

Invk-Future

$$\frac{[\![e]\!]_{(\sigma+\ell)} = o \qquad \sigma(o) = f}{\text{act}(\alpha, o_\alpha, \sigma, \{q_A \mapsto \{\ell \mid x = e.\mathtt{m}(\overline{e}); s\} :: F\} \uplus p, Rq)_S}{\rightarrow \text{act}(\alpha, o_\alpha, \sigma, \{q_P \mapsto \{\ell \mid x = e.\mathtt{m}(\overline{e}); s\} :: F\} \uplus p, Rq)_S}$$

4   Example-Driven Translation Principles

In this section, we informally present the ProActive backend for ABS, that translates ABS programs into ProActive code. Basically, this section shows how the formal translation that will be defined in Sect. 5 is instantiated in practice in ProActive. This backend is based on the existing Java backend for ABS. We keep the translation of the functional layer unchanged and provide a translation of the object and concurrency layers.

Object Addressing and Invocation. To handle the differences between two active object languages, one needs first to define what happens when a new object (active or not) is created. As translating each ABS object into a ProActive active object is not a viable solution (because it is not scalable and because it requires a complex synchronisation of processes), we put several objects under the control of one active object, which fits the active object group model of ABS. To this end, in the translation, we introduce a class COG for representing ABS COGs; only objects of the COG class are active objects in the ProActive translation. We translate the ABS **new** statement that creates a new object in a new COG:

```
1  Server server = new Server();
```

This instruction is translated into ProActive by the ProActive backend:

```
1  Server server = new Server();
2  COG cog = PAActiveObject.newActive(COG.class, new Object[]{Server.class}, node);
3  server.setCog(cog);
4  cog.registerObject(server);
```

Line 1 creates a regular server object. Lines 2 uses the **newActive** ProActive primitive to create a new COG active object. Additionally to the constructor parameters, ProActive allows the specification of the node onto which the active object is deployed. Line 3 makes the local server aware of its COG. Finally in line 4, due to the ProActive by-copy parameter passing, the server object is copied in the local memory space of the newly created remote COG, and is thus locally accessible there. For objects created with **new local** in ABS, the ProActive backend simply registers them locally in the current COG. To enable the same object invocation model as in ABS, we use a two-level reference system in the

---

[5] Wait-by-necessity occurs only in case of method invocation on a future since field access is only allowed on the current object.

ProActive translation: each COG is accessible by a global reference and each translated ABS object is accessible inside its COG through a local identifier. The pair (COG, identifier) is a unique reference for each object and allows the runtime to retrieve any object. When objects are transmitted between COG (e.g. as parameter of method invocations), a lightweight copy is transmitted by the ProActive middleware; it can be used to reach the original object by using its COG and identifier. As only the COG and the identifier are needed to reference an ABS object, we tune the object serialisation mechanism so that only those fields are transmitted between active objects, thus saving memory and bandwidth. The same strategy can be applied to translate any language featuring active object groups into non uniform active objects. For uniform active objects, creating one active object per translated object handles straightforwardly the translation but limits scalability; grouping several objects behind a same active object (proxy) would produce a more efficient program.

In order to explain now how we translate ABS asynchronous method calls in ProActive, consider the following ABS asynchronous method call:

```
1 server!start(param1, param2);
```

In ProActive such a call becomes a remote method invocation. In order to handle it with our object translation model, we perform a generic method call (implicitly asynchronous) named **execute**, on the COG of the translated **server** object:

```
1 server.getCog().execute(server.getId(), "start", new Object[]{param1, param2});
```

When run, the **execute** method of the **COG** class retrieves the target object through its identifier and runs the **start** method on it by reflection with the given parameters. Upon **execute** remote call, objects **param1** and **param2** are copied to the memory space of the retrieved COG. Consequently, two copies of **param1** and **param2** exist in the translation whereas only one of them exists in ABS. However, if method calls occurs on them, the requests for those objects always go to the COG that manages those objects. This callback ensures that only one copy of a translated object is manipulated, like in ABS. Consequently, the behaviour by reference of ABS-like languages can be simulated with the behaviour by copy of ProActive. This mechanism is also applied for future updates.

Cooperative Scheduling. Active object languages often support special threading models and have constructs to impact on the scheduling of requests. Those constructs can be translated into adequate request scheduling of multiactive objects. For demonstration, we consider here the translation that the ProActive backend gives for ABS **await** statements (representative of cooperative scheduling), and for ABS **get** statements (representative of explicit futures).

- **await** statements on futures. An await statement on an unresolved futures releases the execution thread, for example:

```
1 await startedFut?;
```

In order to have the same behavior in the ProActive translation, we force a wait-by-necessity. We use the **getFutureValue** ProActive primitive to do that:

```
1  PAFuture.getFutureValue(startedFut);
```

As in ProActive a wait-by-necessity blocks the thread, we need to configure the ProActive COG class with multiactive object annotations (see Sect. 2.2) in order to qualify the **execute** method and to specify a soft thread limit:

```
1  @Group(name="scheduling", selfCompatible=true)
2  @DefineThreadConfig(threadPoolSize=1, hardLimit=false)
3  public class COG {
4    ...
5    @MemberOf("scheduling")
6    public ABSValue execute(UUID objectID, String methodName, Object[] args) {...}
7  }
```

This configuration allows a thread to process an **execute** request while a current thread that processes another **execute** request is waiting for a future. Indeed, the **hardLimit=false** parameter ensures that the threads counted in the limit (of 1 thread) are only *active* threads. In the example, the thread can be handed over to another **execute** request if **startedFut** is not resolved, just like in ABS.

- **get** statements. The ABS **get** statement blocks the execution thread to retrieve a future's value, as for example on the previous future variable:

```
1  Bool started = startedFut.get;
```

The ProActive backend translates this ABS instruction into the following code:

```
1  getCog().switchHardLimit(true); // the retrieved COG is local: the call is synchronous
2  PAFuture.getFutureValue(startedFut);
3  getCog().switchHardLimit(false);
```

This temporarily hardens the threading policy (i.e. all threads are counted in the thread limit) so that no other thread can start while the future is awaited.

- Other synchronisation constructs. We also tackled the translation of ABS **suspend** statements and of **await** statements on conditions. In this paper, we only provide the formal definition of their translation in Sect. 5. The details of their translation into ProActive code can be found in [19].

Wrap Up and Applicability. In order to finalise the ProActive backend for ABS, we add deployment information in the translation; for that we use the deployment descriptor embedded in ProActive: configuration files binding virtual nodes to physical machines. On the ABS side, **new cog** is followed by the name of a node for deployment. This is the *only* modification that ABS programs must incur to be executed in a distributed way. An experimental evaluation (detailed in the extended version of this paper in [14]) shows that a significant speedup can be achieved by a distributed execution of an ABS program thanks to the ProActive backend. It also shows that the program obtained with the ProActive backend incurs an overhead of less than 10 % compared to a native ProActive application.

We have presented in details the ProActive backend for ABS and discussed the translation of common active object constructs. The concepts applied in the case of ABS are generic and can systematically turn various active object languages into deployable active objects. As an example, JCoBox is similar enough to ABS so that the approach presented here is straightforwardly applicable. The most challenging aspect is that JCoBox features a globally accessible and immutable memory, which could be translated into one active object, or which could rely on copies since the immutable property holds. Regarding Creol, in which all objects are active, the best approach is to group several objects behind a same proxy for performance reasons. Then, preserving the semantics of Creol relies on a precise interleaving of local threads. The transposition to AmbientTalk is trickier on the scheduling aspect, due to the existence of callbacks. However, we found that a callback on a future can be translated as a request that is ready to run but that starts by a wait-by-necessity on the adequate future.

5   Translational Semantics

This section formalises the translation given by the ProActive backend by introducing the translational semantics from ABS to MultiASP. We refer to Fig. 1 for the concurrent object layer of ABS. Runtime syntax and semantics of ABS can be found in [14]. Most of the translation from ABS to MultiASP impacts statements. The rest of the source structure (classes, interfaces, methods) is unchanged except the two following:

(1) We define a new class COG. It has methods to store and retrieve local objects, and to execute a method on a local object; UUID is the type of object identifiers:

```
Class COG {
  UUID freshID()
  UUID register(Object x, UUID id)
  Object retrieve(UUID id)
  Object execute(UUID id, MethodName m, params) { \\
    w=this.retrieve(id); x=w.m(params); return x}
}
```

(2) All translated ABS classes are extended with two parameters: a *cog* parameter, storing the COG to which the object belongs, and an *id* parameter, storing the object's identifier in that COG; methods *cog()* and *myId()* return those two parameters; a dummy method *get()* that returns null is added to each object.

The translation of statements and expressions is shown in Fig. 8. Each of them is explained below. *Object instantiation* first gets a fresh identifier from the current COG. Then, the new object is created with the current COG and the identifier[6]. It is stored in a reserved temporary local variable *no*. Finally, the object is referenced in the current COG and stored in *x*. *Object instantiation in a new* COG is similar to object instantiation in the current COG but method invocations on *newcog* variable are asynchronous remote method calls. The new object is thus copied to the memory space of the remote new COG via the *register* invocation, before being assigned to *x*. *Await future* uses the dummy *get()* method, that all translated objects have, in order to trigger the wait-by-necessity mechanism and potentially block the thread if the future is not

---

[6] The step in which the COG of the new object is set in ProActive is directly encoded in the object constructor in MultiASP.

resolved. *Get future* sets a hard limit on the current activity, so that no other thread starts, and then restores the soft limit after having waited for the future. *Await on conditions* performs sequential *get()* within an activity in soft limit. Conditional guards are detailed later in this section. *Asynchronous method call* retrieves the COG of the object and relies on the *execute* asynchronous method call as described in Sect. 4. *Synchronous local method call* distinguishes two cases, like in ABS. Either the call is local and an execution context is pushed in the stack, or the call is remote and, like in ABS, we perform an asynchronous remote method invocation and immediately wait the associated future within an activity in hard limit. Finally, instructions that do not deal with method invocation, future manipulation, or object creation, are kept unchanged.

In the translation, there exist different multiactive object groups and each group has its own thread limit. Group g_1 encapsulates $freshId$ requests; those requests cannot execute in parallel safely, so g_1 is not self compatible and can only use one thread at a time. Group g_2 gathers *execute* requests. It is limited to one thread to comply with the threading model of ABS, and the requests are self compatible to enable interleaving. Group g_3 contains *register* requests that are self compatible and that have an infinite thread limit. Concerning compatibility between groups, they are all compatible except g_3 and g_2: their compatibility is defined dynamically such that an *execute* request and a *register* request are compatible only if they do not affect the same identifier. In summary:

$$group(freshId) = g_1 \qquad group(execute) = g_2 \qquad group(register) = g_3$$
$$\mathcal{L}_{g_1} = 1 \qquad \mathcal{L}_{g_2} = 1 \qquad \mathcal{L}_{g_3} = \infty$$
$$\forall q, q'. \, (q \neq q' \neq freshId() \wedge (\nexists id.q = register(x, id) \wedge q' = execute(id, m, \overline{e}))) \Rightarrow$$
$$compatible(q, q')$$

In order to support ABS conditional guards, for each guard g, we generate a method *condition_g* that takes as parameters the needed local variables $\overline{x}$. The method body can normally access the fields of the object this. A condition evaluation g is defined as follows: $condition_g(\overline{x}) = $ while($\neg g$) *skip*; return null. We encode the suspend statement the same way with a *True* condition. We define an *execute_condition* method in the COG class; it executes generated condition methods. The *execute_condition* method has its own group with an infinite thread limit because any number of conditions can evaluate in parallel. More formally, we have:

$$group(execute\_condition) = g_4 \qquad \mathcal{L}_{g_4} = \infty$$

6　Translation Equivalence and Active Object Insights

Proving that MultiASP executions exactly simulate ABS semantics is not possible by direct bisimulation of the two semantics. Instead, we prove two different theorems stating under which conditions each semantics simulates the other. We present all technical details on the equivalence and the proof in the research report associated to this paper [14]. We summarise below the highlights of the proof, the principles of the underlying equivalence between MultiASP and ABS terms, the differences between the languages and the restrictions of the proof.

$$\llbracket x = e!m(\bar{e}) \rrbracket \triangleq t = e.cog(); id = e.myId();$$
$$x = t.execute(id, m, \bar{e})$$

$$\llbracket await\ x? \rrbracket \triangleq w = x.get()$$
$$\llbracket await\ g \wedge g' \rrbracket \triangleq \llbracket await\ g \rrbracket; \llbracket await\ g' \rrbracket$$

$$\llbracket x = y.get \rrbracket \triangleq \textbf{setLimitHard};$$
$$w = y.get();$$
$$\textbf{setLimitSoft};$$
$$x = y$$

$$\llbracket x = e.m(\bar{e}) \rrbracket \triangleq a = e.cog(); b = \textbf{this}.cog();$$
$$\textbf{if}(a == b)\ \{x = e.m(\bar{e})\}$$
$$\textbf{else}\ \{t = e.cog(); id = e.myId();$$
$$x = t.execute(id, m, \bar{e});$$
$$\textbf{setLimitHard};$$
$$w = x.get(); \textbf{setLimitSoft}\}$$

$$\llbracket x = e \rrbracket \triangleq x = e$$

$$\llbracket x = \textbf{new local}\ C(\bar{e}) \rrbracket \triangleq t = \textbf{this}.cog();$$
$$id = t.freshId();$$
$$no = \textbf{new}\ C(\bar{e}, t, id);$$
$$z = t.register(no, id);$$
$$x = no$$

$$\llbracket x = \textbf{new}\ C(\bar{e}) \rrbracket \triangleq newcog = \textbf{newActive}\ COG();$$
$$id = newcog.freshId();$$
$$no = \textbf{new}\ C(\bar{e}, newcog, id);$$
$$z = newcog.register(no, id);$$
$$x = no$$

$$\llbracket await\ g \rrbracket_{\bar{x}} \triangleq \textbf{if}(\neg g)\ \{\ t = \textbf{this}.cog(); id = \textbf{this}.myId();$$
$$z = t.execute\_condition(id, condition\_g, \bar{x}); w = z.get\ \}$$

$$\llbracket suspend \rrbracket \triangleq t = \textbf{this}.cog(); id = \textbf{this}.myId();$$
$$z = t.execute\_condition(id, condition\_True, \bar{x}); w = z.get$$

Fig. 8. Translational semantics from ABS to MultiASP

Communication and Request Serving Ordering. The semantics of ABS relies on a completely asynchronous communication scheme while MultiASP ensures causal ordering of requests. The equivalence can only be valid for the ABS reductions that preserve causal ordering of requests. Also, MultiASP serves requests in FIFO order, so similarly we execute a FIFO service of ABS requests, like in the existing Java backend for ABS. Note that those differences are more related to scheduling and communication patterns than to the nature of the two languages.

Shallow Translation. ABS requests, COGs and futures respectively match one-to-one MultiASP requests, active objects and futures. Likewise, except for COG objects, for each ABS object there exist several copies of this object in MultiASP, all with the same COG and the same identifier, but only one of those copies (the one hosted in the right COG) is equivalent to the ABS object.

Futures. Because of the difference between the future update mechanisms of ABS and MultiASP, the equivalence relation can follow as many local future indirections in the store as necessary. A variable holding a pointer to a future object in MultiASP is equivalent to the same variable holding directly the future reference in ABS. But also, the equivalence can follow future references in ABS: a future might have been updated transparently in MultiASP while in ABS, the explicit future read has not been performed yet.

Equating MultiASP and ABS Configurations. A crucial part of the correctness proof consists in stating whether an ABS and a MultiASP configuration are considered equivalent. The principles of this equivalence are the following:

- Equivalence can "follow futures": A MultiASP value v is equivalent to an ABS future provided the future's value is equivalent to v; indeed in MultiASP a future can be automatically updated earlier than in the ABS case.
- Objects are identified by their identifier and their COG name: the value of the object fields are meaningless except in the COG that initially created the object. It is in this COG that we check that fields are equivalent.
- Equivalence between requests distinguishes two cases. (1) active tasks: there is a single active task per COG in ABS and it must correspond to the single active thread serving an *execute* request in MultiASP. The second element in the call stack corresponds to the invoked request. (2) inactive tasks in ABS correspond either to passive requests being currently interrupted or to not-yet-served requests in MultiASP. For each task, equivalence of executed statements, of local variables, and of corresponding future is checked.

Observational Equivalence. The precise formulation of our theorems proves that the ABS behaviour is faithfully simulated by our translation and conversely. This is proven by adequately choosing the *observable* and *not observable* actions in the weak simulation. For example remote method invocation, object creation, and field assignment can be observed and faithfully simulated. The most striking observable reduction in ABS that is not always observable in MultiASP is the future value update. For example, in ABS the configurations (a) $fut(f, f')\ fut(f', \bot)$ and the configuration (b) $fut(f, \bot)$ are observationally different, whereas in MultiASP they are not. Indeed, in MultiASP, there is no process able to detect whether the first future has been updated or not. However, this example is artificial as no information is stored in the first future of configuration (a); any access to the future's value will have to follow indirections and eventually access the value that is not a future. Thus, transparency of futures and of future updates create an intrinsic difference between the two languages. This is why, in the theorem, we exclude the possibility to have a future's value being a future in the configuration. Eliminating syntactically such programs is not possible, thus we reason on reductions for which the value of a future is not a future; this is not a major restriction on expressiveness because it is still possible to have a future value that is an object containing a future (as future wrappers).

In the other direction, namely from MultiASP to ABS, the translation adds several steps in the reduction. However, the added sequences of actions never introduce concurrency so equivalence still holds because we can ignore additional local actions such as assignments and method calls that are not in the ABS program source (e.g. *myId()*).

Theorem 1 (ABS to MultiASP). *The translation simulates all ABS executions with FIFO policy and rendez-vous communications provided that no future value is a future reference.*

Theorem 2 (MultiASP to ABS). *Any reduction of the MultiASP translation corresponds to a valid ABS execution.*

Globally, our translational semantics fully respects the ABS semantics and simulates exactly all executions complying to the aforementioned restrictions, which either are already existing restrictions of the Java backend for ABS, or for which we have given relevant alternatives.

7 Conclusion

This paper tackled the question of providing active object languages, aimed at modelling and verification, with systematic deployment for distributed computing. For that, we have identified the necessary design choices for active object models and languages, involving: object referencing, language transparency, and request scheduling. These design choices have to be considered when implementing any active object language. We have introduced MultiASP, a multi-threaded active object language that has showed to be expressive enough to embody the main paradigms of ABS, featuring in particular cooperative scheduling. We demonstrated how to translate the constructs of an easy to program and verify active object language into the executable code of an efficient and scalable active object middleware. We have instantiated our approach by translating ABS into the ProActive middleware, that implements MultiASP in Java. The immediate outcome of this work is a ProActive backend for ABS. Our approach could be quite easily ported other active object languages since we reason more on active object abstractions than on language specifics. Typically, our work can be straightforwardly adapted to any active object language featuring cooperative scheduling, like Creol and JCoBox. Porting our results on AmbientTalk only requires minor adaptations. A comparison of the ProActive backend against a currently developed Java 8 backend for ABS [21] is ongoing. This analysis focuses on the different implementation approaches for efficiently encoding the ABS semantics. More generally, the provided proof of correctness highlighted the intrinsic differences between active object languages and models. This work will help active object users to choose the language that is the most adapted for their needs, and also help active object designers to identify the implication of specific language constructs and abstractions.

References

1. Agha, G., Hewitt, C.: Concurrent programming using actors: exploiting large-scale parallelism. In: Maheshwari, S.N. (ed.) Foundations of Software Technology and Theoretical Computer Science. LNCS, vol. 206, pp. 19–41. Springer, In Foundations of Software Technology and Theoretical Computer Science (1985)
2. Albert, E., Arenas, P., Flores-Montoya, A., Genaim, S., Gómez-Zamalloa, M., Martin-Martin, E., Puebla, G., Román-Díez, G.: SACO: static analyzer for concurrent objects. In: Ábrahám, E., Havelund, K. (eds.) TACAS 2014 (ETAPS). LNCS, vol. 8413, pp. 562–567. Springer, Heidelberg (2014)
3. Bezirgiannis, N., de Boer, F.: ABS: a high-level modeling language for cloud-aware programming. In: Freivalds, R.M., Engels, G., Catania, B. (eds.) SOFSEM 2016: Theory and Practice of Computer Science. LNCS, vol. 9587, pp. 433–444. Springer, Heidelberg (2016)

4. de Boer, F.S., Clarke, D., Johnsen, E.B.: A complete guide to the future. In: De Nicola, R. (ed.) ESOP 2007. LNCS, vol. 4421, pp. 316–330. Springer, Heidelberg (2007)
5. Brandauer, S., et al.: Parallel objects for multicores: a glimpse at the parallel language encore. In: Bernardo, M., Johnsen, E.B. (eds.) Formal Methods for Multicore Programming. LNCS, vol. 9104, pp. 1–56. Springer, Heidelberg (2015)
6. Caromel, D., Henrio, L.: A Theory of Distributed Objects: Asynchrony — Mobility — Groups — Components. Springer, Heidelberg (2005)
7. Dedecker, J., Van Cutsem, T., Mostinckx, S., D'Hondt, T., De Meuter, W.: Ambient-oriented programming in ambienttalk. In: Thomas, D. (ed.) ECOOP 2006. LNCS, vol. 4067, pp. 230–254. Springer, Heidelberg (2006)
8. Din, C.C., Bubel, R., Hähnle, R.: KeY-ABS: a deductive verification tool for the concurrent modelling language ABS. In: Felty, A.P., Middeldorp, A. (eds.) Automated Deduction - CADE-25. LNCS, vol. 9195, pp. 517–526. Springer, Heidelberg (2015)
9. Flanagan, C., Felleisen, M.: The semantics of future and its use in program optimization. In: POPL 1995. ACM (1995)
10. Giachino, E., Laneve, C., Lienhardt, M.: A framework for deadlock detection in ABS. J. Softw. Syst. Model. (2014). doi:10.1007/s10270-014-0444-y, https://hal.inria.fr/hal-01229046/file/longDF4ABS.pdf
11. Haller, P., Odersky, M.: Scala actors: unifying thread-based and event-based programming. Theor. Comput. Sci. **410**(2–3), 202–220 (2009)
12. Henrio, L., Huet, F., István, Z.: Multi-threaded active objects. In: De Nicola, R., Julien, C. (eds.) COORDINATION 2013. LNCS, vol. 7890, pp. 90–104. Springer, Heidelberg (2013)
13. Henrio, L., Rochas, J.: Declarative scheduling for active objects. In: SAC 2014. ACM (2014)
14. Henrio, L., Rochas, J.: From Modelling to Systematic Deployment of Distributed Active Objects - Extended Version. Research report I3S, April 2016
15. Johnsen, E.B., Hähnle, R., Schäfer, J., Schlatte, R., Steffen, M.: ABS: a core language for abstract behavioral specification. In: Aichernig, B.K., de Boer, F.S., Bonsangue, M.M. (eds.) Formal Methods for Components and Objects. LNCS, vol. 6957, pp. 142–164. Springer, Heidelberg (2011)
16. Johnsen, E.B., Owe, O., Yu, I.C.: Creol: a type-safe object-oriented model for distributed concurrent systems. Theor. Comput. Sci. **365**(1–2), 23–66 (2006)
17. Johnsen, E.B., Schlatte, R., Tarifa, S.L.T.: Integrating deployment architectures and resource consumption in timed object-oriented model. J. Log. Algebraic Methods Program. **84**(1), 67–91 (2015)
18. Lavender, R.G., Schmidt, D.C.: Active object: an object behavioral pattern for concurrent programming. In: Pattern Languages of Program Design, vol. 2 (1996)
19. Rochas, J., Henrio, L.: A ProActive Backend for ABS: from Modelling to Deployment. Research Report RR-8596, September 2014
20. Schäfer, J., Poetzsch-Heffter, A.: JCoBox: generalizing active objects to concurrent components. In: D'Hondt, T. (ed.) ECOOP 2010. LNCS, vol. 6183, pp. 275–299. Springer, Heidelberg (2010)
21. Serbanescu, V., Azadbakht, K., de Boer, F., Nagarajagowda, C., Nobakht, B.: A design pattern for optimizations in data intensive applications using ABS and JAVA 8. Pract. Exp. Concurrency Comput. **28**, 374–385 (2016)

An Interference-Free Programming Model for Network Objects

Mischael Schill[1][✉], Christopher M. Poskitt[2], and Bertrand Meyer[3,4,5]

[1] Department of Computer Science, ETH Zürich, Zürich, Switzerland
mischael.schill@inf.ethz.ch
[2] Singapore University of Technology and Design, Singapore, Singapore
chris_poskitt@sutd.edu.sg
[3] Politecnico di Milano, Milan, Italy
[4] Innopolis University, Kazan, Russia
[5] Université Paul Sabatier, Toulouse, France
bertrand.meyer@inf.ethz.ch

Abstract. Network objects are a simple and natural abstraction for distributed object-oriented programming. Languages that support network objects, however, often leave synchronization to the user, along with its associated pitfalls, such as data races and the possibility of failure. In this paper, we present D-SCOOP, a distributed programming model that allows for interference-free and transaction-like reasoning on (potentially multiple) network objects, with synchronization handled automatically, and network failures managed by a compensation mechanism. We achieve this by leveraging the runtime semantics of a multi-threaded object-oriented concurrency model, directly generalizing it with a message-based protocol for efficiently coordinating remote objects. We present our pathway to fusing these contrasting but complementary ideas, and evaluate the performance overhead of the automatic synchronization in D-SCOOP, finding that it comes close to—or outperforms—explicit locking-based synchronization in Java RMI.

1 Introduction

Inter-device communication is becoming ubiquitous, and the number of connected devices is growing everyday. With this ubiquity comes an increasing demand for programmers to be able to write reliable distributed software, yet this is no simple task. Challenging errors such as data races and deadlocks can arise from subtle mistakes in synchronization code; and the failure of individual devices can block whole systems in the absence of appropriate recovery protocols.

Various language abstractions have been proposed to make it easier to write distributed programs. One such abstraction, natural for the object-oriented paradigm, is that of *network objects* [2]: objects whose methods can be invoked over a network. By handling communication in method calls, network objects allow for local and remote objects to be treated uniformly, without regard to where they are

© IFIP International Federation for Information Processing 2016
Published by Springer International Publishing Switzerland 2016. All Rights Reserved
A. Lluch Lafuente and J. Proença (Eds.): COORDINATION 2016, LNCS 9686, pp. 227–244, 2016.
DOI: 10.1007/978-3-319-39519-7_14

physically located. In principle an elegant generalization; in practice, languages supporting them are often lightweight on synchronization, leaving the user to manage it explicitly, and potentially exposing them to the aforementioned errors.

Many of these pitfalls of synchronization are not unique to distribution: they occur in multi-threaded concurrent programming too. Several languages and libraries attempt to make it easier and safer to write concurrent programs, providing their users with high-level abstractions as diverse as transactional memory [23], block-dispatching [10], actors [1], and active objects [14]. Given the many shared synchronization challenges, a number of these abstractions have been successfully applied across novel distributed programming approaches, exemplified by languages such as Creol [12], JCoBox [21], and AmbientTalk [6].

A family of concurrency abstractions that (until the present paper) had not been generalized to distributed programming were those provided by SCOOP [25], despite their potential to naturally complement the network objects abstraction and to address some of its shortcomings. SCOOP is an object-oriented concurrency model that provides data-race freedom by construction, and strong guarantees about the order in which requests are executed by concurrently running processes. The synchronization provided by its runtime automatically excludes interfering calls, making it possible to reason independently about different blocks of code over multiple concurrent objects, almost as if each block is "sequential". The ethos of the SCOOP approach—stick to the mental models programmers already know well (in this case sequential programming)—is aligned with that of the network objects abstraction, and challenged us to explore how they could complement the strengths of each other.

Our Contributions. The main outcome of this paper is D-SCOOP, a distributed programming model resulting from the fusion of the network objects abstraction with the runtime of the SCOOP concurrency model. The strong reasoning guarantees of the latter are directly generalized to provide interference-free and transaction-like reasoning on (potentially multiple) network objects, without the programmer having to worry about how to achieve it. The basis of this fusion is a message-based protocol for coordinating remote objects, which includes an efficient and novel two-phase locking algorithm for establishing the SCOOP order guarantees without prolonged periods of blocking. Furthermore, we adapt from transactional memory the recovery technique of compensations, in order for D-SCOOP to be able to restore consistency when clients fail mid-computation. This paper presents our pathway to fusing these independent, but complementary ideas. We furthermore evaluate a prototype implementation of D-SCOOP to investigate the performance overhead of its automatic synchronization mechanisms, finding that they come close to—and in some circumstances outperform—explicit locking-based synchronization in the Java RMI realization of network objects.

For the distributed programming community, this paper presents a programming model with interference-free and transaction-like reasoning for distributed objects, and a runtime that effectively handles the synchronization. For the SCOOP community, it presents a generalization of the classical SCOOP concurrency model to distribution in a way that maintains the guarantees of the core abstractions. For language designers, it presents a simple yet effective distributed programming abstraction (and descriptions of how we realized it) that could be transferred to other object-oriented languages.

Plan of the Paper. After introducing the necessary technical background of network objects and SCOOP (Sect. 2), we show how they fuse together in D-SCOOP, our distributed programming model (Sect. 3). We go into more depth on how objects are controlled to avoid interference (Sect. 4) and how compensation helps in managing failure (Sect. 5). Our prototype is then evaluated against Java RMI (Sect. 6), before we review some related work (Sect. 7) and conclude (Sect. 8).

2   Background: Network Objects and Scoop

Our work combines networks objects—a distributed programming abstraction— with SCOOP, a concurrency model that handles synchronization in its runtime and provides strong reasoning guarantees. We present the necessary technical background of these concepts in the context of a running example.

Network Objects. A *network object* is an object whose methods can be invoked over a network. The abstraction is a simple but natural generalization of standard objects to distributed contexts: the programmer interacts with their interfaces in the same way as before, and without regard to where the object is physically located. Communication is handled in the method calls, and is typically synchronous to mimic regular method calls. Network objects first appeared in Modula-3 [2], and have since strongly influenced Java's Remote Method Invocation (RMI) API as well as the Common Object Request Broker Architecture (CORBA) standard.

While implementations of network objects vary, the abstraction is typically light-weight on synchronization, leaving this difficulty to the user, to the point that multiple clients can concurrently execute the same method (introducing the possibility of data races). Simple mechanics such as **synchronized** in Java are not always sufficient to ensure atomicity. Consider for example the simple bank account **transfer** method in Listing 1, which allows some client to transfer an amount (**am**) of money from a source (**s**) account to a target (**t**) account. If the system is single-threaded and the accounts are local, then the method is correct. If the accounts can be accessed concurrently, then locks or other measures are required to ensure the atomicity of **transfer**. If however the accounts are remote and can be accessed concurrently as network objects, then we must adapt again.

```
transfer (s, t: ACCOUNT;              transfer (s, t: separate ACCOUNT;
         am: NATURAL)                          am: NATURAL)
do                                    do
    if s.balance >= am then               if s.balance >= am then
        s.set_balance (s.balance - am)        s.set_balance (s.balance - am)
        t.set_balance (t.balance + am)        t.set_balance (t.balance + am)
    else -- Notify user                   else -- Notify user
    end                                   end
end                                   end
```

Listing 1: Bank account transfer methods: sequential (left) and in SCOOP (right)

One solution is to use locks and expose them as network objects, but this poses risk, e.g. if a client loses its connection before having a chance to release its locks. Another solution is to hide the synchronization within additional methods in the account class, but this is still challenging to implement without introducing concurrency errors such as races or deadlocks. Either way, the simplicity of the network object abstraction suffers with the complexity of synchronizing correctly; hence our aim to elegantly integrate it with a concurrency model that can manage such complexity in its runtime.

SCOOP. SCOOP [25] is a concurrent object-oriented programming model that aims to preserve the well-understood modes of reasoning enjoyed by sequential programs, such as pre- and postcondition reasoning over blocks of code. Programmers are provided with simple abstractions for expressing concurrency, with the runtime itself responsible for correctly handling synchronization. We describe SCOOP in the context of its principal implementation for Eiffel [8], but remark that the ideas generalize to other object-oriented languages (e.g. Java [24]).

In SCOOP, every object is associated with a *process* (which we call its *handler*), a concurrent thread of execution with the exclusive right to call methods on the objects it handles. In this context, object references may point to objects with the same handler (*non-separate* objects) or to objects with distinct handlers (*separate* objects). Method calls on non-separate objects are executed immediately by the shared process. To make a call on a separate object, however, a *request* must be sent to the handler of that object to process it: if the method is a *command* (i.e. it does not return a result) then it is executed asynchronously, leading to concurrency; if it is a *query* (i.e. a result is returned and must be waited for) then it is executed synchronously. Note that processes cannot synchronize via shared memory: only by exchanging requests.

The possibility for objects to have different handlers is captured in the type system by the keyword separate. To request method calls on objects of separate type, programmers simply make the calls within *separate blocks*: these are the bodies of any methods that have separate objects as formal parameters. SCOOP provides guarantees about the order in which calls in these blocks are executed, so as to help programmers avoid concurrency errors. In particular, method calls on separate objects will be logged as requests by their handlers in the order that they are given in the program text; furthermore, there will be no intervening requests logged from other handlers. These guarantees exclude data races by construction, and allow programmers to apply sequential reasoning within separate blocks independently of the rest of the program.

Consider the concurrent version of `transfer` in Listing 1, in which bank account objects have concurrently running handlers. Suppose that a process calls the method `transfer (acc1, acc2, 100)` on separate accounts `acc1` and `acc2`. The body of the method contains two commands on these separate objects—thus, two asynchronously executed requests—that transfer the stated amount from the first account to the second. It also contains `balance` queries which are executed synchronously. The SCOOP guarantees ensure that while the process is inside the body of `transfer`, no other process can log intervening requests on `acc1` or `acc2`. As a result, it would not be possible for another process to observe the balances of the two accounts in an intermediate state, i.e. when the money has been withdrawn from the former but not credited to the latter. The body of `transfer` can thus be reasoned about sequentially and independently of the rest of the program. This additional control over the order in which requests are logged (i.e. that requests cannot be interrupted) is the key distinction SCOOP has over other message-passing-based models such as the actor model, or active objects.

SCOOP provides some more advanced concurrency mechanisms beyond the focus of this paper. Most notable are its generalization of method preconditions to support condition synchronization on **separate** objects, and its support for efficient data sharing between processes sharing memory via "passive" data objects that can be accessed directly (i.e. without the overhead of message passing). We refer to [18,20] respectively for more detailed discussions of these concepts.

SCOOP Runtime. The concurrent programming abstractions presented rely on the existence of a runtime that can correctly and efficiently realize them. At the core of SCOOP's runtime is a simple execution model for managing requests that are sent between processes. Each process is associated with a "queue of queues" [25], that is, a FIFO queue itself containing (possibly several) FIFO subqueues for storing incoming requests. Each of these subqueues represents a "private area" for some other process to log requests, in program text order, and without interference from other processes (since they have their own subqueues). Figure 1 visualizes three processes (p_1, p_2, p_3) simultaneously logging requests (green blocks) on another process (p_0). The process p_0 is handling the subqueues one-by-one in the order that they were created, and handles the requests within them in the order that they were logged there, hence ensuring the SCOOP reasoning guarantees.

Consider again the process that calls `transfer (acc1, acc2, 100)` on two separate accounts, `acc1` and `acc2`. Under the current runtime, the handlers of `acc1` and `acc2` both generate a private subqueue on which the calling process can log requests (i.e. the `balance` queries and `set_balance` commands) without interruption for the duration of the block. Should another process also need to log requests on an account, then a new private subqueue is generated for it and its requests can be logged without waiting.

We remark that earlier versions of the SCOOP runtime additionally provided timing guarantees by not allowing processes to enqueue requests concurrently [17]. A formal comparison with the current semantics is given in [5].

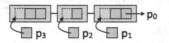

Fig. 1. Three processes (p_1, p_2, p_3) logging requests on another (p_0)

3   Overview of Distributed Scoop

In this section we present D-SCOOP (for Distributed SCOOP), which combines network objects and the SCOOP synchronization semantics into a single, distributed programming model that maintains the simplicity of the original abstractions. We present an overview of its architecture and communication protocol, and explain how separate calls are generalized to potentially remote objects (Sects. 4 and 5 describe in more detail how control of remote objects is achieved in D-SCOOP, and how the system compensates for unresponsive clients).

A prototype implementation of the D-SCOOP model is available online [7]. Our prototype builds upon the SCOOP support for Eiffel in EiffelStudio [8], which implements the model using threads and shared memory. D-SCOOP generalizes the implementation, allowing for multiple instances of potentially remote SCOOP programs to communicate, under-the-hood, by asynchronous message passing.

Architecture. In D-SCOOP, an instance of a SCOOP program is called a *node*. A node can open a connection to another node through a network socket, which is then shared by all of its processes. A node can request the *index object* of another node, which is a user-defined object that typically provides the API of the node, or some form of registry. It is valid for a node to not supply an index object, typically if it is a client in a client-server style setup. To be able to accept incoming connections from other nodes, a node must start a *server* and provide its own index object (or a factory that generates them). Every node in a D-SCOOP network has a unique *identifier* (ID), which is independent of any other IDs such as IP addresses. Object references in D-SCOOP include this node ID, along with their object and process identifiers (as in classical SCOOP), with the latter important for determining the number of processes involved in a separate block.

The nodes in D-SCOOP networks communicate, via their connections, using an asynchronous message-passing scheme. Messages conform to a protocol and can be one of two types: a *request*[1] or a *reply*. Requests are sent from a *client* node to a *supplier*, defining work for the supplier to do. Replies are sent back from the supplier to the client indicating the outcome.

Within nodes, we rely on existing mechanisms of SCOOP for garbage collecting local objects and processes. D-SCOOP however must also account for objects used by multiple nodes. To achieve this, we use a distributed garbage collection algorithm similar to that of Birrell et al. [3].

Requests and Replies. Messages in the D-SCOOP communication protocol have *subjects* which convey their intended semantics. Messages that are requests can have one of many different subjects which we outline in the following. Replies however only indicate success ($\boxed{\text{OK}}$) or failure ($\boxed{\text{FAIL}}$), sometimes with additional arguments, such as the result of a query call.

The simplest request subjects are $\boxed{\text{HELLO}}$, $\boxed{\text{PING}}$ and $\boxed{\text{INDEX}}$, which respectively initialize a connection between nodes, test whether an existing one is still

---

[1] Note that these are distinct from the requests used for inter-process communication in SCOOP.

alive, and request the index object of the supplier node (which typically provides an API of methods for retrieving more objects).

A number of requests are required to realize a separate block involving remote objects. A $\boxed{\text{PRELOCK}}$ request announces that a process in a client node wishes to log calls on one or more processes in a supplier node. When a supplier is ready, the client can issue a $\boxed{\text{LOCK}}$ request to announce it is now entering the separate block. Following this, it can issue requests corresponding to asynchronous method calls ($\boxed{\text{CALL}}$), synchronous calls ($\boxed{\text{SCALL}}$), and queries ($\boxed{\text{QCALL}}$). To announce leaving the separate block, the client sends an $\boxed{\text{UNLOCK}}$ request. (We describe in more detail how these requests establish control in Sect. 4.)

Requests with the subjects $\boxed{\text{SHARE}}$ and $\boxed{\text{RELEASE}}$ are respectively used for obtaining and revoking permission for given object references to be shared with third party nodes. They are used by D-SCOOP for garbage collecting.

Finally, $\boxed{\text{AWAIT}}$ and $\boxed{\text{READY}}$ requests are used to implement condition synchronization on remote objects. In short: if the condition does not hold, the client process issues an $\boxed{\text{AWAIT}}$ request before going to sleep. This instructs the supplier to wake it up with a $\boxed{\text{READY}}$ request once the state of the remote objects changes, so that the condition can be checked again.

Message Handling. Incoming messages are handled by the request handlers of D-SCOOP nodes in multiple stages, depending on their subjects. If an incoming message has the subject $\boxed{\text{HELLO}}$, $\boxed{\text{PING}}$, $\boxed{\text{SHARE}}$, or $\boxed{\text{RELEASE}}$, then it is handled directly. If a message is a reply, then it is relayed to the appropriate process within the node. Messages addressed to other nodes are relayed.

For messages concerning separate blocks and condition synchronization, a more careful treatment is required. In D-SCOOP, every node has a special designated *proxy process* for handling incoming lock and call requests. Associated with these proxy processes are *proxy objects*, which are surrogates (or placeholders) for actual remote objects, holding references to them. This additional layer is used to catch special contexts in which calls are treated differently. For lack of space we do not go into detail, but mention two of the most important: callbacks (see [20]), and a SCOOP extension for passive data objects (see [18]).

To minimize the overhead of proxy processes and objects, they are created only when needed and removed when they are not. For example, if not existing already, receiving a $\boxed{\text{LOCK}}$ request with some given object identifiers will trigger the creation of a proxy process on that node and proxies for those objects. And when no longer in use by local processes, they can be collected by the local SCOOP garbage collector.

Remote Calls in Separate Blocks. The communication protocol presented is ultimately the glue that allows for network objects to be used within the SCOOP framework. Our aim was to make the fusion of these concepts as seamless as possible: programmers should not need to be aware of the communication protocol for network objects, and the core abstractions of SCOOP should not need to be fundamentally reinvented to accommodate the extension.

In D-SCOOP we were able to maintain the original abstractions provided by separate blocks, while also providing a natural generalization to support objects residing on other nodes. When a process needs to make a call on a **separate** object, there are now three possible cases to distinguish. If the target object shares the same process (and thus, obviously, the same node), the call is executed immediately—as in SCOOP. If the target object has a distinct process but on the same node, the process logs a request in a private subqueue for the caller (see Sect. 2)—as in SCOOP. If the target object has a distinct process on a remote node, however, the D-SCOOP communication protocol comes into play, and a $\boxed{\text{CALL}}$ message is sent to the remote node.

4   Controlling Remote Objects

We have presented an overview of the D-SCOOP architecture, its messaging protocol, and its generalization of **separate** blocks to support calls on remote objects. In this section, we describe how control of remote objects and thus distributed separate blocks are achieved.

In D-SCOOP, separate blocks are handled in three phases: (i) the *prelock phase*, for ensuring a correct ordering; (ii) the *issuing phase*, for enqueuing calls; and (iii) the *execution phase*, for executing calls. The issuing phase happens strictly after the prelock phase. While the execution phase cannot start before the issuing phase, the two can otherwise overlap due to asynchronicity.

Prelock Phase. In standard SCOOP, if a process enters a separate block, the processes handling the **separate** objects generate private subqueues for logging calls (see Sect. 2 and Fig. 1). In D-SCOOP however, if a process enters a separate block involving **separate** objects on remote nodes, messages must be sent to trigger the generation of subqueues in a way that preserves the usual reasoning guarantees. We refer to this messaging phase as the *prelock phase*.

A client node seeking to enter a separate block involving remote objects must first announce its intention by sending $\boxed{\text{PRELOCK}}$ requests to the nodes they reside on. This is done in a fixed order (a global order based on node IDs) to avoid deadlocks, and one-at-a-time; an $\boxed{\text{OK}}$ reply must be received before the next $\boxed{\text{PRELOCK}}$ is sent. Once the last such request is successful, the client node announces that it is entering the separate block and will start issuing calls. This announcement is made via $\boxed{\text{LOCK}}$ requests, which can be sent asynchronously in any order. By replying with $\boxed{\text{OK}}$, the supplier nodes are acknowledging that the involved processes have created private subqueues and are ready to enqueue calls from the client. Figure 2 exemplifies this phase for a client node C that wishes to enter a separate block involving remote objects on supplier nodes $N_1, \ldots N_n$. Here, an arrow denotes the transmission of a message, with its subject given at the end (additional parameters are not visualized).

When multiple nodes are entering prelock phases involving common supplier nodes, blocking must occur in order to maintain the separate block order guarantees. In particular, if a $\boxed{\text{PRELOCK}}$ message is sent but the supplier is already involved in the prelock phase of a competing node, then the system blocks on that message. Instead of blocking for the whole of the competing node's separate block, D-SCOOP permits a more fine-grained and efficient solution. In particular,

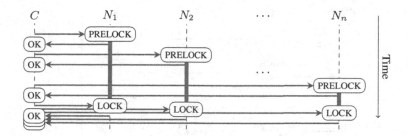

Fig. 2. Prelock phase: a process on node C is entering a separate block involving separate objects on remote nodes $N_1, \ldots N_n$

it only blocks until the competing node leaves its prelock phase and starts issuing calls. That is to say, D-SCOOP only blocks while "setting up" the subqueues in a correct order; competing issuing phases can otherwise safely run concurrently.

Issuing and Execution Phases. The prelock phase ends and the issuing phase begins when the final $\boxed{\text{LOCK}}$ request is successful. At this point, the processes handling all the involved remote objects are ready to enqueue calls. In most circumstances, commands on remote objects are requested via asynchronous $\boxed{\text{CALL}}$ messages, and queries are requested via synchronous $\boxed{\text{QCALL}}$ messages. The supplier nodes enqueue commands and immediately reply with an $\boxed{\text{OK}}$. When a query is received however, the supplier node enqueues it, but only replies once it has been executed (passing the result in an additional parameter of the $\boxed{\text{OK}}$ message).

The execution phase begins with the execution of the first logged call. If all the calls are asynchronous, it can take place strictly after the issuing phase. The issuing phase ends on sending the $\boxed{\text{UNLOCK}}$ message; the execution phase ends on processing it.

```
withdraw (s: separate ACCOUNT; am: NATURAL)
do
    if s.balance >= am then
        s.set_balance (s.balance - am)
    else -- Notify user
    end
end
```

Listing 2: Bank account withdrawal method in D-SCOOP

Example Communication. We return to our running bank account example, which we extend with a simple method `withdraw` (Listing 2) for withdrawing a given amount from a given account that we assume to be remote. The method first synchronously queries the remote object to check that the balance is sufficient, before asynchronously decreasing the balance.

Suppose we have a running D-SCOOP system with two bank accounts on different nodes (A_1, A_2). Suppose now that a client node (C_1) is trying to `transfer` an amount from A_1 to A_2, while another client node (C_2) is trying to `withdraw`

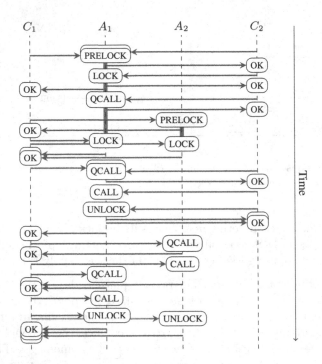

Fig. 3. All three phases: a process on C_1 calls `transfer` on A_1 and A_2; a process on C_2 concurrently calls `withdraw` on A_1

an amount from A_1. Recall that the bodies of both methods are separate blocks (involving, respectively, **separate** accounts on A_1, A_2 and A_1). Figure 3 visualizes the messages exchanged in one possible behavior.

Observe that both clients initially send a PRELOCK request to A_1. The request from C_2 is received first and is therefore answered immediately; meanwhile, C_1 blocks. Since C_2 only seeks control over a process on A_1, it proceeds to send a LOCK request, thus completing its prelock phase and generating its private subqueue on A_1. This allows C_1 to unblock and its first PRELOCK request finally succeeds.

Since the prelock phase of one client can take place in parallel to the issuing and execution phases of another, C_2 already starts issuing calls before C_1 concludes its prelock phase. In particular, it requests the `balance` query (via QCALL) which is executed synchronously (and the balance amount returned). Following this, C_1 requests a PRELOCK on A_2 (which is uncontended), before completing its prelock phase by sending LOCK requests to A_1 and A_2.

At this point, both C_1 and C_2 issue `balance` queries (QCALL)—the former is evaluating its conditional guard, and the latter is evaluating the expression in the input of `s.set_balance(s.balance - am)`. Since C_2 completed its prelock first, its private subqueue on A_1 is ahead of the subqueue for C_1, and so its call is executed first. Following this, C_2 requests an asynchronous command (CALL) to update the balance, and then exits its separate block via an $\boxed{\text{UNLOCK}}$ request. Once acknowledged, C_2 knows that the whole transaction (`balance` and then `set_balance`) was successful, and its effects become visible to other clients. Once the $\boxed{\text{OK}}$ corresponding to its earlier $\boxed{\text{QCALL}}$ arrives, C_1 can resume issuing the remaining calls in its separate block before exiting via $\boxed{\text{UNLOCK}}$ requests to A_1 and A_2.

Note that the reasoning guarantees of the separate blocks have been maintained. The calls are executed in program text order and without intervening calls from other nodes: within a separate block, multiple `balance` calls in sequence thus always return the same result. The combination of the prelock phase and the underlying queue of queues semantics prevents the possibility of interleavings that break this.

5   Compensating for Failure

Our presentation of D-SCOOP has thus far focused on the challenge and intricacies of combining the network objects abstraction with a concurrency model and runtime. In this section, we turn our attention to a topic that cannot be ignored in the setting of distributed computing: coping with failure.

While failure can often be managed simply—a fixed timeout is used, for example, to manage it in prelock phases—failure in the middle of a separate block, when only some of the side-effecting commands have been issued, needs a more elaborate solution. We introduce *compensation*, D-SCOOP's mechanism for reacting to such failure, and demonstrate its use on our running example.

Compensation. In D-SCOOP, upon failure of a supplier, the client is informed using exceptions, and can react to it appropriately in a rescue-clause. However, the suppliers in separate blocks are in general oblivious to the status of the client. Our solution is to introduce *compensation*, a supplier-side mechanism for reacting to client nodes that become unresponsive or disconnect prematurely. The technique registers user-provided closures on suppliers that, before releasing objects controlled by disconnected clients, are executed to restore consistency.

The basic technique is adapted from well-established usage in transactions, in particular, for recovering from long-running transactions or transactions with side effects. It fits naturally with the D-SCOOP model, given that separate blocks are transaction-like in the sense that other clients cannot observe the separate objects in intermediate states. One can think of a $\boxed{\text{LOCK}}$ and $\boxed{\text{UNLOCK}}$ pair as being the beginning and end of a transaction; after $\boxed{\text{UNLOCK}}$ is acknowledged, all changes become visible.

The scope of compensation is the issuing phase, and encompasses all executed calls on processes that have been acquired during the prelock phase (and only those processes). In the case of nested separate blocks, the outer block has to take into account that the effects of the inner block are already visible if an $\boxed{\text{UNLOCK}}$ was issued. This is different to most definitions of nested transactions, in which the inner transaction always finishes together with the outer transaction.

Defining Compensation. Compensation closures are provided by the user as the input of special methods for registering compensation. (We remark that

closures are given with the Eiffel keyword **agent**, and can refer to existing methods.) It is possible to define them in the client or the supplier. A client-defined
compensation closure is registered before the call to the method to be compen-
sated (and is ignored by the supplier if no request follows). A supplier-defined
compensation closure is provided within the called method. The latter comes
with the advantage that compensation is defined together with the method, but
the former allows for more flexibility: different compensations can be defined
depending on where the call is made, which is particularly useful for methods
that do not always need compensation.

(a) Client-defined compensation   (b) Supplier-defined compensation

```
...                                    set_balance (nb: NATURAL)
    t.compensate (agent                    do
        t.set_balance (t.balance))             compensate (agent
    t.set_balance (t.balance + am)                 set_balance (balance))
...                                            balance := nb
                                       end
```

Listing 3: A set_balance method together with possible compensation

Consider the simple method **set_balance** for bank account objects (Listing 3)
which sets the **balance** of an account to some provided input. The listing also
includes examples of how to make it compensable. On the left is a snippet of the
body of **transfer**, now annotated with client-defined compensation before the
call. On the right is supplier-defined compensation, provided at the beginning of
the method body. In both cases, the **balance** argument to the closure (**agent**)
is evaluated to the original balance, so it will restore the old balance if called.

Implementing Compensation. Upon receiving a [LOCK] request, a supplier
node stores the IDs of the newly requested processes in a stack. This stack is
mainly used to identify which processes need to be released upon [UNLOCK]. Each
of the process entries also contains a reference to a set of compensation closures,
extracted from the program text. These closures are accompanied by relative
timestamps, so that within all the sets for this client each number is unique and
a later registration has a strictly higher number than an earlier one. Whenever
a process is unlocked normally (i.e. not due to premature disconnection) the
respective set is cleared. However, if a client node disconnects prematurely, all
sets associated with the client are merged and then ordered by the timestamps.
The execution of the compensation closures is done in reverse order.

Figure 4 shows the call stack caused by a remote client calling the method a
and then h. The targets of a, b, c, d and h are owned by process P_1, while the
targets of the calls e, f, and g are owned by process P_2. During the execution
of c, P_1 acquires control over P_2 to execute. After a is finished, the client sends
another request to execute h before releasing P_1.

We now take a look at three failure scenarios, all of them due to a premature
disconnect by the client. If the client disconnects before a is executed, nothing
happens. The client's control over P_1 is simply lifted. The second case is more

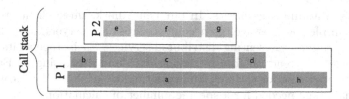

Fig. 4. Example call stack

complex: if the client disconnects while a is executing, the calls a, b, ... g are all executed as requested. Since P_1 is issuing the [UNLOCK] request to P_2 before finishing itself, the changes done by e, f, g are visible. The disconnect then causes the compensation closures of d, c, b, a to be executed before control over P_1 is released. Consequently, the compensation of c has to deal with the fact that the changes due to e, f, g are already visible.

If the client issued the call to h but got lost before sending the [UNLOCK] request, the situation is similar, with the one difference being that the compensation of h is executed before the others.

6   Evaluation

We evaluated D-SCOOP against Java RMI to gauge its performance against a well-established and widely used approach based on network objects. We sought to collect evidence towards answering two questions. First, is there a performance overhead associated with the automatic synchronization in D-SCOOP, and does it become incommensurate with the effort to manually write synchronization code? Second, do the language abstractions of D-SCOOP facilitate simpler code?

Example Selection. D-SCOOP and Java RMI have many differences: not only in the model, but also in terms of the underlying programming languages (Eiffel and Java) which have many points of variation regarding performance and compilers. In this context, we devised a set of four microbenchmarks isolated to comparing the performance of calls: (i) *command call*, in which a single client sends a series of command calls to the supplier; (ii) *query call*, analogous, but with query calls; (iii) *locking and command call*, in which a few clients compete to control a supplier object and send a single command call; and (iv) *locking and query call*, analogous, but with a single query call.

In addition to microbenchmarks, we also evaluated D-SCOOP against Java RMI on three larger examples. First, *dining philosophers*, a classical example where multiple objects (forks) are repeatedly controlled. For this benchmark, all philosophers and forks reside on different nodes, and we assume that eating, using the fork, and thinking take no time. Second, a more practical example: a *log server*, in which various events are logged. Here, there are multiple log servers for redundancy, meaning that copies of logs can still be retrieved if one fails. To ensure a consistent ordering across servers, a client must control all of them before adding the entries. In our benchmark, three clients repeatedly generate a simple log message, gain control across the servers, and then place it. Third, a *pipeline* representing distributed services. Each stage waits until the previous stages are ready before retrieving data and processing it. Each stage provides one operation of the well known formula $\sqrt{a^2 + b^2}$. We measured the time the final stage needed for a specific number of calculations.

For Java RMI, explicit locking was used to establish a comparable flexibility in the clients. Furthermore, the Java code explicitly orders the locks so as to avoid deadlocks. The source code of the examples and of D-Scoop itself can be found on our supplementary material webpage [7].

Performance. Overall, we found that despite the potential overhead of automatic synchronization, D-Scoop's performance is competitive with—and can be superior to—explicit locking-based synchronization in Java RMI. The results of the performance evaluation are listed in Fig. 5 and are the averages of 30 runs; we used two off-the-shelf laptops connected by an ethernet cable. The microbenchmarks show that the performance of both D-Scoop and Java RMI is similar when just issuing commands or queries. D-Scoop commands are a bit quicker than D-Scoop queries due to them being asynchronous, whereas in RMI both are synchronous. When it comes to the control microbenchmarks, the built-in synchronization in D-Scoop allows for a more significant improvement in speed, both for synchronous and asynchronous calls. However, the synchronization overhead prevents the asynchronous advantage of Control/Command translating into faster performance than Control/Query.

For both the dining philosophers and the logging example, the fact that the prelock phase can be done in parallel with the issuing and execution phase of another client proves to be a significant advantage in comparison to RMI. In addition, the logging example shows the advantage of asynchronous calls in D-Scoop. The underlying semantics make it possible to ensure control over multiple nodes and have multiple clients issuing asynchronous calls at the same

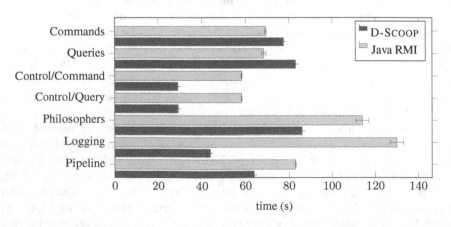

Fig. 5. Benchmark results: each run involved several thousand iterations (see [7])

Table 1. Code complexity

	Classes		Features		Instructions	
	RMI	D-Scoop	RMI	D-Scoop	RMI	D-Scoop
Microbenchmarks	3	2	8	6	19	13
Dining philosophers	3	2	6	3	18	10
Logging	6	3	16	9	23	10
Pipelines	2	1	10	16	62	42

time. The pipeline example has less congestion around the protected objects; here, the advantage of D-Scoop lies solely in slightly fewer messages sent due to more powerful synchronization mechanics.

Simplicity. Our second question asked whether the language abstractions also yield simpler code. For our seven benchmarks, we recorded: (i) the number of classes involved, excluding primitive types, classes, and strings, and ignoring the RMI remote interface; (ii) the number of features (i.e. attributes and methods), ignoring the Java "getters" in RMI since they just return an otherwise counted attribute; and (iii) the number of written instructions, excluding boilerplate code. This ensures that the differences are only due to synchronization. Table 1 lists the results.

As can be seen, the solutions in D-Scoop are much more compact across the three measurements. In the case of advanced techniques such as condition synchronization—an in-depth discussion is omitted for brevity—the complexity of RMI increases further still. Note that not included in the RMI examples are compensation and the automatic releasing of locks, since they are difficult to achieve in that framework. Also, although the usage of a lock or semaphore is counted as a class, its features are not counted in the feature column since they are already provided by the library. We remark that these numbers only indicate that D-Scoop programs are more compact than their RMI counterparts. What we leave to future work is a study of users themselves to determine whether the D-Scoop abstractions are easier to read and program with, regardless of their compactness. (An existing Scoop study is encouraging [19].)

7   Related Work

There is a wide selection of work addressing concurrency and distribution in the object-oriented paradigm. Here, we highlight some work that is closest to our own.

The active object [14] design pattern (which inherits from the actor model [1]), like Scoop, decouples method calls from method executions. Such objects are associated with their own processes, which can send messages to each other asynchronously, introducing concurrency. Despite the similarity to Scoop, active objects lack the guarantee of interference-freedom when multiple objects are involved. Furthermore, non-active objects have to be protected manually, and there is no built-in support for condition synchronization (although it is possible to use the observer pattern to actively notify waiting processes). SCOOP can be seen as an advanced form of active objects: objects are by default active, but multiple objects can share the same process. In addition, the SCOOP synchronization mechanisms ensure the absence of intervening calls and also protect non-active objects [18]. Condition synchronization is simple (via method preconditions) and does not require signaling.

There have been some successful attempts to generalize ideas from active objects and the actor model to distributed programming frameworks, with some prominent examples including Creol [12], AmbientTalk [6], and JCoBox [21]. The latter partitions the object space into "coboxes", each with a common thread of control to improve safety; an approach similar to the processes of SCOOP and D-SCOOP. Caromel et al. [4] consider a way of unifying threads and objects to support simpler reasoning about distributed computing, and provide a formal calculus. An important distinction of D-SCOOP in comparison to other frameworks is the impossibility of interrupting requests sent to multiple (potentially distributed) objects controlled by different threads, giving the model its transaction-like semantics.

Network objects [2] share some similarities with active objects, although calls to them are traditionally synchronous to mimic standard method calls, and calls to local network objects are usually handled by the calling process. Creol exemplifies different synchronization approaches possible with active objects, and their natural extension to network objects. Some languages, such as E [16], avoid blocking entirely to ensure deadlock-freedom. This, in our view, can lead to complex behavior that is difficult to understand from the point of view of classical sequential programming. By making synchronization simpler to use, D-SCOOP potentially reduces (but does not eliminate) the risk of deadlocks.

For dealing with failures, the programming language Argus [15] supports "atomic objects" that can be used in a transaction. In contrast, our compensation approach is not limited to pure data-objects.

8   Conclusion

This paper made a case for combining network objects with synchronization models. We presented D-SCOOP, a distributed programming model obtained by combining the network objects abstraction with the runtime semantics of the object-oriented concurrency model SCOOP. We presented an efficient two-phase locking protocol that generalized the strong reasoning guarantees of SCOOP to network objects, allowing for interference-free and transaction-like reasoning on (potentially multiple) remotely located objects, without the programmer having to explicitly manage their synchronization. Furthermore, we proposed a compensation mechanism by which D-SCOOP programs can recover from failure. The evaluation of our prototype implementation [7] suggested that D-SCOOP remains competitive against—and can outperform—explicit locking-based synchronization in Java RMI, a well-established realization of network objects, with the automatic synchronization mechanisms also allowing for more compact code.

In future work, we plan to improve the efficiency of D-SCOOP with respect to intra-object parallelism [11,13]. We will investigate concepts such as slicing [22], and the possible integration of software transactional memory [9]. We will also investigate whether performance can be improved, by (safely) relaxing the requirement that one node communicates with another via a single connection. Finally, we want to formalize the D-SCOOP semantics using [5] to test extensions, and provide a formal proof that the protocol and algorithms correctly generalize the SCOOP guarantees.

Acknowledgements. We thank Sebastian Nanz for his invaluable support throughout this project. We also thank Carlo A. Furia and the anonymous referees for their helpful comments and criticisms. The underlying research was partially funded by ERC Grant CME #291389.

References

1. Agha, G.: ACTORS: A Model of Concurrent Computation in Distributed Systems. MIT Press, Cambridge (1986)
2. Birrell, A., Nelson, G., Owicki, S.S., Wobber, E.: Network objects. In: Proceedings of SOSP 1993, pp. 217–230. ACM (1993)
3. Birrell, A., et al.: Distributed garbage collection for network objects. Technical report, Systems Research Center (1993)
4. Caromel, D., Henrio, L., Serpette, B.P.: Asynchronous sequential processes. Inf. Comput. **207**(4), 459–495 (2009)
5. Corrodi, C., Heußner, A., Poskitt, C.M.: A graph-based semantics workbench for concurrent asynchronous programs. In: Stevens, P., et al. (eds.) FASE 2016. LNCS, vol. 9633, pp. 31–48. Springer, Heidelberg (2016)
6. Dedecker, J., Van Cutsem, T., Mostinckx, S., D'Hondt, T., De Meuter, W.: Ambient-oriented programming in AmbientTalk. In: Thomas, D. (ed.) ECOOP 2006. LNCS, vol. 4067, pp. 230–254. Springer, Heidelberg (2006)
7. Distributed SCOOP website. http://cme.ethz.ch/scoop/dscoop/
8. Eiffel Documentation: Concurrent Eiffel with SCOOP. https://www.eiffel.org/doc/solutions/Concurrent%20programming%20with%20SCOOP. Accessed April 2016
9. Eugster, P., Vaucouleur, S.: Composing atomic features. Sci. Comput. Program. **63**(2), 130–146 (2006)
10. Grand Central Dispatch (GCD) Reference. https://developer.apple.com/library/mac/documentation/Performance/Reference/GCD_libdispatch_Ref/index.html. Accessed April 2016
11. Henrio, L., Huet, F., István, Z.: Multi-threaded active objects. In: De Nicola, R., Julien, C. (eds.) COORDINATION 2013. LNCS, vol. 7890, pp. 90–104. Springer, Heidelberg (2013)
12. Johnsen, E.B., Owe, O., Yu, I.C.: Creol: a type-safe object-oriented model for distributed concurrent systems. Theor. Comput. Sci. **365**(1–2), 23–66 (2006)

13. Johnsen, E.B., Blanchette, J.C., Kyas, M., Owe, O.: Intra-object versus inter-object: concurrency and reasoning in Creol. Proc. TTSS 2008. ENTCS **243**, 89–103 (2009)
14. Lavender, R.G., Schmidt, D.C.: Active object: an object behavioral pattern for concurrent programming. In: Vlissides, J.M., Coplien, J.O., Kerth, N.L. (eds.) Pattern Languages of Program Design, vol. 2, pp. 483–499. Addison-Wesley (1996)
15. Liskov, B.: Distributed programming in Argus. Commun. ACM (CACM) **31**(3), 300–312 (1988)
16. Miller, M.S., Tribble, E.D., Shapiro, J.S.: Concurrency among strangers. In: De Nicola, R., Sangiorgi, D. (eds.) TGC 2005. LNCS, vol. 3705, pp. 195–229. Springer, Heidelberg (2005)
17. Morandi, B., Schill, M., Nanz, S., Meyer, B.: Prototyping a concurrency model. In: Proceedings of ACSD 2013, pp. 170–179. IEEE (2013)
18. Morandi, B., Nanz, S., Meyer, B.: Safe and efficient data sharing for message-passing concurrency. In: Kühn, E., Pugliese, R. (eds.) COORDINATION 2014. LNCS, vol. 8459, pp. 99–114. Springer, Heidelberg (2014)
19. Nanz, S., Torshizi, F., Pedroni, M., Meyer, B.: Design of an empirical study for comparing the usability of concurrent programming languages. In: Proceedings of ESEM 2011, pp. 325–334. IEEE Computer Society (2011)
20. Nienaltowski, P.: Practical framework for contract-based concurrent object-oriented programming. Doctoral dissertation, ETH Zürich (2007)
21. Schäfer, J., Poetzsch-Heffter, A.: JCoBox: generalizing active objects to concurrent components. In: D'Hondt, T. (ed.) ECOOP 2010. LNCS, vol. 6183, pp. 275–299. Springer, Heidelberg (2010)
22. Schill, M., Nanz, S., Meyer, B.: Handling parallelism in a concurrency model. In: Lourenço, J.M., Farchi, E. (eds.) MUSEPAT 2013 2013. LNCS, vol. 8063, pp. 37–48. Springer, Heidelberg (2013)
23. Shavit, N., Touitou, D.: Software transactional memory. Distributed Comput. **10**(2), 99–116 (1997)
24. Torshizi, F.A., Ostroff, J.S., Paige, R.F., Chechik, M.: The SCOOP concurrency model in Java-like languages. In: Proceedings of CPA 2009. Concurrent Systems Engineering Series, vol. 67, pp. 7–27. IOS Press (2009)
25. West, S., Nanz, S., Meyer, B.: Efficient and reasonable object-oriented concurrency. In: Proceedings of ESEC/FSE 2015, pp. 734–744. ACM (2015)

On Sessions and Infinite Data

Paula Severi[1]([✉]), Luca Padovani[2], Emilio Tuosto[1],
and Mariangiola Dezani-Ciancaglini[2]

[1] Department of Computer Science, University of Leicester, Leicester, UK
pgs11@le.ac.uk
[2] Dipartimento di Informatica, Università di Torino, Turin, Italy

Abstract. We investigate some subtle issues that arise when programming distributed computations over infinite data structures. To do this, we formalise a calculus that combines a call-by-name functional core with session-based communication primitives and that allows session operations to be performed "on demand". We develop a typing discipline that guarantees both normalisation of expressions and progress of processes and that uncovers an unexpected interplay between evaluation and communication.

1 Introduction

Infinite computations have long lost their negative connotation. Two paradigmatic contexts in which they appear naturally are reactive systems [17] and lazy functional programming. The former contemplate the use of infinite computations in order to capture *non-transformational* computations, that is computations that cannot be expressed in terms of transformations from inputs to outputs; rather, computations of reactive systems are naturally modelled in terms of ongoing interactions with the environment. Lazy functional programming is acknowledged as a paradigm that fosters software modularity [13] and enables programmers to specify computations over possibly infinite data structures in elegant and concise ways. Nowadays, the synergy between these two contexts has a wide range of potential applications, including stream-processing networks, real-time sensor monitoring, and internet-based media services.

Nonetheless, not all diverging programs – those engaged in an infinite sequence of possibly intertwined computations and communications – are necessarily useful. There exist degenerate forms of divergence where programs do not produce results, in terms of observable data or performed communications. In this paper we investigate the issue by proposing a calculus for expressing computations over possibly infinite data types and involving message passing. The calculus – called SID after Sessions with Infinite Data – combines a call-by-name functional core (inspired by Haskell) with multi-threading and session-based communication primitives.

In the remainder of this section we provide an informal introduction to SID and its key features by means of a few examples. The formal definition of the calculus, of the

Paula Severi has been supported by a Daphne Jackson fellowship sponsored by EPSRC and her department. All authors have been supported by the ICT COST European project called *Behavioural Types for Reliable Large-Scale Software Systems* (BETTY, COST Action IC1201).

Published by Springer International Publishing Switzerland 2016. All Rights Reserved
A. Lluch Lafuente and J. Proença (Eds.): COORDINATION 2016, LNCS 9686, pp. 245–261, 2016.
DOI: 10.1007/978-3-319-39519-7_15

type system, and its properties are given in the remaining sections. A simple instance of computation producing an infinite data structure is given by

$$\text{from } x = \langle x, \text{from } (x+1) \rangle$$

where the function `from` applied to a number n produces the stream (infinite list) $\langle n, \langle n+1, \langle n+2, \cdots \rangle \rangle \rangle$ of integers starting from n. We can think of this list as abstracting the frames of a video stream, or the samples taken from a sensor.

The key issue we want to address is how infinite data can be exchanged between communicating threads. The most straightforward way of doing this in SID is to take advantage of lazy evaluation. For instance, the SID process

$$x \Leftarrow \left(\text{send } c^+ \, (\text{from } 0)\right) \ggg= f \quad | \quad y \Leftarrow \text{recv } c^- \ggg= g$$

represents two threads x and y running in parallel and connected by a session c, of which thread x owns one endpoint c^+ and thread y the corresponding peer c^-. Thread x sends a stream of natural numbers on c^+ and continues as $f \, c^+$, where f is left unspecified. Thread y receives the stream from c^- and continues as $(g \, \langle \text{from } 0, c^- \rangle)$. The *bind* operator $\_ \ggg= \_$ models sequential composition and has the exact same semantics as in Haskell. In particular, it applies the rhs to the result of the action on its lhs. The result of sending a message on the endpoint a^+ is the endpoint itself, while the result of receiving a message from the endpoint a^- is a pair consisting of the message and the endpoint. In this example, the *whole stream* is sent *at once* in a single interaction between x and y. This behaviour is made possible by the fact that SID evaluates expressions *lazily*: the message $(\text{from } 0)$ is not evaluated until it is used by the receiver.

In principle, exchanging "infinite" messages such as $(\text{from } 0)$ between different threads is no big deal. In the real world, though, this interaction poses non-trivial challenges: the message consists in fact of a mixture of data (the parts of the messages that have already been evaluated, like the constant 0) and code (which lazily computes the remaining parts when necessary, like `from`). This observation suggests an alternative, more viable modelling of this interaction whereby the sender unpacks the stream element-wise, sends each element of the stream as a separate message, and the receiver gradually reconstructs the stream as each element arrives at destination. This modelling is intuitively simpler to realise (especially in a distributed setting) because the messages exchanged at each communication are ground values rather than a mixture of data and code. In SID we can model this as a process

$$prod \Leftarrow \text{stream } c^+ \, (\text{from } 0) \quad | \quad cons \Leftarrow \text{display}_0 \, c^-$$

where the functions `stream` and `display`$_0$ are defined as:

$$\begin{aligned}
\text{stream } y \, \langle x, xs \rangle &= \text{send } y \, x \ggg= \lambda y'.\text{stream } y' \, xs \\
\text{display}_0 \, y &= \text{recv } y \ggg= \lambda \langle z, y' \rangle.\text{display}_0 \, y' \ggg= \lambda zs.g \, \langle z, zs \rangle
\end{aligned} \tag{1.1}$$

The syntax $\lambda \langle \_, \_ \rangle.e$ is just syntactic sugar for a function that performs pattern matching on the argument, which must be a pair, in order to access its components. In `stream`, pattern matching is used for accessing and sending each element of the stream separately. In `display`$_0$, the pair $\langle z, y' \rangle$ contains the received head z of the stream along with the continuation y' of the session endpoint from which the element has been received. The recursive call $display_0$ y' retrieves the tail of the stream zs, which is then combined with the head z and passed as an argument to g.

The code of $display_0$ looks reasonable at first, but conceals a subtle and catastrophic pitfall: the recursive call $display_0$ y' is in charge of receiving the *whole* tail zs, which is an infinite stream itself, and therefore it involves an infinite number of synchronisations with the producing thread! This means that $display_0$ will hopelessly diverge striving to receive the whole stream before releasing control to g. This is a known problem which has led to the development of primitives (such as unsafeInterleaveIO in Haskell or delayIO in [23]) that allow the execution of I/O actions to interleave with their continuation. In this paper, we call such primitive future, since its semantics is also akin to that of *future variables* [25]. Intuitively, an expression future $e \gg= \lambda x(g\ x)$ allows g to reduce even if e, which typically involves I/O, has not been completely performed. The variable x acts as a placeholder for the result of e; if g needs to inspect the structure of x, its evaluation is suspended until e produces enough data. Using future we can amend the definition of $display_0$ thus

$$display\ y = recv\ y \gg= \lambda\langle z,y'\rangle.future\ (display\ y') \gg= \lambda zs.g\ \langle z,zs\rangle \qquad (1.2)$$

and obtain one that allows g to start processing the stream as its elements come through the connection with the producer thread. The type system that we develop in this paper allows us to reason on sessions involving the exchange of infinite data and when such exchanges can be done "productively". In particular, our type system flags $display_0$ in (1.1) as ill typed, while it accepts $display$ in (1.2) as well typed. To do so, the type system uses a modal operator • related to the normalisability of expressions. As hinted by the examples (1.1) and (1.2), this operator plays a major role in the type of future.

Related Work. To the best of our knowledge, SID is the first calculus that combines *session-based* communication primitives [12,29] with a *call-by-need* operational semantics [1,18,30] guaranteeing progress of processes exchanging infinite data. The operational semantics of related session calculi that appear in the literature is call-by-value, e.g. [9,11,28] making them unsuitable for handling potentially infinite data, such as streams. In the context of communication-centric calculi, SSCC [7] offers an explicit primitive to deal with streams. Our language enables the modelling of more intricate interactions between infinite data structures and infinite communications. Besides, the type system of SSCC considers only finite sessions types and does not guarantee progress of processes.

Following [19], we use a modal operator • to restrict the application of the fixed point operator and exclude degenerate forms of divergence. This paper is an improvement over past typed lambda calculi with a temporal modal operator in two respects. Firstly, we do not need any subtyping relation as in [19] and secondly SID programs are not cluttered with constructs for the introduction and elimination of individuals of type • as in [3,14,14,15,26]. A weak criterion to ensure productivity of infinite data is the *guardedness condition* [5]. We do not need such condition because we can type more normalising expressions (such as $display$ in (1.2)) using the modal operator •.

Futures originated in functional programming and related paradigms for parallelising a program [10]. The call-by-need λ-calculus with futures in [25] is used for studying contextual equivalence and has no type system.

In the session calculi literature, the word "progress" has two different meanings. Sometimes it is synonym of deadlock freedom [2], at other times it means lock freedom, i.e. that each offered communication in an open session eventually happens [4,8,20]. Typed SID processes cannot be stuck, and if they do not terminate they communicate and/or generate new threads infinitely often. This means that the property of progress satisfied by our calculus is stronger than that of [2] and weaker than that of [4,8,20].

Contributions and Outline. The SID calculus, defined in Sect. 2, combines in an original way standard constructs from the λ-calculus and process algebras in the spirit of [11,12]. The type system, given in Sect. 3, has the novelty of using the modal operator $\bullet$ to control the recursion of programs that perform communications. To the best of our knowledge, the interplay between $\bullet$ and the type of future is investigated here for the first time. The properties of our framework, presented in Sect. 4, include subject reduction (Theorem 1), normalisation of expressions (Theorem 2), progress and confluence of processes (Theorems 4, 5). Additional examples, definitions, and proofs can be found in the technical report [27].

2   The SID Calculus

We use an infinite set of *channels* a, b, c and a disjoint, infinite set of *variables* x, y. We distinguish between two kinds of channels: *shared channels* are public service identifiers that can only be used to initiate sessions; *session channels* represent private sessions on which the actual communications take place. We distinguish the two *endpoints* of a session channel c by means of a *polarity* $p \in \{+,-\}$ and write them as c^+ and c^-. We write $\overline{p}$ for the dual polarity of p, where $\overline{+} = -$ and $\overline{-} = +$, and we say that c^p is the *peer endpoint* of $c^{\overline{p}}$. A *bindable name* X is either a channel or a variable and a *name u* is either a bindable name or an endpoint.

The syntax of *expressions* and *processes* is given in Table 1. In addition to the usual constructs of the λ-calculus, expressions include constants, ranged over by k, and pair splitting. Constant are the unitary value unit, the pair constructor pair, the

Table 1. Syntax of expressions and processes.

$e ::=$		**Expression**	$P ::=$		**Process**
	k	(constant)		0	(idle process)
	u	(name)		$x \Leftarrow e$	(thread)
	$\lambda x.e$	(abstraction)		server $a\,e$	(server)
	ee	(application)		$P \mid P$	(parallel)
	split e as x,y in e	(pair splitting)		$(\nu X)P$	(restriction)

k ::= unit | return | open | send | recv | future | pair | bind primitives for session initiation and communication open, send, and recv [11,12], the monadic operations return and bind [23], and a primitive future to defer computations [21,22]. We do not need a primitive constant for the fixed point operator because it can be expressed and typed inside the language. For simplicity, we do not include primitives for branching and selection typically found in session calculi. They are straightforward to add and do not invalidate any of the results. Expressions are subject to the usual conventions of the λ-calculus. In particular, we assume that the bodies of abstractions extend as much as possible to the right, that applications associate to the left, and we use parentheses to disambiguate the notation when necessary. Following established notation, we write $\langle e, f \rangle$ in place of pair e f, $\lambda \langle x_1, x_2 \rangle.e$ in place of $\lambda x.$split x as x_1, x_2 in e, and $e \mathbin{>\!\!>=} f$ in place of bind e f.

A process can be either the idle process 0 that performs no action, a thread $x \Leftarrow e$ with name x and body e that evaluates the body and binds the result to x in the rest of the system, a server a e that waits for session initiations on the shared channel a and spawns a new thread computing e at each connection, the parallel composition of processes, and the restriction of a bindable name. In processes, restrictions bind tighter than parallel composition and we may abbreviate $(\nu X_1) \cdots (\nu X_n)P$ with $(\nu X_1 \cdots X_n)P$.

We have that split f as x,y in e binds both x and y in e and $(\nu a)P$ binds a^+ and a^- within P in addition to a. The definitions of *free* and *bound* names follow as expected. We identify expressions and processes up to renaming of bound names.

The operational semantics of expressions is defined in the upper half of Table 2. Expressions reduce according to a standard *call-by-name* semantics, for which we define the *evaluation contexts for expressions* below:

$$\mathcal{E} ::= [\,] \mid \mathcal{E} e \mid \text{split } \mathcal{E} \text{ as } x, y \text{ in } e \mid \text{open } \mathcal{E} \mid \text{send } \mathcal{E} \mid \text{recv } \mathcal{E} \mid \text{bind } \mathcal{E}$$

Note that evaluation contexts do not allow to reduce pair components or an expression e in bind f e, return e, future e, send a^p e. We say that e is in *normal form* if there is no f such that $e \longrightarrow f$.

The operational semantics of processes is given by a structural congruence relation $\equiv$, which we leave undetailed since it is essentially the same as that of the π-calculus, and a reduction relation, defined in the bottom half of Table 2. The *evaluation contexts for processes* are defined as

$$\mathscr{C} ::= [\,] \mid \mathscr{C} \mathbin{>\!\!>=} e$$

and force the left-to-right execution of monadic actions, as usual.

Rules [R-OPEN] and [R-COMM] model session initiation and communication, respectively. According to [R-OPEN], a client thread opens a connection with a server a. In the reduct, a fresh session channel c is created, the open in the client reduces to the return of c^+ and a copy of the server is spawned into a new thread that has a fresh name y and a body obtained from that of the server applied to c^-. According to [R-COMM], two threads communicate if one is ready to send some message e on a session endpoint a^p and the other is waiting for a message from the peer endpoint $a^{\bar{p}}$. As in [11], the communication primitives return the session endpoint being used, with the difference that in our case the results are monadic actions. In particular, the result for the sender is the same session endpoint and the result for the receiver is a pair consisting of the received message and the session endpoint.

Table 2. Reduction semantics of expressions and processes.

Reduction of expressions

[R-BETA]
$$(\lambda x.e)\, f \longrightarrow e\{f/x\}$$

[R-BIND]
$$\texttt{return}\, f \gg= e \longrightarrow ef$$

[R-SPLIT]
$$\texttt{split}\, \langle e_1, e_2 \rangle \texttt{ as } x,y \texttt{ in } e \longrightarrow e\{e_1, e_2/x,y\}$$

[R-CTXT]
$$\frac{e \longrightarrow f}{\mathscr{E}[e] \longrightarrow \mathscr{E}[f]}$$

Reduction of processes

[R-OPEN]
$$\texttt{server}\, a\, e \mid x \Leftarrow \mathscr{C}[\texttt{open}\, a] \longrightarrow \texttt{server}\, a\, e \mid (\nu cy)(x \Leftarrow \mathscr{C}[\texttt{return}\, c^+] \mid y \Leftarrow e\, c^-)$$

[R-COMM]
$$x \Leftarrow \mathscr{C}[\texttt{send}\, a^p\, e] \mid y \Leftarrow \mathscr{C}'[\texttt{recv}\, a^{\overline{p}}] \longrightarrow x \Leftarrow \mathscr{C}[\texttt{return}\, a^p] \mid y \Leftarrow \mathscr{C}'[\texttt{return}\, \langle e, a^{\overline{p}} \rangle]$$

[R-FUTURE]
$$x \Leftarrow \mathscr{C}[\texttt{future}\, e] \longrightarrow (\nu y)(x \Leftarrow \mathscr{C}[\texttt{return}\, y] \mid y \Leftarrow e)$$

[R-RETURN]
$$(\nu x)(x \Leftarrow \texttt{return}\, e \mid P) \longrightarrow P\{e/x\}$$

[R-THREAD]
$$\frac{e \longrightarrow f}{x \Leftarrow e \longrightarrow x \Leftarrow f}$$

[R-NEW]
$$\frac{P \longrightarrow Q}{(\nu X)P \longrightarrow (\nu X)Q}$$

[R-PAR]
$$\frac{P \longrightarrow Q}{P \mid R \longrightarrow Q \mid R}$$

[R-CONG]
$$\frac{P \equiv P' \longrightarrow Q' \equiv Q}{P \longrightarrow Q}$$

Rules [R-FUTURE] and [R-RETURN] deal with futures. The former spawns an I/O action e in a separate thread y, so that the spawner is able to reduce (using [R-BIND]) even if e has not been executed yet. The name y of the spawned thread can be used as a placeholder for the value yielded by e. Rule [R-RETURN] deals with a future variable x that has been evaluated to `return` e. In this case, x is replaced by e everywhere within its scope.

Rule [R-THREAD] lifts reduction of expressions to reduction of threads. The remaining rules close reduction under restrictions, parallel compositions, and structural congruence, as expected.

3   Typing SID

We now develop a typing discipline for SID. The challenge comes from the fact that the calculus allows a mixture of pure computations (handling data) and impure computations (doing I/O). In particular, SID programs can manipulate potentially infinite data while performing I/O operations that produce/consume pieces of such data as shown by the examples of Sect. 1. Some ingredients of the type system are easily identified from the syntax of the calculus. We have a core type language with unit, products, and arrows. As in [11], we distinguish between *unlimited* and *linear* arrows for there sometimes is the need to specify that certain functions must be applied exactly once. As in Haskell [21,23], we use the IO type constructor to denote monadic I/O actions. For shared and session channels we respectively introduce channel types and session types [12]. Finally, following [19], we introduce the *delay* type constructor •, so that an expression of type •t denotes a value of type t that is available "at the next moment in time". This constructor is key to control recursion and attain normalisation of expressions. Moreover, the type constructors • and IO interact in non-trivial ways as shown later by the type of future.

3.1 Types

The syntax of *pseudo-types* and *pseudo-session types* is given by the grammar in Table 3, whose productions are meant to be interpreted coinductively. A pseudo (session) type is a possibly infinite tree, where each internal node is labelled by a type constructor and has as many children as the arity of the constructor. The leaves of the tree (if any) are labelled by either basic types or end. We use a coinductive syntax to describe infinite data structures (such as streams) and arbitrarily long protocols, such as the one betwen sender and receiver in Sect. 1.

We distinguish between unlimited pseudo-types (those denoting expressions that can be used any number of times) from linear pseudo-types (those denoting expressions that must be used exactly once). Let lin be the smallest predicate defined by

$$\mathsf{lin}(?t.T) \quad \mathsf{lin}(!t.T) \quad \mathsf{lin}(t \multimap s) \quad \mathsf{lin}(\mathtt{IO}\,t) \quad \frac{\mathsf{lin}(t)}{\mathsf{lin}(t \times s)} \quad \frac{\mathsf{lin}(s)}{\mathsf{lin}(t \times s)} \quad \frac{\mathsf{lin}(t)}{\mathsf{lin}(\bullet t)}$$

The word "smallest" in the above definition is crucial. For example lin does not hold for the type •$^{\infty}$, because •$^{\infty}$ does not belong to the smallest set satisfying the above clauses. We say that t is *linear* if $\mathsf{lin}(t)$ holds and that t is *unlimited*, written $\mathsf{un}(t)$, otherwise. Note that all I/O actions are linear, since they may involve communications on session channels which are linear resources.

Table 3. Syntax of Pseudo-types and Pseudo-session types.

$t ::=^{coind}$		Pseudo-type	$T ::=^{coind}$		Pseudo-session type
	B	(basic type)		end	(end)
	T	(session type)		?t.T	(input)
	$\langle T \rangle$	(shared channel type)		!t.T	(output)
	$t \times t$	(product)		•T	(delay)
	$t \to t$	(arrow)			
	$t \multimap t$	(linear arrow)			
	IO t	(input/output)			
	•t	(delay)			

Definition 1 (**Types**). *A pseudo (session) type t is a* (session) type *if:*

1. *For each sub-term $t_1 \rightarrow t_2$ of t such that* un(t_2) *we have* un(t_1).
2. *For each sub-term $t_1 \multimap t_2$ of t we have* lin(t_2).
3. *The tree representation of t is regular, namely it has finitely many distinct sub-trees.*
4. *Every infinite path in the tree representation of t has infinitely many •'s.*

All conditions except possibly 4 are natural. Condition 1 essentially says that unlimited functions are *pure*, namely they do not have side effects. Indeed, an unlimited function (one that does not contain linear names) that accepts a linear argument should return a linear result. Condition 2 states that a linear function (one that may contain linear names) always yields a linear result. This is necessary to keep track of the presence of linear names in the function, even when the function is applied and its linear arrow type eliminated. For example, consider z of type Nat $\multimap$ Nat and both y and w of type Nat, then without Condition 2 we could type $(\lambda x.y)(z\ w)$ with Nat. This would be incorrect, because it discharges the expression $(z\ w)$ involving the linear name z. Condition 3 implies that we only consider types admitting a finite representation, for example using the well-known "μ notation" for expressing recursive types (for the relation between regular trees and recursive types we refer to [24, Chap. 20]). We define infinite types as trees satisfying a given recursive equation, for which the existence and uniqueness of a solution follow from known results [6]. For example, there are unique pseudo-types S'_{Nat}, S_{Nat}, and $\bullet^\infty$ that respectively satisfy the equations $S'_{\text{Nat}} = \text{Nat} \times S'_{\text{Nat}}, S_{\text{Nat}} = \text{Nat} \times \bullet S_{\text{Nat}}$, and $\bullet^\infty = \bullet\bullet^\infty$. *En passant*, note that linearity is decidable on types due to Condition 3.

Condition 4 intuitively means that not all parts of an infinite data structure can be available at once: those whose type is prefixed by a • are necessarily "delayed" in the sense that recursive calls on them must be deeper. For example, S_{Nat} is a type that denotes streams of natural numbers where each subsequent element of the stream is delayed by one • compared to its predecessor. Instead S'_{Nat} is not a type: it would denote an infinite stream of natural numbers, whose elements are all available right away. Similarly, Out$_{\text{Nat}}$ and In$_{\text{Nat}}$ defined by Out$_{\text{Nat}} = \ !\,\text{Nat}. \bullet \text{Out}_{\text{Nat}}$ and In$_{\text{Nat}} = $?Nat. • In$_{\text{Nat}}$ are session types, while O'_{Nat} and I'_{Nat} defined by $O'_{\text{Nat}} = \ !\,\text{Nat.Out}_{\text{Nat}}$ and $I'_{\text{Nat}} = \ ?\text{Nat}.I'_{\text{Nat}}$ are not. The type $\bullet^\infty$ is somehow degenerate in that it contains no actual data constructors. Unsurprisingly, we will see that non-normalising terms such as $\Omega = (\lambda x.x\ x)(\lambda x.x\ x)$ can only be typed with $\bullet^\infty$. Without Condition 4, Ω could be given any type.

We adopt the usual conventions regarding arrow types (which associate to the right) and assume the following precedence among constructors: $\rightarrow$, $\multimap$, $\times$, IO, • with IO and • having the highest precedence. We also need a notion of duality to relate the session types associated with peer endpoints. Our definition extends the one of [12] in the obvious way to delayed types. More precisely, the *dual* of a session type T is the session type $\overline{T}$ coinductively defined by the equations:

$$\overline{\text{end}} = \text{end} \qquad \overline{?t.T} = \ !t.\overline{T} \qquad \overline{!t.T} = \ ?t.\overline{T} \qquad \overline{\bullet T} = \bullet\overline{T}$$

Sometimes we will write $\bullet^n t$ in place of $\underbrace{\bullet \cdots \bullet}_{n\text{-times}} t$.

3.2   Typing Rules

We show the typing of expressions and processes. First we assign types to constants:

$$
\begin{array}{llll}
\texttt{unit} & : \texttt{Unit} & \texttt{send} & : \ !t.T \to t \multimap \texttt{IO } T & \texttt{pair} : t \to s \multimap t \times s \quad \text{if } \text{lin}(t) \\
\texttt{return} & : t \to \texttt{IO } t & \texttt{recv} & : \ ?t.T \to \texttt{IO } (t \times T) & \texttt{pair} : t \to s \to t \times s \quad \text{if } \text{un}(t) \\
\texttt{open} & : \langle T \rangle \to \texttt{IO } T & \texttt{future} & : \bullet^n(\texttt{IO } t) \to \texttt{IO } \bullet^n t & \texttt{bind} : \texttt{IO } t \to (t \multimap \texttt{IO } s) \multimap \texttt{IO } s
\end{array}
$$

Each constant $k \neq \texttt{unit}$ is polymorphic and we use $\text{types}(k)$ to denote the set of types assigned to k, e.g. $\text{types}(\texttt{return}) = \cup_t \{t \to \texttt{IO } t\}$.

The types of $\texttt{unit}$ and $\texttt{return}$ are as expected. The type schema of $\texttt{bind}$ is similar to the type it has in Haskell, except for the two linear arrows. The leftmost linear arrow allows linear functions as the second argument of $\texttt{bind}$. The rightmost linear arrow is needed to satisfy Condition 1 of Definition 1, being $\texttt{IO } t$ linear. The type of $\texttt{pair}$ is also familiar, except that the second arrow is linear or unlimited depending on the first element of the pair. If the first element of the pair is a linear expression, then it can (and actually must) be used for creating exactly one pair. The types of $\texttt{send}$ and $\texttt{recv}$ are almost the same as in [11], except that these primitives return I/O actions instead of performing them as side effects. The type of $\texttt{open}$ is standard and obviously justified by its operational semantics. The most interesting type is that of $\texttt{future}$, which commutes delays and the $\texttt{IO}$ type constructor. Intuitively, $\texttt{future}$ applied to a delayed I/O action returns an immediate I/O that yields a delayed expression. This fits with the semantics of $\texttt{future}$, since its argument is evaluated in a separate thread and the one invoking $\texttt{future}$ can proceed immediately with a placeholder for the delayed expression. If the body of the new thread reduces to $\texttt{return } e$, then e substitutes the placeholder.

The typing judgements for expressions have the shape $\Gamma \vdash e : t$, where *typing environments* (for used resources) Γ are mappings from variables to types, from shared channels to shared channel types, and from endpoints to session types:

$$
\Gamma \quad ::= \quad \emptyset \quad | \quad \Gamma, x : t \quad | \quad \Gamma, a : \langle T \rangle \quad | \quad \Gamma, a^p : T
$$

A typing environment Γ is *linear*, notation $\text{lin}(\Gamma)$, if there is $u : t \in \Gamma$ such that $\text{lin}(t)$; otherwise Γ is *unlimited*, notation $\text{un}(\Gamma)$. As in [11], we use a (partial) combination operator $+$ for environments, that prevents names with linear types from being duplicated. Formally the environment $\Gamma + \Gamma'$ is defined inductively on Γ' by

$$
\begin{aligned}
\Gamma + \emptyset &= \Gamma \\
\Gamma + (\Gamma', u : t) &= (\Gamma + \Gamma') + u : t
\end{aligned}
\quad \text{where} \quad
\Gamma + u : t =
\begin{cases}
\Gamma, u : t & \text{if } u \notin \text{dom}(\Gamma), \\
\Gamma & \text{if } u : t \in \Gamma \text{ and } \text{un}(t), \\
\text{undefined} & \text{otherwise.}
\end{cases}
$$

The typing axioms and rules for expressions are given in Table 4. They are essentially the same as those found in [11], except for two crucial details. First of all, each rule allows for an arbitrary delay in front of the types of the entities involved. Intuitively, the number of $\bullet$'s represents the delay at which a value becomes available. So for example, rule $[\to I]$ says that a function which accepts an argument x of type t delayed by n and produces a result of type s delayed by the same n has type $\bullet^n(t \to s)$, that is a function delayed by n that maps elements of t into elements of s. The second difference with

Table 4. Typing rules for expressions.

$$
\begin{array}{l}
[\bullet\mathrm{I}] \qquad\qquad\quad [\textsc{const}] \qquad\qquad\qquad\qquad [\textsc{axiom}] \\[4pt]
\cfrac{\Gamma \vdash e : t}{\Gamma \vdash e : \bullet t} \qquad \cfrac{\mathsf{un}(\Gamma)}{\Gamma \vdash \mathrm{k} : t}\; t \in \mathbf{types}(\mathrm{k}) \qquad \cfrac{}{\Gamma, u : t \vdash u : t}\; \mathsf{un}(\Gamma)
\end{array}
$$

$$
\begin{array}{l}
[\to\mathrm{I}] \\[4pt]
\cfrac{\Gamma, x : \bullet^{n} t \vdash e : \bullet^{n} s}{\Gamma \vdash \lambda x.e : \bullet^{n}(t \to s)}\; \mathsf{un}(\Gamma)
\end{array}
\qquad
\begin{array}{l}
[\to\mathrm{E}] \\[4pt]
\cfrac{\Gamma_1 \vdash e_1 : \bullet^{n}(t \to s) \quad \Gamma_2 \vdash e_2 : \bullet^{n} t}{\Gamma_1 + \Gamma_2 \vdash e_1 e_2 : \bullet^{n} s}
\end{array}
\qquad
\begin{array}{l}
[\multimap\mathrm{I}] \\[4pt]
\cfrac{\Gamma, x : \bullet^{n} t \vdash e : \bullet^{n} s}{\Gamma \vdash \lambda x.e : \bullet^{n}(t \multimap s)}
\end{array}
$$

$$
\begin{array}{l}
[\multimap\mathrm{E}] \\[4pt]
\cfrac{\Gamma_1 \vdash e_1 : \bullet^{n}(t \multimap s) \quad \Gamma_2 \vdash e_2 : \bullet^{n} t}{\Gamma_1 + \Gamma_2 \vdash e_1 e_2 : \bullet^{n} s}
\end{array}
\qquad
\begin{array}{l}
[\times\mathrm{E}] \\[4pt]
\cfrac{\Gamma_1 \vdash e : \bullet^{n}(t_1 \times t_2) \quad \Gamma_2, x : \bullet^{n} t_1, y : \bullet^{n} t_2 \vdash f : \bullet^{n} s}{\Gamma_1 + \Gamma_2 \vdash \mathtt{split}\, e\ \mathtt{as}\ x,y\ \mathtt{in}\ f : \bullet^{n} s}
\end{array}
$$

respect to the type system in [11] is the presence of rule [•I], which allows to further delay a value of type t. Crucially, it is not possible to *anticipate* a delayed value: if it is known that a value will only be available with delay n, then it will also be available with any delay $m \geq n$, but not earlier. Using rule [•I], we can derive that the fixed point combinator $\mathtt{fix} = \lambda y.(\lambda x.y\,(x\,x))(\lambda x.y\,(x\,x))$ has type $(\bullet t \to t) \to t$, by assigning to the variable x the type s such that $s = \bullet s \to t$ [19]. The side condition $\mathsf{un}(\Gamma)$ in [\textsc{const}], [\textsc{axiom}], and [$\to$I] is standard [11].

It is possible to derive the following types for the functions in Sect. 1:

$$
\mathtt{from} : \mathrm{Nat} \to \mathrm{S_{Nat}} \quad \mathtt{stream} : \mathrm{Out_{Nat}} \to \mathrm{S_{Nat}} \to \mathrm{IO}\,\bullet^{\infty} \quad \mathtt{display} : \mathrm{In_{Nat}} \to \mathrm{IO}\,\mathrm{S_{Nat}}
$$

where, in the derivation for $\mathtt{display}$, we assume type $\mathrm{S_{Nat}} \to \mathrm{IO}\,\mathrm{S_{Nat}}$ for g. We show the most interesting parts of this derivation. We use the following rules, which are easily derived from those in Table 4 and the types of the constants.

$$
\begin{array}{l}
[\textsc{fix}] \\[4pt]
\cfrac{\Gamma, x : \bullet t \vdash e : t}{\Gamma \vdash \mathtt{fix}\,\lambda x.e : t}\; \mathsf{un}(\Gamma)
\end{array}
\qquad
\begin{array}{l}
[\textsc{bind}] \\[4pt]
\cfrac{\Gamma_1 \vdash e_1 : \bullet^{n}(\mathrm{IO}\,t) \quad \Gamma_2 \vdash e_2 : \bullet^{n}(t \multimap \mathrm{IO}\,s)}{\Gamma_1 + \Gamma_2 \vdash e_1 >\!\!>= e_2 : \bullet^{n} \mathrm{IO}\,s}
\end{array}
$$

$$
\begin{array}{l}
[\textsc{future}] \\[4pt]
\cfrac{\Gamma \vdash e : \bullet^{n+m}\mathrm{IO}\,t}{\Gamma \vdash \mathtt{future}\,e : \bullet^{n}\mathrm{IO}\,\bullet^{m} t}
\end{array}
\qquad
\begin{array}{l}
[\times \to \mathrm{I}] \\[4pt]
\cfrac{\Gamma, x_1 : \bullet^{n} t_1, x_2 : \bullet^{n} t_2 \vdash e : \bullet^{n} s}{\Gamma \vdash \lambda\langle x_1, x_2\rangle.e : \bullet^{n}(t_1 \times t_2 \to s)}\; \mathsf{un}(\Gamma)
\end{array}
$$

In order to derive the type of $\mathtt{display}$ we desugar its recursive definition in Sect. 1 as $\mathtt{display} = \mathtt{fix}\,(\lambda x.\lambda y.e)$, where

$$
e = e_1 >\!\!>= e_2 \qquad
\begin{array}{l}
e_1 = \mathtt{recv}\,y \\
e_2 = \lambda\langle z, y'\rangle.e_3 >\!\!>= e_4
\end{array}
\qquad
\begin{array}{l}
e_3 = \mathtt{future}(x\,y') \\
e_4 = \lambda zs.g\langle z, zs\rangle
\end{array}
$$

Now we derive

$$
\cfrac{
\cfrac{\vdots}{\Gamma_1 \vdash e_1 : \mathrm{IO}\,(\mathrm{Nat} \times \bullet\mathrm{In_{Nat}})} \qquad
[\times \to \mathrm{I}]\ \cfrac{\cfrac{\nabla}{\Gamma,\Gamma_2,\Gamma_3 \vdash e_3 >\!\!>= e_4 : \mathrm{IO}\,\mathrm{S_{Nat}}}}{\Gamma \vdash e_2 : (\mathrm{Nat} \times \bullet\mathrm{In_{Nat}}) \to \mathrm{IO}\,\mathrm{S_{Nat}}}
}{
[\to\mathrm{I}]\ \cfrac{[\textsc{bind}]\ \cfrac{\Gamma, y : \mathrm{In_{Nat}} \vdash e : \mathrm{IO}\,\mathrm{S_{Nat}}}{\Gamma \vdash \lambda y.e : \mathrm{In_{Nat}} \to \mathrm{IO}\,\mathrm{S_{Nat}}}}{[\textsc{fix}]\ \cfrac{}{\vdash \mathtt{display} : \mathrm{In_{Nat}} \to \mathrm{IO}\,\mathrm{S_{Nat}}}}
}
$$

where $\Gamma = x : \bullet(\text{In}_{\text{Nat}} \to \text{IO } \text{S}_{\text{Nat}})$, $\Gamma_1 = y : \text{In}_{\text{Nat}}$, $\Gamma_2 = y' : \bullet\text{In}_{\text{Nat}}$ and $\Gamma_3 = z : \text{Nat}, g :$ $\text{S}_{\text{Nat}} \to \text{IO } \text{S}_{\text{Nat}}$. The derivation ∇ is as follows.

$$
\cfrac{[\to E] \cfrac{\Gamma \vdash x : \bullet(\text{In}_{\text{Nat}} \to \text{IO } \text{S}_{\text{Nat}}) \qquad \Gamma_2 \vdash y' : \bullet\text{In}_{\text{Nat}}}{[\text{FUTURE}] \cfrac{\Gamma, \Gamma_2 \vdash x\, y' : \bullet\text{IO } \text{S}_{\text{Nat}}}{[\text{BIND}] \cfrac{\Gamma, \Gamma_2 \vdash e_3 : \text{IO } \bullet\text{S}_{\text{Nat}} \qquad \qquad \vdots \quad \Gamma_3 \vdash e_4 : \bullet\text{S}_{\text{Nat}} \to \text{IO } \text{S}_{\text{Nat}}}{\Gamma, \Gamma_2, \Gamma_3 \vdash e_3 \mathrel{>\!\!>=} e_4 : \text{IO } \text{S}_{\text{Nat}}}}}}{}
$$

Note that the types of the premises of [$\to$E] in the above derivation have a $\bullet$ constructor in front. Moreover, future has a type that pushes the $\bullet$ inside the IO; this is crucial for typing e_4 with ($\bullet\text{S}_{\text{Nat}} \to \text{IO } \text{S}_{\text{Nat}}$). We can assign the type $\bullet\text{S}_{\text{Nat}} \to \text{IO } \text{S}_{\text{Nat}}$ to e_4 by guarding the argument z of type $\bullet\text{S}_{\text{Nat}}$ under the constructor pair. Without future, the expression $e_3 \mathrel{>\!\!>=} e_4$ would have type $\bullet(\text{IO } \text{S}_{\text{Nat}})$ and display would be untypeable.

The typing judgements for processes have the shape $\Gamma \vdash P \rhd \Delta$, where Γ is a typing environment as before, while Δ is a *resource environment*, keeping track of the resources defined in P. In particular, Δ maps the names of threads and servers in P to their types and it is defined by

$$
\Delta \quad ::= \quad \emptyset \quad | \quad \Delta, x : t \quad | \quad \Delta, a : \langle T \rangle
$$

Table 5 gives the typing rules for processes. A thread is well typed if so is its body, which must be an I/O action. The type of a thread is that of the result of its body, where the delay moves from the I/O action to the result. The side condition makes sure that the thread is unable to use the very value that it is supposed to produce. The resulting environment for defined resources associates the name of the thread with the type of the action of its body. A server is well typed if so is its body e, which must be a function from the dual of T to an I/O action. This agrees with the reduction rule of the server, where the application of e to an endpoint becomes the body of a new thread each time the server is invoked. It is natural to forbid occurrences of free variables and shared channels in server bodies. This is assured by the condition shared(Γ), which requires Γ to contain only shared channels. Clearly shared(Γ) implies un(Γ), and then we can type the body e with a non linear arrow. The type of the new thread (which will be t if e has type $\overline{T} \to \text{IO } t$) must be unlimited, since a server can be invoked an arbitrary number of times. The environment $\Gamma + a : \langle T \rangle$ in the conclusion of the rule makes sure that the type of the server as seen by its clients is consistent with its definition.

Table 5. Typing rules for processes.

[THREAD] $\cfrac{\Gamma \vdash e : \bullet^n(\text{IO } t)}{\Gamma \vdash x \Leftarrow e \rhd x : \bullet^n t}\ x \notin \text{dom}(\Gamma)$	[SERVER] $\cfrac{\Gamma \vdash e : \overline{T} \to \text{IO } t}{\Gamma + a : \langle T \rangle \vdash \text{server } a\, e \rhd a : \langle T \rangle}\ \begin{array}{l}\text{shared}(\Gamma)\\ \text{un}(t)\end{array}$
[PAR] $\cfrac{\Gamma_1 \vdash P_1 \rhd \Delta_1 \qquad \Gamma_2 \vdash P_2 \rhd \Delta_2}{\Gamma_1 + \Gamma_2 \vdash P_1 \mid P_2 \rhd \Delta_1, \Delta_2}$	[SESSION] $\cfrac{\Gamma, a^p : T, a^{\overline{p}} : \overline{T} \vdash P \rhd \Delta}{\Gamma \vdash (va)P \rhd \Delta}$ [NEW] $\cfrac{\Gamma, X : t \vdash P \rhd \Delta, X : t}{\Gamma \vdash (vX)P \rhd \Delta}$

The remaining rules are conventional. In a parallel composition we require that the sets of entities (threads and servers) defined by P_1 and P_2 are disjoint. This is enforced by the fact that the respective resource environments Δ_1 and Δ_2 are combined using the operator $\_,\_$ which (as usual) implicitly requires that $\mathrm{dom}(\Delta_1) \cap \mathrm{dom}(\Delta_2) = \emptyset$. The restriction of a session channel a introduces associations for both its endpoints a^+ and a^- in the typing environment with dual session types, as usual. Finally, the restriction of a bindable name X introduces associations in both the typing and the resource environment with the same type t. This makes sure that in P there is exactly one definition for X, which can be either a variable which names a thread or a shared channel which names a server, and that every usage of X is consistent with its definition.

4   Main Results

In this section we state the main properties enjoyed by typed SID programs. The first expected property is that reduction of expressions preserves their types.

Theorem 1   (Subject Reduction for Expressions). *If* $\Gamma \vdash e : t$ *and* $e \longrightarrow e'$*, then* $\Gamma \vdash e' : t$.

Besides the usual substitution lemma, the proof of the above theorem needs the delay lemma, which states that if an expression e has type t from Γ, then it has type $\bullet t$ from $\bullet \Gamma$. This property reflects the fact that we can only move forward in time.

As informally motivated in Sect. 3, the type constructor $\bullet$ controls recursion and guarantees normalisation of any expression that has a type different from $\bullet^\infty$.

Theorem 2   (Normalisation of Typeable Expressions). *If* $\Gamma \vdash e : t$ *and* $t \neq \bullet^\infty$*, then* e *reduces (in zero or more steps) to a normal form.*

The proof of Theorem 2 makes use of a type interpretation indexed on the set of natural numbers, similar to the one given in [19]. Note that, since SID is lazy, expressions such as $\mathtt{return}\ e$ and $\langle e, f \rangle$ are in normal form for all e and f.

An *initial* process models the beginning of a computation and it is formally defined as a closed, well-typed process P such that

$$P \equiv (\nu x a_1 \cdots a_m)(x \Leftarrow e \mid \mathtt{server}\ a_1\ e_1 \mid \cdots \mid \mathtt{server}\ a_m\ e_m)$$

By definition, an initial process does not contain undefined names (hence it is typeable from the empty environment) and consists of only one thread x – usually called "main" in most programming languages – and an arbitrary number of servers. In particular, typeability guarantees that all bodies normalise and all open's refer to existing servers.

We say that a process is *reachable* if it is the reduct of an initial process. Unlike an initial process, a reachable process may have several threads running in parallel, resulting from either service invocation or $\mathtt{future}$.

Theorem 3   (Subject Reduction for Processes). *All reachable processes are typeable.*

The most original and critical aspect of the proof is to check that reachable processes do not have circular dependencies on session channels and variables. The absence of circularities can be properly formalized by means of a judgement that characterises the sharing of names among threads, inspired by the typing of the parallel composition given in [16]. Intuitively, it captures the following properties of reachable processes and makes them suitable for proving both subject reduction and progress:

1. two threads can share at most one session channel;
2. distinct endpoints of a session channel always occur in different threads;
3. if the name of one thread occurs in the body of another thread, then these threads cannot share session channels nor can the first thread mention the second.

Next, we show several examples of processes that are irrelevant to us because, in spite of being typeable, they are not reachable. Examples (4.1) and (4.2) violate condition (3), (4.3) violates condition (1), and (4.4) violates condition (2).

The first example is given by the process

$$(vxy)(x \Leftarrow \text{return } y \mid y \Leftarrow \text{return } x) \tag{4.1}$$

which is well typed by assigning both x and y any unlimited type, whereas $(vx)(x \Leftarrow \text{return } x)$, which is its reduct, is ill typed, because the thread name x occurs free in its body (cf. the side condition of [THREAD]). Another paradigmatic example is

$$x \Leftarrow \text{send } a^+ y \mid y \Leftarrow \text{recv } a^- \tag{4.2}$$

which is well typed in the environment $a^+ : !t.\text{end}, a^- : ?t.\text{end}, y : t$, where $t = \bullet(t \times \text{end})$, and which reduces to $x \Leftarrow \text{return } a^+ \mid y \Leftarrow \text{return } \langle y, a^- \rangle$. Again, the reduct is ill typed because the name y of the thread occurs free in its body.

Another source of problems that usually requires specific handling [2,4] is that there exist well-typed processes that are (or reduce to) configurations where mutual dependencies between sessions and/or thread names prevent progress. For instance, both

$$(vxyab)(x \Leftarrow \text{send } a^+ 4 \ggeq \lambda x.\text{recv } b^- \mid y \Leftarrow \text{send } b^+ 2 \ggeq \lambda x.\text{recv } a^-)(4.3)$$

$$(vxa)(x \Leftarrow \text{recv } a^- \ggeq \lambda \langle y, z \rangle.\text{send } a^+ y) \tag{4.4}$$

are well typed but also deadlocked. Again, processes like this one are not reachable hence they are not a concern in our case.

We now turn our attention to the progress property. A computation stops when there are no threads left. Recall that the reduction rule [R-RETURN] (cf. Table 2) erases threads. Since servers are permanent we say that a process P is *final* if

$$P \equiv (va_1 \dots a_m)(\text{server } a_1 \ e_1 \mid \dots \mid \text{server } a_m \ e_m)$$

In particular, the idle process is final, since m can be 0.

We can state the progress property as follows:

Theorem 4 (Progress of Reachable Processes). *A reachable process either reduces or it is final. Moreover a non-terminating reachable process reduces in a finite number of steps to a process to which one of the rules* [R-OPEN], [R-COMM] *or* [R-FUTURE] *can be applied.*

In other words, every infinite reduction of a reachable process performs infinitely many communications and/or spawns infinitely many threads. The proof of Theorem 4 requires to define a precedence between threads and prove that this relation is acyclic.

As an example, let

$$Q = (\nu prod\, cons\, a\, c)(P \mid \texttt{server}\ a\ \lambda y.\texttt{display}\ y)$$

where

$$P = prod \Leftarrow \texttt{stream}\ c^+\ (\texttt{from}\ 0) \mid cons \Leftarrow \texttt{display}\ c^-$$

is the process discussed in the Introduction. It is easy to verify that

$$P_0 = (\nu prod\, a)(prod \Leftarrow \texttt{open}\ a \ggg= \lambda y.\texttt{stream}\ y\ (\texttt{from}\ 0) \mid \texttt{server}\ a\ \lambda y.\texttt{display}\ y)$$

reduces to process Q. Note that P_0 is typeable, and indeed an initial process. Hence, by Theorems 3 and 4, process Q is typeable and has progress. The last property of SID we discuss is the diamond property [24, Sect. 30.3].

Theorem 5 (Confluence of Reachable Processes). *Let P be a reachable process. If $P \longrightarrow P_1$ and $P \longrightarrow P_2$, then there is P_3 such that $P_1 \longrightarrow P_3$ and $P_2 \longrightarrow P_3$.*

The proof is trivial for expressions, since there is only one redex at each reduction step. However, for processes we may have several redexes to contract at a time and the proof requires to analyse these possibilities. The fact that we can mix pure evaluations and communications and still preserve determinism is of practical interest.

We conclude this section discussing two initial processes whose progress is somewhat degenerate. The first one realises an infinite sequence of *delegations* (the act of sending an endpoint as a message), thereby postponing the use of the endpoint forever:

$$\texttt{badserver} \stackrel{\text{def}}{=} (\nu xab)(x \Leftarrow \texttt{open}\ a \ggg= \texttt{loop1} \mid$$
$$\texttt{server}\ a\ \lambda y.\texttt{open}\ b \ggg= \texttt{loop2}\ y \mid \texttt{server}\ b\ \texttt{recv})$$

where

$$\texttt{loop1} \stackrel{\text{def}}{=} \texttt{fix}\ \lambda f.\lambda x.\texttt{recv}\ x \ggg= \lambda y.\texttt{split}\ y\ \texttt{as}\ y_1, y_2\ \texttt{in send}\ y_2\ y_1 \ggg=$$
$$\lambda z.\texttt{future}\ (fz)$$
$$\texttt{loop2} \stackrel{\text{def}}{=} \texttt{fix}\ \lambda g.\lambda yx.\texttt{send}\ x\ y \ggg= \lambda z.\texttt{recv}\ z \ggg=$$
$$\lambda u.\texttt{split}\ u\ \texttt{as}\ u_1, u_2\ \texttt{in future}\ (gu_1u_2)$$

We have that $\texttt{loop1} : \mathsf{RS}_t \to \texttt{IO}\ \bullet^\infty$ and $\texttt{loop2} : t \to \mathsf{SR}_t \multimap \texttt{IO}\ \bullet^\infty$ where $\mathsf{RS}_t = ?t.!t. \bullet \mathsf{RS}_t$ and $\mathsf{SR}_t = !t.?t. \bullet \mathsf{SR}_t$. Since no communication ever takes place on the session created with server b, $\texttt{badserver}$ violates the progress property as defined in [8].

The second example is the initial process $(\nu x)(x \Leftarrow \Omega_{\texttt{future}})$, where $\Omega_{\texttt{future}} = \texttt{fix future}$. This process only creates new threads.

5 Conclusions

This work addresses the problem of studying the interaction between communications and infinite data structures by means of a calculus that combines sessions with lazy evaluation. A distinguished feature of SID is the possibility of modelling computations in which infinite communications interleave with the production and consumption of infinite data (*cf.* the examples in Sect. 1). Our examples considered infinite streams for simplicity. However, more general infinite data structures can be handled in SID. An evaluation of the expressiveness of SID in dealing with (distributed) algorithms based on such structures is scope for future investigations.

The typing discipline we have developed for SID guarantees normalisation of expressions with a type other than $\bullet^\infty$ and progress of (reachable) processes, besides the standard properties of sessions (communication safety, protocol fidelity, determinism). The type system crucially relies on a modal operator $\bullet$ which has been used in a number of previous works [3,14,19,26] to ensure productivity of well-typed expressions. In this paper, we have uncovered for the first time some intriguing interactions between this operator and the typing of impure expressions with the monadic IO type constructor. Conventionally, the type of future primitive is simply IO $t \rightarrow$ IO t and says nothing about the semantics of the primitive itself. In our type system, the type of future reveals its effect as an operator that turns a delayed computation into another that can be performed immediately, but which produces a delayed result.

As observed at the end of Sect. 1 and formalised in Theorem 4, our notion of progress sits somehow in between deadlock and lock freedom. It would be desirable to strengthen the type system so as to guarantee the (eventual) execution of all pending communications and exclude, for instance, the degenerate examples discussed at the end of Sect. 4. This is relatively easy to achieve in conventional process calculi, where expressions only consist of names or ground values [2,4,20], but it is far more challenging in the case of SID, where expressions embed the λ-calculus. We conjecture that one critical condition to be imposed is to forbid postponing linear computations, namely restricting the application of [$\bullet$I] to non-linear types. Investigations in this direction are left for future work.

Another obvious development, which is key to the practical applicability of our theory, is the definition of a type inference algorithm for our type system. In this respect, the modal operator $\bullet$ is challenging to deal with because it is intrinsically non-structural, not corresponding to any expression form in the calculus.

Acknowledgements. The authors thank the reviewers for their valuable comments.

References

1. Ariola, Z.M., Felleisen, M., Maraist, J., Odersky, M., Wadler, P.: The call-by-need lambda calculus. In: Cytron, R.K., Lee, P. (eds.) Proceedings of POPL 1995, pp. 233–246. ACM Press (1995)
2. Bettini, L., Coppo, M., D'Antoni, L., De Luca, M., Dezani-Ciancaglini, M., Yoshida, N.: Global progress in dynamically interleaved multiparty sessions. In: van Breugel, F., Chechik, M. (eds.) CONCUR 2008. LNCS, vol. 5201, pp. 418–433. Springer, Heidelberg (2008)

3. Cave, A., Ferreira, F., Panangaden, P., Pientka, B.: Fair reactive programming. In: Jagannathan, S., Sewell, P. (eds.) Proceedings of POPL 2014, pp. 361–372. ACM Press (2014)
4. Coppo, M., Dezani-Ciancaglini, M., Yoshida, N., Padovani, L.: Global progress for dynamically interleaved multiparty sessions. Math. Struct. Comput. Sci. **26**(2), 238–302 (2016)
5. Coquand, T.: Infinite objects in type theory. In: Barendregt, H., Nipkow, T. (eds.) TYPES 1993. LNCS, vol. 806, pp. 62–78. Springer, Heidelberg (1994)
6. Courcelle, B.: Fundamental properties of infinite trees. Theoret. Comput. Sci. **25**, 95–169 (1983)
7. Cruz-Filipe, L., Lanese, I., Martins, F., Ravara, A., Vasconcelos, V.: The stream-based service-centred calculus: a foundation for service-oriented programming. Formal Aspects Comput. **26**(12), 865–918 (2014)
8. Deniélou, P.-M., Yoshida, N.: Dynamic multirole session types. In: Ball, T., Sagiv, M. (eds.) Proceedings of POPL 2011, pp. 435–446. ACM Press (2011)
9. Dezani-Ciancaglini, M., de'Liguoro, U.: Sessions and session types: an overview. In: Laneve, C., Su, J. (eds.) WS-FM 2009. LNCS, vol. 6194, pp. 1–28. Springer, Heidelberg (2010)
10. Flanagan, C., Felleisen, M.: The semantics of future and an application. J. Funct. Program. **9**(1), 1–31 (1999)
11. Gay, S.J., Vasconcelos, V.T.: Linear type theory for asynchronous session types. J. Funct. Program. **20**(1), 19–50 (2010)
12. Honda, K., Vasconcelos, V.T., Kubo, M.: Language primitives and type discipline for structured communication-based programming. In: Hankin, C. (ed.) ESOP 1998. LNCS, vol. 1381, pp. 122–138. Springer, Heidelberg (1998)
13. Hughes, J.: Why functional programming matters. Comput. J. **32**(2), 98–107 (1989)
14. Krishnaswami, N., Benton, N.: Ultrametric semantics of reactive programs. In: Grohe, M. (ed.) Proceedings of LICS 2011, pp. 257–266. IEEE (2011)
15. Krishnaswami, N.R., Benton, N., Hoffmann, J.: Higher-order functional reactive programming in bounded space. In: Proceedings of POPL 2012, pp. 45–58. ACM Press (2012)
16. Lindley, S., Morris, J.G.: A semantics for propositions as sessions. In: Vitek, J. (ed.) ESOP 2015. LNCS, vol. 9032, pp. 560–584. Springer, Heidelberg (2015)
17. Manna, Z., Pnueli, A.: The Temporal Logic of Reactive and Concurrent Systems. Springer, Heidelberg (2012)
18. Maraist, J., Odersky, M., Wadler, P.: The call-by-need lambda calculus. J. Funct. Program. **8**(3), 275–317 (1998)
19. Nakano, H.: A modality for recursion. In: Abadi, M. (ed.) Proceedings of LICS 2000, pp. 255–266. IEEE (2000)
20. Padovani, L.: Deadlock and lock freedom in the linear π-calculus. In: Henzinger, T.A., Miller, D. (eds.) Proceedings of LICS 2014, pp. 72:1–72:10. ACM Press (2014)
21. Peyton Jones, S.: Tackling the awkward squad: monadic input/output, concurrency, exceptions, and foreign-language calls in Haskell. In: Hoare, T., Broy, M., Steinbrüggen, R. (eds.) Engineering Theories of Software Construction, pp. 47–96. IOS Press (2001)
22. Peyton Jones, S., Gordon, A., Finne, S.: Concurrent Haskell. In: Boehm, H., Steele Jr., G.L. (eds.) Proceedings of POPL 1996, pp. 295–308. ACM Press (1996)
23. Peyton Jones, S., Wadler, P.: Imperative functional programming. In: Deusen, M.S.V., Lang, B. (eds.) Proceedings of POPL 1993, pp. 71–84. ACM Press (1993)
24. Pierce, B.C.: Types and Programming Languages. MIT Press, Cambridge (2002)
25. Sabel, D., Schmidt-Schauß, M.: A contextual semantics for concurrent Haskell with futures. In: Schneider-Kamp, P., Hanus, M. (eds.) Proceedings of PPDP 2011, pp. 101–112. ACM Press (2011)
26. Severi, P., de Vries, F.-J.: Pure type systems with corecursion on streams: from finite to infinitary normalisation. In: Thiemann, P., Findler, R.B. (eds.) Proceedings of ICFP 2012, pp. 141–152. ACM Press (2012)

27. Severi, P., Padovani, L., Tuosto, E., Dezani-Ciancaglini, M.: On sessions and infinite data. Technical report, Universiy of Leicester and Università di Torino (2016). https://hal.archives-ouvertes.fr/hal-01297293
28. Toninho, B., Caires, L., Pfenning, F.: Corecursion and non-divergence in session-typed processes. In: Maffei, M., Tuosto, E. (eds.) TGC 2014. LNCS, vol. 8902, pp. 159–175. Springer, Heidelberg (2014)
29. Vasconcelos, V.T.: Fundamentals of session types. Inf. Comput. **217**, 52–70 (2012)
30. Wadsworth, C.P.: Semantics and Pragmatics of the Lambda Calculus. Ph.D. thesis, Oxford University (1971)

On Dynamical Probabilities, or:
How to Learn to Shoot Straight

Herbert Wiklicky$^{(\boxtimes)}$

Department of Computing, Imperial College London, London, UK
herbert@doc.ic.ac.uk

Abstract. In order to support, for example, a quantitative analysis of various algorithms, protocols etc. probabilistic features have been introduced into a number of programming languages and calculi. It is by now quite standard to define the formal semantics of (various) probabilistic languages, for example, in terms of Discrete Time Markov Chains (DTMCs). In most cases however the probabilities involved are represented by constants, i.e. one deals with static probabilities. In this paper we investigate a semantical framework which allows for changing, i.e. dynamic probabilities which is still based on time-homogenous DTMCs, i.e. the transition matrix representing the semantics of a program does not change over time.

1   Introduction

Over the last 20 years or so probabilistic programming languages, model checking, programming, semantics etc. have become more and more popular. It appears now to be rather straight forward to add probabilities to any language, formalism, calculus, etc. one might be interested in. Most "probabilistic" programming languages, etc. however use **constant** probabilities [10,11] etc., as we also did in our own work [4,7], especially when anything beyond a simple operational semantics is considered.

One of the motivations for introducing probabilities, as a form of quantified non-determinism, into a programming language is to allow for the formulation and analysis of so-called "randomised algorithms" [13], i.e. algorithms where chance is exploited in order to obtain a certain result, may it be probabilistic primality tests, Monte Carlo integration, etc.

However, there is a large class of randomised algorithms in the area of stochastic programming which have dynamic probabilities at their core, such a stimulated annealing, the Metropolis algorithm, Boltzmann machines, etc. [1,17]. All of these try to find global optimal solutions and in order to avoid getting trapped into a local minima (as might, for example, be the effect of a steepest gradient method) there are random perturbations. The effect of these perturbations is decreasing over time, i.e. during optimisation the chances of a perturbation changes slowly to become zero. Without going into the details of such "cooling"

© IFIP International Federation for Information Processing 2016
Published by Springer International Publishing Switzerland 2016. All Rights Reserved
A. Lluch Lafuente and J. Proença (Eds.): COORDINATION 2016, LNCS 9686, pp. 262–277, 2016.
DOI: 10.1007/978-3-319-39519-7_16

schemes or schedules we are in this paper interested in how to formalise dynamically changing probabilities in an appropriate semantical model.

Probabilistic features, e.g. choices, introduce also a subtle, nevertheless extremely important form of coordination. Probabilities have to be normalised, not as a formal requirement but quasi because of the fundamental laws of nature: Something must happen, so the probabilities of all possibilities at any moment must add up to one. Thus, whatever model we employ in order to describe probabilistic choices, assignments, etc. the different options or possibilities are "communicating" in some form via their probabilities: if one option becomes more likely, another one must give up its chances to be executed/realised.

2   A Probabilistic Language

In the following we will denote by $\mathbf{Var} = \{x_1, \ldots, x_v\}$ the set of all variables of a program P and by $\mathbf{Value}(x)$ the range of possible values of a variable x.

Technical restriction: In this paper we assume that $\mathbf{Value}(x)$ is finite for all $x \in \mathbf{Var}$. We will allow below for variables as probabilities which thus also will have to come from a finite set of (possible) values. From a computational point of view probabilities should in any case perhaps be modeled as rational numbers in $[0, 1]$. Using real numbers can, as always, create a number of fundamental problems related to computability etc., e.g. [19].

To simplify the presentation we will go even a step further and only consider positive *integers* in $\mathbb{Z}^+$ as "*weights*"[1]: Given several options with "weights" w_i these correspond to probabilities $p_i = w_i / \sum_j w_j$. As we have to (re)normalise probabilities in any case (even for static probabilities as constants, unless we can trust the programmer that all probabilities in a choice or a probability distribution always add up to one) this does not imply any restriction. It only means that in effect we consider *proportions* or *ratios* rather than rational values.

Conceptual restriction: We do not allow for any kind of pure "non-determinism" as part of the actual execution of the program. The reasons for this are: (i) From a conceptual point of view it seems to be a contradiction to the notions like that of a Turing machine as an unambiguous procedure ("Entscheidungsproblem") to allow for (e.g. angelic) "non-determinism"; (ii) we also do not believe that any physical implementation of a purely "non-deterministic" choice exists (e.g. one could use quantum devices to realise probabilistic but never "non-deterministic" choices); and (iii) there are several mathematical (pseudo-)problems which disappear when one eliminates " non-determinism" during the execution of a program (e.g. related to boundedness, etc. [7]).

However, our semantical model still accommodates "non-determinism" in several aspects such as "non-determinism" as "under-specification" and "openness". Concretely, the semantical model provides for our language (pure) "non-determinism" in two ways: (i) We leave it open which initial configuration will

---

[1] Weights however have to be distinguished from *priorities* in other contexts.

be used, as we have no further interaction with the environment this can also be seen as allowing for an "open" system; and (ii) we also allow for parameters as probabilities, i.e. our semantics allows for "under-specification" in the sense that the concrete probabilities are only determined in a concrete implementation.

2.1 Syntax

The syntax of statements in our language **pWhile** is given in Table 1. We also provide a labelled version of this syntax (cf. [14]) in order to be able to refer to certain program points in a program analysis context, see also Table 1. We will denote by **Label** the set of all labels of a program. For details on expressions $f(x_1, \ldots, x_n)$ (also sometimes denoted simply by e) etc. we refer to e.g. [5,14].

Table 1. The syntax of **pWhile**

$S ::=$ skip	$S ::= [\text{skip}]^\ell$
$\qquad x := f(x_1, \ldots, x_n)$	$\qquad [x := f(x_1, \ldots, x_n)]^\ell$
$\qquad S_1 ; S_2$	$\qquad S_1 ; S_2$
$\qquad$ choose $p_1 : S_1$ or $p_2 : S_2$ ro	$\qquad [\text{choose}]^\ell\ p_1 : S_1$ or $p_2 : S_2$ ro
$\qquad$ if b then S_1 else S_2 fi	$\qquad$ if $[b]^\ell$ then S_1 else S_2 fi
$\qquad$ while b do S od	$\qquad$ while $[b]^\ell$ do S od

For this language we have the usual intuitive semantics: We have an "empty" skip statement, assignment to variables, sequential composition as well as if statements and while loops. The only probabilistic construct is the choose statement which executes S_1 or S_2 according to the probabilities p_1 and p_2 (which we assume to be normalised, i.e. $p_1 + p_2 = 1$, or which will be (re)normalised as part of the execution of the program, mor below). The choose statement can also be extended from its binary version to an n-ary one. We will not consider in this core language random assignments – as in some of our other papers or, e.g., [11] – but just note that obviously one can implement a random assignment (involving finite values) using the choose construct.

2.2 Operational Semantics

The SOS semantics for **pWhile** is given in Table 2. We use the (additional) statement stop to indicate successful termination and (re)normalise probabilities in **R7**, otherwise these are the usual SOS rules for procedural languages. The operational (SOS) semantics of **pWhile** is defined in terms of a probabilistic transition system on configurations. A *configuration* is a pair $\langle S, s \rangle \in$ **Conf** with S a statement in **pWhile** and $s \in$ **State** a (classical) *state*, i.e. a function **Var** $\rightarrow$ **Value**. The SOS semantics is essentially also the same for the labelled version of the language, in this case we can however simplify the presentation

Table 2. The rules of the SOS semantics of **pWhile** (static)

R1 $\langle \text{stop}, s \rangle \longrightarrow_1 \langle \text{stop}, s \rangle$

R2 $\langle \text{skip}, s \rangle \longrightarrow_1 \langle \text{stop}, s \rangle$

R3 $\langle v := e, s \rangle \longrightarrow_1 \langle \text{stop}, s[v \mapsto \mathcal{E}(e)s] \rangle$

R4$_1$ $\dfrac{\langle S_1, s \rangle \longrightarrow_p \langle S_1', s' \rangle}{\langle S_1; S_2, s \rangle \longrightarrow_p \langle S_1'; S_2, s' \rangle}$

R4$_2$ $\dfrac{\langle S_1, s \rangle \longrightarrow_p \langle \text{stop}, s' \rangle}{\langle S_1; S_2, s \rangle \longrightarrow_p \langle S_2, s' \rangle}$

R5$_1$ $\langle \text{if } b \text{ then } S_1 \text{ else } S_2 \text{ fi}, s \rangle \longrightarrow_1 \langle S_1, s \rangle$ if $\mathcal{E}(b)s = $ **true**

R5$_2$ $\langle \text{if } b \text{ then } S_1 \text{ else } S_2 \text{ fi}, s \rangle \longrightarrow_1 \langle S_2, s \rangle$ if $\mathcal{E}(b)s = $ **false**

R6$_1$ $\langle \text{while } b \text{ do } S \text{ od}, s \rangle \longrightarrow_1 \langle S; \text{ while } b \text{ do } S \text{ od}, s \rangle$ if $\mathcal{E}(b)s = $ **true**

R6$_2$ $\langle \text{while } b \text{ do } S \text{ od}, s \rangle \longrightarrow_1 \langle \text{stop}, s \rangle$ if $\mathcal{E}(b)s = $ **false**

R7$_1$ $\langle \text{choose } p_1 : S_1 \text{ or } p_2 : S_2 \text{ ro}, s \rangle \longrightarrow_{\tilde{p}_1} \langle S_1, s \rangle$ with $\tilde{p}_1 = p_{1[p_1, p_2]}$

R7$_2$ $\langle \text{choose } p_1 : S_1 \text{ or } p_2 : S_2 \text{ ro}, s \rangle \longrightarrow_{\tilde{p}_2} \langle S_2, s \rangle$ with $\tilde{p}_2 = p_{2[p_1, p_2]}$

by identifying each statement S with the label of the initial block of S, i.e. a configuration $\langle S, s \rangle$ is identified with the pair $\langle s, init(S) \rangle \in$ **State** $\times$ **Label** (for a formal definition of $init$ see e.g. [5]). Most transitions are in fact deterministic (i.e. the associated probability is 1) just for choices, i.e. rules **R7** do we use the normalised probabilities $\tilde{p}_i$ (more on the actual normalisation procedure below).

The probabilistic transition system defined in Table 2 describes a Discrete Time Markov Chain (DTMC) (cf. e.g. [15,18]) as we obviously have a memoryless process: the transitions in Rules **R1** to **R7** depend only on the current configuration and not on the sequence of the configurations that preceded it. One can also easy to show that the probabilities of out-going transitions from each state sum up to one. It is well-known that the matrix of transition probabilities of a DTMC on a countable state space is a stochastic matrix, i.e. a square (possibly infinite) matrix $\mathbf{P} = (p_{ij})$ whose elements are real numbers in the closed interval $[0,1]$, for which $\sum_j p_{ij} = 1$ for all i [18,20]. We can therefore represent the SOS semantics for a **pWhile** program P by the stochastic matrix on the vector space over the set **Conf** of all configurations of a program P defined by the rules in Table 2.

2.3   States and Observables

For our language we also allow for the specification of the range of possible values of variables, i.e. **Value**(x), via *declarations*. Without going into the details of the formal syntax, we distinguish between parameters, indicated by **para**, and proper variables for which we specify their **Value** as a subset of the integers.

This allows us (also because **Value**(x) are assumed to be finite) to describe the space of probabilistic *states* σ (of a program) as (probability) distributions over classical states, i.e. $\sigma \in \mathcal{D}(\textbf{State})$. We can also see σ simply as a vector in the so-called free vector space $\mathcal{V}(\textbf{State})$ over **State** (distributions correspond to positive vectors with 1-norm 1) cf. [5,7].

For a single variable x we have (the isomorphism) **State** $=$ **Value**(x) and when we consider several variables we can identify a classical state s with an element in the Cartesian product $\mathbf{Value}(x_i) \times \ldots \times \mathbf{Value}(x_v)$. When we consider probabilistic states of a single variable x then we have $\sigma \in \mathcal{D}(\mathbf{State}) \subseteq \mathcal{V}(\mathbf{Value}(x))$. But for more than one variable we have $\sigma \in \bigotimes_{i=1}^{v} \mathcal{V}(\mathbf{Value}(x_i))$, i.e. the so-called *tensor product*, rather than the Cartesian product of $\mathcal{V}(\mathbf{Value})$. This unfortunately leads to a form of combinatorial explosion but is needed accommodate all possible *joint probability distributions* as we have (the isomorphism) $\mathcal{V}(X_1 \times \ldots \times X_v) = \mathcal{V}(X_1) \otimes \ldots \otimes \mathcal{V}(X_v)$.

Concretely, the tensor product – more precisely, the Kronecker product, i.e. the coordinate based version of the abstract concept of a tensor product – of two vectors $(x_1, \ldots, x_n)$ and $(y_1, \ldots, y_m)$ is $(x_1 y_1, \ldots, x_1 y_m, \ldots, x_n y_1, \ldots, x_n y_m)$ i.e. an nm dimensional vector. For an $n \times m$ matrix $\mathbf{A} = (\mathbf{A}_{ij})$ and an $n' \times m'$ matrix $\mathbf{B} = (\mathbf{B}_{kl})$ we construct similarly an $nn' \times mm'$ matrix $\mathbf{A} \otimes \mathbf{B} = (\mathbf{A}_{ij}\mathbf{B})$, i.e. each entry $\mathbf{A}_{ij}$ in $\mathbf{A}$ is multiplied with a copy of the matrix or block $\mathbf{B}$, for further details we refer e.g. to [16, Chapter 14].

In the following we also will use the notion of an *observable* which describes properties a program or system might have (for further details see [7]). Formally, an observable is a linear functional on the probabilistic state space, i.e. an element of its dual space. For finite dimensional spaces, as we have them here, we can identify state and observable space. States and observables are related to each other by the notion of expected value, $\mathbf{E}(x, \sigma)$, which gives the probability that we will observe a certain property x when the state of the system is described by σ. In our finite setting (and by Riesz's representation theorem) we can utilise an inner product $\langle ., . \rangle$ in order to to obtain $\mathbf{E}(x, \sigma) = \langle x, \sigma \rangle$.

3   Static Probabilities

If the probabilities in the `choose` statement are required to be constants (or parameters) then we can us a simple (re)normalisation procedure (at compile time) in order to obtain the effective probabilities that a certain alternative is executed, i.e. we (re) normalise probabilities in the SOS in Table 2 via:

$$\tilde{p} = p_{[p_1 \ldots p_n]} = \frac{p}{p_1 + \ldots + p_n}.$$

Not least because we will allow later also variable values p_i we have to address the issue whether $p_{[p_1 \ldots p_n]}$ is always well-defined. We will exclude negative weights (if the nevertheless appear we could consider the absolute values). However, one problem remains, namely whether or not we allow for $p_i = 0$. One argument – which we will adopt – would be to allow this to indicate "blocked" alternatives, especially when we consider (below) dynamical probabilities. This implies another issue we need to consider, namely the case where all $p_i = 0$. In this case, normalisation would imply a division by zero. To overcome this we set $\tilde{p} = p_{[p_1 \ldots p_n]} = 0$ if we have for all $p_i = 0$.

3.1   Linear Operator Semantics (LOS)

The Linear Operator Semantics (LOS) in [4,7] constructs the generator of the DTMC which represents the dymanics of a program (executions) in a syntax directed fashion. Like Kozen's semantics [11] we can represent the LOS as an operator on the vector space of probabilistic states, i.e. in the finite case as a matrix.

The LOS, $[\![P]\!]_{LOS}$, of a program P is constructed by means of a set, $\{\!\{P\}\!\}_{LOS}$ which associated to a program P is a set of linear operators which describe local changes (at individual labels). From $\{\!\{P\}\!\}_{LOS}$ we can construct the DTMC generator $[\![P]\!]_{LOS}$ then as a linear operator on $\mathcal{V}(\mathbf{Conf})$

$$[\![P]\!]_{LOS} : \mathcal{V}(\mathbf{Value}^n) \otimes \mathcal{V}(\mathbf{Label}) \rightarrow \mathcal{V}(\mathbf{Value}^n) \otimes \mathcal{V}(\mathbf{Label})$$

or simply $[\![P]\!]_{LOS} \in \mathcal{L}(\mathcal{V}(\mathbf{Conf}))$. We obtain it by combining all the individual effects which are described in $\{\!\{P\}\!\}_{LOS}$:

$$[\![P]\!]_{LOS} = \sum \{\!\{P\}\!\}_{LOS} = \sum \{\mathbf{G} \mid \mathbf{G} \in \{\!\{P\}\!\}_{LOS}\}.$$

The $\{\!\{S\}\!\}_{LOS}$ associated to a statement S is given by a set of global and local operators, i.e. $\{\!\{.\}\!\}_{LOS} : \mathbf{Stmt} \rightarrow \mathcal{P}(\Gamma \cup \Lambda)$, cf Table 3. Global operators are linear operators on $\mathcal{V}(\mathbf{Conf})$ i.e. $\Gamma = \mathcal{L}(\mathcal{V}(\mathbf{Value}^n) \otimes \mathcal{V}(\mathbf{Label})) = \mathcal{L}(\mathcal{V}(\mathbf{Conf}))$, and local operators are pairs of operators on $\mathcal{V}(\mathbf{State})$ and labels $\ell \in \mathbf{Label}$, i.e. $\Lambda = \mathcal{L}(\mathcal{V}(\mathbf{Value}^n)) \times \mathbf{Label}$.

Global operators are providing information about how the computational state changes at a label as well as the control flow, i.e. what is the label of the next statement to be executed. Local operators are representing statements for which the "continuation" is not yet known. In order to transform local operators into global ones (once the "continuation" is known) we define a "continuation" operation $\langle \mathbf{F}, \ell \rangle \rhd \ell' = \mathbf{F} \otimes \mathbf{E}(\ell, \ell')$ which we extend in the obvious way to sets of operators as $\{\langle \mathbf{F}_i, \ell_i \rangle\}\} \rhd \ell' = \{\mathbf{F}_i \otimes \mathbf{E}(\ell_i, \ell')\}$ (for global operators we have $\mathbf{G} \rhd \ell' = \mathbf{G}$). We denote by $\mathbf{E}(i, j)$ matrix units: $(\mathbf{E}(i, j))_{ij} = 1$ and 0 otherwise.

Table 3. The LOS semantics of **pWhile** (static)

$$\{\!\{[\mathtt{skip}]^\ell\}\!\}_{LOS} = \{\langle \mathbf{I}, \ell \rangle\}$$

$$\{\!\{[x := e]^\ell\}\!\}_{LOS} = \{\langle \mathbf{U}(x \leftarrow e), \ell \rangle\}$$

$$\{\!\{S_1; \; S_2\}\!\}_{LOS} = ([\![S_1]\!] \rhd init(S2)) \cup [\![S_2]\!]$$

$$\{\!\{[\mathtt{choose}]^\ell \; p_1 : S_1 \; \mathtt{or} \; p_2 : S_2 \; \mathtt{ro}\}\!\}_{LOS} = \{p_{1[p_1,p_2]} \cdot \mathbf{I} \otimes \mathbf{E}(\ell, init(S_1))\} \cup \{\!\{S_1\}\!\}_{LOS} \cup$$
$$\{p_{2[p_1,p_2]} \cdot \mathbf{I} \otimes \mathbf{E}(\ell, init(S_2))\} \cup \{\!\{S_2\}\!\}_{LOS}$$

$$\{\!\{\mathtt{if} \; [b]^\ell \; \mathtt{then} \; S_1 \; \mathtt{else} \; S_2 \; \mathtt{fi}\}\!\}_{LOS} = \{\langle \mathbf{P}(b), \ell \rangle\} \rhd init(S_1)\} \cup \{\!\{S_1\}\!\}_{LOS} \cup$$
$$\{\langle \mathbf{P}(b)^\perp, \ell \rangle\} \rhd init(S_2)\} \cup \{\!\{S_2\}\!\}_{LOS}$$

$$\{\!\{\mathtt{while} \; [b]^\ell \; \mathtt{do} \; S \; \mathtt{od}\}\!\}_{LOS} = \{\langle \mathbf{P}(b), \ell \rangle\} \rhd init(S)\} \cup \{\!\{S\}\!\}_{LOS} \rhd \ell$$
$$\cup \{\langle \mathbf{P}(b)^\perp, \ell \rangle\}$$

We use elementary update and test operators $\mathbf{U}$ and $\mathbf{P}$ (and its complement $\mathbf{P}^\perp = \mathbf{I} - \mathbf{P}$) as in Kozen's semantics. However, the tensor product structure allows us to define these operators in a different (but equivalent) way.

For a *single* variable the assignment to a constant value $v \in \mathbf{Value}$ is represented by the operator on $\mathcal{V}(\mathbf{Value})$ given by $\mathbf{U}(v) = 1$ if $v = i$ and 0 otherwise. Testing if a *single* variable satisfies a boolean test b is achieved by a (diagonal) projection operator on $\mathcal{V}(\mathbf{Value})$ with $(\mathbf{P}(b))_{ii} = 1$ if $b(i)$ holds and 0 otherwise. We extend these to the multivariable case, i.e. for $|\mathbf{Var}| = n > 1$. For testing if we are in a classical state $s \in \mathbf{Value}^n$ or if an expression e evaluates to a constant v (assuming an appropriate evaluation function $\mathcal{E} : \mathbf{Expr} \rightarrow \mathbf{State} \rightarrow \mathbf{Value}$) we have operators on $\mathcal{V}(\mathbf{Value})^{\otimes n}$:

$$\mathbf{P}(s) = \bigotimes_{i=1}^{n} \mathbf{P}(\mathbf{x}_i = s(\mathbf{x}_i)) \qquad \mathbf{P}(e = v) = \sum_{\mathcal{E}(e)s=v} \mathbf{P}(s).$$

We also have operators on $\mathcal{V}(\mathbf{Value})^{\otimes n}$ for updating a variable $\mathbf{x}_k$ in the context of other variables to a constant v or to the value of an expression e:

$$\mathbf{U}(\mathbf{x}_k \leftarrow v) = \bigotimes_{i=1}^{k-1} \mathbf{I} \otimes \mathbf{U}(v) \otimes \bigotimes_{i=k+1}^{n} \mathbf{I} \qquad \mathbf{U}(\mathbf{x}_k \leftarrow e) = \sum_{v} \mathbf{P}(e = v)\mathbf{U}(\mathbf{x}_k \leftarrow v)$$

As we model the semantics of a program as DTMCs we are also adding a final loop ℓ^* (for ℓ^* a fresh label not appearing already in P) when we consider a complete program (DTMC never terminate and thus we have to simulate termination by an infinite repetition of the final state), i.e. we actually have to use $(\{\!|P|\!\}_{LOS} \rhd \ell^*) \cup \{\mathbf{I} \otimes \mathbf{E}(\ell^*, \ell^*)\}$ when we construct $[\![P]\!]_{LOS}$. In this way we also resolve all open or dangling control flow steps, i.e. we deal ultimately with a set containing only global operators.

As said, the operator $[\![P]\!]_{LOS}$ is the generator of a DTMC which implements the dynamic behaviour or executions of the program P. In particular, we can take any (initial) configuration c_0, represented by a (point) distribution in $\mathcal{V}(\mathbf{Conf})$ and compute the distribution over all configurations we will have after n steps as $c_n = c_0 \cdot [\![P]\!]_{LOS}^n$ (using post-multiplication as our convention).

3.2 A Small Example

The LOS semantics specifies the semantics of a program as the generator of a DTMC. We use a simple experimental tool – pwc – which "compiles" a **pWhile** program into an octave [8] script which defines the different matrices/operators. To illustrate this let us look at a simple example involving a probabilistic choice.

Example 1. The concrete program P we consider, for which we also provide the labelling (which is in fact produced by the pwc tool) is given by:

```
var
  p :para; x :{0,1};
begin
  [choose]^1 1: [x:=0]^2 or 1: [x:=1]^3 or p: [skip]^4 ro;
  [stop]^5
end
```

Here we deal with one parameter p, the value of this can be set to any (integer) value before the program is actually executed, and one variable x which can take two values in $\{0, 1\}$. The state space is thus given just by $\mathcal{V}(\{0, 1\}) = \mathbb{R}^2$ (as the parameter p does not change we do not record its value as part of the state). The program is made up from 5 blocks: $[\mathtt{choose}]^1, [x := 0]^2, [x := 1]^3, [\mathtt{skip}]^4, [\mathtt{skip}]^5$. We thus have as the (probabilistic) space of configurations on which the LOS operator acts $\mathcal{V}(\{0, 1\} \times \mathcal{V}(\{\ell_1, \ell_2, \ell_3, \ell_4, \ell_5\}) = \mathbb{R}^2 \otimes \mathbb{R}^5 = \mathbb{R}^{10}$, i.e. $[P]_{LOS}$ is a 10×10 matrix which represents the generator of a DTMC on a space of 10 elements. Each dimension corresponds to a possible configuration, i.e. a tuple $\langle s_i, \ell_j \rangle$ with s a (classical) state $s : \{x\} \to \{0, 1\}$ and a statement or block identified by its label $\ell \in \{\ell_1, \ell_2, \ell_3, \ell_4, \ell_5\}$. Concretely we have the following base vectors e_i in $\mathbb{R}^{10}$ for the state spaces of the DTMC: $e_1 = \langle x \mapsto 0, \ell_1 \rangle, e_2 = \langle x \mapsto 0, \ell_2 \rangle, \ldots, e_5 - \langle x \mapsto 0, \ell_5 \rangle, e_6 = \langle x \mapsto 1, \ell_1 \rangle, \ldots, e_{10} - \langle x \mapsto 1, \ell_5 \rangle$.

For each of the 5 blocks we have a local transfer operator $\mathbf{F}_1, \ldots \mathbf{F}_5$ which are (stochastic) 2×2 matrices, i.e. linear operators on our state space $\mathbb{R}^2$. For blocks 4 and 5 these $\mathbf{F}_i$ are trivial, i.e. the identity 2×2 matrix, for label ℓ_2 and ℓ_3 the transfer operators are slightly more interesting:

$$\mathbf{F}_1 = \mathbf{F}_4 = \mathbf{F}_5 = \begin{pmatrix} 1 & 0 \\ 0 & 1 \end{pmatrix}, \quad \mathbf{F}_2 = \begin{pmatrix} 1 & 0 \\ 1 & 0 \end{pmatrix}, \quad \mathbf{F}_3 = \begin{pmatrix} 0 & 1 \\ 0 & 1 \end{pmatrix}.$$

This allows us to specify the local LOS operators for each basic block:

$$\{\![x := 0]^2\}\!\}_{LOS} = \{\langle \mathbf{F}_1, 2 \rangle\}, \{\![x := 1]^3\}\!\}_{LOS} = \{\langle \mathbf{F}_1, 3 \rangle\},$$
$$\{\![\mathtt{skip}]^4\}\!\}_{LOS} = \{\langle \mathbf{F}_4, 4 \rangle\}, \{\![\mathtt{skip}]^5\}\!\}_{LOS} = \{\langle \mathbf{F}_5, 5 \rangle\}.$$

We could also consider explicitly $\{\![\mathtt{choose}]^1\}\!\}_{LOS} = \{\langle \mathbf{F}_1, 1 \rangle\}$, however this will be covered when we consider the global operators.

The control flow of P is made up from 7 control-flow step triples $\langle i, p, j \rangle$, where i is the initial label, p the transition probability and j the final label:

$$1 - \langle 1, 1, 2 \rangle, 2 - \langle 1, 1, 3 \rangle, 3 - \langle 1, p, 4 \rangle,$$
$$4 - \langle 2, 1, 5 \rangle, 5 - \langle 3, 1, 5 \rangle, 6 - \langle 4, 1, 5 \rangle, 7 - \langle 5, 1, 5 \rangle.$$

For each of these control-flow steps we construct a global operator, typically the tensor product of the local transfer operator $\mathbf{F}_i$ at the initial label i and a control-flow step given by the matrix unit $\mathbf{E}(i, j)$, eventually weighted by a probability. Here we have to consider the (global) operators: $\mathbf{T}_1 = \mathbf{F}_1 \otimes \mathbf{E}(1, 2), \mathbf{T}_2 = \mathbf{F}_1 \otimes \mathbf{E}(1, 3), \mathbf{T}_3 = \mathbf{F}_1 \otimes \mathbf{E}(1, 4), \mathbf{T}_4 = \mathbf{F}_2 \otimes \mathbf{E}(2, 5), \mathbf{T}_5 = \mathbf{F}_3 \otimes \mathbf{E}(3, 5), \mathbf{T}_5 = \mathbf{F}_4 \otimes \mathbf{E}(4, 5), \mathbf{T}_7 = \mathbf{F}_5 \otimes \mathbf{E}(5, 5)$. The first three operators allow us to define the LOS of the choices statement. For this we have to specify a particular value for the parameter p. For example, for $p = 0$ we get after renormalisation:

$$\{\![\mathtt{choose}]^1 \ldots \mathtt{ro}\}\!\}_{LOS} = \{\tfrac{1}{2}\mathbf{T}_1, \tfrac{1}{2}\mathbf{T}_2\} \cup \{\![x := 0]^2\}\!\}_{LOS} \cup \{\![x := 1]^3\}\!\}_{LOS}.$$

If we instead take $p = 1$ we get after renormalisation:

$$= \{\tfrac{1}{3}\mathbf{T}_1, \tfrac{1}{3}\mathbf{T}_2, \tfrac{1}{3}\mathbf{T}_3, \} \cup \{\![x := 0]^2\}\!\}_{LOS} \cup \{\![x := 1]^3\}\!\}_{LOS} \cup \{\![\mathtt{skip}]^4\}\!\}_{LOS}.$$

The LOS $\{\![\texttt{choose}]^1 \ldots \texttt{ro}\}\!\}_{LOS}$ contains global as well as local operators: The global ones represent control-flow steps where the destination is already known, while the local ones (here for the labels ℓ_2, ℓ_3 and ℓ_4 are still unresolved. However, when we consider the whole program then the operation $\triangleright$ resolves the destinations of local operators and turns them into global ones, e.g.

$$\{\![x := 0]^2\}\!\}_{LOS} \triangleright \ell_5 = \{\mathbf{T}_4\} = \{\mathbf{F}_2 \otimes \mathbf{E}(2,5)\}$$
$$\{\![x := 1]^3\}\!\}_{LOS} \triangleright \ell_5 = \{\mathbf{T}_5\} = \{\mathbf{F}_3 \otimes \mathbf{E}(3,5)\}$$
$$\{\![\texttt{skip}]^4\}\!\}_{LOS} \triangleright \ell_5 \;\; = \{\mathbf{T}_6\} = \{\mathbf{F}_4 \otimes \mathbf{E}(4,5)\}$$

Resolving the self-loop for label 5 using $\mathbf{T}_7$ we get the semantics for $p = 0$ as:

$$\{\!P\}\!\}_{LOS} = \{\frac{1}{2}\mathbf{T}_1, \frac{1}{2}\mathbf{T}_2, \mathbf{T}_4, \mathbf{T}_5, \mathbf{T}_6, \mathbf{T}_7\}$$

and for $p = 1$ we have (similarly also for other values of p):

$$\{\!P\}\!\}_{LOS} = \{\frac{1}{3}\mathbf{T}_1, \frac{1}{3}\mathbf{T}_2, \frac{1}{3}\mathbf{T}_3, \mathbf{T}_4, \mathbf{T}_5, \mathbf{T}_6, \mathbf{T}_7\}$$

The DTMC generator in both case is $[\![P]\!]_{LOS} = \sum \{\mathbf{T} \mid \mathbf{T} \in \{\!P\}\!\}_{LOS}\}$.

4   Dynamical Probabilities

The main purpose of this work is to allow for "dynamical" probabilities in programs. That is we would like to allow for variables in choice constructs which allow a change of their values in the course of a computation. Given that our LOS semantics constructs a single operator $[\![P]\!]_{LOS}$ for every program P which does not change during the execution, i.e. represents a (time) homogenous DTMC, this seems to be a hopeless task. On the other hand, the state of the system does obviously contain all the information which could influence how the execution of a program should continue, so if it encodes the values of variables in choices, then this information should somehow be exploitable.

For the SOS semantics it is still relatively easy to extend it towards variable probabilities: We have to replace the normalisation condition in rules **R7** in Table 2 by reference to the current state s, i.e. $\tilde{p}_i = s(p_i)/s(p_1)+s(p_2)$ rather than constant values of p_i. The way to introduce dynamical or variable probabilities into the LOS semantics of the choice construct is to test or check whether we are in a certain state where variables have certain concrete values, if this is the case then the corresponding normalisation is applied.

4.1   Linear Operator Semantics (LOS)

In order to extend the LOS semantics as to allow for variable probabilities we have to consider the way we construct the LOS operator for the choice statement with static, i.e. constant, probabilities: $\{\![\texttt{choose}]^\ell \; p_1 : S_1 \; \texttt{or} \; p_2 : S_2 \; \texttt{ro}\}\!\}_{LOS} =$

$\{\tilde{p}_1 \cdot \mathbf{I} \otimes \mathbf{E}(\ell, init(S_1))\} \cup \{\!\{S_1\}\!\}_{LOS} \cup \{\tilde{p}_2 \cdot \mathbf{I} \otimes \mathbf{E}(\ell, init(S_2))\} \cup \{\!\{S_2\}\!\}_{LOS}$, or more general for n alternatives in a choice statement:

$$\{\!\{[\text{choose}]^\ell \; p_1 : S_1 \; \text{or} \; \ldots \text{or} \; p_n : S_n \; \text{ro}\}\!\}_{LOS} =$$

$$= \bigcup_{i=1}^{n} \{\tilde{p}_i \cdot \mathbf{I} \otimes \mathbf{E}(\ell, init(S_i))\} \cup \{\!\{S_i\}\!\}_{LOS}.$$

In these rules all p_i are known, either because they are constants or because they are constant parameters. We thus can compute the normalised probabilities $\tilde{p}_i$ or, when we need to explicitly record the context in which we normalise, $\tilde{p}_i = p_{i[p_1...p_n]}$ in exactly the same way as in the operational semantics.

When it comes to dynamical probabilities then we need to consider all possible contexts, i.e. all possible values $p_1, \ldots, p_n$ could take, in which we might need to normalise a probability. Formally we define a context for probabilities $p_1, \ldots, p_n$ where each p_i can be a constant value (incl. a parameter) or a variable (name) as a set of sequences $i_1, \ldots, i_n$ of integers:

$$\mathcal{C}[p_1, p_2, \ldots, p_n] = \begin{cases} \emptyset & \text{if n} = 0 \\ \{[p_1]\} & \text{if } n = 1 \text{ and } p_i \text{ constant} \\ \{[c] \mid c \in \mathbf{Value}(p_1)\} & \text{if } n = 1 \text{ and } p_i \text{ a variable} \\ \bigcup_{[i] \in \mathcal{C}[p_1]} \{[i] \cdot \mathcal{C}[p_2, \ldots, p_n]\} & \text{otherwise, i.e. } n > 1. \end{cases}$$

where "·" denotes the concatenation of integer sequences $[i_1, \ldots, i_m]$ defined and extended to sets of sequences in the obvious way.

Example 2. Assume we have a variable x with $\mathbf{Value}(x) = \{0, 1\}$ and a parameter $p = 0$ or $p = 1$ then contexts are given by:

$$\mathcal{C}[x, 1, p] = \{[0, 1, 0], [1, 1, 0]\} \quad \text{and} \quad \mathcal{C}[x, 1, p] = \{[0, 1, 1], [1, 1, 1]\}$$

With this we can now define an extended version of the LOS which also allows for variables as choice probabilities:

$$\{\!\{[\text{choose}]^\ell \; p_1 : S_1 \; \text{or} \; \ldots \text{or} \; p_n : S_n \; \text{ro}\}\!\}_{LOS} =$$

$$= \bigcup_{i=1}^{n} \left\{ \sum_{c_j \in p_i} \sum_{[d_1, \ldots, d_n] \in \mathcal{C}[p_1...p_n]} c_{j[d_1...d_n]} \cdot \mathbf{P}^{p_i[p_1...p_n]}_{c_j[d_1...d_n]} \otimes \mathbf{E}(\ell, init(S_i)) \right\} \cup \{\!\{S_i\}\!\}_{LOS}.$$

To explain this construction: The LOS of the choices is given – as in the static case – as the union of all (global) operators which implement the control-flow step from label ℓ to one of the alternatives $i = 1 \ldots n$ together with the LOS semantics of each of these alternatives defined by $\{\!\{S_i\}\!\}_{LOS}$. However, in the case of static probabilities we have to weight the operator $\mathbf{E}(\ell, init(S_i))$ not just with a normalised probability but instead we test if the values of the probabilities (which can be variables, after all) are described by a particular context and then apply the corresponding normalised weight $c_{j[d_1...d_n]}$. This test operator $\mathbf{P}^{p_i[p_1...p_n]}_{c_j[d_1...d_n]}$ is very similar to the test we apply in order to identify a particular state, i.e. $\mathbf{P}(\sigma)$, except that in a context the same variable can appear several times:

$$\mathbf{P}^{p_i[p_1\ldots p_n]}_{c_j[d_1\ldots d_n]} = \mathbf{P}(p_i = c_j) \cdot \left(\prod_{k=1,\ldots,n} \mathbf{P}(p_k = d_k) \right).$$

The first sum is over all possible values of the guard probability p_i, where we use the short-hand notation $c_j \in p_i$ for $c_j \in \mathbf{Value}(p_i)$ which for constants and parameters reduces to a single term $c_j = p_i$. The second sum is over all possible values of all probabilities in all possible contexts. It might be interesting to note that if a variable appears twice it has to have the same value (as $\mathrm{diag}(e_i) \otimes \mathrm{diag}(e_j) = \mathrm{diag}(e_i)$ if and only if $i = j$ and the zero matrix otherwise). For constant values we can also omit the tests (as $e_i \mathbf{T} = e_i \mathrm{diag}(e_i)\mathbf{T}$ for all $\mathbf{T}$).

It is simple to show that the LOS semantics for choice with variable probabilities is equivalent to the SOS semantics, for the other construct things are unchanged [7].

4.2   A Small Example

In order to illustrate the LOS for dynamical variables let us again first consider a very simple example, similar to Example 1.

Example 3. The program Q we consider is given by:

```
var
  p :para; x :{0,1};
begin
  [choose]^1 x: [x:=0]^2 or 1:[x:=1]^3 or p:[skip]^4 ro;
  [stop]^5
end
```

As we have the same declarations, we have exactly the same state spaces as in Example 1. Furthermore, we also have the same 5 blocks as in the previous example and therefore the DTMC state space of configurations is again $\mathbb{R}^{10}$. We also have the same transfer operators $\mathbf{F}_i$ (and local LOS operators for the basic blocks). However, though the control flow has again 7 control-flow steps and it is nearly identical, except for the step from ℓ_1 to ℓ_2 which here is guarded by a variable probability x:

$$1 - \langle 1, x, 2 \rangle, 2 - \langle 1, 1, 3 \rangle, 3 - \langle 1, p, 4 \rangle,$$
$$4 - \langle 2, 1, 5 \rangle, 5 - \langle 3, 1, 5 \rangle, 6 - \langle 4, 1, 5 \rangle, 7 - \langle 5, 1, 5 \rangle.$$

We can still use the same operators $\mathbf{T}_i$ from Example 1 but the complete LOS semantics now looks slightly different. For $p = 0$ or $p = 1$ we need to work with the contexts given in Example 2. For $p = 0$ we have $\mathcal{C}[x, 1, p] = \{[0, 1, 0], [1, 1, 0]\}$ and thus get

$$\{Q\}_{LOS} = \{ (\mathbf{P}(x = 0) + \tfrac{1}{2}\mathbf{P}(x = 1)) \otimes \mathbf{E}(1, 3),$$
$$(\qquad\qquad \tfrac{1}{2}\mathbf{P}(x = 1)) \otimes \mathbf{E}(1, 4), \mathbf{T}_4, \mathbf{T}_5, \mathbf{T}_6, \mathbf{T}_7 \}.$$

and for the parameter value $p = 1$ we have $\mathcal{C}[x, 1, p] = \{[0, 1, 1], [1, 1, 1]\}$ and:

$$\{Q\}_{LOS} = \{(\qquad\qquad \tfrac{1}{3}\mathbf{P}(x = 1)) \otimes \mathbf{E}(1, 2),$$
$$(\tfrac{1}{2}\mathbf{P}(x = 0) + \tfrac{1}{3}\mathbf{P}(x = 1)) \otimes \mathbf{E}(1, 3),$$
$$(\tfrac{1}{2}\mathbf{P}(x = 0) + \tfrac{1}{3}\mathbf{P}(x = 1)) \otimes \mathbf{E}(1, 4), \mathbf{T}_4, \mathbf{T}_5, \mathbf{T}_6, \mathbf{T}_7\}.$$

Note that test operators like $\mathbf{P}(x = 1)$ should actually be expressed as, for example: $\mathbf{P}(x = 1)\mathbf{P}(x = 1)\mathbf{P}(1 = 1)\mathbf{P}(p = 1)$. However, as said before, in the case of constants (and parameters) these tests are redundant and as projections are always idempotents we also have: $\mathbf{P}(x = 1) = \mathbf{P}(x = 1)\mathbf{P}(x = 1)$.

5 Example: Duel at High Noon

We illustrate the generation of the LOS semantics – i.e. the DTMC generator of a probabilistic program – by considering an example given in [9,10], see also [12, p. 211], which concerns the kind of "duel" between two "cowboys" A and B. We first reproduce essentially the results of [9,10] regarding the chances that A (or B) will win/survive the "duel" with static probabilities. We then also consider the case where one the two duellists (here A) improves his hitting chances during the contest. This situation obviously requires dynamical/changing probabilities.

5.1 Static Probabilities

The idea is that two "cowboys", A (Adam) and B (Boris), have a duel. At each turn one of them is allowed to shoot at the other, if he misses the other one can try, if he also misses it is the first ones turn again until one is "successful". That is, at the beginning one of the two – either Adam or Boris – is allowed to shoot at the other one. Which of the two starts is left open, i.e. decided non-deterministically. We assume that there is a probability a for A hitting B and a probability b that B manages to shoot A. More precisely, we have $a = \frac{ak}{ak+am}$ for a "killing" and a "missing" weight ak and bk, respectively (and similar for b). In the original version it is non-deterministically decided whether A or B starts, but in order to get simple numerical results we will flip a fair coin to determine who has the first attempt. The concrete **pWhile** program is given on the left hand side in Table 4.

The variable c determines whether the duel should be continued, if $c = 1$ the duel continues, otherwise it is over. This is essentially to simulate a **until** statement using the **while** construct. The variable t determines which of the two duellists is allowed to try to shoot, for $t = 0$ it is A's turn, otherwise it is B's turn. As long as the duel is continued (i.e. $c = 1$) it is either A which gets a try (if $t = 0$) or B (for $t = 1$). If it is A's turn he will hit B with probability a – in this case the duel is over and c is set to 0; and with probability $1 - a$ it might be a miss – in this case the next round it will be B's turn. Similarly, for $t = 1$ the duellist B gets his chance.

At the end of the duel the value of t determines who has lost/won – i.e. whose turn it was when the loop terminated, i.e. c was set to zero. In order to extract

Table 4. pWhile programs for the Duel at High Noon

```
var                                   var
ak: para; # A kills                   ak: para; # A kills  (initially)
am: para; # A misses                  am: para; # A misses (initially)
bk: para; # B kills                   bk: para; # B kills
bm: para; # B misses                  bm: para; # B misses
t: {0,1}; # turn     0=A,  1=B         t: {0,1}; # turn     0=A,  1=B
c: {0,1}; # continue 0=no, 1=yes       c: {0,1}; # continue 0=no, 1=yes
                                      akl: {0..10}; # A kills  (learned)
begin                                 aml: {0..10}; # A misses (learned)
# who's first turn
choose 1:{t:=0} or 1:{t:=1} ro;       begin
# continue until ...                  # initialise skills of A
c := 1;                               akl := ak; aml := am;
while c == 1 do                       # who's first
if (t==0) then                        choose 1:{t:=0} or 1:{t:=1} ro;
   choose ak: c:=0] or am: t:=1 ro    # continue until ...
else                                  c := 1;
   choose bk: c:=0 or bm: t:=0 ro     while c == 1 do
fi;                                      if (t==0) then
od;                                         choose akl: c:=0 or aml: t:=1 ro
stop; # terminal loop                    else
end                                         choose bk: c:=0 or bm: t:=0 ro
                                         fi;
                                         akl:=@inc(akl); aml:=@dec(aml);
                                      od;
                                      stop; # terminal loop
                                      end
```

information about the probability distribution describing a particular variable – in our case t – at a given label ℓ, i.e. program point ℓ, we can use an abstraction operator $\mathbf{A}_\ell$. This operator/matrix leaves the first variable (i.e. t) unchanged and "forgets" about all other variables in a particular label ℓ:

$$\mathbf{A}_\ell = \mathbf{I} \otimes \mathbf{A}_f \otimes \ldots \otimes \mathbf{A}_f \otimes (e_\ell)^t$$

with $\mathbf{I}$ the identity matrix for the first variable (for t it is a 2×2 matrix), $\mathbf{A}_f$ a so-called "forgetfull abstraction" for the remaining variables and e_ℓ^t the transposed (column) base vector in $\mathcal{V}(\mathbf{Label})$ which selects or projects the state at label ℓ. The operators $\mathbf{A}_f$ are given by column vectors (or $n \times 1$ matrices) which only contain 1s, i.e. $\mathbf{A}_f = (1,1,1,\ldots,1)^t$ with $n = \dim(\mathcal{V}(\mathbf{Value}(x)) = |\mathbf{Value}(x)|$. This is an instance of a more general framework of Probabilistic Abstract Interpretation (PAI), cf. e.g. [5–7].

With this abstraction $\mathbf{A}_\ell$ we can extract the probabilities that t is 0 or 1, i.e. who has won the duel, if we take $\ell = \ell^*$, i.e. the final label ℓ^8 of the program once the program has "terminated". For this we have to consider the (long-run) input/output behaviour for an initial configuration $c_0 = s_0 \otimes e_0$, i.e. an initial state s_0 which determines the initial values of all variables at the initial label

ℓ_0. We then have to apply the LOS operator $[P]_{LOS}$ until we reach a limit $\lim_{n\to\infty}(s_0 \otimes e_0)[P]_{LOS}^n$. This essentially gives Kozen's input/output semantics [11] of the program, cf. [7].

To obtain numerical results we can stop this iteration for a finite value of n, in our case $n = 100$ is sufficient. Finally, we have to extract the state of t using $\mathbf{A}_{\ell^*}$ and the observable $w = (1,0)$ which gives the probability that $t = 0$, i.e. that the winner is A. In other words, the aim of the analysis is to determine:

$$w = \lim_{n\to\infty} \langle w, (s_0 \otimes e_0) \cdot [P]_{LOS}^n \cdot \mathbf{A}_{\ell^*} \rangle.$$

or a numerical approximation (for $n = 100$). In our case t and c are both initialised, so w is idependent of the initial state s_0. If we consider the "non-deterministic" version, i.e. dropping 'choose 1: t:=0 or 1: t:=1 ro', the value of w would depend on s_0.

We use our tool pwc to construct $[P]_{LOS}$. The program has 13 labels or elementary blocks (with $\ell^* = 13$). The dimension of the DTMC is then $2 \times 2 \times 13 = 52$ as t and c take two possible values. With this we can compute w for different values of the parameters ak, am, etc. The top left diagram in Fig. 1 depicts the chances of A surviving the duel depending on $a = ak/(ak+am)$ and $b = bk/(bk + bm)$.

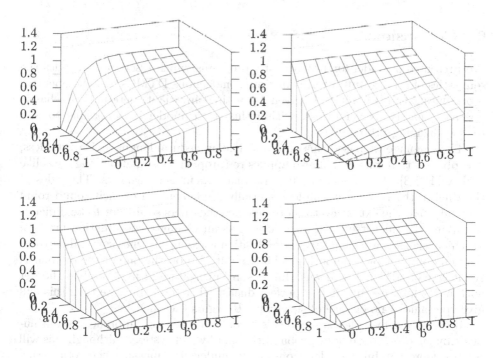

Fig. 1. Survival probabilities w for A with learning rates 0, 1, 2 and 4

5.2 Dynamic Probabilities

If we assume that probabilities (of hitting) are not constant, but that for example one of the duellists is getting better during the shoot-out we have to consider a different model as in the following **pWhile** program as on the right in Table 4.

Here we use the same parameters ak, etc. as in the static case. However for A these are only the initial values. During the duel A will improve his shooting skills (while B's abilities do not change). The (learned) chances of A hitting is given by akl and the chances of missing aml. These are changed using "external" functions @inc and @dec which depend on a learning rate r defined directly in octave as min(max(x+r,0),10) and min(max(x-r,0),10), respectively.

For different values of the parameters ak, am, etc. we can again construct the LOS operator $[\![P]\!]_{LOS}$. In this case we have 17 lables/blocks and two additional variables akl and akm which each can have 11 possible values, thus we have to consider a DTMC on $2 \times 2 \times 11 \times 11 \times 17 = 8228$ states.

The survival chances for A can be computed in the same way as in the static case, using the corresponding abstraction $\mathbf{A}_{17}$, the same w and based on a numeric approximation based on $n = 100$ iterations of $[\![P]\!]_{LOS}$. For different learning rates r we depict the survival rate for A in Fig. 1. For $r = 0$ we get exactly the same as in the static case – after all, A is stuck with his initial shooting abilities and does not improve at all.

6 Conclusions

We presented a model for probabilistic programs which essentially encodes the semantics of a program in terms of time homogenous DTMCs, i.e. the operator representing the semantics is given by a time invariant, "eternal" stochastic operator/matrix. Nevertheless, within this static model it is possible to also realise changing probabilities.

The language we based this on is a simple procedural language. Nevertheless, it is obvious that this model also applies to (proper) coordination languages like pKLAIM [2,3]. This concerns in particular concurrency aspects: The rules of the duel in the cowboy example essentially implement an explicit round robin scheduler and the extension to more general schedulers seems not to be difficult. Surviving the duel itself can also be seen as an ultimate coordination problem in which the role of probability normalisation is essential: Ones survival depends not only on ones own (shooting) abilities but also on the one of the opponent. A hit rate of 50 % for A means almost sure survival for A if B is a bad shooter with a 2 % hit rate, but if B a perfect duelist with 100 % hit rate then this will give the same A no chance of survival if B begins the duel.

It seems also feasible to extend this "probability testing" approach to continuous time models, continuous probabilities and hybrid systems, although this will require more careful considerations of the underlying measure theoretic structure (Borel structure, σ-algebras, measures instead of distributions, integrals in place of sums, etc.).

References

1. Aarts, E., Korst, J.: Simulated Annealing and Boltzmann Machines. Wiley, Chichester (1989)
2. Di Pierro, A., Hankin, C., Wiklicky, H.: Continuous-time probabilistic KLAIM. In: SecCo 2004, ENTCS. Elsevier (2004)
3. Di Pierro, A., Hankin, C., Wiklicky, H.: Probabilistic KLAIM. In: De Nicola, R., Ferrari, G.-L., Meredith, G. (eds.) COORDINATION 2004. LNCS, vol. 2949, pp. 119–134. Springer, Heidelberg (2004)
4. Di Pierro, A., Hankin, C., Wiklicky, H.: A systematic approach to probabilistic pointer analysis. In: Shao, Z. (ed.) APLAS 2007. LNCS, vol. 4807, pp. 335–350. Springer, Heidelberg (2007)
5. Di Pierro, A., Hankin, C., Wiklicky, H.: Probabilistic semantics and program analysis. In: Aldini, A., Bernardo, M., Pierro, A., Wiklicky, H. (eds.) SFM 2010. LNCS, vol. 6154, pp. 1–42. Springer, Heidelberg (2010)
6. Di Pierro, A., Sotin, P., Wiklicky, H.: Relational analysis and precision via probabilistic abstract interpretation. In: Proceedings of QAPL 2008. ENTCS, vol. 220, no. 3, pp. 23–42. Elsevier (2008)
7. Di Pierro, A., Wiklicky, H.: Semantics of probabilistic programs: a weak limit approach. In: Shan, C. (ed.) APLAS 2013. LNCS, vol. 8301, pp. 241–256. Springer, Heidelberg (2013)
8. Eaton, J.W., Bateman, D., Hauberg, S.: GNU Octave - a high-level interactive language for numerical computations, 3rd edn. version 3.8.0, February 2011
9. Gretz, F., Katoen, J.P., McIver, A.: Operational versus weakest precondition semantics for the probabilistic guarded command language. In: Proceedings of QEST 2012, pp. 168–177. IEEE Computer Society (2012)
10. Gretz, F., Katoen, J.P., McIver, A.: Operational versus weakest pre-expectation semantics for the probabilistic guarded command language. Perform. Eval. **73**, 110–132 (2014)
11. Kozen, D.: Semantics of probabilistic programs. J. Comput. Syst. Sci. **22**(3), 328–350 (1981)
12. McIver, A., Morgan, C.: Abstraction, Refinement and Proof for Probabilistic Systems. Mongraphs in Computer Science. Springer, New York (2005)
13. Motwani, R., Raghavan, P.: Randomized Algorithms. Cambridge University Press, Cambridge, England (1995)
14. Nielson, F., Nielson, H.R., Hankin, C.: Principles of Program Analysis. Springer, Heidelberg (1999)
15. Norris, J.: Markov Chains. Cambidge Series in Statistical and Probabilistic Mathematics. Cambridge University Press, Cambridge (1997)
16. Roman, S.: Advanced Linear Algebra, 2nd edn. Springer, New York (2005)
17. Schneider, J.J., Kirkpatrick, S.: Stochastic Optimization. Springer, Heidelberg (2006)
18. Seneta, E.: Non-negative Matrices and Markov Chains. Springer, New York (1981)
19. Stannett, M.: X-machines and the halting problem: building a super-turing machine. Formal Aspects Comput. **2**, 331–341 (1990)
20. Woess, W.: Denumerable Markov Chains. EMS (2009)

Author Index

Printed in the United States
By Bookmasters